D1327859

SPECIAL FORCES BERLIN

SPECIAL FORCES
BERLIN

Clandestine Cold War Operations
of the US Army's Elite, 1956–1990

JAMES STEJSKAL

CASEMATE | publishers
Philadelphia & Oxford

Published in the United States of America and Great Britain in 2017 by
CASEMATE PUBLISHERS
1950 Lawrence Road, Havertown, PA 19083, USA
and
The Old Music Hall, 106–108 Cowley Road, Oxford OX4 1JE, UK

All statements of fact, opinion or analysis are those of the author and do not reflect the official position or views of the United States Government. The material has been reviewed by the DOD, CIA and NSA solely to prevent disclosure of classified material and its release does not imply endorsement or factual accuracy of the material.

Hardcover Edition: ISBN 978-1-61200-444-0
Digital Edition: ISBN 978-1-61200-445-7

A CIP record for this book is available from the British Library.

Printed and bound in the United States of America

For a complete list of Casemate titles, please contact:

CASEMATE PUBLISHERS (US)
Telephone (610) 853-9131
Fax (610) 853-9146
Email: casemate@casematepublishers.com
www.casematepublishers.com

CASEMATE PUBLISHERS (UK)
Telephone (01865) 241249
Fax (01865) 794449
Email: casemate-uk@casematepublishers.co.uk
www.casematepublishers.co.uk

CONTENTS

Foreword   vi
Acknowledgments   viii
Preface   x
Definitions   xv

I   The Origins of Special Forces   1
II   The Formative Years (1956–1971)   18
III   A New Mission and a Midlife Crisis (1972–1976)   78
IV   The Pros from Dover (1976–1981)   101
V   Appointment in Tehran   147
VI   The Final Days (1981–1984)   194
VII   The New Kid on the Block (1984)   220
VIII   Until the Fall (1984–1990)   227
Epilogue: A Casualty of Peace   270

Appendix A: In the Sights of the Enemy   280
Appendix B: Leadership   290
Timeline: Special Forces Berlin, 1956–1990   292
Timeline: Iran Mission, 1979–1981   294
Abbreviations and Acronyms   296
Notes   301
Sources   319
Bibliography   324
Index   327

FOREWORD

With this excellent telling, James Stejskal has made an important contribution on several levels to our acknowledged history of US Army Special Forces and the development of today's American special operations capability.

The book recognizes a unit, the members of which were among the most impactful of giants on whose shoulders the current special operators stand, whether in the SF Groups or in the most clandestine of our special operations "SMU" outfits. My generation of SF soldiers learned how to be effective in a denied area, using a complex mix of tradecraft, ingenuity, common sense, light infantry, and guerrilla warfare techniques in sabotage and subversion, with a nuance and deftness required to survive to accomplish our unconventional (UW) mission. Their exploits, known to few by design, but long rumored can now be shared with the public and SOF professionals. It is fitting too that the unit be recognized and her members honored before time finishes with these great men.

It is also important that as the unconventional pendulum swings back into vogue, that current practitioners and policy makers recognize that as the saying goes, there is little new, more often it is simply the history we don't know. Pushed by longstanding enemies of the West, who have again embraced this ancient form of lethal competition as a natural consequence of our dominance of the conventional battlefield, the US needs to seriously study not only the phenomenon of Russia's use of "little green men" and Iran's manipulation of its surrogates abroad, but also the importance of the West having its own UW capability. James' book reminds us that our own UW roots are deep and that US unconventional warfare units have played important roles since World War II.

More importantly, in the era of counterterrorism, "Det A" teaches us that successfully concluding such campaigns will require investing our best and brightest in deep understanding of foreign cultures and causes, and an ability to work among the peoples who are warring against us. It is hard stuff but not impossible. Further, it is a military task but one that will have close association with intelligence agencies and their paramilitary sections, a relationship that can be strained and counterproductive unless the parties develop a confidence and familiarity with each other. James highlights how in the very close quarters of Berlin such cooperation could be very productive for the country.

Lastly, James rounds out the picture of US military involvement during one of the most unique periods and in the most unique of operating environments, Cold War Berlin. I can think of no other place that served as such a beacon for history's "good guys." For in that fight, that is who we, the West, were. While much is known of the US Army's occupation forces and subsequent storied units, the last being the Berlin Brigade, until now little has been said about SF's role. But it is important to be reminded that even the good guys have had and need their own version of "little green men."

Enjoy this eminently readable and enjoyable history. Get to know the men who over the years moved in the ranks of one of the finest special operations units ever created. With all the hype generated in recent years by far less discreet and less capable special units, it's good to read about a unit who remained in the shadows until history and discretion allowed a public accounting. I was honored to have known many who were in her ranks and humbled by their quiet confidence in the most difficult and underappreciated service to our great country.

LTG Charles T. Cleveland, US Army Retired
Former Commanding General
US Army Special Operations Command

ACKNOWLEDGMENTS

This book is dedicated to that "One Percent" that serve our country and especially the 800+ men who served with Special Forces Berlin from 1956 to 1990. The writing and publication of this work would not have been possible without the encouragement and assistance of many people. The expertise and comments of my friends and comrades, the former members of Detachment "A" and Physical Security Support Element Berlin, assisted me greatly in the re-telling of this story. I especially wish to thank CSM Jeffrey Raker, US Army (Ret), for his friendship and mentorship when we all needed it—it made much difference to all of us and kept several out of Fort Leavenworth. His reading of the manuscript ensured it was balanced and, for the most part, fair. Sadly, on November 10, 2016, CSM Raker entered Valhalla—he was a true warrior leader. The incisive comments of Lieutenant General Charles Cleveland were highly appreciated—his experience and insights made for some interesting conversation and assisted immensely in my descriptions of command issues and the military's upper echelons. I would also like to sincerely thank Colonel Bill "Iron Man" Davis for his help and strength.

Additionally, the staffs of the National Archives and Records Administration at College Park, the US Army Center for Military History at Fort McNair, and the Special Forces Museum at Fort Bragg were extremely helpful and forthcoming.

The staff of Casemate Publishing in Oxford, Clare Litt, Ruth Sheppard, and Hannah McAdams as well as Tara Lichterman in the

USA, did exceptional work to keep the book on track. I would especially like to thank my patient wife, Ambassador Wanda Nesbitt, whose encouragement, along with her incisive reading and commentary, helped immensely in the writing of the work. Finally, I have made all possible effort to locate and acknowledge copyright holders and apologize for any inadvertent infringement. The responsibility for any errors or omissions in this work lies with me alone.

James Stejskal
Alexandria

PREFACE

This book relays the history of a little-known and highly classified US Army Special Forces Detachment that was stationed in Berlin, Germany from 1956 to 1990.

It came into existence in response to the threat posed by the massive armies of the Soviet Union and its Warsaw Pact allies to the nations of Western Europe. The conventional wisdom at the time was that the Soviet hordes would quickly overrun the defenses of the North Atlantic Treaty Organization. US military planners decided they needed a "Hail Mary" plan to slow the juggernaut they expected when and if a war began.

That ace in the hole was Special Forces Berlin. Its primary mission, in the words of the Supreme Allied Commander Europe, was simple: "Buy me time, any time at all."

It was openly known by several names through its 34-year history: Security Platoon, Detachment "A," and finally Physical Security Support Element. Its classified names were 39th Special Forces Detachment as of 1965, and 410th Special Forces Detachment as of 1984. It was a unique unit with skills that combined unconventional warfare (UW) and intelligence tradecraft with counterterrorism (CT) operations. It was a legacy of the Office of Strategic Services (OSS) of World War II and a pioneer of CT tactics and techniques.

Its story began thus:

Shortly after the end of World War II, the United States began to reevaluate cooperation with its wartime "ally," the Soviet Union. George

Kennan's famous telegram outlining the dangers posed by Moscow to the West was a key element that forced a swing in Washington from one of sympathy for the Communist experiment to a realization that the Soviet threat should be contained.

During this "Cold War," the divided city of Berlin was the center of a struggle that pitted the Soviet Union and its Warsaw Pact brothers-in-arms against the United States and its NATO allies. It was one that would last until the fall of the Berlin Wall in 1989.

Situated 110 miles inside the Soviet-controlled German Democratic Republic, the city of Berlin was home to the world's most powerful intelligence services as they played a game of shadows, each seeking advantage over their enemies. But it was not just intelligence services that tussled in this shadow war for supremacy.

In 1956, a small, select group of US Army Special Forces soldiers arrived in the city. Working unseen alongside the conventional American, British, and French combat troops who occupied West Berlin, the SF element's classified, wartime mission was to strike the enemy's rear areas, create chaos and confusion, and provide crucial time for the Allied forces in Western Europe to meet and hopefully check a Soviet onslaught.

These men stayed on alert to meet the threat. The first 40 men who came to Berlin in mid-1956 were soon reinforced by 50 more, and these 90 soldiers (and their successors) would stand ready to go to war in a hostile area occupied by nearly one million Warsaw Pact forces until 1990.

If war came, some of these men would stay in Berlin to fight the enemy, while others would cross the most heavily defended border in the world and disappear into the countryside to accomplish their tasks behind Soviet lines.

Many men served with Special Forces Detachment Berlin over its 34 years. Their presence in that city was cloaked with a banal cover story that obscured the enigmatic truth. There is no good or easy way to characterize what type of men they were. A few were administrative or logistics specialists, some were medics, and most were combat arms experts. Many were native-born Americans, but a good number came from Eastern Europe. Their backgrounds were varied and their cultural differences many. They did, however, have one common ground—a sense of duty and a willingness to defend freedom. One thing is certain, no one became famous because of his exploits in Berlin: they were classified. If a soldier achieved a measure of fame or notoriety, it was for what he did in other theaters and fields of battle such as Vietnam, the Belgian Congo, Somalia, Iraq, and Afghanistan. A disproportionate number of the men who served there rose to positions of great responsibility in other Special Forces and special mission units, and major Army commands. When they moved on, they took their experience and skills with them. Even after the Berlin mission disappeared, they applied those skills to global requirements before and after 9/11. The legacy of Special Forces in Berlin survives through the men who served there.

At the beginning of the Cold War, it was not at all clear which alliance—NATO or the Warsaw Pact—would come out on top. By the time the Cold War ended in 1990, many had forgotten how menacing the Communists had once seemed. The unit's flags were cased and it disappeared as it had arrived, quietly and without fanfare. The unit received no campaign streamers or unit citations for its activities and the record of what it accomplished remained secure in the vaults of the Pentagon. Until now.

Several years ago, veterans of this organization came together for a reunion. Many feared that the story would disappear once the members were gone, so it was suggested a book be written that would preserve the unit's history. Contributing to this decision was the fact that when SF Berlin was disbanded, its files and records were for the most part destroyed or lost. As a member of the unit in both the 1970s and the 1980s, I volunteered to write this book as a necessary and worthwhile endeavor to honor those who served there and to give tribute to their duty and sacrifice.

The history that follows comes from the memories of the men who served there, myself included. It is a narrative that is broad both in its duration and perspective. The anecdotes are coupled with what little declassified, official documentation exists or has thus far been found. Together, they tell more of the history than has ever before been revealed. It has not been an easy journey. After numerous visits and queries sent to the US National Archives, the Pentagon, military commands, and the Center for Military History, I came up with around ten pages of military orders and charts, but little else. Unfortunately, much official documentation has been destroyed. Of the many men I interviewed or who responded to my calls for help, an unfortunate number have passed on. For that reason, this is also a history not likely to be expanded upon in the future. Only these accounts bear witness to their service.

In October 2005, Special Forces Detachment Korea (Det K) was given a new designation: "39th Special Forces Detachment." Many of members of "Det K" objected, knowing little of the exploits and operations of SF Berlin. Perhaps this history will illuminate and rectify that void.

Because of the classified nature of the unit, the Department of Defense and the CIA reviewed the manuscript to ensure national security was not compromised (a trying process for even the most patient). Some material has been omitted and some names were necessarily changed.

Many contributed to this work, providing stories, documents, and images to amplify the history. Many also read it to comment on the accuracy and, in some cases, the veracity of the material presented to eliminate mistakes and questionable details. But, because the history covers a span of more than 30 years, not all worthwhile events could be accommodated in this book. For those omissions, as well as any errors, I alone am responsible. My thanks go to those who shared their memories for this work and to all who served in Berlin.

This is their story.

"No force of its size has contributed more to peace, stability and freedom. The unit has a proud legacy and faced untold risk—fraught with uncertainty. It was involved in some of the most sensitive operations of the Cold War. Its members created techniques that are still in use today."

Lieutenant General Charles T. Cleveland, Commander,
US Army Special Operations Command

"The foremost American urban guerrilla warfare outfit, never used but highly trained, was [Special Forces Berlin], a cold war Army Special Forces 'stay-behind' unit. America stationed an entire Army Special Forces unit in allied occupied West Berlin, deep in East Germany, behind Soviet lines. NATO strategically placed this unit to execute a stay-behind role as the Soviet Army rolled over Berlin, and other Soviet units headed west from occupied East Germany. The men were the consummate practitioners of urban guerrilla warfare both because it was their wartime mission and because they were in the perfect city to train for it. Detachment A [and its successor] remain the least known, most closely held Special Forces operation and is only very rarely in the literature. It stands as the earliest of the future special mission units having been known by a variety of ever changing unclassified unit designations."

Colonel Warner D. Farr, US Army

"[Special Forces Berlin] was one of the premier unconventional warfare and intelligence organizations with the mission to prepare for operations behind the lines in Warsaw Pact countries during the Cold War. This very small organization possessed capabilities and expertise that allowed it to accomplish missions that could be conducted by no other force in DOD."

Colonel David S. Maxwell, US Army

"Prospects of success approximated zero."

Colonel John Collins, US Army

"It would have been glorious."

Staff Sergeant J. J. Morrison, US Army

DEFINITIONS

Guerrilla Warfare (GW)

"Operations carried out by small independent forces, generally in the rear of the enemy, with the objective of harassing, delaying and disrupting military operations of the enemy. The term is sometimes limited to the military operations and tactics of small forces whose objective is to inflict casualties and damage upon the enemy rather than to seize or defend terrain; these operations are characterized by the extensive use of surprise and the emphasis on avoidance of casualties. The term includes organized and directed passive resistance, espionage, assassination, sabotage and propaganda, and, in some cases, ordinary combat. Guerrilla warfare is normally carried on by irregular, or partisan forces; however, regular forces which have been cut off behind enemy lines or which have infiltrated into the enemy rear areas may use guerrilla tactics."

US Army Field Manual 31-21, *Organization and Conduct of Guerrilla Warfare*, Headquarters, Department of the Army, Washington, DC: GPO, 1951.

Unconventional Warfare (UW)

"Activities conducted to enable a resistance movement or insurgency to coerce, disrupt or overthrow a government or occupying power by operating through or with an underground, auxiliary and guerrilla force in a denied area."

Counterterrorism (CT)

"Counterterrorism is activities and operations taken to neutralize terrorists and their networks."

Direct Action (DA)

"Direct action entails short-duration precision strikes and other small-scale offensive actions conducted with specialized military capabilities to seize, destroy, capture, exploit, recover, or damage designated targets in hostile, denied, or diplomatically and/or politically sensitive environments.

Special Reconnaissance (SR)

"Reconnaissance and surveillance actions normally conducted in a clandestine or covert manner to collect or verify information of strategic or operational significance, employing military capabilities not normally found in conventional forces."

Joint Chiefs of Staff Joint Publication 3-05, *Special Operations*, JCS, Washington, DC: GPO, 2005.

CHAPTER I

THE ORIGINS OF SPECIAL FORCES

Berlin—June 16, 1953

The East German construction workers were euphoric but apprehensive as they lay down their tools and descended from their scaffolds. The hardships they had endured in the years following the end of World War II and the empty rhetoric from their masters promising a better life had led to this moment. Nearly spontaneously the workers declared themselves to be free of the yoke of Communism and went on strike, but it was a strike without organization or a plan.

Discontent had been rife in the Soviet-occupied zone of East Germany since early spring that year and even more so after the government announced measures to "accelerate" the move to socialism. But East Germany was already in the grip of an economic downturn that had greatly affected workers and the proposed "New Course" would worsen things even further. The government's announcement was the last straw for workers who saw their quality of life being steadily degraded.

As the workers marched downtown from the city's outskirts, they were joined by hundreds of metal workers from the factories and women from the shops; they were almost exclusively blue-collar workers. First they went to the Alexander Platz and then on to the government buildings at Leipziger Straße. There the mass reached 20,000 men and women, as they demanded the government be abolished. Across East Germany, a spontaneous wave of strikes began and by the next day 500,000 people were protesting. The participants were confident of success, but their confidence was based on a misplaced premise. They thought that because Berlin was occupied by the Allies as well as the Soviets, no military force would be used against them. They believed the West would come to their aid if force was used against them.[1] They shouted slogans but had little idea of what to do next.

The East German government also had no idea how to respond. Their failure to act only exacerbated the situation and further convinced the strikers that the regime was about to fall. But Soviet High Commissioner Vladimir Semyonov and General Andrei Grechko, commander of Soviet Forces in Germany, were not about to let that happen. After consultations with Moscow, they declared a state of emergency.

On June 18, Grechko sent in his forces. Soviet T-34 tanks and troops rolled into the city to crush the unrest, and troops fired tear gas and live ammunition to clear the streets. It was the beginning of the end for the protestors. By early August, all vestiges of the revolt had been erased and the government was again in control.[2]

Although American officials had actively encouraged disaffection with the regime, they had avoided the subject of rebellion and the suddenness of the uprising surprised intelligence officials.[3] The United States' policy had induced many East Germans to believe it would help them. But the Americans did not have the means to support the revolt or any other liberation movement. The message that Radio Free Europe (RFE) and Radio in the American Sector (RIAS) had transmitted was propaganda without teeth. The military had shed its unconventional warfare capabilities after World War II and was only beginning to rebuild them. In Europe, that capability didn't exist at all. In the aftermath of the uprising, the commander of US Forces in Europe wondered why. So did many others.

Rediscovering an Old Art

The origins of Special Forces cannot be traced to an army unit. Rather, they come from a civilian agency. From the beginning, the survival of "Special Forces" was not certain. The "conventional" army resisted the establishment and continued existence of what they saw as an elite unit—something that ran counter to the egalitarian citizen militia that the Founding Fathers envisaged. Special Forces (SF) adapted, proved their worth in fighting complex conflicts, and grew to become the nearly indispensable component it is today.

When the US Army's Center for Military History (CMH) created the official lineage for Special Forces (SF), it established a direct legacy to illustrious military units like Roger's Rangers of the French and Indian Wars, the 1st Special Service Force, and the Ranger battalions of World War II. Colonel Aaron Bank would later call the lineage exercise "nonsense." He stated that the Office of Strategic Services (OSS) was the true precursor of SF.[4] Bank was an OSS veteran, one of the creators of SF, the first commander of the 10th Special Forces Group, and was well placed to judge.

The CMH lineage was established retrospectively in 1960, eight years after the establishment of Special Forces. Because there was no clear military precursor, the 1st Special Service Force and Rangers were assumed to be the closest antecedent. But these units were inappropriate as they were elite, light infantry formations whose operations were intended to support short-term, tactical objectives in concert with conventional units. Special Forces was not intended to be an elite infantry or commando force—its mission was and still is unconventional warfare (UW). For that reason, SF's bloodline can be more directly traced from a quasi-civilian organization, the OSS that operated deep behind enemy lines during WWII.

The OSS was conceived by William "Wild Bill" Donovan in 1941 to "collect and analyze strategic information required by the military's Chiefs of Staff and to conduct special operations not assigned to other agencies."[5] Colonel Donovan, a World War I Medal of Honor winner, got much of his inspiration for this new organization when he visited British Secret Intelligence Service and Special Operations Executive bases and operations overseas. What he saw and heard helped to form his new unit.[6] The OSS was America's first centralized intelligence service, but it also conducted UW missions behind the lines in Europe, the Balkans, and the Far East throughout the war.

According to an early US Army definition, "Unconventional Warfare consists of the three interrelated fields of guerrilla warfare (GW), escape and evasion (E&E), and subversion against hostile states."[7] But UW was a method of war that was scorned in the conventional military because it did not follow accepted rules. In the eyes of the regular army it was something conducted by an undisciplined rabble in dark alleys; it was ungentlemanly. UW was a sideshow to the real wars fought by infantry, armor, and artillery.

The facts tell a different story. OSS provided support in advance of the Allied landings in Africa and France to divert enemy forces from the beachheads and also provided tactical information to the commanders. Along with providing critical intelligence, the OSS's Operational Groups (OG) trained and worked with resistance forces to harass the Axis armies with small unit ambushes, raids, and sabotage missions. The OGs' work with French Resistance was crucial in diverting German forces during the June 6, 1944 D-Day landings.

Other US Army officers conducted similar, if ad hoc, operations during WWII. Following the surrender of US forces on Bataan in the Philippines, Lieutenant Colonel Wendell Fertig and Captain Russell Volckmann stayed behind in the jungles to form Filipino guerrilla bands that tied up Japanese occupation forces on the islands of Mindanao and Luzon until the war ended.

These unconventional units and their operations were the true inspiration for Special Forces.

Donovan's OSS did not survive the end of WWII. President Truman chose to disband it and ordered its functions to be assumed by the War and State Departments. The Strategic Services Unit (SSU) was created in the War Department to integrate the OSS's activities into the military, however, little effort was made to preserve its "special operations" and "morale operations" capabilities. They were quickly abandoned at the end of the war.[8]

The military had distrusted the OSS from the beginning. Even though it was staffed largely with military personnel, the OSS was primarily a civilian agency, and the military had a difficult time accepting its wartime role. Additionally, the secrecy that surrounded the OSS's operations and its unorthodox methods fed suspicions and mistrust. Furthering the problem was a misunderstanding of unconventional warfare and the belief that "regular Army task forces" could perform the same functions.[9]

The OSS was not the only casualty of peace. In the drawdown that followed World War II, the military leadership considered all specialized military units to be a drain on resources. The military would eliminate all special-purpose units after the war, including the Rangers, 1st Special Service Force, and the 5307th Composite Unit known as "Merrill's Marauders."

At the same time, the Central Intelligence Agency (CIA) would become the United States' first centralized intelligence agency and would take on responsibility for covert operations, which included "political, psychological, economic, and unconventional warfare operations" or political warfare—often euphemistically called "subversive operations."[10]

The military did not want responsibility for "political warfare" and the Joint Chiefs of Staff were content to avoid involvement with unconventional warfare in any form, especially anything with the word "subversion" in the definition. For some, the involvement of the US Military Advisory and Planning Group in the successful resolution of the 1947–1949 Greek Civil War seemed to validate conventional thought that the American way of war (i.e. massive firepower, close air support, and mobility) was sufficient to solve any military problem.[11] Others within the US Army disagreed.

By 1946, the United States began to seriously reconsider its wartime assessment of the Soviet Union as an ally. With the death of Franklin D. Roosevelt, the departure of many of his New Deal staff and a growing awareness of Joseph Stalin's intention to permanently occupy Eastern Europe, a more skeptical view of Moscow began to take hold. In the pre-war period, many State Department officers, George Kennan among them, as well as political and business leaders, had warned of the dangers that Stalin and Communism posed. Their warnings had mostly been dismissed by an administration that saw the Soviet Union as a necessary ally for the defeat of Hitler and Nazi Germany.[12]

President Harry S. Truman began to have second thoughts early on. The fraudulent Polish election of 1947 made clear that Eastern Europe was being consolidated under Soviet control. From Moscow, where he was Chargé d'affaires (acting ambassador), George Kennan wrote his "long telegram" in 1946, in which he outlined his belief that the leaders of the USSR considered capitalism to be a menace and that long-term peaceful coexistence was impossible. Two of Truman's senior advisors, Clark Clifford and George Elsey, further distilled Kennan's thoughts into a memo that, along with analysis from other specialists in the government, was presented to Truman in September 1946. These documents contributed to Truman's formulation of a containment strategy that would later be called the Truman Doctrine.[13]

Truman's policies and the growing fear of Soviet encroachment in Eastern Europe, Greece, and Turkey led some in the military to consider other means to fight wars. As a start, the War Department began to take renewed interest in psychological warfare (PW) as a means to combat Soviet disinformation programs. General Robert McClure, who served as General Dwight Eisenhower's psychological warfare chief in the European Theater during WWII, was called upon to comment on the re-invigoration of that capability within the Army. This was a delicate area as the primary responsibilities for PW had been given to the CIA (covert or black PW) and State (overt or white PW). McClure, however, knew that the Army would do the actual implementation of "psywar" in theaters of operations and he counseled that the military needed to prepare and train for that eventuality. Still, the Army's hesitance to get involved with anything that reeked of covert operations led many to shy away. It was only in 1950 that a planning element, the Joint Subsidiary Plans Division, was created as part of the General Staff's Plans Group to prepare training for PW. McClure had been able to argue successfully that PW and UW were operational vice intelligence activities and should be placed under the G-3 (operations), rather than the G-2 (intelligence).

The Korean War would further drive the development of PW and UW capabilities in the army. While the military considered how to create an unconventional warfare capability similar to the OSS in early 1947, the initial studies were a confused amalgamation of airborne reconnaissance, ranger, and commando tasks mixed with OSS capabilities. There was not a clear understanding of what kind of organization was needed and the military had no real desire to be involved in covert operations, especially in peacetime. Then in 1948, under National Security Council

Directive 10/2 (NSC 10/2), the CIA was given responsibility for covert operations that included unconventional warfare. Despite its reluctance to be involved with these activities, the military became concerned with the Agency taking a primary role in planning and training for any type of wartime combat operations.

When the CIA asked for assistance to train personnel for guerrilla warfare in 1949, the Secretary of the Army detailed officers to work directly with the CIA's Office of Policy Coordination (OPC) to ensure the necessary liaison between the CIA and the military was being undertaken. At this point, the Army leadership was content to assist the CIA develop its covert capabilities while the military concentrated on conventional operations. Aside from an agreement to support the CIA with training in guerrilla warfare operations and a lethargic return to planning for "psywar," the USG had not established a credible UW capability by June 1950.

On June 22, 1950, Communist North Korean forces crossed the 38th Parallel into South Korea. This act of aggression would forever change military thinking about the utility of Special Forces.

In August 1950, Secretary of the Army Frank Pace, Jr. showed his impatience in a letter to Army Chief of Staff General J. Lawton Collins asking for action, not a progress report on standing up a psychological warfare organization. To underscore Pace's sense of urgency, General McClure traveled to Washington DC for consultations on the organization of a special staff on the subject. By August 31, 1950, the Psychological Warfare Branch had been approved for activation. General McClure was its first chief.[14]

By January 1951, the Office of the Chief of Psychological Warfare (OCPW) had been fully established as a Special Staff separate from the G-3 and McClure had outlined its functions as "formulate and develop psychological and special operations plans for the Army." With this directive, McClure enshrined his belief that the two activities were intertwined and the military needed its own capability for both. Secretary Pace endorsed this view and institutionalized the relationship of PW with UW in the Army.[15] Pace's support would lead Major General Maxwell Taylor, the Army's senior operations officer (G-3), to direct the development of guerrilla and antiguerrilla warfare responsibilities and to determine which Army units would have those missions.[16]

McClure had already begun to assemble specialists to develop an Army Special Forces capability. His choices showed he understood the requirements of UW well. The officers included Colonel Aaron Bank, Colonel Wendell Fertig, and Lieutenant Colonel Russell Volckmann.

Initial efforts were hampered by terminology. What McClure and his deputies were trying to create did not exist, but there was a tendency to reach back to the Ranger precedent to provide an easy reference point. This was evidenced by the OCPW's naming its first study for the creation of a UW force "Special Forces Ranger Units." This was not exactly what Volckmann and Bank wanted, but McClure felt compelled to use a familiar definition. This further confused the issue as the senior Army leadership tended to view anything "Ranger" as a conventional, tactically oriented, direct-action force, not at all what the OCPW leadership intended.

Then, an opportunity to resolve the issue overlapped with an opportunity to get manpower for the new unit. In July 1951, General Matthew B. Ridgeway, Commander in Chief of Far East Command (FECOM), inactivated all his Ranger units. Soon afterwards, General Maxwell Taylor asked for OCPW assistance to determine the fate of the Army's Rangers. After determining that Ranger training for individual soldiers would become part of the Infantry School, Taylor asked what unit would be able to conduct unconventional warfare operations. McClure and Bank jumped at the opportunity to brief their SF concept knowing that the elimination of the Ranger companies would free up the personnel slots they needed.

Colonel Bank briefed the concept of Special Forces operations with UW as its keystone mission organized to closely resemble the structure of the OSS's Operational Groups. The proposed Special Forces units would be based on 15-man teams that would each act as a nucleus to train an indigenous guerrilla force of up to 1,500 fighters. SF would be a strategic force multiplier working far behind the lines to defeat the enemy. When Taylor agreed to the inactivation of all Ranger units, OCPW had the 2,300 billets necessary to create a new unit. Bank and

Volckmann immediately began the work on a Table of Organization and Equipment (TO&E) and a concept of operations to get Pentagon approval for the formation.[17]

While OCPW was busy creating what would become Special Forces, the war in Korea was forcing General Ridgeway (and later, General Mark Clark) to devise new methods of fighting the Communists. Ridgeway supported the use of propaganda and requested assistance to formulate the message and provide material support. OCPW was eager to help despite differences of opinion on how the activities should be carried out.

McClure was critical of FECOM's conduct of unconventional warfare in Korea. Particularly, he found fault in FECOM's command and control of UW, which had been placed under G-2 (Intelligence) rather than G-3 (Operations). He also faulted FECOM's poor coordination of PW and UW operations with the CIA. The Korean War illustrated the difficulties: although an element existed for coordination at the theater level, the CIA insisted on running its operations largely independent of the military command.[18] These difficulties would be a harbinger of the relationship between the two organizations well into the 21st century.

In 1951, OCPW's planning led to a concept that would be the basis for the future Special Forces Regiment. It would comprise nearly 2,500 troops in three battalions. Importantly, the plan allowed for over half the enlisted men to be Lodge Act recruits, i.e. East European émigrés who would be enlisted into the US Army.[19] It was believed that these indigenous soldiers would be able to operate more easily in Eastern Europe than American troops, who were hampered by cultural and ethnic differences.

Importantly, Volckmann stipulated in his recommendations that the Army should have the responsibility "in peace to prepare and plan for the conduct of special forces operations and in time of war to organize and conduct special forces operations."[20] Although McClure was initially more pragmatic and accepting of a CIA role in UW, he would become less so with time and opposed CIA's role.[21] In part, this change was due to the Agency's refusal to share information about resistance groups with which it was in contact. This issue would remain an obstacle to cooperation and would never be satisfactorily resolved.

The Joint Chiefs of Staff (JCS) finally agreed and gave wartime responsibility for UW to the Army. CIA would retain its capabilities for peacetime operations as delegated under NCS 10/2. But it would be more than a year before the first Special Forces Group would be created and much doctrinal discussion would take place before the final organization and mission details were worked out. The mission statement called for SF "to infiltrate its component operational groups to designated areas within the enemy's sphere of influence and organize the indigenous guerrilla potential on a military basis for tactical and strategic exploitation in conjunction with our land, sea, and air forces."[22]

Colonel Bank's TO&E for Special Forces incorporated both conventional army structure and the organization of the OSS's Operational Groups. The basic unit would be a 15-man team called an Operational Detachment Alpha (ODA) or "A" Team.[23] Ten ODAs would be assigned to each company and three companies would make up a battalion.[24] The company and battalion staffs would make up "B" and "C" Teams that would control the deployed ODAs in the event of war. Each SF Group consisted of three battalions. The intent was to give the group a permanent structure acceptable to the Pentagon, but allow for flexibility. The "A" Teams, for example, could be broken down into two six-man elements or even four three-man elements if needed. This "split team concept" has survived to the present time.[25] Further, the SF Group could be broken up to operate in several locations or work as a whole in a single area of operations (AO) under a theater commander.

The team structure was later modified to comprise 12 men, each a specialist in his primary field. There would be a captain in command with a lieutenant as his deputy, a team sergeant, an operations and intelligence sergeant, two weapons sergeants (one light and one heavy weapons specialist), two engineer or "demolitions" sergeants, two communications sergeants, and two medical sergeants. To ensure the team's operational capability was robust, each man would be cross-trained in the other specialties. This also permitted breaking up the team into small elements when the mission dictated. Along with the "hard skills" of shooting and blowing things up, instruction on intelligence tradecraft and teaching skills were emphasized. The SF soldier was above all else a teacher and had to be able to train and advise a guerrilla force to be effective. This entailed far more than basic combat training could provide. The SF training course touched on everything from revolutionary theory and administration of personnel to advisory techniques and cross-cultural communication.

The first group, the 10th Special Forces Group (Airborne) (10th SFG) was formally established on May 19, 1952 at Fort Bragg, North Carolina about the same time as the Psychological Warfare Center (PWC) was formed there.[26] The PWC was the component school responsible for all training in PW and UW. Although some questioned the incorporation of the two (and the seeming subjugation of SF) under the PWC, it was probably the best choice that could have been made. The PWC was a logical evolution of General Donovan's concepts. Additionally, General McClure understood better than most that SF was a hard sell to military officers who believed the American way of war should not include an "unconventional" aspect.

McClure chose Bank to take command and the latter immediately began to devise intense individual and unit training programs to prepare the unit for full activation. Bank took his post on June 19, 1952 along with seven enlisted men and a warrant officer administrative technician. It was a rather meager beginning, but by the end of the month, the group was at 122 men and by early spring 1953, it reached 1,700 men. Initial recruitment was slow, but the cause was soon discovered and rectified. It seems that some commanders recognized they were about to lose many of their top performers and set out to discourage volunteers or sabotage their paperwork. Only a directive to his subordinate commanders by the Army Chief of Staff eliminated the obstacles.

Individual specialist training began right away. As Colonel Bank later explained, each man would be a volunteer, at least 21 years old with the rank of sergeant or above, airborne qualified, speak or have the aptitude to speak a European language, and willing to serve behind enemy lines, including in civilian clothes if required.[27] Those initial requirements did not guarantee selection for the unit, as each man would be interviewed and subjected to a battery of tests, both academic and physical, to ensure their suitability for the unit. The men were continually evaluated through their individual training and remained on a probation of sorts during the first months of their assignment to a team. As important as technical skills were the abilities to work together on a team or alone far from supervision. The arrangement did seem to keep everyone at peak performance. Standards were high. No one wanted to be returned to the "regular" army once they experienced the unit's *esprit de corps*.

Bank's Army Training Program (ATP) was approved and the group conducted two training tests in 1953: an Army Field Forces Test at Camp McKall, North Carolina and "Operation CLEO" in the Chattahoochie National Forest of Georgia. The training and the field tests drew heavily on the experience and capabilities of the Allied Jedburgh teams and OSS's Operational Groups of WWII.[28] Supported by the US Air Force's 582nd Air Resupply Group, the 10th parachuted 300 troopers into the remote forest areas.[29] The teams practiced operating as guerrilla force organizers and trainers while some civilian volunteers acted as the guerrillas and others provided safehouses or became couriers. The whole gamut of guerrilla warfare operations was played out against a Georgia National Guard unit that filled the role of an enemy "aggressor" force. Escape and Evasion (E&E) nets were set up to exfiltrate "downed pilots" out of enemy territory, while partisans collected intelligence on the "enemy" and carried messages between the guerrilla units hidden in the woods. Once the guerrilla force had been trained, it was used to conduct sabotage missions, ambushes, and raids, simulating wartime scenarios. The test was concluded successfully according to the test observers and the unit certified for operations.[30] Returning to Fort Bragg, the unit was then parceled out for specialist training in mountain, amphibious, and smoke jumper operations.[31]

The 10th SFG had always been destined to be stationed in Europe, but the events of 1953 in the German Democratic Republic (GDR), or East Germany, accelerated the deployment.

Battleground Berlin

When Nazi Germany fell at the end of World War II, its capital Berlin quickly became a point of contention between the Soviets and the Western Allies of the United States, Britain, and France. At the Yalta

Conference, these allies finalized their agreement to divide Germany into zones of occupation. The Americans, British, and French occupied what would be known as West Germany, while the Soviets occupied the East. Deep inside the Soviet-occupied zone, Berlin was also divided into four zones.[32] Soviet leader Joseph Stalin immediately began to put pressure on the Western powers to force them from the city. He directed his occupation forces to blockade routes into the city in 1948, but that gambit failed after the Allies mounted a massive 300-day airlift of supplies. Although Stalin thereafter recognized the Four-Power occupation of Berlin, it was clear that the Soviets and their new ally, the GDR, would never make the occupation easy.

Directly contributing to the GDR's problems, the Federal Republic of Germany had begun its revitalization under the Marshall Plan while East Germany's economy stagnated under Soviet occupation. Many Germans abandoned the Soviet sector in a mass exodus for the western sectors to find jobs and a better life, further hampering progress in the East.

In 1952, following the rejection by the US, UK, and France of Stalin's offer to reunify Germany as a neutral, unarmed state, the GDR government under Walter Ulbricht began a full Sovietization of the country.[33] This meant a crash program of socialization that hit the middle class with high taxes and an emphasis on heavy industry, which led to shortages of personal goods. By April 1953, the collectivization of farms, pressure on churches and opposition parties, and a resulting overall lower standard of living began to cause discontent and resistance. The ruling Socialist Unity Party then decided to increase work requirements by ten percent.[34] With increasing arrests and detentions and signs of impending social unrest apparent, it was clear even in Moscow that a crisis was brewing. Under Soviet instructions to temporarily reverse the socialization measures to avoid a clash, the GDR leadership announced a "New Course" that suspended earlier, unpopular measures. This surprised and shocked the GDR's Communist party faithful and emboldened the populace, who perceived the announcement as government weakness, to demand more.[35] On June 17, 1953, a protest started by East German construction workers the previous day exploded into strikes and unrest that spread to 400 cities, towns and villages across the country. Only a full-scale deployment of Soviet military force that resulted in the deaths of hundreds and arrests of thousands of protestors guaranteed the survival of the GDR.

The United States and its allies were not ready to believe that the GDR was in mortal danger of collapse and never contemplated military or covert action to further destabilize the regime. They were ready, however, to plan for the future and the possibility that war would again visit the European landscape. In 1952, the Psychological Strategy Board (PSB) had called for "controlled preparation for more active resistance" inside the Soviet-controlled zone. This plan was further expanded upon in NSC Report 158.[36] In peacetime, these activities would primarily be the purview of the CIA. Efforts had already begun to organize and support passive resistance movements that would become active in time of war. In order to support these groups should war begin, the Army would need the 10th SFG and, in the early fall of 1953, the unit was ordered to deploy to Germany for permanent basing. On November 11, Colonel Bank and his command set sail for Europe. By the beginning of 1954, they were ensconced at their new home in the Bavarian town of Bad Tölz with a wartime mission to support resistance movements and organize guerrilla forces in the Soviet-dominated Eastern European satellite countries.

The JCS now saw SF as a valuable tool in their plans to defend Western Europe from a Soviet attack. SF's task would be to build a guerrilla capability in Eastern Europe to help "retard" a Soviet invasion. The intent was for SF to make contact with existing underground or resistance organizations, some of which were supported by the CIA, in much the same fashion as the OSS had during WWII and then create havoc in the enemy's backyard.[37]

The future battleground was clear. The eastern borders of the Federal Republic of Germany (FRG) and Austria would be the line of departure for Warsaw Pact forces. NATO expected a spearhead assault of at least 24 Russian army divisions, along with 30 divisions of the satellite states including GDR, Poland and the Czech Republic, to attack through the Fulda Gap. The Soviets could also quickly deploy an additional 38 divisions from its western regions. Supporting attacks were also expected against Norway, Finland, Denmark and through Switzerland, as were raids by Russian "*Spetsnaz*" special operations forces to disrupt NATO's command and control points in the rear areas as the Soviets advanced. NATO also thought the Soviets could expand their forces through mobilization of an additional 145 divisions within 30 days. Soviet planners expected their forces could reach the Pyrenees within a month.[38]

Against this juggernaut, NATO could field approximately 75 divisions. The Soviet superiority in naval and air assets was even more pronounced.[39] The Supreme Headquarters Allied Powers Europe (SHAPE), NATO's military command, planned that arresting a Soviet advance would be a key priority. Nuclear weapons were envisioned for early use. Another key aspect of the defense plan would be to cause disruption in the enemy's rear areas. This is where Special Forces would play their role.

All NATO countries planned for the commitment of special operations forces to take on strategic targets. Most were limited in their ability to deploy units behind the Soviet forces and would rely on keeping them ready for stay-behind roles in their own countries. A stay-behind mission required designated units to remain hidden in place while the enemy pressed forward, emerging only after the Soviets had passed to attack in the rear areas. Even the United States, which planned on parachuting SF far behind Soviet lines, realized that penetration of the enemy airspace by American aircraft would be difficult given the air defenses they would face.

The Far Outpost of Freedom

By the mid-1950s, the divided city of Berlin was the epicenter of the Cold War conflict between the West and the East. The 1948 blockade and the 1953 workers' uprising had demonstrated the true nature of Communist rule and made Berlin a symbol of freedom deep within the Soviet Bloc. The continued presence of Allied forces in the city was a "thorn in the side" of the Communists. The mass exodus of hundreds of thousands of East Germans to West Germany though West Berlin was leading to an economic disaster. Both a political and military problem, the Communist leaders hoped to remove this irritant, first by weakening and then eliminating ties between West Berlin and West Germany. Their goal was to force the Allies to abandon the city so that it could be incorporated into the GDR. Simultaneously, the Allies deliberated on how best to maintain their presence, ensure unrestricted access to the city, and guarantee freedoms for West Berliners.

Militarily, Allied forces in Berlin were initially thought of as a show garrison meant to "keep the flag flying" and to uphold the Four-Power status of the city as set out in the four-power agreements of 1945. In 1955, however, the US Commander of Berlin (USCOB) began to reassess that position and planned not only for a unified defense of the city with the British and French, but a possible breakout to the West. In the fall of 1955, the USCOB proposed that portions of the US garrison in Berlin should prepare for such a contingency in conjunction with Special Forces operations in and around the city.

At a strategic conference in that same year, the three Allied Chiefs of Staff and the three Allied commandants of Berlin agreed that demolition squads should be used to destroy strategic targets outside the city to slow the Warsaw Pact should the Soviets choose to advance on the West.[40] USAREUR planners recognized that if SF elements were stationed in Berlin before any hostilities, they would be "behind the lines" as soon as hostilities began. Better still, they would have time to prepare for a possible Warsaw Pact D-Day in their operational area. Under the concept, the SF teams would destroy strategic targets outside the city to destabilize the enemy and retard his movements. General Anthony C. McAuliffe, Commander in Chief, US Army Europe (CINCUSAREUR) agreed and, in November 1955, plans were made to assign six US Army SF "A" teams to Berlin Command.[41]

The teams would take their orders from the Support Operations Task Force Europe (SOTFE), a new subordinate element of US European Command (USEUCOM). SOTFE was set up in Paris in May 1955 to conduct planning and to provide operational control of all US UW operations. Its primary mission was to use its assets to delay and hamper a Soviet attack. In peacetime, SOTFE set up field exercises, unit evaluations, and coordinated training of the units with foreign SOF units.

During wartime, it would direct the deployment of American SOF units against the Warsaw Pact in accordance with the orders of CINCEUR. For the next 35 years, until the fall of the Wall in 1989, SOTFE would supervise operations of SF in Berlin.

Although the small Allied occupation army in Berlin would be little more than an annoyance to the massive Group of Soviet Forces Germany, it could serve as delaying force to slow their advance. It was with this intent that the idea of placing a Special Forces detachment in Berlin, 110 miles behind the Iron Curtain, was conceived. Although the unit would be part of the occupation forces in Berlin, its mission was not defensive. It was to be a secret weapon ready to strike the heart of the Soviet Army at any moment.

CHAPTER II

THE FORMATIVE YEARS (1956–1971)

If we are mark'd to die, we are enough
To do our country loss; and if to live,
The fewer men, the greater share of honour.
  William Shakespeare, *Henry V*

Berlin was probably the last thing Major Edward Maltese was thinking about that day in the spring of 1956. Having recently arrived at Flint Kaserne, Bad Tölz from the United States, he fully expected to take command of a company of the 10th Special Forces Group (SFG) and settle into the regimen of living and working in southern Germany. He would get his company, just not at Bad Tölz. Colonel William E. Harrison, the 10th's commander, ordered Maltese to set up a new Special Forces Detachment in Berlin. It would have a modified SF company organization—six teams and a small headquarters staff—and a skeleton crew of 40 men to start. Most important, its true name, organization, and especially its mission were classified.

The unit would be attached to Headquarters, 6th Infantry Regiment, which was already stationed in the city as part of the American Berlin Command occupation force.[1]

It would be a formidable job, but "Malt" was ready. As an infantry officer during World War II, he jumped into St Mere Eglise, France on D-Day with the 1/505th Parachute Infantry Regiment and again into the hellfire of Operation MARKET GARDEN in Holland. He was with General James Galvin when the 82nd Airborne entered Berlin as part of the first occupation force. In the Korean War he was a company commander and made his third combat jump with the 187th Airborne Regimental Combat Team. He joined Special Forces in 1953 and was assigned to the 10th when it moved to Germany. "Malt" cared more about his men's welfare than his own advancement. They felt it and reciprocated with great respect and loyalty and he advanced steadily in rank anyway. Maltese would be instrumental in dealing with the staff at Berlin Brigade while his men plunged into the details of building a clandestine unit in the city.

His first task was to select the men who would go with him.[2] The initial group consisted of a major (himself), a captain, and six Operational Detachment "A" Teams simply designated Team One through Team Six.[3] Initially, the teams were manned at half strength with six non-commissioned officers, commanded by a master sergeant. A captain would eventually fill that position and the teams would be increased to 11 men.[4] All were SF qualified and a Top Secret (TS) security clearance was required (a step above the Secret clearance usually necessary for SF duty) as well as the ability to speak German or another Eastern European language.[5] This was mostly unnecessary as about 45 percent of the men were Lodge Act soldiers.[6] Perhaps the most significant requirement was for each volunteer to understand the clandestine nature of the job. While in Berlin, no one was to identify himself or the unit as SF or allude to the nature of their mission. They were there to "support the Berlin Brigade," a phrase that said everything and nothing at the same time. There were problems with this rather ad hoc cover mechanism that would come back to haunt the unit. Having no officially approved cover meant the unit had no established cover for status (its alleged reason to exist), and second, the men had no cover story for their day-to-day jobs, their reason to be in the city. The inevitable result was that everyone came up with his own story resulting in a patchwork of inconsistent covers, which gave the opposition something to focus on: a mystery unit. Working outside the confines of the base, the men would put on their ad hoc covers, but an in-depth check would have quickly revealed their falsity. Other mechanisms would later be developed to better conceal the men and the mission.

While many of the officers and senior non-commissioned officers (NCOs) were selected by hand, enlisted volunteers were requested by the simple means of posting a notice on the unit bulletin board in the late spring of 1956. The notice asked for men in specific military occupational specialties (MOS) and qualifications who wished to be considered for a new unit in Berlin. Those who responded were interviewed and told they would be notified in several weeks if selected. Henry Bertrand was one who saw the notice and volunteered. An SF medic in Bravo Company of the 10th, he was given orders for Berlin in June.[7]

Getting There

Once the men were selected, the next order of business was to get everyone to the city. Bertrand remembered that in July 1956, Major Maltese ordered the men to travel to Berlin in small groups of three to four. They drove personal cars north to Helmstedt, a small West German town on the border where the *Autobahn* crossed into the Soviet zone. Helmstedt was near the Checkpoint Alpha crossing site, where Allied travelers processed first through the MPs and then the Soviets before entering the German Democratic Republic (GDR) to get to Berlin.

When they arrived at Helmstedt, they dropped off their cars and rode the US Army Duty Train through the Soviet zone to Berlin. At that time, no one with a TS clearance was permitted to drive a car though the Soviet zone because the Army did not want to risk having a soldier detained and interrogated by the Russians. The Duty Train was the more secure route. Traveling in civilian clothing under classified CINCUSAREUR orders attaching them to the 7781st Army Unit, the men rode to Berlin and went straight to McNair Barracks, their new home in the American sector.[8] The rest of their equipment was to follow by guarded truck and military train into the city.

The cars they had driven to Helmstedt were brought to Berlin by the MPs themselves. They followed the long straight drive through the Soviet zone to the next stop, Checkpoint Bravo, where the drivers and their cars were checked out of the Soviet zone and into the American sector of West Berlin.[9] After several days in Berlin, the men were still without their vehicles and they began to wonder what had happened. When they looked around the various barracks, they found that the cars had arrived and had been appropriated and used as personal transport by the MPs who had driven them to the city. The cars were swiftly returned after the MPs were confronted and the consequences were fully explained.

Working out of the regimental headquarters of the 6th Infantry, the new unit's cover as the "Security Platoon" provided a reasonable amount of latitude for a clandestine Special Forces unit to operate in the city both in uniform and in civilian clothes without raising suspicions. Only about ten officers in the Berlin Command knew the true makeup of the "platoon" and its mission. The men of the Detachment did not have much contact with 6th Infantry units other than to participate as "aggressor forces" in the field exercises that took place in the Grunewald forest. The Det was conducting its own preparations for war.

In April 1958, the unit moved again, this time several kilometers across town to Andrews Barracks. It was a location that would permit expansion and better security. The unit was renamed Detachment "A" and was simply called "the Detachment" or Det "A" for short. This would be the unit's cover name until its inactivation in 1984.

After the move was completed, the unit needed to be filled to its authorized strength and the search began for qualified men. Two methods were used: the standard army method of someone in the Pentagon scouring records for experienced men to take the assignment and the commander's "direct approach."

Jim Wilde was at Bad Tölz waiting to be assigned to one of 10th Group's teams in 1957. He was a junior NCO and had recently arrived from Fort Bragg as part of a levy from the 77th SFG. One day he and Karl Helmle were ordered to report to the day room where "a major" awaited them. Wilde's first panicked thought was along the lines of "I've never talked to a major and why would one want to talk to me?" So it was with some trepidation that he reported to the officer. Wilde entered the room, reported in, and was told to sit down. The commander said, "I have only two questions for you. Do you speak German and do you drink?" Wilde said later that he thought about his answers for a moment and then lied a bit. His German was OK, but not fluent he said, and he drank, but he thought it was better to say he didn't. The major seemed to measure Wilde up for a moment and then said, "Pack your bags, you're leaving with me for the train station in two hours."

Wilde hesitantly asked, "Where are we going, sir?"

"Berlin," came the reply.

Wilde blurted out, "But I don't want to go to Berlin!"

It was not negotiable, "You are a radio repairman. I need radio repairmen. We're leaving for Berlin." With that the interview was over.[10]

In later years, if an aspirant wanted the assignment (assuming he even knew of the unit's existence) it helped to contact SF Branch at "DA" (Department of the Army) and talk very nicely with the personnel specialists about the assignment. Gifts of alcohol, candy, and flowers made a positive consideration of the request more probable.[11]

In the early years, a few enlisted men and officers were recruited for the unit who were not "SF" qualified. Some, like parachute riggers, admin specialists, and supply sergeants, would work on the headquarters staff. A small number would be assigned to teams where they would be trained up on the job, as there were simply not enough SF-qualified soldiers in the Army at the time.[12] Wilde would receive his "S" as a radio operator and be cross-trained in demolitions and weapons after a year on the team.[13] Not only did a soldier need to be individually and technically qualified, he had to fit in with his mates.

Language was always important and early on the inside joke was that English wasn't heard much in the team rooms. In fact, it may have been the least common language! Although German was the primary language requirement, the teams had a decidedly eastern European flavor. And, the Lodge Act soldiers were clannish—they called themselves the "10-8-12 Club," a reference to their identification numbers that all began with "10812." One American-born sergeant who joined the unit early on said he was assigned to a team made up of 10812 men. It was several weeks before anyone but the team sergeant spoke to him. But, once he was accepted, it was like being adopted into a family. The unit had several cultural layers and each "A" Team had a decidedly different personality.

"In the Event of a General Outbreak of Hostilities . . . ."

1956 was a turbulent year in Europe. Popular uprisings in Communist Poland and Hungary were ruthlessly put down by their Soviet occupiers. In the GDR, the Group of Soviet Forces Germany occupied the country with between 382,000 and 423,000 troops. The GDR's newly formed army, the *Nationale Volksarmee* (NVA) had about 75,000 men.[14] In contrast, the Allied force made up of Americans, British, and French numbered only around 10,000 in West Berlin. Despite the fact the Allies could count on "Force B," an additional three detachments of heavily armed, paramilitary *Bereitschaftspolizei* (Readiness Police) and their German Labor Service guard battalions, the odds were not in their favor.[15] Det "A"—in their Security Platoon guise—trained the *Bereitschaftspolizei Notstandzug* (Emergency Platoon) in the use of the American heavy weaponry it had been issued, primarily the 60mm mortar. In the late 1950s, the *Bereitschaftspolizei* were a small but crucial part of Berlin Brigade's defense plans.[16] Allied reinforcement of Berlin in time of war would not just be infeasible; it would be impossible, as Warsaw Pact air defenses would quickly close all air corridors. NATO would be occupied with holding off the Soviet onslaught expected to slam through the Fulda Gap onto the plains of Western Europe. In effect, the Allies in Berlin would be on their own. Some believed the city would become the world's largest POW camp.

The Area of Operations

Berlin in the late 1950s was a study in contrasts. East Berlin, under Soviet occupation, seemed not to have come far since the final battle of the war in Europe. The damaged shells of public and private buildings still bore mute testimony to the destructive fury the Russian army and the Allied bombings had brought down on the city. Much of its industrial capacity had been simply ripped out and transported to the Soviet Union while the rebuilding of the city progressed slowly. Where it was rebuilt, especially along the newly renamed Stalinallee, the buildings reflected a socialist style considered both ponderous and ugly. It had been a cosmopolitan city ravaged in war that now lived day-to-day anticipating the next cataclysm. Brown lignite coal smoke from East Germany hung thickly, while cold winds from the steppes of Russia penetrated the soul through the long, cold, gray winters.

In the western sectors occupied by the Americans, British, and French, it was a different story. Although there were huge depots of coal reserves stored in strategic locations, a legacy of the Berlin Blockade of 1948, the West responded with a rebuilding plan designed to reflect the "new, democratic western Germany to the outside world."[17] International architects were invited to design and build a modern city with public parks and improved living accommodations. The United States presented the city with a conference hall that was quickly nicknamed the "pregnant oyster." It was clear the city was more than a political flashpoint, it became a cultural and social counterpoint between the Communist East and the Democratic (and Capitalist) West.

For the men of the Detachment, it was an unbelievably unique experience. Serving in the divided city, whether in 1956 or in 1985, was unlike duty anywhere else. Walking along Bernauer Straße next to the Wall in the early evening fog, S-Bahn trains rattling along on the overhead tracks, you could easily think you were taking part in a film noir adaptation of *The Third Man* or *The Spy Who Came in From the Cold*. Not 50 meters away was the front line of an existential struggle between two cultures that stood ready to go to war. The front line encircled you, your home, your family—everything—there was no rear area for a safe retreat. You lived deep inside what was already enemy territory. Yet, across the street you could walk into a *Kneipe* and order a beer and schnitzel and sit quietly reading a book, completely oblivious to the conflict.

The history of Berlin weighed down oppressively at times. A sign on a building facade commemorated the events of *Kristallnacht,* the night of broken glass when the anti-Jewish pogroms started in 1938. The march of jackboots through the narrow streets echoed in not-so-distant memories. To escape, there were the beaches of the Wannsee where many came to forget they were locked inside a huge cage. Spring and summer seemed to signal both renewal and survival.

The Detachment's men moved through the city in civilian clothes, carrying the briefcases, shoulder bags, or, later, day packs, that contained the tools of their trade; whatever they needed for the tasks they were to undertake that day. They walked alongside ordinary Berliners with the uneasy knowledge that they could well be called upon to fight on those very streets. At the same time, it was hard not to smile inside—for these men were among the privileged few Special Forces soldiers given the opportunity to serve in this far outpost on such an important mission. The glory of the Spartans was often recalled at unit events, but not unforgotten was the unequivocal ending that befell them at Thermopylae.

Soviet War Plans

In the mid-1950s, the Soviet Union continued to consolidate its control of the countries of Eastern Europe. The integration of the Federal Republic of Germany into NATO's ranks gave the USSR the justification it needed to form the Warsaw Pact. And, although the alliance had a political dimension, its primary purpose was to off-set NATO militarily. Ostensibly, the Soviet Union sought only to legitimize and protect "political-territorial results of World War II," in other words to achieve the inviolability of its borders.[18]

NATO leaders saw it otherwise. The brutal suppression of freedoms in East Germany, Hungary, and Poland showed the true dimensions of the Soviet Union's rule. Furthermore, intelligence indicators led NATO to believe the Soviet Union sought to expand beyond its borders into Western Europe and assessed the Soviets would go to war on a massive scale, possibly leading off with "massive nuclear strikes that would totally, and irreparably, destroy the losing side's entire social and political system."[19] These attacks would be followed with a massive thrusts into Western Europe using conventional armored and motorized infantry forces, along with attacks against strategic targets such as airbases and fixed facilities using air, missile, and special operations assets.

The Supreme Allied Commander Europe (SACEUR), General Alfred Gruenther knew NATO's military forces would be severely disadvantaged if the Warsaw Pact was able to achieve surprise. He relied heavily on intelligence sources to provide him with indications of Soviet preparations for war. When and if war came, NATO would rely on its own air assets to destroy key choke points such as rail marshaling yards and bridges crossing the Elbe and Oder Rivers to slow the enemy's advance and follow-on logistics. In support of NATO, US Army Special Forces—along with special operations forces from Allied countries—planned to conduct missions that would disrupt the Warsaw Pact military forces in their rear areas. Some fifty "A" teams from the 10th Special Forces Group at Bad Tölz were allocated to conduct unconventional warfare operations in Western Germany and Eastern Europe, while the six teams in Berlin would conduct direct-action missions against the rail, road, and canal infrastructure around Berlin before beginning UW operations. A key element of these operations would also be to report on Warsaw Pact activities and movements to enable air strikes against them.

Det "A" Plans for War

As a result of the move, Maltese's unit came under the direct supervision of the US Commander of Berlin (USCOB) and the Detachment's formal ties with 10th Group were broken. During peacetime, the Detachment was administratively responsible to the USCOB, but during wartime, it was responsible to two commanders. The operational concept was "upon the outbreak of general hostilities or under certain conditions of localized war," the teams would first attack targets in East Germany selected by the USCOB as vital to his successful defense of the city, as well as priority targets in the US European Command (EUCOM) Unconventional War Plan.[20] Once that tasking was completed, the teams would conduct UW operations as directed by Commander, Support Operations Task Force Europe (SOTFE).[21] The concept was for each team to link up with local guerrilla forces and to assist them to organize, train, and fight the Soviet forces. It was an ambitious and extremely dangerous mission, some would call it suicidal.

SOTFE was charged with unconventional warfare (UW) planning, training, and operations for all US special operations forces (SOF) in Europe. These included the 10th SFG, the new Detachment "A," the early Air Force special operations squadrons and later the Navy Special

Warfare units.[22] Now, with another tool in its chest, SOTFE planners began to devise the role the Detachment would play in a future war.[23]

At first, the Detachment's six teams worked separately on their specific missions, but in late 1959, the organization was changed, primarily due to a lack of officers. Three task groups (TG), designated North, South, and Central, were formed to ease administrative control. In time of war, however, the six teams would conduct their combat missions separately.[24] TG North was oriented towards the French sector of Berlin and beyond, TG South would use the American sector as their launch point. The two teams of Task Group Central would remain in Berlin to conduct urban UW or "stay behind" operations after neutralizing their designated in-city targets.[25]

The unit would first conduct sabotage attacks on vital targets such as rail marshaling yards, bridges, military command and control systems, telecommunications, petroleum oil and lubricant (POL) facilities, power plants, and inland waterways. Most of the rail targets were on the *Berliner Aussenring,* a 125-kilometer rail line that circled West Berlin just outside the city and would carry the overwhelming majority of Soviet traffic westwards to the front. Once those targets were destroyed the teams would then conduct the CINCEUR's mission of unconventional warfare behind the lines of the Warsaw Pact armies, the so-called "stay behind" mission. It was also prepared to arm and direct civilians inside Berlin against an occupation force—there were 10,000 weapons in the Brigade's Emergency Arms Reserve stored specifically for that purpose.[26] It was clear that the Detachment's mission was based on the "worst case" scenario of an all-out war with the Warsaw Pact.

Each team was assigned a sector of the city to work in and an area beyond the frontier inside the GDR where their targets were located. Very detailed target folders with all available intelligence, maps, and aerial photos were assembled and models of the targets were constructed to plan their mission. Each team's preparations were compartmented from the other five—only the unit commander and his operations and intelligence staff knew all the targets.[27]

A number of factors went into target choice. First, was the target critical to the Warsaw Pact? Second, was it accessible; could the team get to it? Then, would the enemy be able to repair or replace the damage quickly? Would the target's destruction have any effect on the enemy?[28] Obviously, destroying a bridge that could be easily bypassed or a railway line that would be quickly repaired would have little long-term effect—those were scratched from the list. The mission concept was straightforward, however, its execution would be another story.

Teams spent a lot of time along the city's perimeter in their assigned sectors looking for suitable crossing points. The EGs (East Germans) were expecting people to escape out of the GDR, not into it, which made the prospect of crossing this fortified barrier somewhat easier. When the Wall was built in 1961, the mission became quite a bit more difficult for the teams tasked to cross over. Even then, crossing the border was just the first hurdle. Once outside Berlin, the teams faced a cross-country march to the target that would require them to avoid enemy rear area security forces. The teams had to be prepared to deal with local guard forces; a bridge or a railway junction might not be defended, but an enemy headquarters would be guaranteed to have heavy security.

For the teams remaining in the city, the targets were easier to reach. West Berlin's power plants, canals and locks, and radio stations could be put out of action quickly. Detachment members conducted in-depth studies of their targets that included arranging tours of the facilities and in some cases working at the site. The popular radio station, Radio in the American Sector (RIAS), was designated a target because it was assumed the enemy would want to use it in the critical first days of their occupation. To develop the target folder, a Detachment communicator, Jim Wilde, got a job there, ostensibly as a student intern. Over several months he was able to study the facility closely and identify which components needed to be sabotaged to put the station out of action, but not destroy it completely. He then helped put together information that would be kept up to date with periodic visits by other unit members. The teams that remained in the city had a relatively easier mission, in that they would be able to immerse themselves among the population quickly. The four teams designated to cross into East German territory would find survival quite a bit tougher. Once the teams crossed the border, found and destroyed their targets, they then were to link up with underground groups that had either been set up by or were in contact with US intelligence agencies, but as that information was closely held, no one was entirely sure how that was to happen. Failing all else, the teams had escape plans to make their way to friendly territory. According to some of the men assigned to the unit at that time, there was a general feeling they probably would not make it that far.

In 1957, Major Maltese was reassigned to USAREUR Headquarters and Major Roman Piernick replaced him. Piernick was born in the United States, the son of Polish immigrants, won the Silver Star in World War II, and spoke Polish and German fluently. The language ability came in handy with the Lodge Act soldiers. Piernick, like most men of the Detachment, had no illusions about the enemy across the frontier. Piernick had been part of the US occupation force in Berlin in 1946. During his stay he went to visit his grandfather and extended family in postwar Poland. For unknown reasons, he was arrested and interrogated by Russian officers for five days. Piernick's experience of seeing his relatives "terrorized by the Russians and fearing to speak the truth" motivated his sense of mission.[29] Piernick's feelings were shared by some of the Lodge Act recruits whose anti-Communism was often extreme. This was understandable as most of them came from countries that were now under the boot of the Soviets. Many still had family, relatives, and even friends back in their homelands who they couldn't visit or even write to, for fear of endangering their lives. Theirs was a visceral feeling that didn't compare to that of native-born Americans who hadn't experienced the deprivation and oppression of a Communist or Nazi regime.

Unlike Maltese, Piernick was more distant in his command style and not as close to the men. Piernick spent most of his time at the Brigade Headquarters and left the day-to-day running of the unit to his XO, Captain Bliss Croft. What Piernick did have was a solid background in intelligence tradecraft and his biggest contribution was making sure everyone in the unit knew these skills. He also ensured that Uncle Sam paid for the men's civilian clothing by getting the USCOB's approval on paper. Piernick had a talent for using Army regulations for the common good, but that didn't prevent the occasional glitch. The first batch of clothing was purchased by one of the unit's native Germans, Gerhard Frick, who apparently had no sense of style. The clothing was issued to everyone in the unit piece by piece. As Harry Brown put it, "We looked like a bunch of clowns." After that, everyone shopped for his own clothing, but it took a while for the guys to blend into the local population. Some still looked like clowns.

Raising the Stakes

In November 1958, Khrushchev announced his readiness to turn over the USSR's control functions of Berlin to the government of the GDR. Shortly thereafter, he demanded the Western Allies pull their forces to make Berlin a demilitarized city. Khrushchev's motivations were complex, but in essence centered on countering the growing influence of West Germany (FRG) in NATO and forcing international recognition of the GDR. A secondary effect would be to remove "the thorn" and allow the Communists to gain control of the western sector of Berlin, which Khrushchev alleged was a base for the Allies to attack the USSR.[30] Khrushchev said his "suggestions" would further the cause of peace in Europe, however, the Allies did not respond as Khrushchev had hoped and saw his posturing for the threat it was.

The underlying reason for the Soviet concerns was the steady stream of East Germans fleeing the country for West Berlin. The outpouring of refugees was seriously debilitating to the GDR's economy as manpower shortages were affecting everything from manufacturing and agriculture to medical care. The tide would have to be stemmed or the country would be facing a difficult future. When increased numbers of border guards and negative propaganda against the West did not affect the flow, a more concrete solution would be found.

The Allied assessment was that giving the GDR control over access to Berlin would certainly lead them to shut down the routes into the city and precipitate a renewal of the Berlin blockade. Evacuating West Berlin and making the city a "demilitarized zone" would effectively hand the East the keys to the city. The Allies would not accept Khrushchev's unilateral declarations, which would heighten tensions in Europe for the next three years.

For the Detachment, little had changed. Khrushchev's ploy only reinforced the reasoning for their presence in the city and added urgency to their preparations. Now, the trips into the city to set up communication nets and conduct surveillance of border crossing points were real. The only question was when they would be called on to execute the mission.

Four teams prepared to go over the Wall into East Germany. Two would stay behind and conduct urban UW. If the city was occupied by the enemy there would be targets to destroy—both hard and soft—and that mission would require the men to use all their tradecraft skills if they were to survive and be successful. In many ways, the cliché that one man's terrorist is another man's freedom fighter is quite true. Political motivations may define the differences between the two and how they are perceived, but their methods are largely the same. The Detachment embraced the tactics of the underground freedom fighter and any other trick or skill that would help them accomplish their mission in the face of a numerically superior enemy and, with luck, survive.

Day X in Berlin

If and when war came, it was assumed that the Soviets and East Germans would lead off with a surprise attack to quickly seize control of the city and neutralize the Allies' ability to resist. That meant key facilities, units, and personalities would be targeted for capture or destruction. The headquarters of the American, British, and French forces and their colocated communications centers, civilian radio stations, power plants, and transport hubs were all expected to be early targets.[31] The American facilities in the southern part of Berlin, consisting of McNair, Andrews, Roosevelt, and Turner Barracks with their combat and combat support units, and the Clay Headquarters Compound that housed the USCOB, US Army Berlin Commander, the State Department and the CIA's Berlin Operations Base (BOB) were all on the Soviet list. The Allied military units, including the Detachment, would have little time to escape being trapped in their facilities if the Warsaw Pact successfully launched a surprise attack. These assumptions turned out to be fairly accurate.

After the Wall fell in November 1989, East Germany's planning documents called "*Fall X*" surfaced and showed their intent to capture West Berlin when and if war began. Although the earliest dates show planning began in 1969, it is probable the mission was under consideration long before that date. The East Germans estimated it would take three days to overcome Allied defenses. Key to their plan was the use of shock troops to capture West Berlin's three airfields, Tempelhof, Tegel, and Gatow, along with key bridges inside the city to prevent the Americans, British, and French from linking up to present a unified defense. The NVA's elite 40th Air Assault Regiment along with *Stasi* special operations units would have played key roles in the initial phases of the operation.[32] The Wall would have been penetrated by heavy armor and infantry units at nearly 50 locations to consolidate the first attacks and these elements would have been followed by 600 *Stasi* intelligence officers to arrest leading politicians, security officials, and journalists for internment. Interestingly, the Wall would have been left standing to facilitate control of the western half of the city's "capitalist" population—several million souls—for the duration of the conflict. The East Germans and Soviets considered West Berlin to be a *"Stachel im Fleisch des Sozialismus"*—a thorn in the flesh of Socialism—and planned to neutralize it quickly in any conflict with the West.

In hindsight therefore, maintaining the Detachment on a high alert status was the correct precaution. From its inception until it was disbanded, the unit was able to assemble and move out quickly. This required the unit to be kept in readiness on a rotating basis with a third of the unit on alert and the balance on a lesser status or in training. A "cascade" roster was used to alert unit members. If someone couldn't be reached by a phone call, the person preceding him on the list would have to go to his residence to find him. As technology improved, radio pagers were used to call in the entire unit, selected groups, or individuals in a matter of minutes. The standby alert requirements also limited the number of personnel who could be outside the city at any time. If hostilities erupted, it would obviously be difficult to get back to the city.

Contemplating Unconventional Warfare

Beyond the planned destruction of their initial targets, preparing for UW was conceptually extremely difficult. Using the Allied experience from WWII, military planners at SOTFE relied on the CIA to provide support for SF operations behind the Iron Curtain. The premise was that the CIA would recruit dissidents in hostile states who would then form resistance groups in time of war or be able to contact existing resistance movements inside East Germany. It was members of these groups who would meet SF teams on the ground and provide the foundation for a guerrilla army. But the CIA would not provide any information on these assets to the Army until it was evident that war was imminent. It was a serious leap of faith to trust this methodology and, over time, it would become clear that the system had serious flaws. By the late 1950s, however, these flaws remained unknown to all but a privileged few inside the Agency.[33]

According to its 1957 Global War Plan for Clandestine Operations, the CIA had "the responsibility for supporting the unconventional warfare operations of the military in wartime and for peacetime preparation for such support, including operation of, and planning for conversion of, assets to satisfy military UW requirements insofar as its capabilities permit."[34]

As part of that global requirement, in Eastern Europe[35] the CIA would:

Assist U.S. armed forces to
(1) Retard from the *outset* of hostilities, the Soviet advance, attack the Soviet forces, destroy their lines of communication, and exert the maximum pressure on them during the period that the Allied forces are engaged in the defense of Western Europe. *This is of highest priority.*
(2) Incite discontent amongst Soviet peoples with the Kremlin-controlled government and keep alive and strengthen their hope for eventual liberation therefrom.
(3) Develop the resistance potential of opposition elements within the USSR and countries under its domination....
(4) Priority in CIA preparations for wartime operations insofar as Western Europe is concerned will be in areas *east* of the Rhine–Alps line.[36]

In order for the CIA to accomplish those goals, its officers in Europe were tasked to locate and recruit members of the opposition in

Soviet-controlled areas with the intent of developing these assets into potential guerrilla force members—a "paramilitary apparatus." These projects were known by various code names and three in particular were concerned primarily with Germany: LCSTART, LCPROWL, and KMHITHER. Initially, plans called for in excess of 400 agents to be recruited. This would form the basis of anti-Communist stay-behind and resistance nuclei that would be trained and prepared for "the outbreak of a general conflict when the East German Apparat [would] engage in retardation, industrial and scientific sabotage, and general resistance activity. ... attention [would] be devoted to penetration of strategic installations as well as enemy security and active border crossings and caching operations will be carried out now and drop zones, sabotage targets, and holding areas will be earmarked for military forces."[37]

This typically involved the recruitment of a principal agent who would recruit like-minded sub-agents. Another program, called TPEMBER, began in the early 1950s, but by 1955, the Agency recognized the assets were often unqualified for the work and posed a risk to each other because of poor vetting, bad operational security, and bad tradecraft. The Agency phased out the TPEMBER program and replaced it with more selective recruitment of independent "sleeper" assets that could be activated in time of need. The program may have been feasible in the 1950s, but as the East Bloc intelligence services improved their internal security, the odds of this program's success dwindled. The failure of the Agency's paramilitary networks elsewhere in Eastern Europe, especially Albania, in the 1950s was perhaps a harbinger of what would happen in the GDR, especially after 1961. The Agency also felt that the few assets it could recruit behind the Iron Curtain were better employed in the collection of current intelligence, not left idle.

The Agency then tried another recruitment and training program, called WUDEPOT, for external assets of Eastern European origin, usually emigrés in the US. These volunteers lived outside the target country and would infiltrate into it when required. This closely mirrored the OSS's WWII experience in Europe and would be the way the CIA hoped to support its wartime responsibilities.[38] The basic plan called for three-man WUDEPOT teams to drop into selected UW operational areas (UWOA) just before or at the outbreak of war and receive Special Forces teams who would follow them.

How these assets could have been quickly infiltrated into the UWOAs around Berlin to meet and support the Detachment's "A" Teams was a question that was never satisfactorily addressed. Although the Agency professed that they would provide contacts for the Det's UW mission, no details on the contacts or networks were ever provided, ostensibly because of security concerns.

Tools of the Trade

Before 1963, the Detachment was equipped with standard (if old) US weapons: M2 carbine, M3 submachine gun—better known as the "Greasegun"—and the M1911 automatic Colt pistol. Some of the M3s were equipped with silencers—better described as "noise suppressors."[39] The unit's weapons were kept in its basement, but it was recognized the Detachment could potentially be cut off from its headquarters, making the arms stored there useless.

The solution was to prepare something euphemistically described as a Mission Support Site (MSS). In this case a MSS was a burial location in a remote area, better known as a cache, where supplies could be hidden and recovered when needed. Captain Bob Deshler, the Det's S-3 officer, began an extremely compartmented plan named Project "Under" for each team to establish a number of cache sites in the city. These contained "sterile" weapons (9mm Sten submachine guns and Walther P-38 pistols), ammunition, medical gear, demolition materials (usually C-3 plastic explosive, fuse and igniters), and radios.[40] The teams carefully waterproofed the gear and then sealed it in special aluminum containers. Locations were chosen and cased in remote areas of the Allied zones including the Grunewald and Spandau forests, as well as in built-up or "urbanized" parts of the city. Before emplacement, the Detachment S-2 (intelligence) and S-3 (operations) officers reviewed the proposed site and the Detachment commander gave final approval. Then came the fun part.

In 1960, Sergeant Rolf Kreuscher's team began the planning for their first cache emplacement as they would for any mission. The team decided that the best cover for action would be a contrived military exercise, like the ones the Brigade's infantry units often conducted in the city's forests. They would set up a "headquarters" under a big general-purpose tent to hide their activities in plain sight. The entire emplacement process, along with contingency plans in case of a compromise during the process was briefed to the commander and the staff. Invariably, someone would toss in a curve ball "what if" question to test how well the team anticipated all the possible problems. Once the plan was approved, the teams set out to put their containers in the ground in the spring. The numerous emplacements were staggered over days and months and the sites were placed under surveillance to determine if anyone had any interest in the location or the activities.

The tent was set up and a deep hole for the cache dug under the cover of the olive drab canvas. Outside, several team members watched for unwanted intruders. Further out, other team members with radios wandered through the forest and acted as a forward picket line. Kreuscher's team placed their containers at least one meter underground. Before filling in the hole completely, a large paving block was placed to permit the sites to be located with a long probe. Then the hole was completely filled in and the site cleaned up. If other unit members could not locate the emplacement site visually, it was deemed "good to go."

Another team outfitted themselves as construction workers for their emplacement. They used German trucks with all the appropriate tools and a case of beer—standard equipment on all civilian job sites. Once the cache was in the ground and the site carefully sterilized and returned to its original condition, the location was logged in detail using maps, reference points and multiple compass readings so it could be found and recovered if needed for war. The existence of the caches was highly classified and the files carefully maintained in the S-2's vault for reference.[41] The cache plan had one critical weakness, but it was never tested. While the S-2 had the site files, the teams—once the original personnel had rotated out—did not have exact information on the locations. They only knew that sites were out there somewhere in their area. The intent was to issue the files during the run-up to a conflict so teams would be able to review them and locate their sites. That weakness did not deter anyone and, given the emphasis so many placed on being prepared for a "surprise attack," most teams came up with creative solutions that involved the acquisition and hiding of "war materials" like explosives, grenades, and ammunition in locations they knew and could get to in an emergency. The location of these unofficial caches would be passed on to other team members as their previous "owners" rotated out. The unit's officers were kept in the dark, ostensibly to protect their careers, but in reality the NCOs didn't want their personal caches to be compromised to the commander by an uneasy officer's conscience.

Along with weapons, explosives, and radios, the other essential ingredient to support UW was money. Up to 1960, the unit's contingency fund was paper money, but West German marks would probably be worthless in wartime and US dollars would be dangerous for anyone to carry, use, or accept. A stable, untraceable currency was needed and the new plan called for the acquisition of gold, a lot of it. It was called the "Bluebird Fund" and consisted of around 1,500 coins purchased for around 12,000 US dollars, which at 1960 prices was around 350 ounces of pre-World War I gold coins—Austrian ducats, German marks, and Russian rubles of varying denominations. It all fit in a shoebox-sized cash box. The coins could not be put into the caches because the Army's restrictive regulations required periodic audits, nor could it be stored at the unit, so the coins were kept in a vault in the Brigade's Clay Compound Headquarters. The commander would order the coins be withdrawn from the vault if enemy action was deemed imminent, but a two-man rule was enforced and only a few designated custodians had access to the box.[42]

Sitting behind the lines, the need and the motivation for good mission planning and training was clear. For a soldier at a stateside assignment, or even in Bad Tölz, the threat was not immediate. That was not the case in Berlin. No one knew exactly when the "balloon would go up" and the Russians were very close, too close for comfort. Rolf Kreuscher later remembered "We could see them across the border every day and we planned to get them before they could get us."

Rolf Kreuscher served three tours in the Detachment, his first as a sergeant in 1957; his last as captain and Team Leader in 1974. He was born in the German town of Pforzheim and, despite the fact that Allied bombs destroyed his home (and town) in WWII, he knew who his enemy was: the Soviets had killed his father on the Eastern Front. That and the differences in the politics of East and West made his choice both visceral and clear. On 17 August 1962, Rolf was at the Wall and heard shots on the East Berlin side. Climbing up to an observation point, he saw Peter Fechter lying at the base of the Wall on the East German side. Fechter had tried to escape the Communist zone by brazenly trying to climb the barrier in the light of day. The *Grepos* (border police) fired on Fechter as soon he began his run across the aptly named "death strip." Fatally wounded, he lay at the base of the Wall. No one on either side of the Wall moved. Kreuscher was in civilian clothing and could do nothing as American MPs and West Berlin police officers approached the scene. The officer in charge of the MPs made contact with his superiors and was told to do nothing, while the West Berliners and the East Germans faced off. Neither would move closer, fearing the other side would open fire and as the minutes, then hours ticked by, Fechter slowly bled to death. Kreuscher's resolve to fight the Communists was further hardened that day.

Training—Preparing for War

The Detachment ran on a cycle and training followed a predictable schedule, especially if there was no crisis underway. There were field training exercises, demolitions training, ski training for all, and combat diver training for some. Then there was shooting at the ranges, communications and medical training. Physical fitness was a given and daily workouts were routine and usually done alone—running, swimming, and with weights. About once a week, the teams would train together in a remote section of the Grunewald or on the soccer field. Maintaining the standards for airborne duty were the absolute minimum requirement.

Learning about the enemy, called Warsaw Pact Identification (WPID) training, through the study of their order of battle, tactics, equipment and uniform recognition was tedious in the classroom but became more interesting when one could actually observe the Russians and

East Germans through binoculars. The daily routine was more varied and thorough than any conventional army unit or regular SF units. It had to be.

Sergeant John Blevins recalled,

> We would scout out targets, like rail junctions, bridges, telephone and electricity towers, canals, highway bridges, looking at anything that could be destroyed to slow the enemy down. We had classes on sabotage, foreign weapons, improvised explosives, surreptitious methods of entry, lock-picking, secret writing, improvised codes, disguises, surveillance, agent communications, cell organization, drop zone setup, emergency medical treatment, and caches.

The instructors were either in-house experts like Hilmar Kullek, or trainers from other organizations that often used throwaway names like "Team 10." They were usually retired Agency operations officers (many with OSS experience), who set up classroom and practical work in the city using techniques that had their roots in the OSS but which had been refined over the years by the Agency.[43] The most important subject was communications as it was the most dangerous activity in clandestine or underground operations.[44] After the classroom theory of intelligence tradecraft was given, many days were spent on the streets setting up "non-technical" communications systems, which enabled teams to communicate with each other clandestinely without the need for personal contact or radios.

Sites were cased for dead letter drops (DLD) and their corresponding load and unload signals, as well as for locations suitable for a quick personal meet or a brush pass. Each location was looked at from all angles to determine how to get into the area and out (especially if under pressure) and for plausible reasons to be in the location to develop a cover for action. The devil was always in the details, small things like store opening hours or changing traffic patterns could ruin a plan. Each site was rechecked periodically to note changes like this. Doing the necessary legwork and writing the reports was time consuming, but necessary, and the observation skills developed through casing were very useful. With practice, a walk through an area could reveal important details and revisits at different times of the day filled in any gaps in the information. At the same time, casing was a clandestine art and it was important not to "burn" a site by spending too much time or showing obvious interest by photographing or sketching a location in the open. In a denied area, i.e. one that was controlled by heavy security like East Berlin, memorization was often the only way to collect the information.[45]

Getting to a meet or servicing a dead drop required the participants be free from surveillance. That meant a lot of street time was spent learning how to follow and observe a person, as well as how to detect hostile observation. Generally, it is easier to be the "rabbit" than the "hound" and practice sessions could degenerate rapidly when trying to follow someone through a train station or along the Kurfürstendamm in and out of department stores during rush hour. For a change, teams would pick an unsuspecting civilian and follow them through their day's activities. Berlin during the Cold War was unique and strange things often happened, as Kim Kendle remembered. One day, his team picked a man they saw crossing Checkpoint Charlie into West Berlin to practice their newly learned surveillance techniques:

> There were four of us and we had no trouble picking up the individual and immediately put a tail on him using standard techniques, which we soon learned were not good enough. After several hours of being led all over downtown West Berlin, through several big department stores and the Berlin Zoo, we realized that he was on to us and would stop and let us find him and then continue the game. As midday approached, he led us back towards the border crossing at Checkpoint Charlie and entered a *Gasthaus*. I debated whether we should all go in or leave two members outside and then switch off. I decided that since we had been made, it made no sense to leave anyone outside. We entered, spotted our target, split up and sat at different tables. Our target had already ordered a meal and a beer. We placed our orders and after about 15 minutes, he stood and approached my table. I was dumbfounded. I started to get up and he motioned for me to sit back down. He introduced himself in perfect English and asked if we could all sit together and enjoy a beer, which we did. He critiqued us on our amateurish efforts and gave us some pointers. We later went out and continued our mission with our target actually trailing us and we switched off and on for the rest of the day until it was time for him to return to the east. No names or organizations were exchanged.

Kendle and his team had better luck as their skills improved. They were later detailed to help officers from the Agency's BOB surveil two East

German *Stasi* intel officers who crossed into West Berlin. Through the evening they tracked the two and finally followed them into a nightclub popular with American GIs. The Agency officers observed the East Germans try to elicit information from the American soldiers and then tapped Kendle and his group to get close and find out what kind of questions they were asking. It was a simple job to get the spies interested and the Det soldiers learned they were looking for basic, low-level order of battle information. The Agency officers then waited for the spies to leave and confronted them on the streets, effectively ruining their future usefulness in the West.[46]

Berlin was full of spies and it was not unusual for one country's intelligence operation to cross paths with another. Suspected clandestine meets were sometimes observed and photographed by Detachment members. Encounters were usually reported to the 766th Military Intelligence Detachment for exploitation. As expected, responses were only occasionally forthcoming and usually limited to a comment that the information was useful for ongoing investigations.[47]

Another hazard was operating in the areas where criminal activities were common. It was easy to get into trouble and guys tended to go out in pairs if they were headed into the more notorious sections of town—it was much better to have a cover man or two when withdrawing from a brawl than to wing it alone. Detachment operations often took place in areas not recommended for tourists.

Nevertheless, there was always one guy who didn't listen. A senior supply sergeant named Bob was in the Kreuzburg district one night when four knife-wielding Turks confronted him. They certainly expected him to hand over his money, but he was not the easy target they expected. A burly former weapons sergeant, Bob took on his attackers one by one. The end result was four attackers lying in the street, having been danced on by Bob's infamous mountain boots. Operating in the city required both street sense and a martial attitude that avoided confrontation, but dealt with it definitively when other options were exhausted.

Army life was more often than not "boredom, punctuated by moments of sheer terror" and Berlin was no different, even for the Detachment.[48] But those moments were memorable.

When Bob Olson remembered his tour sixty years later, he said,

I like to think that I was part of the reason that there was no Third World War, but it is a hard position to defend. Our job was to blow the rail lines surrounding the city if war began and then make our way towards Allied lines. For three weeks out of every month, we went to classes and drank beer. On the fourth week, we flew to Bavaria, parachuted into the mountains at night and ran around in the woods. It was a lovely way to live.

Sometimes, at night, we went out onto the border. Remember that this was before the Berlin Wall. Instead of the Wall, they had plowed fields planted with machine-gun towers and high barbed wire fences. We sometimes heard shots, but I don't believe that anyone tried seriously to kill me. In those days people would try to escape across the fields and often they were shot while doing it. It was also possible to take a subway across the border and I never knew why the people who were shot on the wires didn't take the subway instead. I remember, one night with a big moon, sitting under the bottom of one of those high towers, listening to the East German guards above me and thinking of how like a dream it was.

Part of our job was to walk the border and report on anything unusual that might be happening. Late one winter afternoon in Berlin, Pappy Barnett and I were doing exactly that. The ground was spotted with dirty snow and we walked along a barbed-wire border fence. The border fence by East German standards was a line of telephone poles strung with tight single-strand barbed-wire at about eighteen-inch intervals. Looking at a fence like this from a little way, off you would think that you could fit between the strands, but you couldn't, and while you were trying, the East German guards could machine-gun you at their leisure. Pappy and I walked across a deep plowed pasture and on the opposite side of the fence, covered with beautiful, long pink, blue and yellow ribbons flying from four foot sticks, was a newly planted mine field. There was a mound of earth in the right corner of the field, and I noticed a black slot in the mound. When I put glasses on it, I saw two pairs of little rat eyes looking at me down a long machine-gun barrel. On the left end of the field was another slot in a mound, two more pairs of rat eyes, and one more long Russian machine-gun barrel.

Pappy should have said, "Don't bother running, Graceful, you'll jest die tired."

What I believe he actually said was: "Keep walking, Graceful, and think about the funniest thing that ever happened to you."

We were in civilian clothes, and we had no real business being where we were; had the guards been sufficiently bored, or if their quotas had not been met, they could have spread us all over that pasture, but apparently neither of these conditions held, so we just walked the [seeming] seventy or eighty miles to our car.[49]

About That Woman

Berlin in 1959 was still in the midst of reconstruction, but in the Western zones, there was a huge demand for workers, by which was meant young men. As a result of this, the young men who got over the border made their way almost immediately to West Germany. The young women, on the other hand, were faced with the choice of laying cobblestones or hanging out with foreign soldiers. Many may have been prompted by monetary incentives to work for the East German security services. Unlike the infantry units, "Det" soldiers were not subjected to a curfew, which led many of the younger soldiers to prowl the streets of Berlin at night. While some of the Detachment's men returned home with German brides, others did not, but not for lack of trying. Bob Olson also remembered a German woman that he was interested in named "Black Christina." She kept him at arms' length and had a reputation; supposedly she had syphilis and was a Russian spy, but more importantly she didn't like Bob. Still, they drank beer together and when he asked why she didn't like him, she retorted, "Olson, zer iss nothing wrong with you. Come back Thursday and we haf fun." Unfortunately, Olson knew—and, per-haps so did Christina—that Thursday was the day the unit was scheduled to parachute into the Hartz Mountains for a month in the field.

Olson didn't see Christina for another year and then it was time for him to go home. He went by sea and the ship he left Hamburg on was the oldest and smallest troop ship still in service with the United States Army. According to a plaque on the cargo mast, it had been sunk just outside of the Panama Canal in 1942, then it was raised, recommissioned and used to transport dignitaries like Olson and 400 other sick, dirty, young men, who slept on bunks stacked five high in the depths of the old rust bucket. The secret was to be on the top bunk, the fifth: the roll of the ship was worse there, but nothing undesirable could fall on you. One day he was lying on top of the cargo hatch and looked up to the top deck where the officers and their wives lived, and there, on the bridge with the officers taking in the crisp sea air was Black Christina looking pregnant.

Olson called out: "Hey, Christina, you came out pretty fat."

She called back: "Hey, Olson, I did come out fat. I haf married a major, but luf to you anyway."

As the time passed, many Detachment members began to morph into "citizens" of Berlin. They followed the grooming styles of their age group, and dressed accordingly. For the most part German was spoken amongst the team members and they tried to blend in, but it was not always easy, as some replacements were not fluent German speakers. Some had to adopt a different country for their cover story, whether it was as a Greek guest worker or a Spanish student. In extreme cases, a non-linguist could adopt a legend of being Irish or South African, preferably any non-aligned country. Some men got involved with off-post activities, such as attending church, working at restaurants, joining local sport teams, or going to college. Along with learning the culture, many friends and contacts could be made who might be useful when the balloon went up.

Jim Wilde played basketball with a Berlin League team for four years and then took on the job of coaching the team because they wanted to play American-style basketball. That year, the team won the league championship. During the final game, the opposing team coach told him that he felt like they were playing against an American college team. He didn't recognize that Wilde was an American.

Wilde would later say, "First and foremost in everyone's minds was that, in order to accomplish the mission, they had to survive, and to survive you had to blend in. One mistake, one misspoken word, or action could compromise the team and the mission."

In addition to their government-supplied quarters, many team members acquired an apartment "on the economy," that would serve as their safehouse. These were usually nothing more than studios with the bare minimum of furniture and a hot plate for cooking. It would do for the first days of conflict, but not much longer. Other safehouses were acquired by recruiting German nationals to act as a "keeper." The real Berliner would often live in the property and ensure it was maintained and secure. The sites took different forms—apartments, garden houses in the woods, warehouses—and were used by the teams during exercises and held for the eventuality of conflict.

One such keeper was a man named "Lothar," a senior official of the postwar German administration in Berlin. Rolf, a unit member, met Lothar while playing on the same football (soccer) team. Over time,

Rolf determined Lothar was politically anti-Communist and supportive of the American presence in Berlin and "recruited" Lothar to help the unit. Lothar controlled access to a building that he provided for Rolf's team to use as a safehouse, drop site, and training site.

Outwardly, Lothar was a typical brusque, officious German—so much so that no one suspected him of helping the Americans. He kept his clandestine life separate from his official and family lives, all the while providing a crucial service to the Detachment. To say he was recruited is actually a misnomer, as Lothar was a patriotic German who saw his role as helping his own country, not as collaboration. There were many like him.

This "safehouse" practice fell off in later years as budgets became tighter and the economy more expensive. The only way for a soldier to live downtown was to give up government quarters, which some family men were loath to do, or find a local girlfriend. As usual, budget restraints limited operations to essentials, safehouses were determined to be a long-term, recurring expense that might never be used. The more satisfactory (read: bureaucratic) solution was to wait until conflict broke out then simply occupy an available place that would probably provide safety for what would only be a short stay anyway.

Making Commo

In wartime, the teams in their operational area would use high-frequency (HF) radios to communicate with the higher headquarters whether it was located in France or, in later years, the UK. Given the capabilities of the Soviet and East German counterespionage services, it could also be the most dangerous clandestine activity to attempt. Before digital burst transmission devices existed, radio operators had to send the shortest and fastest message possible, then get off the airwaves and move. West Berlin was a good practice ground because both Allied counterintelligence and the German *Verfassungsschutz* (internal security service) tracked illegal radio transmissions with mobile RDF (radio direction finding) units. As the Detachment was operating the radios clandestinely, it was a game of cat and mouse. The radio operators knew they were the only link between the team and higher headquarters and could not be compromised.[50]

The first radio used by Det "A" was an OSS "spy" radio set dubbed the RS-6. Small and easy to transport, the set included four pieces, each about the size of a paperback book; a crystal controlled half-watt transmitter, a receiver, an AC power supply, and a power inverter for use with a hand-cranked generator or battery.[51]

When radio procedures were tested, a two-man cell would often operate out of a hotel "safehouse" in a different location than their fellow team members. One would check in for a full night's stay or two, fully intending to use the room only for the radio transmission. The tricky part was always convincing the clerk to give them a room placed where they could send and receive best. While propagation charts gave the optimum times for radio operations, the operator usually transmitted at night. A long wire antenna would be hung out an open window down the side of the building and the transmission begun.[52] The receiving base station copied the message, but typically did not answer until 24–48 hours later.

Occasionally, things didn't go quite to plan. During one test, Frank, a team communicator, checked into a hotel and was later joined by a teammate to send a situation report. After hanging the antenna in the room, they decided not to use the radio's batteries and plugged the power supply directly into the hotel's electrical supply. The message had been encrypted elsewhere and the clear text destroyed to lessen the chance of compromise should they be "captured." Frank tapped out the message, initiating the blind broadcast at the appointed time with a series of the letter "V" in Morse, then a five-letter authenticator group, and finally the message. The text would always include a code word that indicated the sender was free of duress, its absence or the use of a substitute code word would tell headquarters the team or the radio operator may have been captured. If the operator forgot, he was given a chance to acknowledge the mistake in the next message from headquarters. The messages were always numbered and each station could acknowledge which one they had received in their subsequent message so everyone could keep track of the conversation.

The entire transmission took only minutes, but that was enough to give the enemy a chance to lock on to their signal. They quickly packed up the equipment and opened the door to leave only to find all the lights in the hotel had gone out. The radio's power supply had apparently blown the circuit breakers. This was another reason to check out early and, having already paid the bill, they slipped out a side exit. Within minutes of their departure, they saw an RDF unit cruising the streets looking for their signal. It was a close call but, as they say, good training.

Piernick was also big on escape and evasion (E&E) training and he tasked the teams to plan training events. Each team would try to outdo the other with diabolical twists. One took place in Berlin's Grunewald, a 25-square-kilometer forest in the western part of the city. The exercise took place at night and each man had 3 kilometers to traverse. Just for fun, the controllers arranged for the *Berliner Polizei* and their Alsatian guard dogs to patrol the escape corridor. Stealth and good field craft were key to not being caught; some evaders covered their scent by rolling in the forest mulch while others relied on the police making too much noise as they crashed through the forest searching for them. At one point, the police and their dogs were chased from the scene by a wild boar that decided they too were fair game. That gave a couple of evaders the space they needed to move. Everyone made it through the gauntlet by morning.

Then Piernick ramped up the difficulty. Five "volunteers" were taken by truck to a spot south of Bremerhaven in West Germany and dropped off. Dressed in sterile army uniforms with no money and no IDs, they were told that they had just escaped from a POW camp and now had to make their way to Bad Tölz, 850 kilometers to the south, by any means and without getting caught. To make things interesting, every policeman along the route was alerted and a bounty was offered for the capture of the "escapees." With no other instructions or time limit, the men first separated to make the trackers' job difficult, and headed out. Each took his own counsel on direction and method of movement. By the end of the first night, all had managed to acquire civilian clothing and shed their uniforms to blend in with the German population. One evader found a couple of days' work as a manual laborer and earned some spending money before continuing his travel. Another caught a ride with some college students who were heading out on holiday in their VW microbus, while a covered beer delivery truck provided transport for a third. Within ten days, all five arrived at Flint Kaserne, home base for the 10th SFG, where they were debriefed on their experiences. A lot of German *Polizei* went home disappointed they had missed out on the reward.

E&E training was essential for the individual soldier, but more importantly for the Detachment's wartime mission. The unit would be required to recover pilots and aircrews shot down behind Warsaw Pact lines. If they could be found before the enemy got to them, the crewmen would be put into a network and sent home. The Det practiced these skills during their UW exercises in Berlin and West Germany. Most importantly, the annual exercise allowed the Detachment to role-play and organize a UW support structure that closely replicated the building of a guerrilla force auxiliary behind enemy lines, exactly what they would need to do in wartime.

As part of his training to set up an E&E net, Mike Kelly experienced what it was like to be run through one. He traveled to a small town in West Germany and was dropped off with instructions to find and unload a DLD that contained a message written on water-soluble paper. The note gave him directions to follow a route through the forest and to whistle *Lili Marlene* at a certain point. Mike didn't know the tune, so he whistled *Dixie* instead.

He was suddenly surrounded by strangers and "bagged" with a cloth hood. Taken to a safehouse, his fingerprints were taken and encoded into a message that was sent to the SF Operational Base (SFOB) in West Germany to verify his identity. He then spent ten days moving between different locations, usually in the trunk of a car, and staying in safehouses where no English was ever spoken and the "keepers" themselves spoke a language he could not understand. At the end of the line, he was taken to a landing zone in West Germany and put onto to an evacuation aircraft, a deHavilland U-6A Beaver, for his return "home" to Berlin.[53]

In the Zone

To prepare for the wartime UW mission, the Detachment participated in exercises that usually took place in West Germany, as Berlin did not lend itself to large-scale field maneuvers. A key part of UW would be the training of guerrillas (Gs). The theory was that a 12-man SF A team would be a force multiplier in time of war and could train a 1,200-man "G-Force" to battle the Soviets. SOTFE staff officers wrote the scenarios for operations and the Detachment took part with German *Bundeswehr* (army) infantry soldiers playing the role of the G-Force.[54]

Typically, the teams would go into isolation several weeks before deployment to begin planning for their "mission." Lesson plans were developed to teach the "guerrillas" about weapons, demolitions, communications, and medical subjects, as well as small unit tactics—all in German. At times, the lead instructor give his class in English with another NCO translating it into German to refine skills and technique. All the while, the Germans believed their teachers came from Bad Tölz or the States. The subject of Berlin was scrupulously avoided.

Generally, the exercises would last 10–14 days and would test how the team would organize and employ their Gs tactically. Small missions, such as reconnaissance and ambush patrols, would be run to practice tactics and teach tactical intelligence collection, which in turn would lead to larger operations. The exercise would culminate in a large raid to destroy an enemy target. The Detachment would also participate in UW exercises that ran as part of larger conventional force maneuvers.

In the fall of 1958, Team Two prepared for its annual exercise. The men were flown from Berlin to the NATO airbase at Evreux-Fauville, France where they went into isolation. For a week, the team reviewed an Area Study that described their target in detail. The exercise would take place in southern Bavaria, but the study portrayed the area as occupied Eastern Europe. The team would parachute into the countryside at night and be met by a guerrilla band that was operating in "Aggressor" territory, as the enemy was then called.[55] A series of events designed to test the team's capabilities would be played out. The "guerrilla chief" and his deputy were senior noncoms from 10th Group at Bad Tölz and would act as graders. Their job was also to throw up occasional obstacles to see how the team reacted to the unexpected, while 20 *Bundeswehr Fallschirmjäger* (paratroopers) played the part of the untrained, rag-tag militia. This wasn't a difficult task as most were German draftees with bad attitudes who didn't want to be playing army in the woods. The aggressors, on the other hand, came from the US Army's 11th Airborne Division, a group of serious soldiers who did not like to be shown up in the field.

Preparations went uneventfully and the team conducted a mission brief-back to the staff to show it was fully prepared. After the requisite inquisition, the commander cleared them for deployment. The team conducted a night airborne infiltration, jumping from an USAF Air Transport Command C-124, and hit the ground running. After making contact with the G-Force, training to give the German soldiers skills in small unit tactics was begun. During the first week, they practiced reconnaissance and combat patrols. During the second week, the team would ambush an aggressor force truck convoy to obtain the food and supplies necessary for the remainder of the exercise. When it came time to spring the ambush, all went according to plan except one small detail. The Gs were in place, undiscovered, on a remote section of road in the forest. The team had placed the Gs in a standard linear ambush with their weapons covering the "kill zone." There was an outpost on one end to signal the convoy's approach and security placed to protect their backs. Then the convoy approached. The first trucks drove into the zone and the Gs opened up. Unfortunately, the "aggressors" decided that blank ammunition and grenade simulators were not sufficient to stop their trucks. They just kept going, ignoring the explosions and rifle shots, leaving the team and the Gs standing by the road hungry, low on ammunition, and scratching their heads. Pete Astalos, aka the "Mad Bomber," was the team's senior engineer and demo sergeant. A Lodge Act soldier, he had served in the Romanian and German armies during WWII. Standing by the side of the road, he muttered in his adopted language, "Next time, I make them stop."

The convoy was scheduled to run daily, so the team made its preparations for another ambush the following day. While the team got the guerrillas into position, Astalos and his sidekick, the team's junior engineer, took off down the road with their rucksacks. After what seemed an interminable time, the two slowly returned, reeling out wire behind them. They settled into position and everyone waited.

At the appointed time, the aggressor convoy again came trundling down the road and entered the kill zone. Explosive simulators were fired to initiate the ambush and the Gs opened up with their blank-firing rifles. As before, the aggressors ignored the commotion and kept rolling. Astalos stood up and hurled several epithets at the convoy as he twisted the handle of his blasting machine. Down the road, white puffs of smoke appeared in a line along the uphill side of the road and several trees crashed down across the road in front of the lead truck. It was a perfect *abatis*: a roadblock of entangled tree trunks and limbs. The convoy screeched to a halt and the Gs closed in to finish the job. With the concussions of the explosives still reverberating through the forest, Astalos grinned and gleefully yelled "You see! I stop them."

Mission accomplished. The supplies were "captured." The team melted back into the woods leaving "dead" 11th Airborne troopers to clean up the road. It was a success in general terms, but the staff officers back at SOTFE went into apoplectic fits. Bilateral agreements required the US Army to pay the German government for property damaged or destroyed during maneuvers and so, Astalos' engineering excellence cost the army the price of a brace of trees and all their conceivable off-spring for the foreseeable future. The Detachment commander refused to punish the team and suggested the aggressors were at fault because they refused to play dead properly.[56]

Putting on the Brits

When the British Command wanted to test one of their own units in 1958, they turned to the US Army. The Detachment was tasked to infiltrate a British Army of the Rhine (BAOR) brigade headquarters element that was encamped near Soltau in West Germany. The brigade was undergoing an evaluation exercise and its commander did not know his security was about to be tested. Team Two was given the operations order and a plan was made using intelligence provided about the "enemy" position. The team would infiltrate the area by parachute and contact a guerrilla force once they were on the ground.

An aircraft dispatched from Bad Tölz with 10th Group riggers and parachutes picked up the team at Berlin-Tempelhof. After taking off, the team rigged up while flying through the air corridor to the western zone. Their night jump was into a drop zone about 20 kilometers from the British brigade's location. As the aircraft approached, the team's "guerrilla" reception committee—who were actually two role-playing SAS troopers—lit DZ markers for the pilot to guide his approach. Once on the ground, the team quickly collected their gear and stashed it in a forest hide site to be picked up later. Then the "Gs" guided them to a barn, their safehouse, where they would spend the night and prepare for the mission.

After securing the site, everyone settled in for the night. Everything was quiet until the crack of rotting wood told one team member his cozy spot wasn't so good. He plunged through the hayloft into a very muddy pigpen. Luckily, he had a clean set of clothes in his rucksack. The team spent the next day in hiding and then left the barn after dark the next evening. They had to travel several kilometers to close on the headquarters but they moved slowly, walking for five minutes and stopping another five to listen for enemy movement before proceeding. As they neared the camp they slowed to a crawl and moved into several concealed observation points from which they watched the British through the night and all the next day. By observing the comings and goings in the British camp, the team was able to pinpoint the brigade commander's quarters and other key locations. Around 0200 hours, most of the team set out in small groups, moved slowly through the surrounding forest and ravines, and infiltrated the camp's perimeter without being seen or challenged by the British sentries. The balance of the team remained outside the camp to cover the teams' withdrawal.

A two-man team approached the commander's tent and waited out-side, listening for movement. Satisfied that the commander was asleep, one man slowly crawled under the flap. Once inside, he carefully placed a calling card onto a table next to the colonel's cot and quietly backed out of the tent. The other sections had, in the meantime, placed small explosive charges near other targets in the camp. On cue, the charges were set off and the team exited the camp firing blanks. The team returned to their rally point several hundred meters from the camp. They then followed a route intended to mislead any trackers before diverting off on a meandering route to a new hide site.

The next day, the Gs told the team that they were to return to the headquarters for a "discussion" with the commander. Arriving at the brigade's tactical operations center, the colonel came in and, with a bit of embarrassment, quipped "You chaps gave us quite a start last evening." He laid the team's calling card on the table, its inscription "YOU ARE DEAD" face up, and acknowledged he was indeed dead. A good-humored exchange of ideas took place as the commander seemingly took on recommendations to improve his headquarters' security. The team was thanked and, seeing a chance to depart gracefully, left the scene to be picked up at the nearest airfield for a return to Berlin. There can be no doubt the commander received less humorous comments from his higher headquarters.

Smile and Wave, Boys, Just Smile and Wave

Airborne operations are a way to get somewhere. Other methods include walking, swimming, or hopping a ride on a bus. Although this is a simplistic way to describe methods of infiltration, the fact remains that they are only a delivery method to get soldiers to a destination. That said, a bit of fortitude is required to step out the door of an airplane into a 110-knot slipstream in the black of the night with 100 pounds of gear (not counting parachutes) strapped onto your body. And that's just to get to the start point of a mission. After that, it's all uphill.

In reality, the Detachment had little operational use for its airborne status. When war came there would be no airplanes departing from Tempelhof to drop paratroopers behind the lines. They were already behind the lines and the Warsaw Pact antiaircraft guns and missiles that ringed the city would make life difficult for all but the lowliest pigeon. Walking, sloshing through sewers, and swimming across the lakes and canals would be the better, more survivable routes to get into the East.

That said there were reasons to maintain airborne status. First, keeping everyone on jump status precluded the necessity for retraining and no one wanted to lose his monthly jump pay. Second, it was always possible that a peacetime mission requiring an airborne infiltration would pop up. Above all, the Detachment jumped because it was a designated airborne unit and was required to keep its personnel up to date to maintain that status.

Soon after it arrived in the city, the unit began airborne operations. Initially, the teams rigged for parachute operations inside one of the huge hangars at Tempelhof or flew to a supporting airfield at Neubiberg or Fürstenfeldbruck where they were met by riggers from 10th SFG with parachutes. Later, the procedure changed to in-flight rigging. In-flight rigging was always a challenge because of the space limitations in a cramped C-119 or C-124 cargo plane, but necessary as rigging on the ground in Berlin was not the best security procedure. Sometimes the exercise would be to fly out of Berlin in the morning, jump onto Karen DZ outside Bad Tölz, and then be trucked to the airfield at Fürstenfeldbruck west of Munich for the pick-up and flight back to the city. All of this made for a long day and the troopers began to call themselves the "Munich for Lunch Bunch."

Captain Adam Klys, a Polish immigrant who was one of the first two non-native American officers to join the unit in the early 1960s later recalled one of the times when things didn't go quite as planned.[57] On one flight, a "leg" captain from the Berlin Brigade was put on the only flight leaving Berlin because he needed to get home to his family. It just happened to be a Detachment jump flight, but no one thought to mention it to him. When the other "passengers" began to pull their parachutes off a covered pallet and suit up for the jump, he began to panic. Thinking there was an in-flight emergency, he went to the jumpmaster (JM) and asked for a parachute. The JM jokingly told him he was out of luck—there weren't enough to go around.

Finally, the Air Force loadmaster told him not to worry—the airplane was not in danger. The captain was sent to sit in a corner and stay out of the way while the JM and his assistants went down the checklist for the drop. The C-124 slowed to jump speed—110 knots—and the crew opened the doors. The wind howled through the cabin and the turbulence and the roar of the engines compelled the hapless officer to squeeze even tighter into his corner. The green light came on and the paratroopers were gone, out the door and into space. The aircrew pulled the static lines back into the cabin and buttoned up the aircraft. A relative quiet returned to the cabin when the doors slammed shut. The captain found himself completely alone with nothing to do but contemplate what he had just witnessed. When the aircraft landed, the crew told him to forget what he had just seen. That would have been the end of it except that two weeks later, he was riding back to Berlin on the Duty Train and noticed a group of civilians passing his section of the carriage. Realizing they were the same guys who jumped from his airplane, he could only shake his head. The team had finished their field exercise and was returning home. They just smiled and waved.[58]

The Exploding Trash Can

In the late 1950s when the prospect of another world war seemed real, nuclear weapons became America's panacea to slow the Soviet hordes pouring off the steppes of Russia into Western Europe. Nuclear bombs, missiles, and artillery projectiles topped the list as part of President Dwight Eisenhower's "New Look" strategy of deterrence. Less well known among these were the devices called "atomic demolitions munitions" (ADMs). These were small nukes, relatively speaking, with a yield in the low kilotons, originally designed to be used by combat engineers to mine routes and destroy bridges in front of the approaching enemy. Someone in the Pentagon came up with what they undoubtedly thought was a bright idea: stop an invasion by dropping SF teams armed with nukes into Eastern Europe and letting them wreak havoc in the Russian backyard.[59] Special Forces actually received this mission as early as 1956 and began testing infiltration techniques with the devices.[60] Early on, SF worked with ADMs that were much bigger than the later Special Atomic Demolitions Munitions (SADM), the so-called "trash can nukes." The ADM-4 was the first such weapon adapted for the task. It consisted of four major components, each piece weighing 40–50 pounds.

The Detachment was tasked in early 1957 to participate in the tests for two reasons: first, its men had the requisite Top Secret clearances and, second, Lieutenant Colonel Piernick had very close ties with USAREUR staff. Ben Linschoten, the Detachment's first intelligence sergeant, coordinated the planning at Frankfurt and Team Five was given the mission to test the theory. The ADM-4 was the weapon they would carry. Being on the mission was both a source of pride and a severe challenge. Security restrictions meant that no one could discuss any aspect of the operation. The other teams were not even aware of the full details of the exercise, only that a team was being deployed. Team Five spent several weeks training up on the device and then prepared to conduct a practice mission.

The team went into isolation at Bad Tölz and was given a target folder that showed their objective to be an aircraft factory with an adjoining airfield. The exercise planners had chosen a winery complex next to a section of highway in the Heilbronn area of Baden-Württemberg, north of Stuttgart. The winery lay in the Neckar River valley and offered good terrain for a team to maneuver through undetected. There were 11 men on the mission, two of whom were actually part of 10th SF from Bad Tölz who would participate as team members. The "enemy" were all American forces as no one wanted to take chances with a compromise of the ADM or the mission if the team was "captured" during the exercise by German or Allied troops.

A day before the team was to parachute in, two team members infiltrated into the target area to set up surveillance and to mark the DZ. The night of the drop, the team was trucked to the departure airfield where they rigged for the drop. Each man carried his personal gear that included rucksack and weapons, but four of the men would also carry the ADM-4 components plus the timer device. Weighed down with well over 100 pounds of gear, not including the weight of their parachutes, the four had to be assisted into the airplane to finish the final rigging on board. The rest of the team members were only burdened with 60-pound rucksacks. A JM and two assistants from Bad Tölz would put the team out over the DZ and return with the aircraft to base.

The C-119 departed on time and began a long flight over Germany and into France before turning to make the low-altitude approach for the drop. On the ground, the advance party had laid out the lights for the pilot and JM to identify and orient the plane on the correct flight path over the DZ, which they lit minutes before the anticipated drop. There would be no radio contact; the team would have to rely on the markers and hope they identified the correct set of lights. Six minutes out, the JM stood his charges up and began the pre-jump hook up and inspection routine. He then turned to the open door to look for the marker lights. The assistant JM, the Air Force loadmaster and his assistants stood behind holding onto his harness and watching the jumpers who were standing by. They were especially watchful to ensure no equipment got too close to the doors where it could be sucked out along with everything attached.

The pilot was flying on the plotted approach azimuth when the JM spotted the markers and called out a correction to the loadmaster who relayed it to the pilot. Satisfied, he turned to the team and barked out "Stand in the door!" With jumpers positioned in the doors on either side, the JM resumed his perch to line up the DZ lights to determine the release point. Seeing them come into line, he stood up and gave the order to jump, "Go!" The ten men shuffled like a waddle of penguins, more falling than jumping out the door. Everyone hoped to be in somewhat of the correct position as they hit the aircraft's slipstream and engine wash. In less than ten seconds everyone was out the door and the JM and aircrew pulled in the static lines and closed up the aircraft.

The team was under canopy at 1,000 feet above the ground. The parachutes had opened hard for the heavily laden men but there were no malfunctions and only a couple of guys were twisted up, a condition reversed by some cycling of legs and pulling of parachute risers. With the plane long gone, there was only silence and darkness. There was no horizon to orient on, so everyone was looking at the ground, orienting themselves on the marker lights to determine wind drift and speed to prepare for the landing. When they were about 100 feet above the ground, each man released his rucksack on a drop line so that it would swing about 15 feet below him. The equipment would hit the ground first and remove most of the danger of trying to land with too much weight. The heavier ADM containers were let out carefully by hand to prevent the drop line from snapping and the precious cargo smashing into the earth below.

Oscillating slowly back and forth, each man felt rather than saw the ground rush up in the darkness and did his best to execute a proper landing. Fortuitously, no one was hurt and all the packages were intact. After the team rallied together, the advance party led the team off the DZ to the edge of the forest where the parachutes and harnesses were cached. They then took off through the woods towards the target about two hours away.

Movement through the brush was slow and deliberate. The heavy rucks and ADM components made each step difficult, especially in the hilly terrain, and no one wanted to be discovered at this stage of the mission. Finally, the team arrived near the target and encamped at a site chosen by the advance team. It was out of range of security patrols, but close enough to get to the target quickly with the heavy components. Two men in a forward observation post watched over the target through the next day and the leader's reconnaissance determined the final plan.

The advantage of the nuclear device was clear, its placement did not have to be precise, it needed only to be well concealed and reasonably close to the target. Half the team would approach the target the following evening while the other half provided security to their rear. The team would not be captured. If capture seemed imminent, the device could be assembled and fired. The team understood that if they were detected they would not be going home.

The following evening, the plan went like clockwork. The attack team moved into position without being discovered by sentries and assembled the weapon under cover about 100 yards from the target buildings. Assuming the timer worked as advertised and not instantaneously as some surmised, the team would have an hour to exit the area and get as far away and under as much cover as possible before the weapon went off. Pushing the fire button, the timer started and the team backed out of the area carefully. Reaching the OP, they joined up with the other half of the team and started to move away.

At this point that victory was declared and the exercise ended. The team had not been compromised going in and the weapon was put together and "fired" without a problem. Returning to the weapon, the operators demonstrated the firing sequence to the exercise controllers and then dismantled the device so it could be returned to a secure bunker somewhere in Germany. Relieved both figuratively and literally of their burden, the team was let go to celebrate their success. From there, it was a truck ride back to Bad Tölz, clean up and turn in of weapons, a bit of rest, and a trip into town for some Bavarian *Gemütlichkeit*, schnitzel, beer, and whatever the night would bring. There was only one warning, don't miss the ride to the airfield.[61]

In the final analysis, the ADM mission concept proved viable for SF, although it was clear that a smaller device with fewer components would be easier to infiltrate into the enemy's space. Team Five's experience, however, was the last of its kind for the Detachment. The weapons could only be stored in Western Europe. Due to the political environment and security requirements, nuclear weapons could not be stored in the city. The unit would not be tasked to maintain the ADM mission. It was simply not operationally feasible to conduct it from Berlin.[62]

Red Team

When Willy Brandt became the mayor of Berlin in 1957, he was an extremely popular man in West Berlin, less so on the other side of the city. He was a supporter of the Allied Forces in his city and extremely vocal in his contempt for the East Bloc. The Communists, naturally, hated Brandt. By early 1961, there was a growing concern for the mayor's safety and, although he was well guarded by uniformed and plainclothes officers of the Berlin police, intelligence reporting led the Americans to believe that either the Soviets or the East Germans might try to assassinate or kidnap Brandt.

The USCOB, Major General Ralph Osborne, asked Lieutenant Colonel Piernick to have his men evaluate Mayor Brandt's safety. Jim and "Gerhard" were assigned to clandestinely shadow the mayor and check his security precautions. The two set about the task and watched him from morning to night each day. They quickly noted that Brandt followed the same routine almost every day going to work and returning to his residence. It was only during the day that his schedule and movements varied, depending on the demands of his job.

Understanding that the enemy would be looking to kidnap or kill the mayor they approached the problem from a perpetrator's view and developed attack scenarios based on his vulnerabilities. After several days of surveillance, the team were able to devise four possibilities, the first being an attack at close range. The second was a stand-off or long-range attack by sniper fire. Brandt's driving route was the third, as it never varied. And last was his habitual stop for a "BZ"—the *Berliner Zeitung* newspaper.[63]

Gerhard, a native German, decided he needed to get really close and connived his way into meeting the mayor's maid. She lived in a small cottage adjacent to the main house and he managed to introduce himself and work his way into her heart. Before long, his interest was being reciprocated and he began to spend time with the woman at her home. The mayor had security at his house but they got used to seeing the maid's "suitor" and only made note of him arriving and leaving. From his intimate vantage point, Gerhard was able to survey the compound and the house and put together a mock plan to kill the mayor. While this would have been the most time-consuming option for an assassin to undertake, it was recognized that a "suitor" could easily use such an opportunity to eliminate not only the mayor, but also his entire entourage in his home.

As the team looked for other vulnerabilities, they found the mayor normally ate dinner with his family in a dining room that overlooked a lake through a large window. From the other side of the lake, Jim would watch the house using a rifle telescopic sight at a distance of roughly 300 meters and observe Brandt with his family. The observation point was secluded in the evenings and would have been an ideal spot for a singleton assassin to shoot the mayor. Escape would have been easy; the assassin could dump the rifle in the lake and quickly disappear into the surrounding forest.

Their most detailed and logistically intensive plan was for an attack on the mayor's car. There were several choke points en route to and from the mayor's residence and the mayor's car passed over several sewer covers along the route. The team devised several scenarios including a command-detonated device in a sewer or a direct assault on the vehicle at a choke point.

The final scenario involved the mayor's habitual newspaper stop. Every morning he would stop at the same street kiosk. He would roll down the window, and extend his arm with the correct change, and accept the BZ from the dealer. It was an excellent place for an assassin, who could approach the kiosk as the mayor's exchange was happening. With a silenced weapon through the open window, the assassin would easily have been able to shoot the mayor. Escape from the kill zone would have been difficult, but possible, as the element of surprise and confusion at the scene would have given a shooter cover to melt away into the crowd.

When the operation was completed a report outlining the team's findings was presented to the USCOB. The report was quickly classified and Mayor Brandt's routine changed in short order. The Wall went up later that year and Brandt's security became even tighter.[64]

The Detachment's work in probing and testing security vulnerabilities and then devising countermeasures was a hallmark of its existence. The techniques developed in this field provided its soldiers with unparalleled skills in UW and, later, counterterrorism operations.

The Wall

As 1961 unfolded, Berlin remained the focal point of the Cold War. Its occupied status presented Moscow and East Berlin with a serious problem. The continued mass exodus of East Germans through the city's porous border into West Berlin drained precious manpower from the Communist state. As the crisis became more urgent and Allied military and political leaders made plans to show their determination to remain in Berlin. In June, President John F. Kennedy met with Khrushchev in Vienna and told him that the United States was committed to the people of West Berlin. Khrushchev restated his intent to sign a peace treaty with the East German government that was clearly intended to force the Allies from the city.

On the night of August 12, 1961, East Germans closed the border between East and West Berlin at all but a few crossing points and the next day, construction of a wall that would encircle the city was begun.[65] The confrontation that ensued was a test of wills. For the moment, the Allies counted on their militaries to make a show of force that would deter a Soviet move to recognize the GDR or to encroach on West Berlin's status as an occupied city.

The JCS gave instructions to CINCEUR who issued the following orders to the USCOB:

> Mission: Conduct intelligence, operational, planning, logistic, and informational activities in Berlin during the period 1 July 1961–30 July 1962, in support of the following specific objectives:
> a. Maintain a U.S. power position, which will permit the United States to negotiate from a position of strength.
> b. Create an international environment in which the values of freedom can be sustained and enhanced.
> c. Deter general and limited war without sacrifice of U.S. security interests.
> d. Maintain Berlin's status and security, and its communications with the West.
> e. Foster as close an association between Berlin and the Federal Republic of Germany as Berlin's situation permits.
> f. Maintain Berlin as a symbol of the contrasts between freedom and communism, and of the will and the ability of the Free World to resist Soviet imperialism.[66]

Berlin had emerged as a symbol of Western resolve in the face of Soviet aggression during the blockade and resultant airlift of 1948. The morning after construction of the Wall began in August 1961, it became clear the city would remain at the forefront of the struggle between two ideologies. The Western press flooded the city and the Wall was shown to represent all that was wrong in the Soviet system. Berliners on both sides of the Wall could only stare in shock as their hometown was brutally cut in half. While President Kennedy would privately say, "better a wall than a war," the US would continue to stand fast with Berlin.

The United States began to build up its forces in Europe. The Berlin Brigade became more visible as its troops conducted more frequent exercises and Wall patrols of the city and war plans were updated in expectation of a showdown and possible conflict.

The city saw a stream of visitors that would include the US Vice President Lyndon Johnson shortly after the Wall's construction. President Kennedy appointed General Lucius D. Clay to be his personal representative and he would act as Chief of Mission Berlin through the crisis. Along with an additional 1,500 US troops sent from West Germany, Kennedy was determined to show that the US had no intention of abandoning the "Island of Freedom."[67]

The East German propaganda machine called it "the Anti-Fascist Protection Wall." Its true purpose, however, was to halt the mass exodus of the GDR's population across the last open border in the Iron Curtain. It worked as designed.

Although the Western Allies could not stop construction of the Wall, they wanted to ensure they still had access to East Berlin under existing treaties made with the Russians. In late October, two months after the Wall had been put in place, a US diplomat attempted to cross into East Berlin. He was stopped and turned back when he refused to show his identification to an East German guard. That incident occurred on October 22 and within a few days General Clay devised a plan to push the Allied treaty rights by having another US citizen attempt to cross into the East. This time US Forces Berlin would be ready if the Soviets and East Germans attempted to impede the access of US personnel to East Berlin.

On the morning of October 27, 1961, a young American NCO, Herman Halterman, a young infantryman working with the Berlin Brigade G-2 (Intelligence), woke up and prepared for work. The office he was assigned to ran access patrols into East Berlin to patrol the sector and observe daily events. The East Germans would usually attempt to follow the patrols' Chevrolet sedans with their EMW 340 and Wartburg 311 cars, but they were easily left behind.

After the Wall was constructed, the G-2 patrols and all other Allied traffic were restricted to one crossing point: Checkpoint Charlie. But the new requirement to show an ID was contrary to existing agreements. To drive home that point, General Clay directed that an American soldier was to cross the border and, if challenged to show an ID, he was to turn around, return to the West to pick up an escort of Military Police and M-60 tanks and proceed again through the checkpoint.

Halterman was told not to carry a weapon, but he ignored the order. He later said he wasn't going to be the only person without a gun and he certainly was not going to be the only one to go down. He drove his own VW "Bug" that day and got as far as the first guard before he was stopped. Turning around he went back to pick up his escort and the force rumbled back to the checkpoint. This idea didn't really work either as the Russians seemed to have read the American playbook. As soon as the American tanks entered the street, a company of Soviet T-55s rolled out from behind cover into positions on the other side. Now Halterman, accompanied by a squad of armed MPs and gun jeeps, was sitting between the barrels of 20 tanks. Knowing the big guns were locked and loaded and remembering that discretion was the better part of valor, the troops and Herman in his VW carefully returned to the West. Meanwhile the tanks sat facing each other for 16 hours before they mutually agreed to pull back. It was the first and last time that US and Soviet tanks faced off during the Cold War.

Herman's performance got him noticed. By November that same year, he had been recruited for duty in the Detachment.

During the crisis period of 1961, the Detachment was prepared to support the Brigade in the defense of West Berlin if required. The USCOB tasked the unit with two separate missions if the invasion took place. The first was to block the S- and U-Bahn lines which entered the American sector from East Berlin and East Germany with explosives to stop the Soviets and East Germans from reinforcing Communist elements in the American sector. It was code-named OPLAN STRANGLE. The second mission was for the "Special Forces Detachment to execute covert demolitions of portions of the Wall." This was intended to assist US forces execute a breakout from the city.[68]

The crisis passed, the unit was not required to put its skills to use, but the calculus had changed. With increased security on the frontiers, crossing over became more difficult and plans would require revision. There was time for that to be done as everyone's tour was extended 12 months because of the crisis.[69]

Another aspect of the Wall's construction was that tensions between East and West, which were already high, became even more acute.

When the unit's men conducted operations near the frontier, it had to be done carefully because a mistake could be deadly. The East German border guards treated their section of the Wall as a "no go" zone and were prone to react nervously. On more than one occasion, the *Grepos* fired a round when spooked by a noise. Their instructions were to shoot anyone trying to escape or found in the death strip without hesitation or prior warning. As the guards were subject to imprisonment if they didn't shoot at an escapee, they tended to take their orders seriously.

Life in the City

Getting to Berlin was an experience in and of itself. In the early 1960s, most personnel shipped out from the States by boat to Bremerhaven. On arrival, representatives from the army's personnel replacement depot separated those soldiers assigned to Det "A" to be briefed. They rechecked their gear to ensure they had no Special Forces insignia on their uniforms or green berets in their bags. The next stop was the US Army Duty Train, the nightly "not so" express that took American personnel, both military and civilian, and their families on an overnight journey from Frankfurt through the Soviet-occupied zone to Berlin. Riding the train was a memorable experience, usually a negative one. Flag Orders printed with the traveler's name and rank were presented along with an identification card and the reservation made at the travel office to get on board.

Passengers shared a cramped four-person compartment in a carriage that would equate to third-class accommodations on a train in the States. Once moving, the train made for the frontier with East Germany where the locomotives were changed for the Communist variety. There would be no West Germans running trains into the East, it seemed. While stopped, the American MPs on board would present each passenger's Flag Orders to the Russians who would industriously copy all the names and stamp the papers. Then the MPs and their Russian counterparts would exchange salutes and the train would clank forward, carriages protesting and groaning as speed was gained. The Russians never came on board the train, they were there to keep East Germans from hopping a ride to freedom. The routine was repeated at the other end when the train got to West Berlin and the Russians compared the numbers they had received from the first inspection and then stamped the orders once again. It was a routine that repeated itself daily with travelers moving east to west or west to east on either the train or the *Autobahn*. The only difference was that on the *Autobahn* the Russians came in direct contact with the traveler and his vehicle. The Russian privates often surreptitiously offered pieces of their uniform in exchange for cigarettes, West German marks, or US dollars to augment their meager earnings—getting five dollars for a belt buckle would double their monthly income. But the *Autobahn* was off-limits to the Detachment's men until the early 1960s because of the Army's travel restrictions.[70] The procedures were the same for the British and French trains. The French train was just as uncomfortable, but had the advantage of wine and beer being sold in the dining car. The American train was dry, apparently because the leadership thought GIs might get drunk and give the Russians a hard time. This assumption was probably correct.

On arrival at Berlin's Lichterfelde-West train station, the new guys were met by a senior non-com who would direct them to an unmarked civilian van. A quick "Welcome to Berlin" would often be the only words spoken during the short ride to Andrews Barracks where the newcomers were unceremoniously off-loaded and installed in their barracks rooms. If the new arrival was unlucky enough not to have his "TS," he was not briefed on the full scope of the mission. Occasionally, a soldier would not even have a completed Secret clearance, in which case he would be quarantined away from operations until cleared. In either case, an OPSEC briefing would be the first thing the men would receive. Not having a clearance was the rare exception, however, and the teams integrated each new man into their routines as quickly as possible.

It was 1963 and Sergeant Kim Kendle had just spent a year in Laos with the White Star program. He was looking forward to another assignment to Okinawa and the 1st SFG, when his orders were suddenly canceled and replaced with ones assigning him to the 6th Infantry in Berlin. Although he tried to get them rescinded, the Army didn't want to hear any arguments, so Kendle and five other SF troopers were assigned to escort 300 recent basic training graduates to Germany. After they arrived in Bremerhaven, the six were separated from their charges and continued on by train to Berlin fully expecting to serve in a "leg" unit.[71]

Once in Berlin, Kendle and the others were met and taken to Andrews Barracks and put in their rooms with instructions not to go anywhere. Even a visit to the latrine required an escort. Now, totally "pissed off" because he was no longer in SF and off jump status, Kendle stewed in his room until he and the others were rounded up for a meeting several hours later. They were assembled in the unit conference room and the commander, the executive officer, and sergeant major briefed them on their new home. Kendle and the others were totally surprised to discover they were members of a "secret" SF unit. Before that moment, none of them had any clue of the unit's existence.[72]

Arriving officers first met with the commander, while the enlisted men would meet with the sergeant major after being met and briefed by a team sergeant. The newcomer was welcomed, then told what to expect if he screwed up. Few ever experienced the sergeant major's closed-door counseling sessions. When these were necessary, they were short and to the point. Minor infractions were handled in house and often ended up with a contribution to the *Hühner Freitag* (Chicken Friday) fund. Though rare, very serious infractions were followed with a quick packing of bags and a one-way train ticket out to the "Zone" as West Germany was called. If an officer was relieved, a very quiet and quick departure back to the States was arranged and a career abruptly ended.

Looking for Targets

While operating in the city posed little problem for the Detachment, the Wall made reconnaissance of the targets in the GDR very difficult. For the most part, teams relied on aerial photography and intelligence reports from military or civilian intelligence agencies. Occasionally, the East Germans would unwittingly help by publishing pictures of their socialist collective factories and railways, but military targets were never shown in detail. Even the CIA had difficulty collecting intelligence in the East as the intensive internal security and counterespionage environment made the recruitment and handling of agents very difficult. The CIA permitted only its case officers assigned to East Berlin to run operations in the East and, because scrutiny was so intense on Western visitors, officers in West Berlin and West Germany had to be content with doing their work on the "friendly" side of the Wall.[73]

Luckily, the Allies and the Soviets had agreed after WWII to permit monitoring of military activities in their occupation zones by what were called Military Liaison Missions (MLM) from a compound a short distance outside Berlin at Potsdam. Set up in 1947, these missions ostensibly existed to foster good relations, but they also served as legal spy platforms.[74] The Soviets tried to observe the Western Allies' forces in the FRG, the Allies did the same in the GDR. Looking for new equipment was one task, the other was to serve as an early warning mechanism. A similar, but separate, mechanism run by the Brigade G-2, exercised the right of passage within East Berlin.

The American MLM or USMLM, like its Allied counterparts, sent vehicles into East Germany each with a Foreign Area or Intelligence Officer who spoke Russian and a NCO intelligence analyst who spoke German.

These Military Liaison Missions provided the Detachment with an opportunity to look at their targets up close. Beginning about 1966, the unit began to exploit them by assigning men to accompany the "tours" as they were called. Traveling in modified Mercury Cyclones, Opel Ambassadors, Ford Broncos and—later—Mercedes sedans or *Geländewagons* (4 × 4), the tours would enter the "East" and conduct patrols ranging in duration from a half-day in East Berlin to a week in the Soviet zone of Germany—the GDR. The NCO would drive and the officer would act as recorder and photographer. The East German *Stasi* often tried to follow the cars, but the tour vehicles could outrun most anything the Soviets or East Germans could field and a burst of speed and evasive driving generally put them far behind. The tour teams traveled on preplanned routes looking for troop concentrations, field exercises, and military facilities with each trip based on previous visits and current intelligence reporting. The work required an expert knowledge of the Soviet and East German order of battle, as well as an ability to recognize specific military vehicles and equipment, sometimes with nothing more to go on than an antenna, the shape of a tarp draped over a vehicle, or a partial view of a tank's track guide.[75] It was extremely esoteric work and required fast thinking as well as a good memory, although tape recorders were used to augment pencil and paper. If a team was lucky they would encounter troops training or a convoy of vehicles, in which case the team would drive along the convoy snapping pictures and reciting the nomenclature and serial number of each piece of equipment seen. With that information, a determination could be made of the type and which unit was moving and often where it was going—either returning to barracks, going to a training area, or rotating home. More significant were the new units when they arrived, especially if they had new equipment.

The work could also be dangerous. The poorly trained Russian soldiers guarding a facility or onboard a military train sometimes felt it their duty to snap off a couple of potshots at the Western "spies" they encountered. Even more disturbing were the attempts to disable the Mission's vehicles by ramming them with armored personnel carriers or trucks.

The Detachment sent a number of NCOs to ride along as officially accredited members of the MLM. It was an ideal way to get close to their targets. This cover required them to be fully trained to conduct all the duties of the normal MLM personnel, as well as target reconnaissance. The USMLM (as well as those of the other allies) provided a wealth of intelligence throughout its existence that benefitted the NATO Alliance. It also assisted SF Berlin's mission preparation greatly. Training for the Mission required learning nearly the entire order of battle for the Soviet and East German armies, including being able to identify vehicles and the myriad variants for each one. This enabled analysts to identify units by the composition of a convoy's trucks or the model of tank it was assigned.

Driving was a key skill that needed to be mastered. It was no ordinary driving, it was driving through fields, forests, across rivers, and mud safely. High-speed, cross-country driving in forward and sometimes reverse gear needed to be second nature, Recovery techniques were also taught for those occasions when nature overwhelmed a vehicle's forward (or backward) momentum.[76]

Another tool was the "Ring Flight" conducted by Berlin's Aviation Detachment. Detachment soldiers would periodically fly along on the daily UH-1H and deHavilland Beaver (later Pilatus Porter) flights along the Wall not only to look at targets that lay close by, but to survey the frontier for suitable crossing points. Every bit of information that could be gathered, from hand-held photography and satellite imagery to old maps, was useful for their mission planning.

Along with their official penetrations into East Berlin, Detachment men often made personal visits to the "capital" of the GDR just as did the soldiers and families of the Allied occupation forces. After the confrontations of the early 1960s, an accepted routine for crossing Checkpoint Charlie into the East was adopted. After showing a special pass, the soldier's vehicle was allowed to proceed through the barriers. East Berlin was a complete contrast to the vibrant western sectors. Dominated by Soviet-style buildings that replaced the destruction of WWII bombing, much of the city was still scarred by the bombings and the final battle of 1945. Most Allied soldiers went shopping for bargains, ate at a decent restaurant and quickly return to the West. With an exchange rate that averaged 11 East German marks to one West German mark, everything from high-quality Czechoslovakian crystal to precision Zeiss binoculars could be purchased on the cheap. Ironically, the American MPs were more stringent in checking out the returnees. They insisted on vehicle inspections, ostensibly to make sure soldiers hadn't bought all the goods from the stores and antagonized the locals. More to the point, they wanted to ensure no East Germans were in the trunk of the car. Rumors that some Detachment men may have smuggled East Germans across the border into West Berlin in exchange for compensation were never conclusively proven. For what it's worth, the motto of SF is, after all, *De Oppresso Liber*—Free the Oppressed.

Life on the Kaserne

Andrews Barracks had a long military history. It began life as the Prussian Main Cadet Academy under Kaiser Wilhelm I in 1872 and in 1933 it served as the headquarters of the *Waffen SS* Body Guard Regiment "Adolf Hitler." It was seized by the Americans after WWII and turned into a barracks for primarily support troops, which included the 42nd Combat Engineers, the 287th Military Police, and the Army Security Agency's (ASA) soldiers who manned the signal intercept station on Teufelsberg.[77]

One always had the feeling that there were ghosts nearby. The main gate opened up onto a cobblestone parade ground where SS formations, with men like Adolf Hitler and *SS-Oberst-Gruppenführer* Sepp Dietrich presiding, had taken place.[78] The Gestapo had used the basement of another building as a detention and interrogation center. Yet another had served as a backdrop for the executions of conspirators following the attempted assassination of Hitler in July 1944. The building now housed the Enlisted Men's Club but the bullet-chipped walls were still visible. There was a coldness to the place that not even the warmest Berlin day could entirely sweep away.

In 1964, John Blevins experienced some of the barracks' hidden history. Near the Detachment's building was what appeared to be an abandoned building with a chain link fence around it. Curiously, there was always a guard posted there. One day the unit was detailed to provide a levy of men with TS clearances. They were taken to the train station where they offloaded crates marked as school supplies and books. The crates were then loaded onto trucks and taken to the abandoned building.[79]

Inside this vacant shell, they schlepped the crates down three flights of stairs to the basement, which apparently had been left untouched since the end of World War II. The Germans who had been stationed there during the war apparently did not like to see a blank wall, so most of them were covered with murals. It was a startling revelation about those who had lived there. One mural showed an SS soldier kicking an obviously Jewish man in the backside with a caption in German that read, "Kick them all back to Palestine." Another showed a bunch of SS soldiers sitting around a table drinking beer. One of the SS soldiers had his hand up the waitress's skirt with a caption that read, "The only thing Jewish women are good for." Along with the bullet holes, these grim reminders of the Third Reich were inescapable.

Living beside the ASA barracks was another "interesting" experience. The Army Security Agency (ASA) tended to recruit highly intelligent young men and women for signals intelligence work. Most were language adept and spent their days at the Teufelsberg (Devil's Mountain) facility listening to and transcribing the signals of the Warsaw Pact countries. Teufelsberg was one of the US's most important signals collection sites. Its technicians listened in on everything from Russian tank commanders in the field to high-level Warsaw Pact conversations during the Prague crisis of 1968 for indications that hostilities might be imminent.

A few of the ASA soldiers were a bit naïve. For some strange reason, these highly intelligent but rather paranoid kids chose to believe the Det's sole reason for existence was to kill them if the Russians started a war. There were other indications of paranoia among the ASA personnel, including some papering their sleeping quarters with aluminum foil to block the intrusive Soviet radio waves directed at them, while others refused to go off post for fear of being kidnapped. Rather than disabuse the youngsters of their misguided fears, some of the Det's NCOs choose to encourage them. This went as far as a promise of clemency being given to the better-looking females. *Verbum sap.*

The Detachment was an anomaly in another regard—it was not integrated, unlike all other army units since 1948. The reason was a simple matter of survival. All other things being equal, an African-American soldier had little chance of successfully passing himself off as a German or European at an enemy checkpoint or, for that matter, a West Berlin police checkpoint. Although several African-American soldiers did serve in the 1970s and later, they did so in support roles and not on the operational teams. Quite frankly, it was hard enough for a trooper who came from the hill country of Tennessee to be seen as anything other than an American. If a "southern gentleman" from the unit was pulled into secondary, he had an iceberg's chance in hell of fooling an experienced *Stasi* interrogator.

Learning how to get around the city was a priority for newcomers. The average Berlin Brigade soldier knew how to find their barracks, the location of the Post Exchange (PX), the best downtown bars, but little more. The Detachment's troopers were expected to know the city well, to navigate to any point in the city without resorting to tourist maps and to be completely acquainted with their area of operations (AO). To develop this knowledge each man was subjected to a scavenger hunt of sorts called "transportation training." Each man was given a set of questions pertaining to obscure places and objects in the city that could only be answered by going to the location in question. With questions in hand, a fistful of German marks and a time limit, they set out to fulfill the quest. After running several of the tests, travel in the city by bus, subway (*Untergrundbahn* or U-Bahn), and street car (*Straßenbahn* or S-Bahn) became much less intimidating. Part of the test included meeting team members at out-of-the-way bars. It was easy to select a meet location as there were about 5,000 *Kneipe* and *Bierstuben* in the city and German workmen and businessmen alike loved to spend their after-work hours trading stories and drinking beer and schnapps. After an evening of revelry, the key for the newbie as well as the old hand was to know when it would become difficult to navigate the transportation system. The 0600 morning formation was not voluntary.

The Quiet Time

While Germany was a focal point for the Cold War in the 1960s, it can't be forgotten that "small" conflicts were happening elsewhere. In 1961, the Soviet KGB put into action a plan to launch "armed uprisings against pro-Western reactionary governments" with the aim of "diverting the attention and forces of the United States" and began to do so, supporting revolutionary groups in Africa and Latin America.[80]

More importantly, another war on the other side of the globe began to exert its influence on the US military. The Vietnam "War," which started out as an advisory mission in 1954, became a police action in the early 1960s, and finally, a full-scale conflict around 1964 with around 50,000 American troops in action.[81] Special Forces first became involved in 1957, initially operating out of Okinawa where the 1st SFG was stationed. When the 5th SFG was established at Fort Bragg in 1961, additional teams began operating in Vietnam on temporary duty until the entire group was forward based to Na Trang in 1965.

At the same time, smaller brush fires were being dealt with in South America, where the 7th SFG was assisting the Bolivians to achieve a satisfactory outcome against Che Guevara. In Africa, the 10th SFG assisted the Belgians in a non-combatant evacuation of civilians to get them out of harm's way in the Congo. These operations proved that SF was very adaptable to a variety of missions beyond its core task of UW. It also set the stage for counterinsurgency and "foreign internal defense" to take precedence as its primary mission in the future.

As the counterinsurgency role for SF grew in the 1960s, the training at the school in Fort Bragg also evolved. The paradigm taught by the World War II experience of the OSS in Europe, specifically the necessary tradecraft to work with resistance forces behind the lines was de-emphasized. While there were some instances of UW operations in Southeast Asia, specifically the White Star and Montagnard programs, it was fighting Communist insurgents that was of paramount importance. Because of this, it would be 10th SFG, and especially SF Berlin that would keep the unconventional warfare mission alive through the 1960s until its disbanding in 1990. Training for the urban UW mission in Berlin required additional skills not taught at Bragg, including intelligence tradecraft and how to organize and operate clandestinely, the things needed to survive as a secret unit. The CIA brought in teams to instruct and the Detachment used that training to prepare for its wartime mission. As proficiency was gained, the Det would provide the same training to SF teams who came to Berlin to "relearn" UW operations.

The Detachment's manpower pool was greatly affected during this period both by the limited number of SF-qualified personnel and by

Vietnam. The teams were consolidated from six teams to three task groups because there were not enough officers to command them and the reduced number of available NCOs. Although this did not alter the planned wartime employment of six teams, it was necessary for administrative control. At the same time, those who served in the 39th seemed earmarked for success. Nearly 30 of the men who served in the unit between 1958 and 1963 were commissioned as officers and most of those who stayed in the service made the senior NCO grades. Although the unit's mission was classified, having "Detachment A" noted in a soldier's record was a very positive addition when it came to promotion time.

Most of the men who served in Berlin from around 1962 until 1972 also served in Vietnam. A number did multiple tours in the war zone and many came out of the war highly decorated. Too many lost their lives there. Regrettably (and blasphemous to say) there were a very small number who did their best to avoid Vietnam and used their assignments with the 10th SFG, 7th SFG, and Berlin to stay out of Southeast Asia.

After 1972, most of the senior NCOs had Vietnam experience in counterinsurgency, direct action, or strategic reconnaissance roles and that changed the way SF Berlin went about its business. They tended to infuse more reality into both training and mission preparedness. There was less rosy optimism and more of a darker "let's do this, but do it right" attitude. And, as before, no one talked about being the "baddest dudes" on the block or that they were looking at a suicide mission. Now it was a pragmatic "this is what has to be done to ensure success, now give us the tools to do it."

SF Berlin operated at a comfortable rhythm as the Cold War was still cool and tensions were low in Europe. Training ran in its usual cycle: "city training," skiing in the Alps, diving in the Baltic, demo training at Murnau and UW field exercises in West Germany. Then there were hours of classroom learning German, Morse code, surreptitious entry techniques, and Warsaw Pact uniform and equipment identification. Often giving the training was the training. When a team sergeant told one of the team to teach how to hot wire a car or to do low-light surveillance photography, it tested the soldier's ability to conduct the kind of short-notice "hip pocket" training so necessary for times when schedules fall apart.

Range training included all the unit's standard weapons, the Walther MPK submachine gun and P-38 pistol, 40XB and M21 sniper systems, plus the odd MAC-10, British Sten, and AK47 for familiarization. Occasionally, special devices from the "Mudslow" list were brought out for training.[82] The Mudslow items were mostly WWII-era OSS sabotage and escape and evasion (E&E) gear. These toys included the Welrod Mark I Hand Firing Device—a truly silent pistol, the suppressed High Standard HDM, and the Stinger—a .22 caliber pen gun that came packaged in what looked like a toothpaste tube. It had an effective, accurate range of about one foot. Demolition materials like explosive coal and chemical-time pencil fuses were brought out occasionally so the operators could familiarize themselves with every piece of equipment. Some of the items didn't require explanation, like caltrops, steel spikes that were to be strewn out on a trail by an evader to discourage pursuit, or the suppository that held small tools useful for escaping confinement—assuming one was not well searched after capture.

Hühner Freitag—the Tradition of Chicken Friday

One general officer visitor noted that the Detachment must have been elite, because it was the only unit in the American sector that had its own bar. It was not a sterile day room like other units, but a real bar with beer taps, refrigerators, and a semi-circular wood bar for which a walnut tree from the Black Forest sacrificed its life. The bar had been liberated from the old Army hospital when it was slated to be demolished. The setup was completed with a tournament-size pool table and dartboard that allowed some mostly good-spirited competition, and a smoke-filled, back room for the card games (mostly Pinochle) and shuffle board players. Almost every week's training schedule culminated with a Friday afternoon cleanup of the building and the maintenance of weapons and equipment—unless a field exercise was underway. One team was given the responsibility for *Hühner Freitag*—a bonding exercise that entailed the burning of meat on the grill and the drinking of beer. The actual origin of *Hühner Freitag* has been lost to history, but it was a tradition that had a clear purpose: comradeship among the men and, rarely, women invitees. Once in a while, frustrations and perceived injustices were worked through in an intricate ballet of combatives known as "Drunk-Foo," not always to protagonists' satisfaction, but usually to the observers' amusement. On the whole, it was a good place to be at 1600 on any given Friday. It was important to remember though that cars do not drive themselves home, and that "driving by Braille" was not a good solution for those with alcohol-impaired visual and motor skills.

Berlin was unfortunately not as well endowed with good beers as Bad Tölz or Munich—*Berliner Kindl* and *Schultheiss,* the two local brews, were rumored to be crafted with formaldehyde, and the East German beers were equally bad choices. The best option was to travel into East Berlin and buy 50-liter kegs of *Budweiser Budvar* or *Pilsner Urquell,* two Czech beers that won taste tests hands down in comparison. Besides, even when paying the rent on the kegs, the total price in East marks converted to about 10 US dollars—a bargain at twice the price.

CHAPTER III

A NEW MISSION AND A MIDLIFE CRISIS (1972–1976)

Sergeant Major D. A. Smith stood tall in front of the morning formation and surveyed his empire from left to right. The Detachment's day began with a formation and Smith was ending his usual daily instructions with an unusual announcement.

"All right, you guys know the Army celebrates D-Day every year at Normandy with a big memorial party. Anyone who took part in the invasion gets to go to France on the taxpayers' dollar and participate. Now, before I send in the list of eligible men, is there anyone else but ME who was there?"

Once again he looked his formation up and down, certain he was the only one eligible.

At first there was just silence.

Then came a voice from the back of the formation, "SGM, can I go too?"

D. A. looked a bit surprised and answered, "Wolf, is that you? Were you there?"

"Yes I was SGM. I was on the welcoming committee!"

And so began a typical day in the Detachment.

In 1972, Major Sid Shachnow was working as the G-3 at Berlin Brigade when he was reassigned to take command of the Detachment from Lieutenant Colonel Bob O'Malley. Despite his Irish surname, O'Malley had a distinctly Asian heritage. He was also infamous because of an encounter he had with General William Westmoreland in Vietnam. It was 1967 and O'Malley, a team leader at the Xom Kat Special Forces camp, had just returned from a long patrol with his Vietnamese counterparts. Dirty and tired, he just wanted to get a shower. Inside the camp perimeter, Westmoreland approached O'Malley and, thinking he was a Vietnamese officer, asked in his best pidgin English if he had a good patrol and if "he kill many VC." O'Malley looked at the general and replied in his best Harvard accent, "Yes General, we kill vely, vely many." Then he continued, "Captain O'Malley reporting, Sir."

O'Malley's stock went up with everyone but Westmoreland that day.

Jim Wilde was O'Malley's XO at the camp and remembered the incident well.[1] Wilde also lost points with the general when he directed him down into the operations center bunker for a briefing but forgot to tell him to duck his head. "Westy" smacked his head on an ironwood header in the dark stairwell. Stunned from the blow, the general asked if all VIPs were so treated. Wilde wanted to say, "No, only you," but held his tongue. When the general left the camp, he was not pleased.

Several years later, O'Malley took command of the Detachment. His duty there, however, was like that of most officers—each spent two or at the most three years in the unit and then moved on. Unless the officer was a very notable leader or something significant happened under his watch, only he himself remembered his service. After Piernick departed in 1961, came Francis Mahan. A bit rotund, Mahan was known as "Bouncing Frank" and was regarded as a pudgy martinet and not well liked. Then in 1964, came James Johnson and in 1967, Burl McDaniel. Neither left much of a legacy in the shadow of the Vietnam conflict. O'Malley served from 1969 to 1972. The next man, Sid Shachnow, would be remembered, mostly for his later service, but remembered still.[2]

Shachnow had had both a difficult and fortunate life. As a Jew born in Lithuania, he survived the genocidal horrors of World War II and the postwar Soviet occupation of his homeland. When his family realized life would be just as bad under the new regime as it had been under the Nazis, they escaped to the western zone of Germany and then immigrated to the US. Like the Lodge Act soldiers, Shachnow found a home in the US Army, joined Special Forces, and rose through the ranks. With combat experience in Vietnam and fluency in several languages he was a good fit for the command position. Shachnow threw himself into the assignment.

Before Shachnow's arrival, the Detachment was in a number of ways still treated as a subordinate unit of the 10th SFG. This was due in large part to the extraordinary amount of control exercised by the 10th's commander, Colonel Ludwig Faistenhammer Jr, aka "King Ludwig," who ran Bad Tölz like a personal fiefdom. Born in Munich, Ludwig was even asked to become the city of Bad Tölz's mayor. He didn't accept the job, probably because it would have taken him away from his cherished command. When Shachnow visited Flint Kaserne shortly after he took command of SF in Berlin, he had an ugly confrontation with Faistenhammer. Faistenhammer thought he controlled SF Berlin as well as Bad Tölz and tried to cow the Det's commanders into doing what he wanted. Shachnow saw things differently and told him that he was in charge of Berlin and would run it as he saw fit. He told the "King" that he was not in his chain of command. Colonel Faistenhammer was livid. Shachnow was, however, entirely correct and his standing up to Faistenhammer broke the last remaining bonds of control that the Bad Tölz commander thought he had over the Detachment.

The Vietnam Hangover

The Detachment was well versed in its mission, but unsure as to what the future would bring. The US Army of the early 1970s was suffering a crisis of confidence, a result of the war in Vietnam and its effects on the home front. With the combined effects of indifference and hostility from the American people, as well as severe budgetary and manpower cutbacks, morale plummeted in the conventional force. The draft had ended and the new All-Volunteer Force had taken over, but pervasive indiscipline, drugs, and racial issues that strained all levels of the military remained. To make things worse, a reduction in force (RIF) was hitting the officer corps and some of the youngest and best were being jettisoned into civilian life. It was not the best of times for the Army.

Special Forces did not go untouched. The RIF meant there were few young, able captains and majors. Although most were simply put out of the military, some opted to stay in as NCOs. The resulting reduction in rank from officer to staff sergeant (at best) greatly tested the mettle of the man and often his wife. The joke was that one look at her husband's first pay stub as an enlisted man was enough to convince a wife to bail out. Overall, SF went from around 10,000 men during Vietnam to around 4,200 in the mid-1970s.

Another deterrent to serving with SF was a conventionally minded Army leadership that saw SF as undisciplined and elitist, anathema to an egalitarian notion of the American citizen-soldier.[3] Many senior officers did their best to hamstring and disadvantage SF units and their personnel; service with Special Forces was often considered the "kiss of death" to an officer's career. While one or two tours with SF might be acceptable, officers were expected to serve with their regular branch or risk not being promoted.[4] NCOs could also be "tapped" (selected) for drill instructor duty or be sent to regular units when personnel shortages occurred. But, for the most part, despite the surrounding adversity, morale remained at high levels in Special Forces. It was in this environment that Detachment "A" operated in the mid-1970s.

In the early 1970s, the Warsaw Pact juggernaut was still on Western Europe's doorstep, but the threat of war seemed slightly less imminent. German Chancellor Willy Brandt's "*Ost Politik*" and the "triangular diplomacy" of US President Richard Nixon and Henry Kissinger had altered the foreign policy landscape of Europe for the better and "détente" seemed to be leading towards a brighter future. But peace was by no means assured. Following the American withdrawal from Vietnam, the Soviets viewed the United States as a diminished power and began again to assert themselves globally. Moreover, for the peoples of Eastern Europe, little had changed and the oppression of Communism still hung heavily over their heads.

The atmosphere in West Berlin was hyperactive compared to the depressed and drab East. It had a lively economy and vibrant nightlife that harkened back to the 1920s. Despite their seeming optimism, there was an anxiousness on the part of citizens who knew everything could change on the decisions of leaders in Washington and Moscow. Berlin held constant reminders of the proximity of the Communist East, from the formalities of taking a road trip to West Germany to the acrid smoke that blanketed the city in winter, a signature by-product of the low-quality brown coal used in the DDR. There was an underlying seriousness to the West Berliners that a mask of frivolity could not obscure.

Shachnow spent his first days considering how the UW mission would best be handled. The irrepressible Rolf Kreuscher, now a captain, was back for his third tour and told Shachnow about the miles of tunnels that permeated the underground landscape of Berlin. It had long been thought the tunnels could be used as a method to cross the Wall, if they were properly checked out. There were tunnels for the subways, sewers, and electrical systems and, while most were mapped, some of the older ones were not. Most intriguing was that many did not respect the East German border. The EGs had blocked most of the tunnels where they passed under the Wall, but the passages could be opened again. There were also active lines of the U-Bahn that passed under East Berlin. While all but one of the stations in East Berlin had been abandoned, the tunnels were still open and provided another possible method of getting into the East. The tunnels close to the Wall had never been accessed because the EG border guards kept armed sentries at all the underground platforms and periodically patrolled the tracks on their side of the border. No one wanted to bump into a patrol and alert the EGs to US interest in the area.[5]

Following a chance meeting with a Berlin official who told him more details about the underground water system, Shachnow decided to look into it himself. Taking a small team down into the canals, he spent several hours navigating the tunnels to find where the system crossed into the Soviet zone. Unfortunately, when they approached a barrier gate, they may have set off an alarm on the other side. They withdrew from the area without encountering anyone and believed they had accomplished a valuable reconnaissance. The next day Shachnow received a call and was told he needed to be in the commanding general's office later that day. When he arrived, he could see that General Bill Cobb was not happy. Cobb told him the venture into the canals had possibly compromised an intelligence operation. An alarm had alerted the EGs to a presence in the tunnels and they had responded with an alert force on their side of the barrier.

There are pros and cons to compartmentalization, and one of the cons was that neither organization trusted the other enough to tell them what they were doing beforehand. As a result, Shachnow had a General Officer Letter of Reprimand in his file and clear instructions not to go underground without written permission. In the future, the general instructed, the Detachment would coordinate with the "appropriate" elements to make sure no one would endanger someone else's secret project.[6]

The teams were not deterred by this speed bump and continued on with mission preparations as before. The training cycle followed the usual cycle of activities outside Berlin that included alpine skiing in the winter months, the annual UW field training exercise—now called FTX FLINTLOCK—in the spring or fall, combat diver training, and parachute jumps. Then there was sniper and demolitions training, communications exercises, and the occasional exchange training with NATO allies.

Alpine skiing was done in the Italian Dolomites, Spanish Pyrenees, and southern Germany, usually at Berchtesgaden, although teams occasionally trained with the 10th SFG at Lengreis or Mittenwald. Each year, one or two soldiers would go to the German Alpine ski or mountain climbing schools, and the best of these went to the ski instructor course. There were no better schools if you wanted to be a good military skier or climber (of course, the French, Italian and Austrian schools were not bad). Although there was little use for mountain climbing in Berlin, the technical rope skills taught at those schools were useful for urban warfare training, specifically building assaults. The skiing and winter warfare training, on the other hand, were necessary for operations in the winter terrain of northern Germany and Eastern Europe.

Swimming for Your Dinner

Unlike the Navy's UDT/SEAL teams, Army Special Forces did not have a maritime combat mission beyond using the water as a means to infiltrate their operational area. At the time, each SF battalion (ODC) had at least one dive team that trained to use either underwater or surface swimming to achieve land-fall and commence their primary mission of Unconventional Warfare (UW). Therefore, underwater operations (UWO) were a skill enhancement for the ODA's capabilities rather than its main purpose. Typically, if the target was wet, it belonged to the Navy. In Berlin, however, there was no Navy, so the Det had the mission to itself.

Since the unit was already in its "stay behind" location, traditional infiltration requirements like parachute or helicopter infiltration did not apply. Furthermore, there were limited operational capabilities available to support and sustain missions, especially with the density of air defense systems behind Soviet lines. There was no on-call fire support and no deep-penetration helicopters that could pull a compromised Special Forces team's bacon out of the fire. The basic premise that everyone understood was, "You're on your own, son."

Because of the high-threat environment, the Detachment fell back on tried and true infiltration technologies that had been around since the beginning of warfare. These included walking and the use of waterways as avenues into a target area. Self-reliance, imagination, and initiative was the essential alchemy for success and survivability. So leveraging any advantage available from the waterways in and around Berlin required some thoughtful deliberate planning and operational adaptation. The probability of surviving the walk into East Germany was improved through stealth and camouflage (using East Bloc weapons and equipment). Swimming into enemy territory required having the best training and equipment available.

Beginning in the mid-1960s, a small amount of dive and scout swimmer training was done in Berlin's lakes, the Wannsee and Havel River. Team Two was the Detachment's dive element and, along with its UW mission, it carried the added responsibility for maintaining and instructing other unit members in those skills. Det "A" would be one of only a few units, the others being the 3/7th SFG in the Panama Canal Zone and the 1st SFG on Okinawa, certified to train Special Forces divers, outside of the formal SF Underwater Operations (UWO) school at Key West, Florida. Many of the men on the team had been instructors at Key West anyway. The Detachment was also lucky to have an Olympic-size pool at its disposal—it was right out its front door on the compound. The 50-meter-long pool had been built for the German team to practice prior to the 1936 Berlin Olympics. With a 10-meter dive tower and a 7-meter deep end, it was suitable for UWO training and equipment tests. The team did physiological training/testing with the Air Force in Weingarten, while in the city the German Lifesaving Society's dive tower and compression chamber in the French sector on the Tegeler See were also available for testing and treatment if there was a dive emergency. There wasn't too much need for that as the dive depths in Berlin rarely exceeded one atmosphere, which pretty much eliminated the danger of getting the "bends."

In 1972, the Det sent ten men to Crete for a dive course run by a team from the 10th SFG. The following year, Team Two, the Det's dive team, ran a scout swimmer course, while another composite group traveled to Crete for a basic SCUBA course run by six members of SEAL Team Two. The SEALs taught the course with open-circuit SCUBA rigs and practiced a lot of demolitions against shore and underwater targets. However, army regulations specified that Special Forces divers were also to be trained on closed-circuit SCUBA gear. The SEALs used Emerson rigs while the Detachment had Dräger LAR-IIIs. So a second phase was run with the German equivalent of the SEALs, the *Kampfschwimmerkompanie* (KSK), who also used the Dräger.[7] The KSK also taught underwater reconnaissance and demolition tactics. After successful completion of both basic open-circuit SCUBA with the SEALs, and the follow-on closed-circuit tactical training with KSK, the men were awarded the military's SCUBA Diver Badge.[8]

After Crete, the Det "A" reciprocated by inviting the SEALs along for ski training and then to Berlin for the Urban Unconventional Warfare Course, also called the "City Training Course." It covered surveillance and countersurveillance techniques, intelligence tradecraft, target analysis, along with familiarization firing of the unit's foreign-sourced weapons and the museum pieces from OSS caches that still had operational utility. The SEALs also did their best to prove they could drink more than the Detachment and quite often won the bet, but then failed the evasion practical exercise when fun got excessive.

Larry Niedringhaus was Team Two's Team Leader (TL) and responsible for updating the unit's gear. Larry realized he could buy state-of-the-art equipment because the German government was obligated to pay for all equipment used by the Allied forces in Berlin as part of the occupation agreement. The only proviso was that the equipment had to be German. This worked out to the unit's advantage as the best equipment at the time was German. Niedringhaus purchased Dräger LAR-III closed-circuit oxygen rebreather systems along with German open-circuit SCUBA rigs for the team. The Dräger was superior to the vintage American Emerson system in both simplicity and service reliability. With all the new gear, a dive locker was established to store and maintain it properly; the responsibility for that went initially to SFC Bob Picknell, while MSG Wolfgang Ostertag did most of the liaison with the KSK. The Dräger would be the equipment of choice to cross over into East German waterways or sabotage the locks and canals on Berlin's Havel River.[9]

Eckenförde

Team Two was the only team in the unit that routinely practiced UWO. In order to sustain training and skill competency, in 1975, the team traveled to the northern German town of Eckenförde near Kiel on the Baltic Sea. It was the home of the KSK, and the *Kampfschwimmer* (combat swimmers) were among the world's best marine commandos or "frogmen." Their facility was an outstanding place for the team to train outside of Berlin.

The team arrived and immediately fell in with KSK's daily physical training regimen and familiarized with their equipment, which was largely the same as the Detachment's. The men swam in pairs and did long surface swims that were followed by dives of increasing distance using both open- and closed-circuit SCUBA. Then came compass dives that required precision timing and navigation. A diver could not surface to confirm his position, but had to end up on his target point when he surfaced or the dive was considered a fail. Accurate compass swimming was important inbound from a release point, which for US

Special Forces in wartime might be a submarine, a small boat off of a mother ship, or casting into the water from an aircraft. That said, swimming back out to sea to find your ride home after a mission was a hell of a lot harder than finding a moored vessel in a harbor. Additionally, the extreme cold water made the swims uncomfortable and quickly tired a swimmer. The Baltic Sea's strong currents compounded the challenge.

The KSK did not practice swimming to a point on the shore or land target from a boat; they practiced swimming from one ship to another, because their mission preference was to attack ships moored in harbors. During one early exercise, two Det divers, Sergeants Juan Renta and Ron Bruce, either weren't paying close attention or misunderstood the KSK dive master who was giving their mission brief in German. As a result, they thought that they would be swimming against the current, when in fact the opposite was true. Launching from one ship, they kicked extra hard to make sure that they made it to their target on time. The "target" was a West German Navy torpedo boat, lying several kilometers away, and marked with a small light. At night and underwater, the marker light was nearly impossible to see. Much sooner than anticipated, the team realized they were on the far side of the target ship's hull. Luckily, the instructors did not detect their approach until they returned and surfaced at the target.

Increasing levels of endurance were tested as the swims became longer and more complicated. The KSK swimmers usually put the kilometers behind them quicker than the Detachment's men—something to do with continual conditioning in the Baltic—but they lacked tactical acumen once on land. Therefore, exchanges of operational techniques ensured the KSK saw the training as mutually beneficial.

Although the Detachment had been conducting limited water operations since the late 1960s, those were only fully integrated into its formal war plans after Niedringhaus's efforts.[10] In the 1970s, the Detachment began to run its own training course that stressed underwater navigation, long-distance underwater and surface swimming from a release/start point without surfacing and with multiple underwater course changes. Then full mission profiles were practiced. Successful graduates had to show they could approach, attack, and withdraw from a target without being detected.

Training "Tourists"

The men gathered near the edge of the river, watching the barges glide silently past on the ink-dark waters. Four men had already entered the water, climbing down the man-made embankment protected from the cold in their wet suits, weapons and explosives in waterproof satchels. They had swum off about an hour after midnight, heading towards a oil storage depot—the mission target. The remainder of ODA 311 waited tensely and as patiently as they could for their turn.

It was October 1974. ODA 311 had arrived in Berlin nearly two weeks earlier from Fort Devens, Massachusetts for the Detachment's city training—14 days of instruction and practical work in the finer points of urban unconventional warfare—a sort of special ops tourism course. The team was a SCUBA detachment from 10th SFG under Lieutenant Steve Philbrick and MSG Alvin Young. Because of this, the Detachment's Team Two had the "duty" to run the course with an emphasis on waterborne ops.

As usual, all the "esoterics" were presented: urban surveillance, target analysis, tradecraft, along with weapons and demolitions familiarization. It was called "familiarization" because most everyone was well versed with guns and explosives, but the equipment the Detachment used was non-standard, foreign, and somewhat unusual.

At the end of the course, the team was subjected to a final tactical exercise. The ODA was tasked to conduct an amphibious raid on a sprawling oil tank farm that lay along the Havel River. The team had conducted surveillance on the site for five days and noted that there were only two or three guards. After the team determined the guards' patrol plan, they decided on a plan of attack and briefed it back to the Det commander as part of their evaluation. During war, there would be no brief-back; it would all be done at the team level.

Given the go-ahead, the team dispersed from the safehouse into the city. They were to meet with an "asset" who had a hide site near the river with a cache of equipment. Slipping into the hide site individually and by twos, they assembled and were given wet suits, training explosives, and Walther MPK submachine guns. Steve and Alvin, his team sergeant, went through the drill to ensure their team was ready. Then it came time for the advance element to lead the way. The team sergeant led a small team to find and secure the site where they would enter the facility. About twenty minutes later, Steve and the remainder of the men entered the water and followed to link up and carry out the raid.

The river was surprisingly dark and forbidding. With its level about five feet below the banks and the bright lights of the city, it was difficult to see and the river barges were surprisingly quiet. Some of the team, swimming on their backs and not always looking ahead, had to quickly maneuver out of the way to avoid being run over. As he swam into the night, Steve felt the cold seep into his wet suit. Luckily, winter was a month away.

As the main party closed in upon the target, the second element could see there was a problem. The landing point was covered with 15–25 guards. Not only had the number of guards increased, the lead swim team had been compromised as it approached the target. As they were already backing off the shore, Steve and his swim buddy, Bob Johansen, swam ahead to meet them. They quickly decided to abort and swim to their pickup site. They had to get out of the area by using the shadows and barges that were tied up along the bank for cover. Not all of the team made it, one man was picked up close to the target. A patrol boat's searchlight swept the river, but the rest were able to evade to the exit point. Making dry land in an area heavily overgrown with scrub and abandoned structures, they cached their gear and got back into civilian clothes. The team made their way back to the rendezvous point as they came in: singly and in pairs, taking care to watch their backs as they went.

Later, a second run would allow the team to practice its actions on target, but on this night the unexpected came between the team and their goal. The exercise controllers sometimes stacked the odds against a team just to give them the experience of failure.

Wet Work

In 1976, the UWO mission was shifted to Team Three. Along with Team Four, the two teams were assigned central Berlin as their area of operations—they were the stay-behind teams.[11] With more kilometers of canals than Amsterdam, Berlin was a city of waterways that were critical to the movement of supplies. The canals provided Team Three with an excellent system of inter-connecting routes that could be used to access targets in the city and serve as a way out when necessary.

Team Three planned to use the Dräger to support their operations. The compact packaging of the LAR-III made it a very versatile rig and adaptable for more than underwater operations. Closed-circuit gear like the LAR-III that did not leave telltale bubble trails in the water was essential to avoid detection and was the ideal technology as long as the diver maintained a safe depth. What is a safe depth? Without getting too technical, oxygen (O_2) becomes toxic over 29.4 psi or two atmospheres, which is deeper than 33 feet or 10 meters of depth for a pure O_2 rebreather. Tolerance for this toxicity is influenced by individual physical conditioning and psychological composure.

When swimming for training in Key West, it was possible to swim 2,000 meters or more, one way, without being in water over 30 feet deep. Often the moonlight reflecting off light-colored sand enabled terrain recognition to aid navigation for both ingress and egress from a target on the long swims and the bioluminescence was a distraction to the monotony.

This was not the case in Eckenförde, where the water was deep and clouds often blocked out the moon. You were alone, accompanied only by the rhythm of your slow, measured breathing as you tried to balance the inhalation and exhalation volume into the rebreather. As each two-man team swam, one man was on the compass and depth gauge, the other was straining to hear or glimpse anything discernible in the blackness to avoid compromise or worse.

The swimmers' concern for surface craft was common to all operations. The sound of a small boat approaching quickly meant the team might have been detected. Worse, in an active harbor, the turbulence from a large ship passing overhead could pull the diver up into the propellers. Special Forces infiltration planning typically selected routes in remote undeveloped areas where a diver could easily hide at a safe depth to avoid a small craft. In the deep, cold dark waters of the Baltic, however, the thrashing thrum of a big ship's props was much more worrisome.

The KSK response was to go deep and dig into the bottom and hold on until it passed. This could be an excursion to 70 feet of depth and presented a new paradigm for the Det "A" divers who had been trained in Florida. Once below 33 feet, a diver could become affected by O_2 toxicity, but the Dräger system included a buoyancy compensator with separate compressed air bottles that could be breathed if required. The KSK training experience reinforced the requirement for good physical and psychological conditioning. This influenced the dive courses that Team Three ran compared to how the courses were taught in Florida. Since there was not any standard-issue closed-circuit SCUBA equipment to replace the obsolete Emersons withdrawn from US Army Special Forces, the Detachment's LAR-IIIs gave the unit a unique capability, which was shared with other SF units that cross-trained in Berlin.

Team Three studied the storm drains that emptied into the lakes and rivers and determined that they could be used to access many parts of the city from underground. These also could provide temporary hiding places or caches for equipment or even people (eternal darkness and rodents notwithstanding). The resident Team Three tunnel rat was SFC Rick Bucho who, before taking over as the unit's Senior Engineer, put much thought into how to sustain operations literally underground.

The waterways penetrated both the intercity border between East and West Berlin as well as into the countryside of the GDR. Although they were heavily guarded and barriers were in place, it would still be possible to use them to infiltrate the East. Where boat traffic crossed between the two zones, a single or several divers could accompany a barge through the opened barriers. Hanging onto a slow-moving barge, a diver would be less likely to lose his handhold at an inopportune moment if a line could not be secured. The canal crossing points at Dreilinden, Teufelsee, and Potsdam-Niedlitz were all regarded as possible exfil points.

Ron Sheckler and Rick Patrick arrived around the same time, late 1976 and early 1977. Both were most recently from 3/7th SFG in Panama and brought years of SCUBA/Scout Swim experience with them. They quickly influenced the Underwater Operations training techniques and methods. Additionally, Sheckler was able to provide civilian dive cer-tification to complement the rigors of the military dive training. Prior to that, it had been ironic that a qualified Special Forces diver could not rent gear while on vacation because he did not possess a civilian certification card. This was extended to the dive teams at 1/10 SFG in Bad Tölz as Sheckler and Joe Gadzik, previously of 5th SFG, provided Dräger closed-circuit enhancement training to their basic open-circuit SCUBA course to enable military certification.

To reduce attention, open-water swims and deep-dive requirements for initial and recertification were conducted outside Berlin, often at Chiemsee or Starnbergersee in Bavaria. But Berlin's tunnel environment was outside the typical dive profile of a regular ocean infiltration—it was usually totally dark and using lights was compromising.

To prepare for this, drills were developed that specifically addressed spatial disorientation and obstacle negotiation well beyond the confid-ence exercises in other military dive courses. The lights of the Andrews' pool were turned off to approximate the low visibility conditions in the canals, lakes, and storm drains. Pool training emphasized ditching, donning, and swimming from rig to rig through hoops coated with glow paint tethered at different levels and orientations in a blacked-out pool after entering from the 10-meter platform. The compact chest mount of the LAR enabled a rucksack to be worn normally. Its fiberglass shell and neck strap enabled it to be easily removed and hand carried or pushed ahead through a confined space. That made it ideal for negotiating the underground, water-filled tunnels of Berlin.

Of course, these were an entertaining break between flutter kick sessions on the side of the pool with a water-filled face-mask that reinforced breathing through the mouth and not the nose. The last thing you want is to choke on water through your nose and flood your closed-circuit rig with water because the dry chemical that absorbs CO_2 creates a caustic solution that is not to be ingested. Turbidity in many of the waterways was so bad that the compass and depth gauge had to be held against the face mask in order to see it. Consequently, claustrophobia was a challenge for those that had never experienced it. To screen each diver's capabilities and help overcome this fear, the Det

"A" equipment inventory included a one-man recompression chamber, which all divers had to successfully endure. This was mandatory for initial training as it was how the team would transport an injured diver to medical treatment. However, a coffin is more spacious and the exercise was a humbling challenge for all experience levels. It seemed sized to fit Europeans, who were typically smaller than most Americans. Folks like "Poncho" Liner who had spent time in the weight room had to be greased to even slip in. Given time and team medic Juan Renta's gentle bedside manner, all were coaxed through, except "Joe" who never made it past his waist. Lucky for him, he was already qualified from Key West and a capable diver but it was like holding a cat over water and as a result more than a few free beers were provided at his expense.

Operationally, no one expected to live long in an occupied Berlin. But the flexibility provided by the Dräger LAR-III opened new dimensions for movement, access, and when necessary evasion.

Terror in the City

A new threat was looming on the horizon. Prior to World War II, Berlin was home to a number of Socialist and Communist movements that found strong support in the city as it was a center of industry and Karl Marx's working class. That was until the National Socialists (Nazis) wiped most of them out. After the war, the city returned to its status as a haven for left-leaning thinkers and rebels. Many students came to West Berlin to escape West Germany's military service requirement. They attended the Free University where many joined activist movements opposed to the "bourgeois capitalist system" and protested against the "*Amis*'" occupation of Western Europe and the war in Vietnam. By the end of the 1960s Berlin was again a hotbed of radicalism.

Many Germans saw their country as a pawn in the middle between two foreign camps—the Soviets and the Warsaw Pact against the Americans and NATO. Most were not revolutionaries; they were simply antiwar. A very small number, however, went underground to form terror movements dedicated to bringing down the West German government and forcing the American forces in Germany to go home.

These were the Baader-Meinhof Gang, later known as the Red Army Faction (RAF), and the Revolutionary Cells (RZ) operating throughout Germany. Berlin had another attraction for these groups and that was the relative ease with which they could pass into Eastern Germany where the GDR government tolerated their presence. The East German MfS's Main Department XXII encouraged and provided material assistance to these groups in order to destabilize the West—if and when their activities were in line with the GDR's interests.[12] Today, this would be called "state-sponsored terror."

Terror attacks against individuals and US facilities in West Germany prompted the Germans to reinforce their capabilities to combat terrorism. At first, this consisted of reinforcing the investigative capabilities of the *Bundeskriminal Amt* or BKA (Federal Criminal Office), but no specialized counterterrorism (CT) force existed at that point. The police forces of the individual states (*Länder*) were responsible for reacting to terrorist incidents. That changed after the Palestinian group Black September took Israeli athletes hostage at the 1972 Olympic Games in Munich. The failure of the Bavarian police forces to resolve that incident resulted in a German government decision to create a dedicated CT force, *Grenzschutzgruppe* 9 or GSG-9 (Border Protection Group 9).[13]

Other countries reacted in similar fashion. The Israelis created a domestic CT force *Yagav* and gave the army's *Sayeret Matkal* (General Staff Reconnaissance Unit) and navy's *Shayetet* 13 (Flotilla 13) the additional mission of CT operations. In France, the *Groupe d'Intervention de la Gendarmerie Nationale* or GIGN (National Gendarme Intervention Group) was created. The fact that GSG-9, GIGN, and YAGAV were all civilian police units was indicative of their home countries' concern with the use of military forces for the resolution of civilian law enforcement issues.

In the United States, city police forces created Special Weapons and Tactics (SWAT) teams to deal with hostage barricade incidents, drug gangs, and terrorists. The FBI also created a CT division to deal with the issue, but it concentrated primarily on domestic terrorists. Although Army SF personnel often advised local police forces with their tactics and training, the military was not yet specifically tasked with the CT mission.[14] Up to that point, the mission was handled on an ad hoc basis—plans were made up as things happened—and DOD policy gave Military Police units the responsibility to prepare for what were then seen as criminal incidents.[15]

It was only after the 1976 Israeli raid on Entebbe that General John Hennessy, the CINC of US Readiness Command (REDCOM), was directed by JCS to revise a CT concept of operations plan that his staff had written the summer before and to develop a joint force capability for the mission. It would prove to be a difficult task. While the national capability would require two years to achieve operational status, EUCOM was given the formal tasking to develop its own capability. Shortly thereafter, the Detachment received authorization to expand training and increase logistical support, specifically more ammunition and equipment that would be necessary to prepare for the tasking.

In CONUS, both the Army and Navy rebuffed Hennessy's request for forces saying Special Forces and the SEALs were overcommitted. Hennessy was able to set up a skeleton force consisting of REDCOM's JTF 7X, a special staff for contingencies, and elements of the Army's 2nd Ranger Battalion and USAF's 1st Special Operations Wing to begin planning and training. A second push came from JCS in 1977 after Dutch commandos successfully resolved a terrorist hostage incident on a train in Holland and GSG-9's spectacular takedown of an airliner in Mogadishu. The Army and Navy again refused to "play jointly" with General Hennessy and, instead, began to set up their own specialized CT forces. The SEALs began to train at Norfolk, while MG Robert C. Kingston, then commander of the Army's John F. Kennedy Special Warfare Center (USAJFKSWC), ordered the creation of a temporary force called "Blue Light" as a stopgap measure.[16]

In June 1977, Colonel Charlie Beckwith was given authorization to set up a new unit that would be called 1st Special Forces Operational Detachment—Delta, something he had been advocating for a long time. Better known as "Delta" or "Delta Force," it would require two years to be operational.

In the interim, "Blue Light" was created in 1977 from five Operational Detachment "A" (ODA) teams from 5th SFG and 7th SFG, and a composite Operational Detachment "B" (ODB) from the 5th. Many of the men in the unit were veterans of the Son Tay POW Camp raid and were superlative shooters and operators.[17] The project was given an area at Mott Lake on Fort Bragg where the men built their own pistol and rifle ranges, along with a reaction shooting range, simulated buildings, and other targets. Ultimately, Blue Light would be shut down after Delta came on line.

Major General Jack V. Mackmull, who followed Kingston at USAJFKSWC, tried to keep Blue Light operational, but the CJCS, General Edward "Shy" Meyer, overruled him. Mackmull was able to keep the Blue Light facility and its very qualified personnel to form the core of a new training program called Special Operations Training (SOT) that was meant to keep their direct-action skills alive and available to train the men of the SF Groups.[18]

Ahead of the Curve

Several years before, in February 1974, USEUCOM's special operations directorate, SOTFE, had tasked the Detachment to provide sniper teams to support antihijacking operations at Berlin's airports. In case of an incident involving American aircraft, the Det's sniper/observer teams could assist the military or city police with precision, long-range rifle fire. The Detachment had already been training with the Army's Advanced Marksmanship Unit at Vilseck, West Germany to master the art of "one shot, one kill." In wartime, the teams also planned to use their "long guns" to damage material targets such as Soviet mobile rockets on their launchers from a long way off, so the CT mission only required solutions to a few new challenges. Under this new tasking, the Detachment's snipers began to practice scenarios and work out how to shoot accurately and effectively through obstacles like automotive safety glass and Plexiglas windows with their M-21A and 40XB rifle systems. Timed practice sessions by an experienced marksman at 300 meters often yielded 10-round shot groups that could be covered with a silver dollar.

But, the Military Police's (MP) methods of engagement differed greatly from the Detachment's concept of how things should be handled and problems came up immediately. The coordination of sniper fire with the MP "assault" teams was difficult even with good communications, as the MPs had not been trained in the "kinetic resolution" of hostage situations or terrorist incidents. It was a new art form that required a great deal of preparation and training. The US military as a whole was not well prepared to deal with terror, which was still largely viewed as a law enforcement problem, not a military threat.

After the 1972 Munich debacle, the Detachment leadership anticipated counterterrorism tactics and skills would need to be developed and refined to counter future threats. Shachnow used the sniper mission tasking as justification to send six unit members to a special FBI Counter Air Crimes course in the spring of 1974. The FBI, at that time, was the most experienced US agency dealing with "skyjackings" and terrorism. Their training was a variation of the SWAT training course the FBI gave to other national police forces and included courses presented by various experts in criminal psychology, relevant legalities, and case studies of incidents presented by the agents who had resolved them. Mostly, however, the training was team and tactics oriented. A lot of marksmanship and weapons firing drills, quick reaction, target discrimination, precision shooting, team tactics and tactical exercises, including clearing of buildings and rooms and an aircraft fuselage—a so-called linear target. The course included physical training, both as conditioning and for team building, hand-to-hand combat, along with leadership, situation reaction, and problem-solving drills.

The SOTFE staff started to plan for contingencies that would require more tactical skill than a MP company could supply. They were monitoring GSG-9 for organizational and operational insights and doing the same with the Israeli CT units.

Later in 1974, SOTFE requested the Detachment provide an estimate of its ability to conduct "very surgical military operations." The unit had to break down exactly what SOTFE was asking for and then answered with a message describing Det "A's" capabilities and training. Beyond precision direct-action operations, the unit's skills in urban UW operations and intelligence collection rounded out the proposal.

SOTFE liked what it saw and, in early 1975, requested the unit write a plan to form a CT force for EUCOM under Contingency Plan 0300 (CONPLAN 0300).[19] Captain "Mac" Dorsey, Team Three's commander, was given the responsibility to develop the proposal that outlined what the Detachment required in material and training resources. Sergeants Farr, Niffenegger, and Shedlock were instrumental in producing a proposal requesting equipment that was mostly already available in the Army inventory and a training POI that was accepted on its first submission.

The development of training began with a study of terrorist methods, including aircraft skyjackings, and hostage barricade incidents, as well as the techniques used by security forces to resolve those incidents. The Detachment's mission and organization was adapted to include these kinds of activities. This mission would periodically vie for dominance with the unit's other requirement to plan, prepare, and train for OPLAN 4304's UW taskings.

In November 1975, a second composite team went to Quantico to attend the FBI's antiterrorist training course, a two-week course which involved extensive range time, tactics, analysis of weapons effectiveness, and much physical fitness time. However, the Detachment's attendees had been selected based on experience and not on their ability to run fast and jump high like most of the other teams at the course. The others came from city or state police SWAT teams and their average age was perhaps 25/26 years. The Detachment's men were senior NCOs and averaged more like 40 years of age. At 37, Captain Darrell Katz was the youngest member of the team and they consistently struggled against the even younger policemen in the physical events. But, the "old hands" brought back advanced operational techniques for "resolving" terrorist incidents that added to the unit's program.[20]

Things were progressing well. Then came an unexpected blow to the unit's leadership.

An Ignominious Downfall

Lieutenant Colonel Moran A. "Moon" McKenzie had taken command in early 1975, but would not complete his tour. McKenzie was not SF qualified and no one was sure how he got the assignment, but from the beginning he had issues with his deputy, Major John Langston, who had also served under Lieutenant Colonel Shachnow as his XO. Langston did not like McKenzie. The reason was never clear to the personnel of the unit, but Langston, who also was not SF, wasn't liked by the men anyway. The relationship was not toxic to the point of disrupting operations, but it was evident the two officers didn't get along.

McKenzie was not familiar with German culture or clandestine operations, but he knew enough not to interfere with operations and let his sergeant major and Captain Don Gentry, the S3, run the Detachment. Both were highly competent and the unit was functioning well. At least until the Berlin Brigade's Deputy Commander, Colonel Richard J. Kattar, a man with no love for Special Forces, decided that the Detachment should provide instruction to the Brigade's 6th Infantry Regiment. Who better to teach the infantry than a bunch of over-qualified senior NCOs? The Det was detailed to instruct a leadership school and conduct adventure training like cross-country ski training and a scout swimmer course.

The requirement that the training should be given in uniform only added more insult to the tasking and eroded the unit's cover. Kattar's "official position" was that the Detachment NCOs would be good role models for the infantry troops, but everyone suspected he just wanted to keep the unit on a short leash.

The unit had taught several two-week classes and after one class graduation, a party was held at the Det "A" dayroom. *Bier, Wurst und Brötchen* were served for a party that was to last perhaps an hour. However, someone used the event as an opportunity to inform Kattar that McKenzie was drinking with the enlisted men, an affront to the officer corps in most conventional officers' view. It was apparently also distasteful to Kattar, who showed up unannounced, went straight to the dayroom and found McKenzie there drinking a beer with the enlisted men. It was after 1700 hours, but this behavior did not go down well and Kattar called McKenzie out to the hallway and relieved him.

The official reason for McKenzie's relief was "loss of confidence" and there was never any proof that Langston was behind the relief, but there was strong suspicion. Langston, seemingly aware of that everyone blamed him, took the prudent step to be quickly reassigned.

That was not the end of the story, however, as Kattar installed his own choice of commander, another non-SF officer, Lieutenant Colonel Raymond Rau, an aviator. Rau was not a bad guy, he had won the Distinguished Service Cross and Silver Star flying in Vietnam, but he was not an appropriate choice to command a SF unit. Not that it mattered to Kattar, he just wanted his man in charge. Kattar, through a pliant Rau, then put the entire Detachment back into uniform and continued to use them as professional skills instructors for the Brigade.

In a matter of a few weeks, Kattar nearly succeeded in destroying the unit's morale as well as disrupting its operations. The Brigade tasking put an enormous strain on the unit and training for its two classified missions, UW and CT, suffered. Nearly a year would pass before the Brigade Commander, Brigadier General R. Dean Tice, who accepted McKenzie's removal, would be transferred out. Soon after the new commander, Brigadier General Walter E. Adams, arrived in June 1976 the Detachment was put on his briefing schedule.

When Adams came to the unit in the late fall of 1976, Master Sergeant Terry Swafford, the Detachment's S-3 NCO, was detailed to brief him. After Swafford described the unit's wartime and peacetime missions and how its current additional tasking was undercutting readiness, the general cut him short. He wanted to know what had happened and how. After hearing the story, he told Swafford to get the unit out of uniform and back on the streets. It wasn't a victory, but it was a relief. The full resolution would come with the New Year.

CHAPTER IV

THE PROS FROM DOVER (1976–1980)

"Colonel Olchovik, are your men going to kidnap me tonight?"
Soviet Army General Yevgeni Ivanovski[1]

In the fall of 1976, Acting Sergeant Major Jack Fulp felt that a change was coming.[2] He was right. The new sergeant major, Jeffrey Raker, arrived the first week of January 1977 and immediately set out to reverse the damage Kattar had wrought. Raker first met with the current Detachment commander, Lieutenant Colonel Rau, the team sergeants and members of the staff to get an orientation on the unit's status and current operations. With those facts in hand, he set out to meet with Colonel Pawlik, the new deputy Brigade commander (DBC) for his initial interview. The DBC was the rater for the Detachment commander and he endorsed the sergeant major's efficiency report. Raker quickly established rapport with the DBC—both began their careers as infantrymen—and then shifted the subject to the question of leadership. He got the DBC to agree that soldier training, and to some degree training of junior officers, was the business of each unit's NCOs. That made it easy for him to point out that sending the Detachment's SF sergeants to train the Brigade's soldiers while their own NCOs stood in the back of the room with their hands in the pockets undermined the authority of those NCOs and was detrimental to good order and discipline. As it turned out, the colonel was not fully aware of Det A's role in the training. Telling Raker the Detachment should be training for its own real world missions, Pawlik said he would cancel the Det's task of training the 6th Infantry.

The two men then relaxed and settled back to enjoy cigars, which filled the room with blue smoke. Pawlik then mentioned that he had yet to have any Brigade soldier graduate from the German Ranger School, the *Einzelkämpferlehrgang*. He admitted he was embarrassed because he thought that the Brigade had been sending good infantry soldiers to the course.[3] SGM Raker asked him to give the Detachment eight quotas for the next course and promised the DBC that they would all graduate and restore the reputation of the Brigade.

In early February 1977, eight men made their way to Schongau to begin the strenuous course. Four weeks later, all eight came back having completed the course with flying colors. The school *Kommandant* Major Dieter Roelle wrote a letter to Brigadier General Adams praising their achievements and noted the Detachment's men had helped many of the German soldiers to make it through as well. It probably didn't hurt that the Det "A" soldiers sang German Army marching songs, including the *Fallschirmjäger Lied*, throughout the course.[4]

Now that the unit was freed of its albatross, Raker set out to find a new commander. He knew he could not get the Detachment to a higher standard of readiness by himself. What was needed was a commander with the right credentials: SF qualification, European background and language qualification, and, most importantly a true believer in UW.

This is where Raker's skill as a "fixer" came into play. Raker outlined his ideas to his friend, former SF battalion commander: Albert Deprospero, who was in a position to help. Deprospero had been since been promoted to colonel and was the Deputy Director of Army Materiel Systems Analysis Activity, an activity of the Army Material Command, which was headed by a super-grade Department of Defense civilian employee. The civilian was on a first-name basis with the Army's Deputy Chief of Personnel and could therefore influence officer assignments worldwide.

Colonel Deprospero heard the SGM out and hesitated only a moment before suggesting Stan Olchovik. He volunteered to do the legwork for Raker, and if Stan agreed, to send him a copy of his Officer Record

Brief (ORB), which arrived in Berlin a week later. Raker had also established a soccer game relationship with the Brigade commander, General Walter Adams that was equally important. General Adams' and Raker's sons were on the same soccer team and the two men watched them play each week. During one of their conversations Raker mentioned that the Detachment was in the market for a new commander since Lieutenant Colonel Rau had recently been reassigned and Major Dahlia was only in interim command. Adams asked he had an officer in mind and the sergeant major told him that he had just received the ORB of a highly qualified officer for the post. In short order, Raker delivered the ORB to the commander's office and waited for matters to take their course.

At first, nothing came of it. At the next soccer game Adams said, "Oh, by the way sergeant major, I had to rule against your prospective new commander." Adams noted that Olchovik was an artillery officer who had served almost exclusively in SF. Raker didn't try to change his mind (an exercise in futility in any event) but thanked him for his consideration and mentioned that Stan might still get the assignment, to which Adams replied, "Then, so be it, but I had to turn him down."

The wheels had already begun turning, the Pentagon had decided to assign Colonel Olchovik to Berlin despite Adams' comments. Olchovik and his charming wife, Amika, soon became favorites at Brigade social events.[5] Later, in another soccer game conversation with General Adams, Raker mentioned that Colonel "Scottie" Crerar had been promoted retroactively with four years in grade because, for some reason or another, he had been overlooked. Raker wondered out loud if the same thing might have happened to Lieutenant Colonel Olchovik. The seed had been planted; General Adams requested a relook and Olchovik was promoted to full colonel with four years' backdated rank and pay.

Raker and Olchovik, or "Col O" as he was known, made quite a pair. Raker, a native German, was the gruff senior NCO never without a cigar nearby or a pithy comment to share. His laugh penetrated the halls of the unit and he rarely raised his voice. He didn't need to. Raker was a mostly affable, sometimes hard-nosed "Smaj" that kept the men on track and in good spirits. Raker knew each man and what they were capable of and took that into account if one of them screwed up. If he decided the culprit was beyond redemption it was a different story, as one young soldier found out. That man, Steve, was caught with a young woman in his barracks room. Brought before the sergeant major, he didn't get a chance to say a word. He was told to pack his bags; a spot on that evening's "Olchovik Express," the Duty Train to West Germany, had been reserved for him and orders for Steve to be reassigned to a conventional unit were already prepared by the ever-efficient Danny Goldman, the S-1 Admin NCO. Steve tried to argue that it wasn't fair because other guys had gotten off with lesser punishment for the same infraction. Raker just looked at him for a second and then pointedly crushed out his cigar in the ashtray, "You know, Steve, you are right. But that's what we call a double standard."

If Raker was the hammer, Olchovik was the anvil. The tall, burly Czech émigré seemed to speak through his sergeant major, but when he did talk the conversation was short, to the point, and heavily accented.

Olchovik was the kind of leader who made things happen at higher levels without anyone seeing what had transpired. He would come down to the day room for most Chicken Fridays and became one of the guys—to a point—there was always distance between him and everyone but Raker. Raker later explained why Olchovik had been sent to the unit, he said, "He was a brain surgeon sent to fix things, not a dentist like his predecessor."

Col O inspired the same loyalty as Raker. When someone from another unit parked in the commander's marked spot, the offending VW Bug was picked up and stuffed nose to tail between two trees within minutes.

The snowball began to roll as operational readiness returned to being the unit's priority not the Berlin Brigade's make-work tasking. Both the colonel and the sergeant major saw that the 39th SFD had a key role to play in Europe. Most importantly, while a general war with the Russians was possible, terrorism was a clear and present danger.

Over the years, the composition of the teams had changed. There were fewer Lodge Act and more American-born soldiers on the teams. But there were still many immigrants and first-generation sons of immigrants, along with a few country boys that could never quite jettison their distinctive accents. The teams were tight-knit and everyone was on a first name basis. Although some officers tried to maintain their status, the older NCOs usually made them accept the fact that they were going to called by their given name rather than their rank. The rivalry between teams was still intense, but there were alliances as well. And there was the usual horseplay. After one day of training, Team Five's "Styk" decided he would annoy Team Six. He snuck into their team room and filled the ashtrays with some chemical powder that he had scraped out of smoke grenades. Later, when "Stefan Wolpack" went to put his cigarette out, the flash and huge ball of smoke that filled the room did indeed annoy the team. Several days later, while Team Five was cleaning its weapons, retaliation came. A Team "Sixer" named "Bobo" opened the door a bit and tossed a French training grenade into room. The French grenade did not explode, it popped, sending a white marking powder over everything in its bursting radius, which in this case included people, papers, and just-cleaned weapons. The war would continue so, until the two teams decided they should direct their energies at other rival teams and not each other.

The calendar year 1977 began with the usual "holistic" training. Winter warfare training took place near the small village of Berchtesgaden in the Bavarian Alps and one last round of cross-country ski training was presented to the 6th Infantry Regiment. The commanders had chosen to conduct annual ski training since the unit was established and it was one reason so many soldiers kept coming back. It was good training, but it was also a reward for a year's hard work. The commander could have chosen field training with cross-country ski marches and camping in snow caves. Instead it was Alpine skiing punctuated with short stints of cross-country skiing. It was the same theory, but a more relaxed approach that pushed everyone to willingly master the skills.

The Detachment had stayed at the *Alpengasthof Vorderbrand* so often, it had become the de facto Bavarian headquarters of the unit. The hotel lay on the slopes above the town not far from the so-called "Eagle's Nest" and the rubble of what was once Hitler's southern home, the *Berghof.* The *Vorderbrand* was typically Bavarian, the family traced its ownership to long before 1933.[6] There was a small locked room off the main hall that was used for special events. The family's souvenirs were kept here, including a photo album. The matronly proprietress would sometimes bring it out and proudly show off the pictures of "Uncle Adolf's" visits before and during the war. At times, the owners seemed to think the Detachment soldiers were long-lost kinsmen—sort of Teutonic warriors from the New World.

The Jenner mountain rose behind the hotel and every morning the instructors would drag their students out of the hotel and hike up the trail to catch the first lift to the top of the mountain. Several hours of formal instruction would follow, broken only by rest stops at the different tea houses on the slopes. Depending on which type of courage was being imbibed, some skiing styles became markedly more fluid towards afternoon.

A few of the Detachment men were top-grade instructors: Bob and Sid were among those who were envied for their graceful and seemingly effortless skiing ability, while the rest of the group skied somewhere between snowplow and almost open parallel skiing. The instructors would take their fledglings to a certain comfort level and then push on to more and more challenging slopes. Often, after one of the long "tea" breaks, they would lead their thusly reinforced students into the *Spinnergraben* (fool's ditch). The route down through this extremely challenging ravine was littered with boulders the size of small cars and false moves were sometimes followed by minor avalanches and some spectacular crashes. To the skiers' credit no one was seriously injured, killed, or buried there.

As the muscles grew weary and the sun descended below the top of the western mountains, the intrepid skiers would head down the trail—this time on skis. Making it down the hill was infinitely more challenging than the trek up because it was dark, everyone was tired, and some were skiing at the ragged edge of their capabilities on an icy track. Patrick, one of the more accomplished instructors, came down the hill and "shushed" to a halt in front of the *Vorderbrand* to count his "ducklings" as they returned to the nest. All but one were accounted for. Hiking back up the trail, Patrick found Nick half-buried in a snow drift next to the creek below the track. Nick's eyes were about the only thing visible. After being pulled from the slush, Nick gave "I didn't see the curve" as his lame excuse. Then again, *Jägertee* (hunter's tea) was known to affect a skier's vision.

Back in the warmth of the hotel, an evening of Bavarian *Gemütlichkeit* (roughly translated as: good food, beer and schnapps, and lots of hospitality) followed before each fell into several layers of feather bedding to sleep it off until morning. Only once or twice did someone attempt to sleep outside in the snow, but they were always rescued by the waitresses who needed their bar bills paid.

A full 14 days of hard training was almost enough to make one want to return to Berlin, despite the fact that life there was not always as exciting as being on the slopes. A case in point was the classroom training that covered stupefyingly monotonous subjects like Soviet uniform recognition or Morse code that was pounded into everyone's heads (unless you were a communicator). The students' interest was affected by what he had experienced downtown the night before, or the skill of the instructor. No matter how interesting the subject though, everyone looked forward to training outside, even in the cold Berliner weather.

New unit members were given their scavenger hunt questions so they could learn the city in detail. Then came the instructors from "Team 10" to teach surveillance and intelligence tradecraft skills. Target folders were studied intensely, which led to discussions on where and how to cross the Wall. Old assumptions were called into question as the East Germans improved the border's forbidding construction and new ideas for surviving the first 24 hours of war were debated. Much time was spent studying the Wall and rivers of the city, while non-technical communications sites and safehouse locations were checked or new ones sought out and recorded.

The Wall had evolved over 15 years into a very formidable obstacle. The inner city barrier between the western and eastern sectors consisted of a 10-foot-high concrete structure topped with a round, concrete pipe that made it difficult to gain a hand-hold. There was a secondary barbed-wire fence on the GDR side of the Wall and the two were separated by a strip of manicured sand that made footprints stand out. Light poles and guard towers completed the obstacle. Existing buildings and canals were incorporated into the line in a fashion that made escape from the East nearly impossible. The Wall around West Berlin's border with East Germany was just as dangerous. The separation between the main wall and the inner border of the GDR side was generally wider, sometime 75 meters, with a road that the *Grepos* used to patrol the perimeter as well as deliver the guards to their posts. There was also a tertiary fence in the center of the so-called death strip that would slow down a would-be escapee or make any guard who might contemplate emigrating to the West think twice. But in Berlin, unlike the border between the GDR and the FRG, anti-personnel mines like the SM-70 shrapnel mine were not used to deter *Republikflucht* (defection). There was one serious deficiency in the design, which for the most part did not concern the Communists, and that was the Wall was meant to prevent escapes from East Germany not break-ins. Sections of the Wall were vulnerable and those were the areas Det "A" studied as potential crossing points. Knowing what lay beyond the security strip was equally important as it would not be prudent to cross over only to unintentionally end up inside an East German Army compound, of which there were many.

Teams also discovered that the East Germans had built their own crossing points into the Wall. These were used by the *Stasi* to surreptitiously transfer people and material across the frontier. Unsophisticated, they usually consisted of nothing more than a door or gate in the inner fence and outer wall that remained locked until needed. The passage would normally be used in the dead of night when *Stasi* officers would arrange for the observation towers to be unmanned and the lights along that section of the perimeter to be turned off. These sections of the frontier were studied extensively for use because they were located in areas that were secluded on both sides of the Wall. Occasionally, a team would find a way to spook the East Germans into an alert, causing a reaction force to be sent to a specific location. Response times and actions could be gauged for planning with the added benefit of upsetting the border troop's quiet evenings.

Because the unit's initial operations in wartime would be carried out in civilian clothing, each man required identity documents. It was assumed that everyone's names had been compromised to the opposition, either by the process of assigning soldiers to Berlin or the simple crossing of the inter-German borders. The chaos of war would level the playing field somewhat in the early days of a conflict—background checks would be unlikely and communications limited. That meant a few simple identity documents would suffice to pass cursory examination at checkpoints. Failing that, guns would be necessary. A solution was found in the expertise of an euphemistically named "Other Government Agency." Each man developed a cover legend, choosing a name and a country of origin that was backed up by his own heritage and language capabilities. Where Germany would not work, another country such as Greece, Cuba, or South Africa might be chosen as many foreign businessmen, guest workers, and students lived in Berlin. The completed packets would be sent out and months later a set of documents would return—enough to pass muster at a checkpoint early in a conflict. The documents were held in the S-2 to ensure no one decided to do something stupid, like trying to use them for travel to another country.

For day-to-day work in the city, each man had his official credential that ostensibly served as a "Get out of Jail" card. Except the cards didn't always work as advertised. Although the identification was emblazoned with the word *Ermittlungsdienst* (investigative service), which insinuated a police connection, getting caught someplace where it was necessary to produce the card meant you already had failed. Second, the cards worked fine with the American MPs, but the Berlin police, the Brits, and the French were suspicious by nature of men lingering near the Wall. They would pull people into secondary whenever they could. The idea was never to have to pull the card out. Nevertheless, a few managed to test the theory. In 1974, Ed Trout and Larry Niedringhaus were detained by the British while doing a "recce" close along the Wall in the British sector. The Brits disregarded the men's identification and took them to their headquarters near the Olympic stadium for an extended interrogation. It was only after a telephone call was placed to the number on the card that they were released. Tensions tended to be high whenever or however the Wall was involved and the Brits were always on alert for Irish Republican Army (IRA) terrorists in Europe.

The Army Intrudes

No matter what standard the unit held itself to, the "real" army had its own ideas of what kind of physical shape and technical proficiency each man had to uphold. At least twice a year, everyone took the Army Physical Fitness Test (APFT). At that time, the Pentagon said individual units could not enforce their own "standards," so the unit's "goal" was for each man to achieve a 300—the max score.[7] It was difficult for a combat arms soldier to fail unless he swore off sports, physical activity, or had several broken bones. Constant fitness training let each team's leadership monitor their men's performance so no one had issues when the unit ran the test.

Technical proficiency was another requirement that was measured through a combination of a hands-on performance evaluation, a written test, and the supervisor's performance certification of specific tasks through what was called the "Skills Qualification Test" or SQT. The unit prepared for that test like it was a mission. The skills were generic across the Army; infantrymen with the military occupational specialty (MOS) 11B had the same test if they served with a regular infantry unit or were a Special Forces weapons sergeant. It was the same for engineers with the 12B MOS. As the test was administered by the Infantry Regiment, everyone had to meet the same standard. Several weeks of combined study and practice was necessary because many of the men hadn't touched regular army weapons or techniques for years. The unit underwent the SQT for the first time in 1977. When the results came back, Sergeant Major Raker passed on the Berlin commander's congratulations; the entire unit scored in the top 6% of the Army. Then it was back to preparing for the real missions.

GSG-9 and Magic Fire

The Detachment first trained with GSG-9 in April 1977, when a group of nine men spent three weeks at their facility at Sankt Augustin/Hangelar, south of Bonn, in the FRG. These nine were the first Americans to work with the unit other than some FBI agents who had done an orientation visit. Captain Claude Kelley led the team, which was a composite of men from Teams Three and Four.

GSG-9 focused solely on CT and had the vast resources the mission required—really nice resources. It looked like Porsche Designs was somehow involved with putting together their uniforms and equipment; if they weren't, Mercedes' Advanced Motor Group certainly was. GSG-9's patrol cars were Mercedes W123 sedans, modified with more horsepower, better brakes and complete with gun ports. Their weapons were straight out of Heckler & Koch's latest sales brochure: MP5 SMGs, P9S pistols and the G3 SG1 and PSG-1 sniper rifles. That said, the occasional Mauser 66 sniper rifle and Remington 870 shotgun were to be seen and a Smith & Wesson .357 magnum revolver was favored by the commander, *Polizeidirektor* (Colonel) Ulrich Wegener.[8] Their stuff was surgical, but perhaps more suited for city rather than field work.

The Det's team began with marksmanship on the GSG-9 ranges. It was a way for the Germans to familiarize the Americans with their weapons and to see how well they could shoot. It was the basis to gauge how fast training should proceed. First pistols, then the MP5s, and finally the G3 SG1 on the sniper range.

Several days were spent sharing information on breaching tactics—breaching being the art of entering a building, plane, train, or bus by explosive means, that is when using the door handles will not suffice to gain quick access to a target. Flexible explosive detonation cord—"det cord" for short—was used on portable frames to cut through doors and blow off handles and hinges, while shotguns were demonstrated for their utility in keyless entries.

Then came the cars. The Germans were very proud of the "Mercs" and proceeded first to a test track near their base to exhibit the finer points of handling the big four-door sedans. Then came the turn of the boys from Berlin who were, for the most part, more used to the handling of Ford Escorts in the city rather than the open track.

The Berlin police had recently run a high-speed driver course on Tempelhof airfield using whatever trash cars they could get their hands on, mostly confiscated vehicles. The Detachment students only rolled one VW during that course and the driver won the coveted broken mirror award.

Once the GSG-9 instructors were comfortable, the team made the transition to high-speed convoy driving on the *Autobahn*, with signature European blue lights and sirens and all. The exercise paused one day when one of the GSG-9 drivers blew a tire and trashed his Mercedes. It was good that a German was at the wheel, because the Detachment probably couldn't have afforded the car's replacement cost.

Assault tactics played a large part in the training. After chalkboard talks, the team watched their German counterparts and then practiced the techniques. GSG-9 did not like to use live ammunition in training, but they had an excellent substitute that was even more useful—plastic-tipped training ammunition. The cartridges were blue in color to prevent them being confused for live rounds, but they were still dangerous. When fired, the plastic "bullets" traveled at high velocity for the first 50 meters and were capable of penetrating uniforms and flesh, but they didn't ricochet, a key safety factor.

The Germans used the ammo to run scenarios without the worry of damage. For their typical training, they set up a series of targets in an abandoned factory and then ran room-clearing exercises. First, a four-man GSG-9 ran the scenario while their compatriots hid behind concrete pillars and exposed targets on sticks for the team to engage and eliminate. Multiple rooms could be cleared and shooting in any direction (except at live humans) was permitted.

The Americans started running through the course and then the Germans upped the ante by tossing grenade simulators for a little shock effect. All went well until a simulator was tossed into a confined passageway between two sections of the factory. John, the first man in the hallway had nowhere to go and dove for a semi-shielded corner, while Ron, the tail gunner, threw himself backwards out of the corridor. The grenade went off and both men shook themselves off to continue when John realized he was wounded in the lower leg. Mike, one of the Det's other assaulters, called a halt and began to get agitated, thinking the Germans had accidentally shot John. The moment was about to get ugly when a team member noticed powder burns on John's pants. In the melee, John had accidentally shot himself and now he had a plastic bullet in his leg. Apologies given and accepted, John was taken to the infirmary while everyone else discussed the finer points of gun safety. Training continued, and John returned, sheepishly, to face his team's ridicule. He would be marked as a dangerous man from then on and would soon depart the Detachment.

Training moved on despite the interruption. The Germans were reassured by the team's reactions during the training and their competence shown minus one bad bit of weapons handling. The course concluded with Commander Wegener presenting the GSG-9 qualification badge to the members of the team along with a joke about not having a wound badge to present to John. GSG-9 was doing it right and soon got to prove it soon afterwards in the rescue of hostages from Lufthansa Flight 181 in Mogadishu, Somalia in October 1977.[9]

Although GSG-9 was a police organization, its skills and facilities were an ideal fit for the Detachment and several more teams would train with them in the next two years. GSG-9 was not permitted to operate in Berlin. In the city, Det "A" worked with the Berlin police's *Sondereinsatzkommando* (SEK). SEK units in Berlin and other German cities, along with the federal CT force GSG-9, were created following the tragedy of the 1972 Summer Olympic Games. The failed rescue attempt by an unprepared police element at Fürstenfeldbruck airfield led to the creation of specially trained units tasked to conduct counterterrorism operations. In Berlin, the SEK was the premier CT unit because federal German units like the GSG-9 and the *Bundeswehr* (defense forces) could not operate in the city under the existing Four Power Agreement.

A Night on the Town

Gil was talking quietly with Peter in the dark apartment. The shades were drawn and the lights were out, everything was just as it had been when the team picked the lock and entered two hours before. There were five of them, three Germans, including Peter, and two Americans including Gil, all sitting on the dilapidated furniture facing the entry.

Their pistols were drawn and held in their laps, barrels pointed generally towards the door. Every once in a while, a static hiss could be heard as Peter's radio came to life. Peter was the leader. The Americans, both from the Detachment, had been invited to observe the arrest of a criminal. It was armed observation as they had their pistols out as well. The perpetrator was a heavy hitter in the drug world thought to be responsible for the violent demise of several ring members. The *Polizei* decided it was time to take him off the streets and thought his apartment was a good place to wait.

Peter was a SEK section leader. It was natural that the Detachment would find points of affinity with the SEK. When it began the intensive train-up to take on the CT mission, the unit came in contact with members of the SEK. For one, both units used common training areas, the Berlin Brigade's Rose and Keerans Ranges among others, and it soon became clear that both units were cut from similar cloth. The officers of the SEK watched closely whenever the Detachment was at the range. The SEK were easy to spot as they were always in civilian clothing and carried submachine guns, while the regular Berlin police wore hideous green uniforms and were armed with Walther P-1 pistols, a newer production version of the old P-38. The P-38/P-1 was a fine general-purpose police pistol, but limited in several respects. First, it had only an eight-round capacity. Second, it tended to break, and last, it wasn't well suited for close-quarter battle (CQB) techniques. The Detachment abandoned the P-38 when it was discovered that its alloy frame had a lifespan of around 5,000 rounds. After months of intensive CQB training and shooting thousands of rounds, malfunctions increased and frames were cracking at an alarming rate. The pistols were swapped out for a newer weapon—the Walther P5, which had issues of its own. Some would have preferred the Colt 1911 in .45ACP caliber, but it was clearly an American weapon and the choice was made to stay with German pistols.

Before long, a certain comradeship developed between the two units. The Detachment's wartime mission was never discussed, but it was clear that CT was a common ground between the units. Further, if the Detachment was employed within the geographic confirms of

West Berlin for a terrorist incident involving Americans, the SEK would be there as well. Some members of the Detachment developed close relationships with SEK officers that would have been useful in wartime.[10]

That close cooperation had brought Gil and his sidekick to the apartment. Pauli, another Detachment operative, was downtown at the SEK's command center near Tempelhof airport listening to the exchanges over the radio. Peter listened closely as the volume on his set was turned down as far as possible. Several more SEK were outside watching the streets for the "perp's" arrival. Finally, nearly three hours into the wait came the call they had been waiting for—the man was on his way up. Everyone rose as the jangle of keys gave away his approach. The locks turned, the door swung open, and the man stepped into the doorway.

What happened next is disputable, either Peter yelled "Freeze!" or one of the other SEK guys punched the criminal in the side of the head with his lead-lined sap glove. What is not disputed is that the bad guy dropped like a rock. There was silence and then, "*Mist!* I wanted to shoot him."[11]

Afterwards, Gil thanked Peter for the invitation to tag along and said it would be best if Peter didn't mention to the sergeant major the fact they had all carried weapons.[12]

Pauli was already on notice with the SGM for instigating a running "gunfight" with the SEK in the British sector. After an exercise that simulated a prisoner snatch, the SEK had chased the car Pauli was driving, all the while exchanging blank submachine-gun fire and a couple of grenade simulators before the Germans wisely broke off the wild ride. The British MPs made some desultory enquiries with the Americans but no one in the Brigade headquarters could answer their question. Naturally, the staff had an inkling the Detachment might've been involved and asked SGM Raker if his troops had anything going on in the area. Raker, as usual, denied everything and suggested the French might be up to no good. He knew full well that Team Five was probably behind the incident but chalked it up to training since no one got caught.

Some combined training followed as a way to share techniques and benefit from experiences. The SEK began to ask for Detachment men to accompany them on operations. In small groups, usually one or two men, the teams would ride along with the SEK and in some cases operate with them on criminal stakeouts and, rarely, an arrest of a dangerous criminal that was beyond the capacity of the regular police. The experiences were invaluable for the Det soldiers, exposing them a segment of society that could prove invaluable should the balloon go up. There was also a great deal to be said for the *Bier und Wurst* shared after training or the occasional soccer game, which the Detachment invariably lost.

Relations between the units were good and there were ample opportunities for social as well as operational events. One memorable Thanksgiving included roast pheasants that had been liberated from the Berlin zoo. Nick had decided the turkey available in the stores was too expensive, so a lightning raid was conducted and several birds vanished. When the SEK guests mentioned the theft at the party while gazing at the sumptuous repast laid out in front of them, Nick did what every SF trooper was trained to do, deny everything, admit nothing, and deflect the argument somewhere else. The food was good.

The SEK often trained at the British Army's Ruhleben urban warfare facility, an area built as a mock city within Berlin. It was smaller than the huge American Parks Range "Doughboy City" and resembled a quaint village neighborhood more than a modern city. There, assault teams could practice entry techniques and critique each other's methods or possibly adopt best practices. There was one area, however, where the Germans had no experience—helicopter assault operations.

In the fall of 1977, the SEK was tasked to demonstrate their counterterrorism skills to the Allied military commanders and the officials of the Berlin government and police. The scenario was be a hostage incident that would take place in a multi-story building on a police compound in the northern part of the city. With several weeks to prepare, "Reinhard," their commander, requested the Detachment's assistance to teach them helicopter rappelling and how to conduct air insertions onto buildings. Team Five was given the job.

The first phase of training began on top of a five-story building at Parks Range and started with the basics of equipment rigging and rope handling, then progressed to rappelling or *Abseilen* as the Germans called it. The instruction was in German backed up with hand signals to ensure the message was clear inside the deafeningly loud aircraft. The team demonstrated each step before the police officers did it themselves, both to show how it was done and to give the officers confidence in the equipment and the instructors. Rappelling is not difficult, but it does require a certain amount of coordination, strength, and trust to hang out over a sheer wall with only a rope to keep you from a long fall. The officers first had to hook up correctly and then position themselves on the edge of the roof with two 120-foot nylon ropes weighing down their "brake" arm. Getting comfortable took practice and when they had enough time on the wall, training began with the helicopters. First, rigging and the finer points of how to stand on the skid were taught inside the Berlin Aviation Detachment's hangar at Tempelhof. Then it was back out to Parks Range for the serious training.

The officers were first taken up in the helicopter and shown what it looked like when a four-man team did an assault rappel over a building. At first, many found it quite unnerving to lean back on the skid of a helicopter with the rotor down wash and the scream of the turbine engine in their ears, so they practiced first at low altitudes. Then the levels were raised steadily until the ropes were extended completely about 100 feet off the ground. Ground safeties were used to belay the rappellers in case anyone lost their grip.

Once everyone was comfortable, the building assault training began. There are significant differences with assaulting a building and static rappelling from a wall or a helicopter that goes up and down like an elevator. The helo approaches the target at a low altitude and relatively high airspeed before it flares out to hover 40 to 50 feet over the building. The rappel master in the aircraft spots the building to make sure it is directly under him and then orders the ropes, now packed in deployment bags, to be tossed down onto the building. The assaulters then must climb onto the skid and begin their rappel within seconds to achieve surprise. Safety was paramount—if the pilot drifted off the spot, the ropes would be hanging free in the air and the rappeller could look forward to a fall equivalent to the height of the building if he reached its end in free space. As parachutists say, it's not the fall that kills you it's the sudden stop and it would not do to kill one of the unit's German allies. Needless to say, the stress factor went up by a factor of ten and in the first attempts the Germans' eyes were as wide and wild as one would expect. With practice, however, they began to enjoy it.

The time had come to show off their new skills. On the day of the demonstration, the designated four-man SEK assault team met the Detachment instructors, Jon and Styk, at Tempelhof, where the UH-1H stood ready. The SEK officers were rigged up and safety checked before being hooked up in the aircraft. By that time, the pilot was ready for departure and asked to start the engine. Only the two pilots up front and Styk and Jon in the back would ride along on the flight to the exercise location in the Reinickendorf district of Berlin. With rope bags securely stowed under the assaulters and everyone belted in, the rotors began to turn and heart rates rose as the bird began its hover and then dipped forward to skim across the airfield as it lifted into the sky. Very little compares with low-level flying over Berlin in a Huey, but there was not much time to enjoy the flight. As the facility came into view, Styk was holding on to the doorframe leaning out to spot the target. Identifying the location, he came back inside to watch the pilot and gave the command for the bags to readied. At the same time, the SEK's ground commander gave the OK for the helo to start its run to the target. Its arrival overhead would signal the start of a full assault that consisted of two additional SEK teams covered by police snipers from the MEK.[13] The four unbuckled their safety belts and all the ropes and harnesses were quickly rechecked to ensure they were properly hooked up and clear of entanglements. Looking out the door again, the target was about 30 seconds out. The helo came in quickly over the building and flared before settling back level with the ground. Verifying the target, Styk signaled the SEK to drop their deployment bags and then to stand on the skid. A quick check ensured the ropes were on the target and the "Go" was given. The two assaulters on opposite corners dropped away from the skid, then the second pair leapt into space. They swung underneath and began their descent; the helicopter rocked slightly but did not drift off the spot. A couple of seconds passed and the assaulters were on the roof. Shedding their ropes, they disappeared into the building with their MP5s at the ready.

In the air, the job was finished. The ropes were de-rigged and dropped, and the helo turned and began its flight back to base. Styk asked the pilot to take the long route home. With the doors open, he leaned against the pilot's seat back and enjoyed the view over the divided city during the slow return ride before touching down at Tempelhof. It was a good day in the neighborhood.

Touring the East

Detachment operators were again riding with the tours in East Germany. The Military Liaison Mission (MLM) was the single best producer of ground-truth intelligence on the Group of Soviet Forces in Germany (GSFG) and its East German counterpart, the National People's Army (NVA). The Detachment was continually updating its holdings on targets such as headquarters and weapons storage facilities in the East and working with the tours provided an opportunity to see things up close. The Det's interest was ancillary to the MLM's primary mission, but either way, it gave the men who worked with the tours an unparalleled view of their possible future enemies. The "Sovs" and "EGs" weren't always that impressive and it was clear the alliance between them was often one of tolerance rather than friendship. That said, neither was to be trusted. The East Germans would talk disparagingly to the Americans about the Russians, but when the conversation turned to the NVA, they clammed up. And the *Stasi* surveillance cars that followed them could be quite evil when it came to making things difficult for the tour teams. The tour teams called them "Narks."

The Russian soldiers were also a sorry lot. The officers lived in fear of their superiors and were often drunk; the NCOs uneducated but brutal; and the enlisted men—all draftees—were victims. The basic soldiers were paid the equivalent of about 10 US dollars a month, but they didn't have anything to spend it on. What they wanted most was alcohol, in almost any form. They foraged for mushrooms and stole gasoline to sell or trade for it. They distilled aircraft antifreeze and strained shoe polish through bread to get something to drink. Still, there were several hundred thousand of them led by men who were not afraid to use the whip or the pistol to move them forward, and they had a lot of pretty good equipment. These potential enemies bore considerable watching.

The tours were stressful for the MLM officers and NCOs, not so much physically (other than they had to live out of their cars for three to four days at a time) as psychologically. There was constant stress from watching out for and avoiding ambushes. Although the Missions had been set up as a legal mechanism to "liaise with" and monitor each other's activities, both sides took steps to restrict their movements by setting up permanent and temporary restricted areas (PRA/TRA). The Soviets used the TRAs prolifically, so much so that the USMLM, as well as the British and French missions, chose to ignore them. The teams would start out from their base at Potsdam on a non-contentious route and make sure their Russian or Stasi minders lost their scent and then disappear off the radar into the TRAs to find out what was going on. "What" was often a training exercise or the deployment of sensitive equipment the Sovs wanted to conceal from observation. That sort of thing was exactly what the MLMs were looking for and quite often found.

In the mid-1970s, the new versions of the T-64 and T-72 began to appear, along with new mobile missile launchers. The Defense Intelligence Agency wanted information and photographs of everything and that's where the MLM did its best work.

Although the tours were considered a nuisance to the respective powers and the reactions or countermeasures they undertook to limit what these "legal spies" could see was markedly different. In the Allied zone, an encounter usually meant the Soviet vehicle would be blocked in place for several hours and then eventually be released with a protest to their commander. In the East, it was a very different story. Soviet soldiers guarding facilities or on rolling military trains would sometimes fire live rounds at the MLM tours that appeared in front of them or cars would often be forcibly run off the road to trap the tour team. In the vernacular, this was a "clobber." Once, a US Air Force officer and NCO on a tour made the mistake of parking their vehicle in the same spot near a Soviet airbase for several days running to photograph a new swing-wing fighter aircraft. On the third day, a Soviet *Spetznaz* team ambushed them when the NCO got out to relieve himself in the woods. The Russians had closed in around the tour car during the night and were waiting in the brush in full camouflage. They took down the NCO and rushed the car while the doors were unlocked and pulled the officer from the car. The two were physically beaten and all their maps, notes, and camera equipment were stolen. It was typically thuggish Russian behavior to which the Allied response was composed rectitude—good for the politicians; infuriating for the men on the ground.

In the spring of 1978, Ron was assigned to the MLM as a driver of one of the MLM's new Mercedes sedans. They were very nice cars right out of the factory, but the mission tricked them out with switches to shut off the brake and taillights, heavy-duty suspensions, long-range fuel tanks, and flat olive-drab paint among other things. They were capable of participating in the Paris to Dakar Rally and performed wonderfully in the East German hinterlands. There was nary a Trabant or Gaz that could keep up with them. However, there were other ways to stop them.

One day, Ron and his partner, a Russian-speaking military intelligence major, were cruising down a two-lane country road near a TRA after having observed some GSFG maneuvers. As they proceeded out of the area, they encountered a stopped Russian convoy and moved left to pass the vehicles parked on the shoulder of the road. As they came abreast of the lead vehicle, a Soviet armored personnel carrier shot out of the woods and rammed the MLM car in the rear quarter panel causing it to flip off the road and roll at least once before it came to rest on its roof. The passengers were dazed and disoriented as a group of Russian soldiers surrounded the vehicle and started to pull the Americans and all their belongings out of the car. The major said he was injured and it was only through Ron's protests that the Russians stopped trying to drag the officer out of the car by his arms. At one point, after righting the car, the Russians began to loot the vehicle. When Ron tried to intervene he was restrained by a Soviet officer and the barrels of several weapons.

The car was trashed. All the windows were broken and the area around it was littered with everything that had been inside the car. It took several hours to get the major to a hospital and when Ron made it back to the Potsdam House, he still had to file a report. It was clearly an intentional ambush, but the Russians would later respond that it was the Americans who were at fault due to "high speed and erratic driving." Rick, another Detachment operator who drove with MLM, later said that "clobbers were part of the initiation process and everyone expected at least three during their time there."

There were successes though, and those greatly outweighed the setbacks. Close-up photographs of new Soviet equipment like the T-80 tank, along with souvenirs appropriated in training areas like a bandolier of Russian magazines filled with the previously unseen 5.45 × 39mm ammunition for the newly issued AK-74 assault rifle. Being chased by a Russian mobile rocket launcher permitted one team to determine how fast the vehicle could move. It was all in a day's work. Luck was sometimes a factor in the collection, as was being in the right place at the right time. Earlier that year, during a search of an empty training area at Buchenwald, Ron and his partner noticed a number of strange objects partially obscured by the early morning fog. As the fog lifted, a brand-new Soviet air assault regiment with its equally new HIND-D helicopters sitting like a flock of malevolent geese in the field greeted their eyes and camera.

The MLM provided a good mechanism for the Detachment to get eyes on the terrain and their targets. It was also a reminder of the formidable enemy they could face. An enemy that was also doing its best to prepare for the eventuality of war, not only through their own MLM in the FRG, but with commercial trucks traveling the same *Autobahns* they would use for their advance—driven by the men who would command the Soviet tanks.

Occasionally, the Soviets were just out for harassment. It was one thing to be near a military base or a convoy when they clobbered an Allied vehicle, it was another when a driver was trying to get to work. In one incident, Rick drove alone across Glienecke Bridge one afternoon to make his way to the Potsdam House, the USMLM's base inside East Germany, in one of the brand-new Mercedes sedans. Painted flat olive green and outfitted with a 6.9-liter engine, it was a formidable road car. Not so much against armored vehicles.

He came up on the tail-end of a convoy of Soviet student drivers in the narrow streets of the city and stayed back a distance so the Russians wouldn't get jumpy. Unfortunately, they did anyway. Soon the Russians attempted to box in his vehicle to detain him. Rick wasn't having anything to do with a detention as, in addition to the standard camera and video equipment, he was carrying some sensitive notes for the duty officer at the house. Rick was tried to force his way out of the box, but didn't want to damage the new car. The Soviets had no such compunction and as he later described it, "They didn't destroy the vehicle, but they did shorten and narrow it significantly."

An armored BMP tracked vehicle has a decided advantage in a narrow corridor. When Rick finally came to a halt, he ate the four pages of classified notes, while the Russians pounded on his windows and forced open the trunk. When the local Soviet commandant arrived on the scene, he naturally wanted to know what was on the notes and accused Rick of spying. He denied everything and refused to sign any documents and was finally released following eight hours of detention. Arriving at the Potsdam house in the early morning, everyone wanted to know where he had been. He only wanted some water to get rid of the taste of paper.[14]

An American Terrorist (or four) in England

In late 1977, the Secret Intelligence Service (SIS), aka MI6, sought out assistance from the United States to train local British security forces how to better identify and track terrorist teams that might try to carry out operations in the UK. Since the early 1970s, the Irish Republican Army had successfully infiltrated small, sabotage teams into the "mainland" that would select a target, conduct surveillance, and then attack it with explosives or firearms. Up to that point a number of attacks had been carried out by the IRA including bombings in London, Birmingham, and Bristol.

SIS wanted to use outside "specialists" to simulate a terrorist operation in order to make the training more realistic, as opposed to using the British SAS, who had the home-field advantage. The exercise would test inter-service capabilities to track a terrorist team in and around Southampton, a large port city on the south coast of England. The

SIS/MI6 officers acted as exercise controllers, while MI5 and local police were the local security force learning from the exercise. But, as was often the case with the British "cousins," there was a larger agenda.

When the request was received, SOTFE tasked Detachment "A" to conduct the exercise that was then code-named RED SAILS. The first team to go consisted of Gil Turcotte, Ron Braughton, Frank Closen, and Tom Powell. All four had extensive experience; Powell and Closen participated in the Son Tay Prison Camp raid, while Turcotte was a three-tour veteran of Vietnam, and Braughton was an SF medic and martial arts guru with experience elsewhere in Southeast Asia.

At first, Gil thought it would be a canned exercise, but he began to have doubts when he was first directed to a safehouse in Germany to show his communications skills to an American intelligence officer. There, Gil was told to set up an AN/GRC-109 radio and send a message to another station. Asking where the station was so he could set up his antenna, he was told he didn't need to know. After convincing the officer that a compass azimuth was needed to send the radio waves in their proper direction he finally got a point of the finger. Then he was given an unsuitable send frequency and Gil had to request another. Finally, he set up his encoded message on a one-time pad without the use of any aids, which fully confused the officer. Questioned about whether he had done this kind of work before, Gil—who had at least 15 years' experience working as a communications sergeant—said he thought he could handle it. The message was sent. After the officer received a call that it had been received "5 by," meaning loud and clear, Gil was released to rejoin his team. The point of the test would only become clear later.

The team arrived in Southampton and was given a rental car. They were then shown to a hotel where rooms awaited them by name and they settled in for the night. Several hours later, Gil heard the elevator arrive on his floor and the footsteps of several people walking down the hallway. They knocked on his door. When he opened it, two policemen and a civilian clothed officer confronted him. Gil knew he was about to be set up.

The leader of the group told Gil that there had been reports of "silver thieves" in the area and that he should be sure to keep his door locked and his belongings safe. The leader then asked, "Oh, by the way, may we take a look inside your room?" Gil's sense of danger had been set off when the group came directly to his door instead of rooms closer to the elevator or the end of the hall, so he just said, "Thank you for the information." And "No, you may not come in, I'm trying to sleep."

The police went away.

The next morning, the team was taken to the local SIS headquarters. They were given a notional mission to sketch the basement interior of a local police station for use by another team to rescue a comrade. The team now understood that they were being used as bait for some sort of security force training exercise and they started to use extreme caution. They moved out of the hotel into separate accommodations and quickly set up a clandestine communications system to maintain contact.

The team decided that Gil and Ron would do the reconnaissance of the station. Figuring simple was the best solution, the two walked into the station arguing about the location of a local tourist attraction and stopped at the duty officer's desk, still arguing. After a moment, the duty sergeant managed to quiet the two down and asked if he could help. While the officer was telling Frank the proper directions, Gil interrupted and asked after the toilet. He wandered off down the hall managing to get lost several times so that he could collect the needed information. Returning to the front desk where Ron was still in animated conversation with the sergeant, Gil looked at the bulletin board behind the desk only to see his own ugly mug staring back at him. On the wall were wanted posters with artist's renderings of the team members among all the other criminal faces. Knowing that it was critical to get out of the station quickly, Gil thanked the sergeant and quickly drug Ron out of the area.

The British had gone from outright cheeky to cheating at this point. The Americans couldn't quite figure the British logic, as they had gone from expecting to instruct in a classroom to finding themselves on a publicly displayed wanted list. They could have prepared better had they known it was a game to be played out.

The next stop was a meet with the SIS controller where Gil turned over the sketches of the station to a somewhat astonished reception.

The next assignment was their last: plant a bomb at a power distribution station and then escape and evade from the area. SIS informed them they were on their own now; that they would be arrested and interrogated if they were picked up. It now seemed the point of the exercise was to test them, not the local police.

The team left in their rented car and got onto the motorway to return to the city. Traveling in moderate traffic, they were suddenly in the sights of a police car. They were pulled over by two officers who approached the car. One kept the team covered, while other went to the driver's window and requested Ron's identification. Ron was polite and asked why they had been stopped. It was obvious the police knew who they were because they had been driving with the flow of traffic and were singled out for no good reason.

The officer stated that there had been a robbery. Silver thieves had broken into a church and "Oh, by the way, may we search your vehicle?" Nothing was to be found as the team had hidden all their compromising tools in a cache, so the police didn't have the chance to arrest them. But the Det "A" Team realized the rental car was a liability. Back in town, they parked the car and dispersed, with a plan to meet later. After several hours, Ron returned to the area where the car was parked and watched the area. He soon picked out a surveillance team. He approached the car when it was concealed by a delivery truck, opened the hood and pulled several distributor wires, and closed the hood before the truck moved away. A call to the rental agency arranged a replacement car to be delivered to another location.

They knew they had to work fast and accelerated their plan. With a new vehicle, the team made a hurried reconnaissance of the target and selected an entry point. They then located and assembled the components of a simulated explosive device that had been hidden for them earlier by their SIS controller. The following night, Frank, the engineer sergeant, and Gil approached the target while Ron and Tom provided outside security. Entering the facility through a neglected fence that abutted an abandoned factory, they were able to get into the building through a back door. The device was placed under a central transformer. Had the device been real, it would have destroyed the transformer and ignited the cooling oil within its case. There would have been enough damage to knock out the facility for several days.

The team then cleared out of the area and signaled their SIS controllers that the deed had been done. They then dispersed to their respective bed downs. When they showed up at SIS headquarters the next day, their spy host wanted to know why they hadn't hit the target—the Brits couldn't find a trace of the bomb. Gil, being his usual irascible self, told him in less than diplomatic language that he was obviously mistaken and that they should look again. A second search by the SIS was more successful.

The team returned to Berlin less than enthusiastic about how they had been treated, but willing to accept the exercise as valuable under more clearly defined rules and instructions. Several weeks later, the confusion was cleared up. Gil, the senior NCO on the team, was called down to the commander's office where he found Colonel "O" ranting. When Gil asked what the matter was, the colonel handed him a letter and said, "You are not going anywhere for these guys." Gil looked at the letter from the chief of SIS and suddenly understood the game. It requested the team be seconded to the SIS for service in Northern Ireland. The radio test and the exercise were intended to see whether they were suitable for the task of trying to infiltrate the IRA. Colonel "O's" answer was succinct, "Not just no, but Hell No!"

The Shooting House

Kidnappings, aircraft hijackings, and terrorist incidents were on the rise in the early 1970s, and the UW mission was sliding back on the priority list. CT training was sexier—when you put rounds into a target, you could see tangible results. That was not so much the case with the urban skills. At the time, it was necessary because the threat of a terrorist attack was higher than the Soviets coming over the Wall.

Throughout 1977 and into 1978, there were many varied things happening in the unit. Alongside the UW, ski, combat diver, and airborne training, the teams were spending much more time on the ranges. CT training was accelerated, and shooting the older weapons—the Sten, Welrod, and High Standard—along with the MPK and sniper systems took on new urgency. A lot of ammunition was used to bring everyone up to the marksmanship standard required for CT operations. In 1978 alone, the Detachment's basic ammunition allocation exceeded that of the entire Berlin Brigade. The unit generally used shooting facilities at Rose Range, which were standard pistol and rifle stands. The pistol/submachine-gun stands were 25 to 50 meters long with heavy walls, overhead baffles, and dirt backstops, while the rifle ranges were 300 meters with target pits at varying ranges. A longer rifle range called Keerans was located near the *Autobahn* a few kilometers away. A sniper could use that one to practice 500-meter shots if the range safety rules were circumvented. That required some very good persuasive skills to convince the range officer that the unit's marksmen would not pick off any Germans in the surrounding forest and end his career. If really long ranges were needed, there was always Vilseck and the British ranges at Sennelager in West Germany.

In late 1977, the Detachment decided to adopt the Brigade's Range 5 as its own and, after the headquarters consented its exclusive usage by the unit, construction was started to convert it to a more suitable close quarter battle (CQB) training range. At that time, the accepted technique for constructing a shooting house was to use car or truck tires laid flat over poles to a height of about ten feet and filled with sand. The poles were laid in a staggered pattern which resulted in a barrier that permitted shooting in four directions or even tossing grenades into the enclosed space. But that required a lot of space as the tire walls were 6 to 8 feet thick. A multiple room structure would require about half an acre of land to build—land that was not readily available in the city.

A solution was required and, as one would expect, some of the unit's more devious minds like Nick Brokhausen and Brad Cooper came up with designs that turned the range into a closed facility consisting of a number of small rooms with walls that could be reconfigured as required. The shooting direction was still restricted as the movable walls would not stop a projectile, but the rooms permitted fairly extreme shooting angles up to 90 degrees off the main axis. That meant room-clearing procedures could be practiced as long as no-one fired back up the range.

Above: Some of the first: Vuckovitch, Daugherty, Nugent, and Sanchez, 1957. *(US Army; JFK Museum)*

Below: Convoy ambush in West Germany circa 1956. *(US Army Photo: 10th SFG Yearbook 1956)*

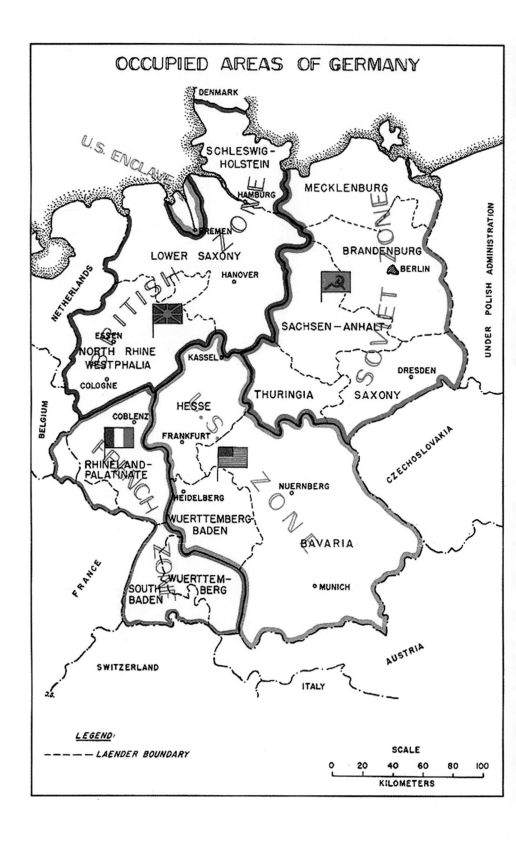

OCCUPIED AREAS OF GERMANY

DENMARK

U.S. ENCLAVE

SCHLESWIG-HOLSTEIN

MECKLENBURG

HAMBURG

BRITISH ZONE

SOVIET ZONE

BREMEN

LOWER SAXONY

BRANDENBURG

BERLIN

HANOVER

NETHERLANDS

ESSEN

NORTH RHINE WESTPHALIA

KASSEL

SACHSEN—ANHALT

DRESDEN

COLOGNE

THURINGIA

SAXONY

BELGIUM

HESSE

COBLENZ

FRENCH ZONE

FRANKFURT

U.S. ZONE

RHINELAND-PALATINATE

CZECHOSLOVAKIA

UNDER POLISH ADMINISTRATION

HEIDELBERG

NUERNBERG

WUERTTEMBERG BADEN

BAVARIA

ZONE

WUERTTEM-BERG

SOUTH BADEN

MUNICH

FRANCE

SWITZERLAND

ITALY

AUSTRIA

LEGEND:

----- LAENDER BOUNDARY

SCALE

0   20   40   60   80   100

KILOMETERS

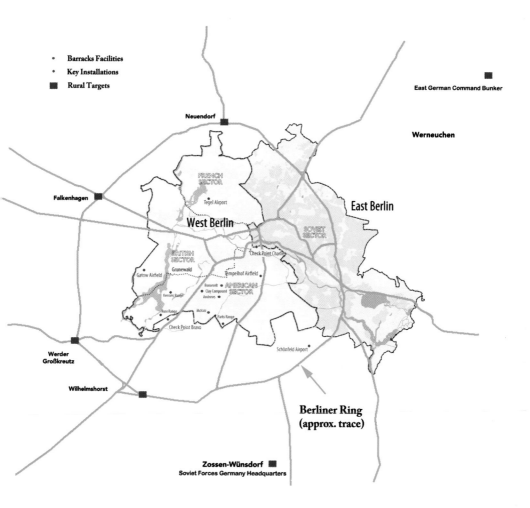

Above: Map of a divided Berlin showing the Aussenring railroad and targets. *(Adapted from a map by de:Benutzer:Sansculotte; author's collection)*

Opposite: Map of a divided Germany with occupation sectors, 1945. *(Source: The American Military Occupation of Germany 1945–1953, by Oliver J. Frederiksen; USAREUR, Hist Div.; Darmstadt, Germany; 1953; USAREUR, public domain)*

Preparing for a jump inside a hangar at Tempelhof airfield, 1959. *(Jim Wilde)*

Harry Brown's Team 5 after its special ADM exercise in 1957. The two men standing at left rear are from 10th SFG. *(Harry Brown)*

FTX SEA RULER at Fürstenfeldbruck Airfield in Bavaria, 1963. Back row, from left: Thomas Twomey, Roy Pace, Sam Huggins, Leslie Besci, Frank Webber, Earle Peckham. Front row, from left: Adam Klys, Hugh Miller, Herby Ladd, Bob Helton, David Scoville. *(Adam Klys)*

SFC Ponds teaching demolitions with German *Bundeswehr* soldiers in Baumholder, 1968, and the results. *(H. D. Halterman)*

H. D. Halterman returns to Checkpoint Charlie after East Germans refuse him entry into East Berlin without ID, October 27, 1961. *(H. D. Halterman)*

Practicing the art of *Bratwurst* eating at an Imbiss stand. *(Jim Wilde)*

Detachment "A's" Headquarters. Building 904, Section II, Andrews Barracks. *(John Blevens)*

SFC Bren explaining RS-6 Radio and HF Commo to the Brigade commander, Brigadier General Hartel, circa 1961. *(Jim Wilde)*

The Wall in 1965—
French Sector border
with East Germany.
(Mike Kelly)

The Wall as observed
from a Ring Flight
helicopter. *(Bob Schreiber)*

Looking into East Berlin
near Checkpoint Charlie
in 1977. East German
border guards were as
interested in us as we
were in them. *(Author's
collection)*

Above left: Feeding the socialist dogs, 1977. The shepherds were good for alerting the border guards to human presence. *(Author's collection)*

Above right: Plowing the Death Strip, 1986. *(Author's collection)*

Below: A team's model of a Wall crossing site. *(R. Hopkins)*

Getting close up and personal:
surveilling the East German border
guards, circa 1988. *(Author's collection)*

Following the "Dark Man"—Surveillance of a subject in the Rudow U-Bahn Station, 1977. *(Author's collection)*

The Berliner sewer system. *(Sid Shachnow)*

Above left: Underwater ops in Berlin's Wannsee, 1968. MSG Tatman and Sgt George Wieck. *(Roger Sherman)*

Above right: Team Three with Dräger LAR-III Rigs in Andrews' pool, 1978. *(Doug Snow)*

Below: Team Three just before a training jump into the Chiemsee in southern Germany, 1978. Standing, from left: Ron Sheckler, Frank Closen, MSG Tom Briggs, Howie Fedor, Rick Patrick. Kneeling, from left: Dennis Warriner, Joe Gazdik, Ron Cornell, CPT Smith. *(Joe Gazdik)*

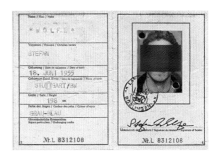

Some of the official
and unofficial IDs
used for operations.
*(Mike Stephens and
author's collection)*

Below: Test firing
a suppressed
Ingram M10, 1978.
(Author's collection)

Left: Berlin SEK officers demonstrate their entry technique. Door kicker with ballistic shield and armed with pistol, number two man armed with Walther MPL, 1978. *(Author's collection)*

Below: Group photo of Team Five and Berlin police SEK squad, 1978. *(Author's collection)*

Det "A" Team running to board a German helicopter at German Ranger School, 1977. *(R. Gigl)*

Roger Sherman with two of the local ladies at the Alpen Gasthof Vorderbrand during ski training, 1967. *(R. Sherman)*

Cross-country skiing in southern Germany, 1978. *(Author's collection)*

Right: Rappelling from Berlin Aviation Detachment UH-1H, 1977. *(Author's collection)*

Below: Russ Krajicek and the "Welrod" 9mm Mark I hand-firing device—a true silenced pistol—circa 1977. *(Author's collection)*

Left: Team Sergeant MSG Russ
Krajicek practicing urban combat at
Parks Range, 1978. *(Author's collection)*

Below: Team Five mountain climbing
in Bavaria with 10th SFGA ODA-8
mountain guide, Donald Ringley,
1979. *(Author's collection)*

GSG-9 demonstrates emplacing a door charge at the "factory," 1977. *(D. Snow)*

GSG-9 Colonel Wegener awards GSG-9 qualification wings to Team Three, 1977. From left: Captain Claude Kelly, John Probart, Henry Zelinski, Gentry Deck, Mike Mulieri, Ron Braughton, John Franson, and Ron Sheckler. *(D. Snow)*

Ron Braughton and Sid Williams demonstrate their driving techniques at Tempelhof airfield after winning the Berlin Police's "Broken Mirror Award" for best roll-over, 1978. *(Sid Williams)*

Below: Jon Roberts and Close Quarter Battle training with Ron Braughton as line coach—Range 5, 1979. *(J. Roberts)*

Getting familiar with an Air Berlin Boeing 737 on the tarmac of Tegel Airport, 1978. *(Author's collection)*

Above: Det "A" Team Five trains with GSG-9 in 1978. Standing, from left: Nick Brokhausen, Jon Roberts, author, "Hawkeye" Thomas, Russ Krajicek, Howie Fedor, Frank "*Der Speiß*" Midlil. Kneeling, from left: Paul Piusz, Captain Chris Feudo. *(Author's collection)*

Left: The Det's Iran Raid assault team: John Mims, Billy Krieger, Colonel Stan Olchovik, Stu O'Neill, Corky Shelton, Jim O'Callaghan, Brad Cooper, Bob Kuenstle, "Sam." *(US Army)*

Below and opposite: Operation EAGLE CLAW. *(Author's collection)*

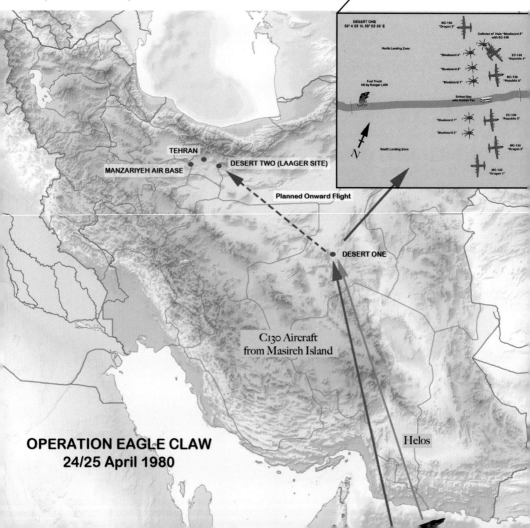

OPERATION EAGLE CLAW
24/25 April 1980

TEHRAN

MANZARIYEH AIR BASE

DESERT TWO (LAAGER SITE)

Planned Onward Flight

DESERT ONE

C130 Aircraft
from Masireh Island

Helos

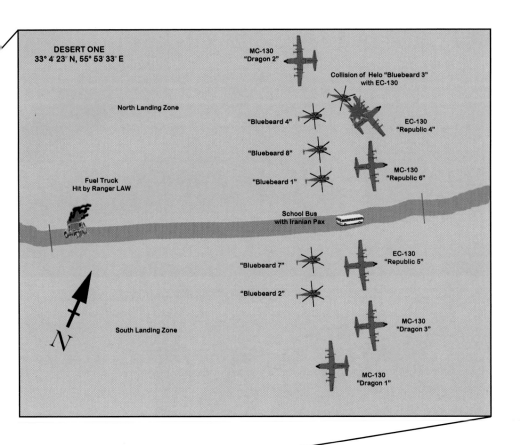

DESERT ONE
33° 4′ 23″ N, 55° 53′ 33″ E

MC-130 "Dragon 2"

Collision of Helo "Bluebeard 3" with EC-130

North Landing Zone

"Bluebeard 4"

EC-130 "Republic 4"

"Bluebeard 8"

MC-130 "Republic 6"

Fuel Truck Hit by Ranger LAW

"Bluebeard 1"

School Bus with Iranian Pax

"Bluebeard 7"

EC-130 "Republic 5"

"Bluebeard 2"

N

South Landing Zone

MC-130 "Dragon 3"

MC-130 "Dragon 1"

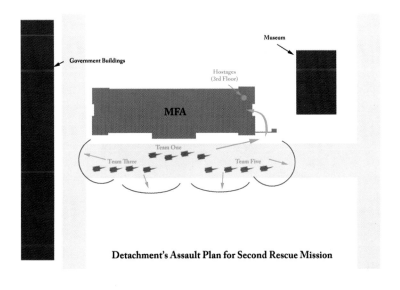

Government Buildings

Museum

Hostages (3rd Floor)

MFA

Team One

Team Three

Team Five

Detachment's Assault Plan for Second Rescue Mission

Above: Author and Jon Roberts during night training for Iran II—Operation STORM CLOUD, summer 1980. *(US Army)*

Left: Det "A" Team Three trains in Florida for Iran II—security team: Glen Watson, Phil Brown, John Mims, Dave Boltz, Ron Cornell, Captain Werner Krueger, and Howard Fedor. *(H. Fedor)*

Left: Rick Hendrick and Tony Abernathy (both Team One) in OH-6; part of the MFA building assault team for Iran II. *(R. Hendrick)*

Right: Det "A" practicing for Iran II at Eglin AFB with OH-6 helos. *(Author's collection)*

Right: Practicing for Iran II at Florida Ranger Camp—Bringing the hostages out of the "Foreign Ministry." *(Author's collection)*

Below: "Nick" underway in mufti. *(Jeff Raker)*

Above: Commemorative patch for Det participants in Operation EAGLE CLAW and STORM CLOUD. *(Author's collection)*

Left: Stu O'Neill decorated for his actions at Desert One during Iran Rescue attempt. Awards are the Soldier's Medal, Joint Service Commendation and Army Commendation Medals. *(Stu O'Neill)*

Detachment "A" commander Col O decorates SGM Raker with Meritorious Service Medal upon his reassignment to Fort Bragg. *(Jeff Raker)*

PSSE-B's Section P17 circa 1984 with transitional CT gear (before the switch to the MP5 sub-machine gun): Safreed, Tripp, Raby, Schreiber, Billingslea, Boggio, and Hopkins. *(B. Schreiber)*

Left: Thermal door-opening device. *(D. Baty)*

Below: Flame On! Thermal torch door-opening device in use. *(Author's collection)*

Nighttime CT exercise at Tegel airport on Pan Am aircraft. Images taken from sniper/observer position, circa 1986. *(B. Schreiber)*

PSSE-B Section P-34
clears a room—CT
scenario training at
Range 5, 1986.
(J. Roberts)

An unnamed surveyor
checking out an
Ugandan Air Force
MiG-21, during a survey
of Entebbe airfield,
1986. *(Mike Stephens)*

Rick Hendrick taking
a look at a Russian
troop train inside East
Germany, circa 1985.
(Rick Hendrick)

Russian T-80 tank. Note hollow track guides (white circle), a signature feature for the tank when under a tarp, 1985. *(R. Hopkins)*

Observation point—a typical hide site along the Rhine for counting trains—REFORGER 1985. *(Carl Franquet)*

PSSE-B Section 17, circa 1988. Dick Safreed, Bob Wallace, Dave Buie, Bill Billingslea, Doug Fordham, Tony Gleason, Pat Griffen, Jim Morgan, Les Thaxton, Chief McDonald, Dave Baty. *(D. Baty)*

PSSE-B Section P-23 at the "Bridge of Spies," circa 1986. Edgar Smith, Alex Hernandez, David Gensiejewski, Terry Malgrem, Dennis Bohen, Gary Jones, Sam Edgar, John Schuler, Alex MacRae, David Farmer, Wally Wing. *(David Gensiejewski)*

PSSE-B Section P-43 in full assault gear—A patriotic team photo with the "borrowed" Berlin Brigade Headquarters flag that was to be taken into Iran during Operation STORMCLOUD *(Author's collection)*

PSSE-B Section P-52 with daytime sniper weapons: McMillan rifle in 7.62 or 300 Win Mag, HK-21, M-21 system. Standing: Edgar Smith, Lee Blackwell, Tim Barker, Joe Ward, unnamed, Harry Reed II, Steve Gasper. Kneeling: Bud Odom, Uwe Duchow, Gordon Cvach, unnamed. *(Bud Odom)*

The CINC's In Extremis assault force in front of C-141B. PSSE-B's annual Ellipse Bravo certification exercise, 1986. *(Author's collection)*

Entrance to PSSE-B headquarters, Building 817, Roosevelt Barracks, Berlin, and the sign the East German security service couldn't figure out. *(D. Baty)*

A sniper team prepares to move out—Ellipse Bravo in northern UK, 1988. *(D. Baty)*

The PSSE-B S-3, Major Bruce Hoover, making commo with homebase during Ellipse Bravo, 1988. *(D. Baty)*

November 10, 1989—The Wall falls. *(Author's collection)*

Major Steve Philbrick takes the flag of command shortly before PSSE-B is closed down. USCOB and former Det "A" Commander Brigadier General Shachnow presides. *(Sid Shachnow)*

The whole facility was built for around 10,000 marks (2,500 US dollars) and it served the unit well.

After studying the techniques of the FBI and the Israelis, there was another unit to be studied. In Britain, the Special Air Service (SAS) was in action against the Provisional Irish Republican Army (PIRA) in Northern Ireland using fighting techniques that originated with William Fairbairn in 1920s Shanghai. Several of the Detachment's soldiers trained with the SAS at Hereford (and elsewhere) and brought the techniques they learned to the table. Probably the most important of these was the art of CQB.

CQB was just one technique of combatives, but it offered a holistic approach to training that had one aim—to guarantee success in killing. The SAS, in their usual straightforward manner, outlined its premise as follows:

> CQB is much more a personal affair than ordinary combat and it is just not good enough to temporarily put your opponent out of action so he can live to fight another day. He must be quickly and definitively killed so that you can switch your whole attention on the next target. Besides obvious physical abilities, the CQB operator must be cool-headed and, above all, remorseless. The pistol and the SMG [submachine gun] are the main weapons used by the CQB operator. These weapons are generally regarded by the ignorant as "dangerous" and "useless." In the hands of a trained CQB operator these weapons are extremely lethal. However, for the CQB operator to maintain a high degree of professionalism he must train continuously in an aggressive manner. The end product ... must be automatic and instantaneous killing.[15]

The six key areas of concentration during training were surprise, confidence, concentration, speed, teamwork, and offensive attitude.

The Det had also determined the name for its CT teams and, although the moniker fast action group (FAG) found favor with some, special action teams (SAT) was the final choice. The assault force as an entity was called the special action force or SAF.[16] Training was conducted building block style, each component serving as a foundation for the next. Weapons handling was key. It would take days of shooting before the instructors were comfortable enough with a shooter to put him into the more dangerous scenarios. The shooter had to demonstrate he could handle his weapons with exacting familiarity, focus, precision, and deliberate speed.

Although everyone had a reasonable familiarity with their assigned weapons, it was another thing altogether to shoot live rounds while moving quickly through a target area as a group. Many hours and thousands of rounds were spent on the line shooting at standard targets and then graduating to smaller targets and conducting rapid, target discrimination shooting with friendly and hostile targets at ranges of 7–25 meters. Several shooters moving together down the range on line preceded room-clearing training where two or more shooters entered a room to engage targets at various angles and depths in the confined space. Only seconds were needed to clear a room of all hostile targets.

There were near misses. In one scenario, two shooters entered a room with their MPK submachine guns to engage targets. In the early days, the shooters dove through the door and hit the ground as they engaged the targets. This was before it was realized that accuracy was hard to maintain while flying through the air, ricochet bullets hugged floors and walls, and mobility was sacrificed if a man was on the ground. In this particular instance, two shooters burst through the door and hit the sandy ground, and began to engage targets. When bullets stitched the sand on both sides of one shooter's outstretched arms, the range master called a cease-fire. Besides shooting low, the errant gunner had set his weapon to automatic, rather than using the preferred semi-automatic "double tap." It was quickly realized that this system didn't work.

The CQB techniques taught by the SAS were incorporated into the unit's tactics and a more deliberate method of quickly flooding a room with four to six men in a controlled manner was practiced. It turned out to be the best method as the shooting was more accurate and safer for everyone but the bad guys. The SAS called this the "Careful Hurry." With sufficient time and ammunition, shooters trained to double-tap multiple targets with very tight shot groups in the kill zone of the target, quickly and consistently. As the shooters and teams refined their skills and became more confident, the scenarios became more complex, from single to multiple rooms with larger four- and six-man teams moving through the range in a deadly ballet of precision shooting. Then the teams moved to scenarios simulating buses, trains, and aircraft—so-called linear targets—that were flooded with teams moving down aisles with guns covering passengers right, left, and forward while sniper teams covered any terrorists foolish enough to show themselves in the windows. The unit began to do extensive assault scenarios that went from two assaulters clearing one room, to multiple teams entering and clearing rooms sequentially.

An especially vivid demonstration of shooting skills was used for the VIP visitors who wanted to see the Det's skills up close. It was decided that holes in paper targets or punctured balloons were not adequate for showing the shooters' accuracy, so mannequins were scrounged from some German department stores by various means and dressed up as terrorists. To finish things off, sacks of red paint were inserted into the mannequins' heads before the show began. Then, with the generals or admirals watching from a more-or-less safe location the teams would execute a room-clearing exercise. Most of the VIPs fully expected blank ammunition would be used. They were quickly and violently disabused of that notion when the men blasted their way into the rooms and began shooting the dummy terrorists. Each head shot resulted in a plume of paint spray that shocked the onlookers back into reality. One visitor remarked that he thought the training looked exceptionally dangerous, to which Col O replied, "It is, but only for the targets."

For a change of scene, the unit used Parks Range at night. Two teams would start from opposite ends of the "city" and move through the center towards the other side in a variation of capture the flag similar to today's paintball wars. Using blanks, smoke, and the occasional grenade simulator, each team would stalk the other for several hours inside and outside the buildings until it was agreed that everyone was dead and it was time to go home.

Target discrimination (shoot/no shoot) and reduced visibility (night/ smoke) training was also practiced. Jim Robinson and Frank Closen put together a slide show that was projected onto a screen for timed shooting at an underground range on Andrews Barracks. The images depicted everything from little old ladies and children with guns to terrorists reading books in order to better exercise the shooter's powers of observation. The shooter faced a screen onto which a slide would be projected for a short time; he had to make the decision whether to shoot or not and then hit the target before the screen went dark. It was a basic but effective beginning.

The indoor range would later be closed down because it didn't have adequate ventilation. By that time, most of the Detachment's shooters had probably inhaled enough carbon and lead to qualify for a lawsuit, but no one thought about that then. They were too intent on tightening their shot groups. Two in the chest and one in the head was the mantra and after several thousand rounds most could routinely double-tap twenty rounds—with magazine changes—into a saucer-sized area from 10–15 meters. A team of ten shooters would easily expend several thousand rounds per day at the range.

The Remington 870P shotgun also came in handy for ballistic entries—opening doors with slugs or clearing elevators with "double-aught" buckshot. It was routinely carried, usually by the breacher or the assault team leader, in addition to an MPK and pistol. Most operators trained with a single pistol, the assigned P-38 or the later P-5, but whenever a load-out occurred, a second personal pistol found its way into his gear. The Smith & Wesson Model 59 and CZ-75 were two favorites, but the short-barrel .357 Magnum revolver was also well regarded.

All the other required skills for CT operations were trained on and in some cases devised. Rope work; rappelling and climbing techniques; helicopter operations, communications, emergency medical treatment, explosive breaching, to name a few, were taught and practiced by all members of the force. It was vital that each man could take over the duties of another when necessary.

Charlie B Comes to Town

Something was brewing on the other side of the big pond. Colonel Charlie Beckwith had found fertile ground at Fort Bragg [Redacted], and he was looking for inspiration.[17] Besides visiting the boys at Hereford (SAS) and Hangelar (GSG-9), he came to Berlin with his senior NCO. He knew the Det had the CT mission for Europe and wanted to benefit from its experiences and training. Having priority as the Army's new special mission unit, he took full advantage of his prerogatives. When he showed up, he simply asked for everything. He took copies of the unit's CT training plans, standard operating procedures (SOP), and equipment inventories; appropriated the shooting slide shows; and then went to Range 5 and other facilities to photograph and sketch the set ups. Much of what Detachment "A" pioneered in CT operations ended up being integrated into the [Redacted] program. It was frustrating for those in the unit at the time, but in retrospect, it was better for everyone, as the material later helped [Redacted] to move quickly towards their operational validation in late 1979.[18]

With Charlie gone, the ops tempo did not slack off. The unit operations officer connected with the country manager for Pan Am airlines and arranged for the unit to use their aircraft for training. Teams first visited Tegel international airport at night to conduct static training on Pan Am's Boeing 737 and 727 passenger aircraft in the hangars and on remote parts of the airfield. Everyone first learned the layout of the aircraft, how to cut power to the aircraft and disconnect the front landing gear steering. From there they learned how to open the doors, emergency exits, and stairwells from inside and outside the plane. Once aircraft entries were mastered, teams would practice assaults using ladders on single and multiple entry points. This was always a tricky maneuver as a ladder set in the wrong position made opening the door difficult and it could easily be knocked down if the emergency slide inflated. Using the concealed access points from the cargo areas into the cockpit and galleys was also considered, but generally proved a very last option because of the difficulty maneuvering through the passages. The Pan Am crews were extremely accommodating as the teams crashed through emergency exits practicing rapid entries. The pilots assured the team that the seals were still good, but a lot of passengers might have been disturbed to know that the wing exit windows they were sitting next to had been punched open the previous evening by a bunch of men with guns. Several operators were taught how to conduct an aircraft power up and engine start for an emergency taxi, which led to some "white knuckle" moments for the instructor pilots as well as the rest of their team.

Full assault scenarios by two or more assault teams were rehearsed on a remote corner of the airport under the cover of night. With sniper/observer teams covering their approach, teams practiced approaching the aircraft from the rear, carrying ladders that had been padded to prevent metal on metal noise. The ladders were placed on the sides of exit doors and at the trailing wing edges near the fuselage, while role-players roamed inside the aircraft watching and listening for any noise or rocking movement that would compromise the assault force. Several men would inch their way up the wing root to be in place under the exit windows while the teams climbed the ladders and positioned themselves to open the doors without getting blown off their perch by the inflating escape slide if it was engaged. On a prearranged signal, often an explosive charge near the window of the cockpit, the exit windows would be punched in while the doors were pulled open—a difficult maneuver, but one that can be executed quickly if well practiced. The teams flooded the aircraft from the front, rear, and sides to clear the cockpit and cabin of any hostiles while controlling the passengers and getting them off the aircraft as soon as the terrorists were eliminated. The passengers would be herded off under careful watch and searched to ensure a terrorist hadn't slipped into the crowd. It was excellent training that honed both individual and team tactics as well as overall control of several teams in a very complex scenario.

Amazingly, the cooperation between the Detachment and Pan Am was arranged with a handshake and without any legal paperwork being thrown in to complicate matters. The Pan Am base manager risked his career when he permitted the use of the company's aircraft, but he understood the training's necessity and its value. He had witnessed the looming dangers of skyjackings and wanted to ensure he did everything possible to prepare.

Once tactical training had been completed, teams began rotations onto the airfield during routine commercial flight operations. The Det's men worked in the positions of ground guide and baggage handler at the Pan Am gates. At first, the unionized employees balked at training the strangers in their procedures, but once assured the men were not strike-breakers they were quite helpful. The idea was to have men trained who could get close to the plane to conduct an emergency take down if a hijacking situation deteriorated before the SAF's full assault element could move. One wondered what the passengers would have thought had they known the men on the tarmac handling their flight were American SF soldiers.

Time off in Berlin

Free time was always a bit dodgy in Berlin: there were just too many distractions. Although there were some good places to go further afield, across the street from Andrews Barracks there were several pubs, bars, and restaurants frequented by GIs and Germans alike (although most Germans knew enough to give the GI locales wide berth). There was the *Goldene Sonne* (Golden Sun), which later became the "Home Bar," the "Nashville," and the "Speak Easy," all of which catered to the American crowd and were far too conveniently located to ignore. The *Sonne* was the Detachment hangout in the 1960s, but the "Speak" took its place in the 1970s and early 1980s, especially as fewer Lodge Act soldiers were in the unit. Run by an effervescent British expat woman, it was an after-work relaxation point for those who didn't have to make their way home or an aversion to alcohol. There were the occasional displays of fisticuffs outside the bars, generally following an ill-advised intrusion into the Detachment's area of operations by members of the 287th MP or the 42nd Engineer Companies. The altercations usually went badly for the intruders.

The neighborhood bars were favored primarily because they were close to home and comfortable territory. Most of the Detachment preferred to hang with their own; drinking with blue-collar Berliners lost its luster after an argument or two. Germans love to talk and debate, but they could be extremely restricted in their worldview and caustic about Americans.

One team was enjoying an evening out downtown when a bunch of students from Berlin's Free University at the next table began to harangue the *Amis* about everything from the crimes of Vietnam to race relations in America. One of the team came back with a logical counterpoint that ran something like your points are valid, but America has made progress in the field of race and prejudice. He then asked, "How about the way Germans treat the Turkish guest workers?"

One of the students replied, "That's different, Turks aren't human!" It was an alarming but unfortunately typical comment and effectively ended the debate.

The city's best time of the year was the two weeks of summer when Berlin went from drab gray to colorful. Then it was mandatory to head out to the Wannsee beaches or the Ku'damm to watch the young women. Rarely was anyone successful in picking up a date as the over-consumption of beer tended to interfere with the smooth delivery of even the best lines.

Our Friends

The British 2nd Parachute Regiment came to Berlin in 1977 and, naturally, the Detachment found them in the Irish Pub in central Berlin. After drinking with them and not falling into any fights, there followed training and shooting competitions. These, in turn, oft led to convivial evenings of carousing. The "2 Para" soldiers were eventually lured to the Detachment's Day Room for a number of BBQs following training events or just because. It was probably the closest Allied unit-to-unit connection made during the Detachment's time in the city—the SAS only rarely appeared in Berlin and then usually in four-man teams on relatively short reconnaissance trips. They were usually identifiable by their long hair, leather jackets, and the concealed Browning High Powers they carried. They were much like the Detachment, but with different accents.[19]

A final party was held at the Detachment for what seemed to be a company-sized group of the Paras before they departed for Northern Ireland in early 1979. It was a good farewell, but of course no one anticipated that many of their new friends and comrades would be killed in the Warrenpoint ambush several weeks later. That operation was carried out by PIRA who also assassinated Lord Mountbatten on that same day. The loss of 19 men that August 27 confirmed the threat that existed to soldiers involved in guerrilla wars.

VIP Security

Before the Warrenpoint ambush, another terror group had grabbed the headlines by trying to kill General Al Haig in Belgium as he was being driven to work at SHAPE Headquarters. The incident took place on June 26, 1979. The Red Army Faction (RAF) carried out the attack. Andreas Bader and Susan Albrecht trained in a Palestinian Black September camp in Aden for the hit, but the attack failed. Haig's driver was too erratic, alternately speeding up and slowing down, and the bomber couldn't time the firing of the explosives for the correct moment. Fifty pounds of plastic explosive had been buried in a culvert and the terrorists were connected to the bomb with a 600-meter stretch of cable. The blast blew a hole in the road behind Haig's car, tossing a 6-foot slab of asphalt into the air that landed on the following car, but no one was severely injured. Haig's driver ignored his order to stop and headed for the headquarters. Scheduled to retire in a couple of days, Haig would pass the USEUCOM colors to General Bernard Rogers during a change of command (CoC) ceremony at Patch Barracks near Stuttgart. The event planners at Patch were convinced terrorists would storm the compound's fences and called for reinforcements to provide additional security. The Detachment's Team Five and sniper teams from Team One were alerted and within two hours the teams were ready with their equipment and weapons uploaded. The trucks rolled for Tempelhof where a C-130 was waiting on the tarmac. Once loaded, the plane immediately rolled out and took off, heading for Stuttgart's military airfield. The teams arrived the day prior to the ceremony and set out to conduct a rapid survey of the compound, keying in on the two event areas: the main plaza where the CoC would take place and the Officers' Club that would be used for a reception. It was decided to place sniper/observer teams in buildings surrounding the plaza. But before that happened, the local MPs were asked if they had checked the buildings. Getting a noncommittal shrug of the shoulders, the Detachment took the task in hand. The buildings surrounding the plaza were searched and then a perimeter walk was done to determine weak areas. With an MP major and captain in tow to take notes, weaknesses and blind spots in the fence were noted for repair and monitoring. As the men walked along they found a large hole in the fence near the officers' club that was used by some of the dependent children to take a short-cut to the outside. As they stood on the hill overlooking the spot, they were surprised to see a woman enter the compound carrying a large shoulder bag. Watching her disappear into the "O" club through a basement door, the men could only look at each other in disbelief. Following her into the building, they were able to confront the woman and verify her identity. It turned out she was an employee of the club that also used the shortcut.

The MPs thanked the Det "A" men and shooed them off so they could get work fixing the holes before the installation commander found out there was a problem.

The next day, the teams were in place above and around the plaza. Three sniper/observer teams were watching from the attics of the barracks while Team Five's assault team was using the post chapel that stood at the edge of the plaza for an operations center. Men were wandering around the edges of the parade ground discreetly armed with pistols and briefcase submachine guns, while others acted as backup inside the chapel with the heavy artillery.

As the guests began to arrive, it seemed every German VIP in the world, including the mayor of Stuttgart, Manfred Rommel, was present.[20] Disconcertingly every VIP was accompanied by a protection team and more guns. All that needed to happen was for one firecracker to explode and the whole neighborhood would have gone up in smoke.

As the crowd grew, the team just watched, while the Germans tried to figure out who the other guys were. It was a stand-off, with clean-cut, Hugo Boss-suited Germans on one side and the leather-jacketed "Snake-eaters" on the other. Retrospectively, the word "cowboys" comes to mind, but that could apply to either side.

All of the four-star generals—Haig, Rogers, James Allen and Robert Huyser—were resplendent in their glory that day. The change of command went without a hitch or an attempted terrorist takeover, and the reception afterward was just as terror free, that is, if you don't count the waitresses and waiters who were frightened to death by a bunch of longhairs running around the officers' club with loaded guns looking for something to shoot.

Team Nick and the "Pensioner Beaters"

Back in the city and after all the bullets had been accounted for, Col O was assured that General Haig was not looking for him, so life went back to its frenzied normality.

One of the first things to crop up was another RED SAILS exercise. This time two three-man teams were detailed to infiltrate the UK. This exercise had the clear rules and objectives that were lacking in the first version that ran in 1978; it was a sudden death competition and the first Detachment team identified by the Brits would be eliminated.

One team chose to infiltrate the UK by air. After landing at London Heathrow, they made it out of the airport and down the road towards Southampton before being stopped at a checkpoint. The police supervisor didn't like their cover story and pulled them into secondary. Game over, one team was gone.

It was up to the second team to carry the ball. This team, made up of Nick, Klem, and "Houston" had already infiltrated the UK individually to break the "team" profile. One traveled from France by ferry carrying some of the team's "unusual" equipment concealed in objects like a home-baked loaf of bread—still a viable option in the days before X-ray scanners. The other two men came in by air, got together in London to rent a car and headed for Southampton, where they all met at a pre-arranged, secluded personal meeting place (PMP).

Once in Southampton, each found their way into a secluded bed and breakfast by ignoring the Brits' admonition to use only the assigned hotels. The first thing to do was meet their MI6 case officer and receive their first tasking.

Nick went to the meeting after following a detection route to make sure he was free of surveillance. His "CO" asked after the rest of the team saying they hadn't been seen at the hotels. Nick only responded that they shouldn't plan on seeing them either. A bit nonplussed, the handler outlined the first mission. It was identical to the task given the previous team, case a local police station and provide the CO with detailed plans that would enable a prisoner to be rescued. Nick thought this would be a piece of cake and he and Klem started out the next day. On the initial approach, all appeared normal but, as they got closer, they realized not all was well. Standing next to a bulletin board on the street, Klem nudged Nick and nodded towards the board. Nick saw the problem right away. Their portraits were prominently displayed on wanted posters describing them as having beaten and robbed a pensioner of his money. Furthermore, there was a little old lady looking at the posters and glancing sidelong at them. It was time to leave.

Making for the nearest druggist, they bought razors and hair coloring and proceeded to a public toilet where they shaved off their mustaches and exchanged clothing. They hoped their profiles were changed enough to fool anyone who had seen them before.

They then contemplated the task. They knew it would be foolhardy to return to the station, but how to collect the intelligence they needed was a mystery. Then Klem had an idea.

"Who knows about the inside of a police station besides a policeman?" he asked.

The light went on for Nick, "A criminal."

"Or a homeless person," Klem responded.

The next hours were filled with buying sandwiches and cheap wine and hunting out homeless people under bridges and in parks until they got a clear idea of the layout of the station. They even had the names and badge numbers of the policemen.

The following day, Nick met his CO who was suitably impressed with their product. Nick did not give up his secret sources. They might be useful later.

The next task was a bit more complicated: deliver a package of explosives to their team mate "Houston" in a park. This would prove to be a bit of a challenge as Houston had been compromised. He had made the mistake of hiding his VHF radio—a "walkie talkie"—under the sink in his room. Unfortunately, the landlord was a former Special

Branch detective who made it his habit to nose around the rooms of his renters.

Houston failed to meet with Nick and Klem several times and they now suspected he was lost to the game. Meeting him in the park would be suicidal, but they wanted to show the Brits they were on to them.

Nick put together a package for Houston, wrapping it with construction paper and placed it in a bag. Approaching the park, he encountered a young man and asked him if he wanted to make some money. The waif said yes and Nick gave him a one pound note to take the package "to the man on the bench," promising two more pounds on his return. The child took off with the package and slowly walked up to the bench where Houston sat.

Predictably, the police pounced. The young man and Houston were taken to the ground and the package seized by the police officers who thought they were dealing with actual terrorist suspects. A detective—who should have known better—ripped the package open, only to have a bloody pig's head roll out and bounce across the ground. There was only silence save the shuffle of footsteps as Nick and Klem retreated from the area.

The next task was the target attack on a communications tower that was carried off without much difficulty. But then, the two surviving members of the team had to find their way to a remote beach where, Nick had been told by the handler, they were to be picked up by submarine and taken to their safe haven.

The two decided to travel in light disguise. Nick with a big hat and Klem with a bigger woman's wig. Later stories have Klem in a simple dress as well, but that point remains disputed to this day.

As they approached the beach, a police roadblock came into view. It was the obvious end of the line for the exercise and the team, but they had to make an attempt. They stopped at the barrier and two policemen approached the car and began to ask questions about their life histories and where they were going. Finally, one of the policeman blurted out, "You've certainly got one ugly girlfriend," and grabbed Klem's wig off his head. Asked why he was wearing a wig, Klem responded calmly, "My head was cold."

At this point, the exercise was over and the team was taken to an MI6 training base located somewhere on the coast. The base facility was a

medieval castle with moat, drawbridge, and probably a wizard somewhere within the walls. A "hot wash" was conducted where everyone
got the chance to critique and be critiqued. Klem and Nick came off
well; Houston, on the hand, was rather depressed after the session. The
police and MI5 came out of the session rather worse for wear at the
hands of the SIS and the team.

With all the blood spilled that was to be shed, a rather English feast
took place to celebrate the exercise. As might be expected, Klem made
off with MI6's crystal glassware—all emblazoned with Her Majesty's
seal. To cap it off, the Brits all stood up with their backs to the team
and when they turned around, they were all sporting fake mustaches—a
toast to the team's ingenuity.

Nous Defions[21]

In August 1979, Rodney and Styk were ordered to attend Special
Operations Training (SOT) at Fort Bragg to conduct an assessment of
the training site for the unit. Arriving at Mott Lake for the training,
the two created a bit of stir with their "relaxed grooming standards,"
which didn't quite meet the scrutinizing approval of many officers, but
official orders signed by a general officer were the ticket to turning their
criticism off.

The SOT facility provided a good, if distant, alternative training
option for the unit as it offered longer ranges and the ability to conduct
larger-scale live fire exercises than were possible in the confines of Berlin.

The most attractive aspect of the training experience was the instructors, many of whom were veterans of the Son Tay raid and very good
weapon handlers. SFC Paul Poole was a master of the M1911A1 Colt
.45 pistol and able to tighten everyone's shot groups with his instruction.
One of his favorite antics was to make his students practice their trigger
pull by having them rest the barrel of their loaded pistols on the wooden
barriers that stood in front of the shooters. He would then tell the
students to take the slack out of the trigger until they felt the weapon
was on the verge of firing but no further. Invariably, one student would
squeeze just a bit too much and blow a hole in the wood.

"Trigger control," he would intone with a twinkle in his eye, "is everything." Of course, Poole could hit a bull's eye ten times out of ten at 100 meters with an arms room pistol—not a super-accurized, national match special.

The SOT facility also permitted assault teams and sniper/observer elements to work together at the same time on the same range, something not yet possible in Berlin. The high-velocity rounds that cracked over the students' heads as they assaulted a target were a good incentive for snipers and assaulters to focus clearly on the task.

The training also emphasized helicopter operations, both insertion and extraction of teams using assault "landings" (jumping off the skid while five feet above the ground), rappelling, ladders, and McGuire/STABO rig techniques. Some of the pilots enjoyed scaring the hell out of the passengers by simulating an engine failure at 200 feet, letting the bird plummet with a stomach-churning drop and going into an auto-rotation just to "familiarize" the students. One of the instructors who had been severely burned in a Vietnam helicopter crash was not so amused and nearly choked the pilot.

Another instructor, "Tiny" Young, who wasn't tiny, enjoyed tipping his fellow junior instructors for their spare change. He would literally pick them up by their ankles and shake them upside down. Whatever money came out of their pockets paid for his snacks that day. He was famously remembered for his part at Son Tay, where he carried a heavy oxyacetylene torch and its gas bottles into the compound to cut the POWs out of their cages. When the raid concluded he carried the equipment out again because he had been told he could keep it if he did.

All the training was documented and, after the "Berliners" returned to home base, a briefing was presented on the program. It was decided to rotate teams back to the course to enhance both marksmanship and team operational skills as an adjunct to the unit's existing methods.

Certification

In early fall of 1979, the Detachment was required to prove its CT capability through an operational certification. It had been conducting similar exercises for SOTFE and EUCOM throughout 1978, but now the requirement came from the national level. Another outfit and GSG-9 were to be evaluated about the same time but in different locations and both would be tested with similar missions, a simulated aircraft hijacking. [Redacted] got an additional target of a small building thrown into the mix as it had a larger assault force. They both passed their tests.

The Detachment was alerted for its exercise and within the required two-hour window, all personnel were assembled, the equipment was uploaded onto two Mercedes trucks, and everything was headed for Tempelhof where the trucks were put onto a C-141. The aircraft departed immediately for Ramstein Air Force Base in the FRG. At the airbase, the Detachment was escorted to an empty hangar where the command group received a situation briefing.

Naturally, the evaluators threw the unit a curve ball. Its test target was a passenger train. Apparently, someone was enamored with the 1977 Dutch resolution of the South Moluccan train hijacking crisis and wanted to see if the Detachment would fare as well.[22] The evaluators came from SOTFE headquarters at Stuttgart, a couple from the Pentagon, and a British SAS officer who had CT experience with one of the 22nd SAS's special projects teams.[23] The SAF went through its operations checklists to make sure all the equipment was ready, radios were communicating, and weapons prepared. At the same time, the S-2 was quizzing the exercise staff about the target to find out everything the teams needed to know about the layout of the train, who the terrorists were and what kind of weapons they carried, as well as the number of hostages and their condition.

The train, made up of an engine and four passenger cars, a baggage car and a caboose, was located on an isolated rail siding inside the air base; there would be no outsiders watching. A team of six "terrorists" were on board, as well as about forty "hostages" being role-played by air force personnel. It was the classic linear target in its most difficult form. While aircraft present a difficult target to approach and access, once in the doors, the CT operatives have a simple target compared to the many separate cars, compartments, and interior doors that make up a passenger train. Trains can be equally daunting to approach and in this case the size of the assault force necessitated a phased operation.

The Detachment's SAF quickly set up teams to observe the train as planning began. There would not be time for much rehearsing as the test required quick resolution. Radio communications between the observer teams and the command element established the terrorists' patterns of movement through the train and the details of where most of the passengers were located. The terrorists had confined their hostages to two central cars, but maintained security by walking up and down the train through the cars. It was clear the target would need to be flooded with assaulters while sniper teams would neutralize as many of the terrorists as possible in the first seconds. Small teams would approach the train from the ends, entering through side doors blown open with small explosive charges, while the main assault force would concentrate on the center cars.

When the release order was given, Col O let loose his teams. It was nighttime, which permitted small teams to approach each end of the train undetected. There they halted and then one section went under the train to crawl forward to the center section to assist the main force entry. The remainder of the SAF was positioned along the edge of the forest and would rush the train once the assault began.

As the teams moved into position, the sniper/observer teams kept overwatch and reported movement on the train. When the teams were in place everyone waited tensely. It was a typical German autumn evening—cool and damp as the day had been overcast and wet. The men waited for a seemingly interminable stretch in the damp grass with little to keep them warm except their adrenaline, which wore off as the night progressed.

The SAF commander was in constant contact with the different assault teams and the snipers. He spoke the code word for all elements to confirm they were in position and ready. In turn, each team acknowledged. Then he asked the snipers to confirm targets and waited until all six terrorists were in the crosshairs of the rifles, before again calling out, "Standby, Standby." Seconds ticked by and then, "Execute, Execute, Execute!"

The explosives were set off and the teams under and near the cars rushed their doors while the main force charged the other entries. This was the crucial moment as the main force had 25 meters to cross before they reached the train. One or two men went down, falling in the rough terrain before picking themselves up and carrying on. Crucial seconds passed before all the doors were breached and the teams had flooded the cars. But the terrorists were all taken down quickly and the passengers were taken off under guard to be searched and segregated. The test was over.

Most everyone was satisfied with the plan and its result—most importantly the SAS officer was happy. One SOTFE colonel was tempted to put some derogatory comments in his report to the effect that the main assault force being exposed for too much time, but Olchovik pointed out to him that the snipers had probably killed all the bad guys before that. Moreover, he would be "happy to give the colonel an ass-whipping he'd never forget if he didn't take the comment out." Somehow, it didn't make it into the report.

The unit was certified for its CT mission. Back at the hangar, the Det's supply sergeant made some friends when everyone arrived to find beer icing in 55-gallon drums and the BBQ blazing. The "Smaj" let everyone slept in the next morning.

The Fire on the Horizon

The year 1979 would prove to be a significant one in special operations history. Along with the Soviet invasion of Afghanistan, the Iranian revolution began in February and by early fall the country was in the hands of supporters of Ayatollah Ruhollah Khomeini. There were indications of trouble ahead, but no one knew exactly where it would lead. In November, it would become quite clear.

CHAPTER V

APPOINTMENT IN TEHRAN

September 1979

Team Five headed out that evening, traveling west with the night. They were on the US Army Duty Train that connected Berlin to West Germany. The train clanked out of Lichterfelde-West station and made its first stop just after it crossed into East German territory at Potsdam. The West German capitalist locomotive was swapped for an East German communist locomotive in one of the strange vagaries of East-West diplomacy. Noisier and dirtier than the "*West Lok*," the GDR locomotive heaved its cargo up to speed and rolled on. The next change would be several hours later at the border near Helmstedt where the locomotives would again be exchanged and then it was straight on to Frankfurt.

The ten men had three compartments to themselves. The snacks were broken out along with a thermos of "tea." The MPs occasionally wandered through the corridors to make sure no alcoholic beverages were being consumed. Everyone knew alcohol could lead to calamitous behavior and the men from the Det were always suspect in the eyes of the MPs. The two units never got along well together; it was always just when the party got fun that MPs would blunder in and ruin it.

The train was no different, so a measured prudence took form on the claustrophobic run across East Germany. Don't drink beers in front of the MPs; drink "tea" instead. The cards came out, or the men settled back into the rock-hard bunks to read a paperback or just nod off. Twelve hours for the run to Frankfurt, then the next leg would come.

A comfortable rhythm rocked the car, the MPs stayed away, and soon it was dark and everyone was asleep—excepting those who were in that twilight zone between wakefulness and full REM sleep, maintaining a wary eye out for something, anything that might be out there. Nick was staring out the windows in this drone state and suddenly pulled back shaking his head. Jon and Styk watched him from the darkness. "Shit," he muttered, looking around to see if anyone had noticed, "I was looking for an ambush." Too much time on recon with CCN in Vietnam.[1] Jon and Styk settled back and closed their eyes. It was too hot in the car and the windows were stuck closed.

The next morning, the team was up and ready as the train rolled into Frankfurt's Hauptbahnhof. The baggage came off and the men sauntered down the platform towards the place where they were to meet their liaison man. Ten men walking together with purpose, long hair and leather jackets aside, signaled something to those in front of them. "*Die Bundeswehr marschiert,*" remarked one perceptive onlooker. "The Army is on the move." People tended to clear out of the way.

The liaison officer was met and keys were handed over. The team headed out in two Ford Taunus vans, northwest toward Bonn; Sankt Augustin/Hangelar to be precise, the headquarters of GSG-9.

It would be a short course, five days, to get insights and practice with an ally. Many of GSG-9's techniques, along with those of the SAS and the Detachment's own were now fully integrated into unit training. From here on it was continual adjustment and fine-tuning of tactics, techniques, and personnel. The positions on the assault teams would change as individuals demonstrated particular skills and proclivities. Some were better suited for the sniper/observer section, while others served best as assaulters. Breachers were almost always the engineer/demo sergeants, but other than that, the teams were fully adjustable. SAT team leaders tended to be the most experienced, not the highest ranking as with the ODA. There was no room for error and a captain could not roll in and expect to lead an assault team. Col O made that clear when the officers reported to the unit. He put it like this: "You will listen to your team sergeant or you won't be on a team. Period."

Team Five, like the other teams in the unit, had two assault teams, each with four to six men, plus a sniper/observer team. This time, the element was mostly Team Five plus Howie from Team One. It was a young team, except for the team sergeant, Frank, who was a Yugoslav émigré. Four were Vietnam vets.

The team was met by Border Patrol Captain "Dieter" at the front gate and escorted to the main building. Colonel Ulrich Wegener was waiting on the steps and greeted the team before turning them back over to Dieter. Then Wegener was off to meetings in Bonn and the team was left in the hands of his men.

Walking across the compound to the barracks, the team passed several of GSG-9's big gray Mercedes sedans and a formation of young men in their pressed, dark blue-green uniforms. Russ summed it up for everyone when he commented, "They look pretty, but can they fight?"

GSG-9 was essentially an elite police unit, not like the SAS or Special Forces, but a special purpose paramilitary unit. Still, they were good at what they did, which was counterterrorism and combating heavy crime in a permissive environment.

The team first familiarized with the Germans' weapons, and then did room- and building-clearing tactics for the first two days. The third day was a trip to the factory for the obstacle-cum-terrorist-shooting course. It started out well enough—until the first obstacle. A GSG-9 trooper went over a hurdle, actually a log that served as the front gate into the facility, with a deft hand placed on the bar and jaunty kick over. The team knew they were in trouble when Captain Chris looked back at the others with a "watch this" gleam in his eye and then proceeded to slip off the log into a puddle. Howie turned green trying not to choke to death while laughing as did the rest of the team, while the Germans looked on politely until they figured it was OK to laugh as well. Onward then, leaving adversity behind, the team stormed the factory impatiently waiting for the Germans to show them how it was supposed to be done.

With a "You think you can handle this?" look, the Germans said, "Your turn," and the team was off. And they did handle it, the exclamation point being a 75-meter off-hand MP5 shot that took a target out a moment after it was revealed. The look the Germans gave was a

"You *Amis* are not so bad after all." Chris got his redemption as well by double-tapping his way into the Germans' hearts.

Day Four

The GSG-9 officer stood up in front of the team and said, "We heard you guys were good in the field so we arranged a little excursion."

"Tonight we fly to hit a target somewhere here," said the captain pointing at a map. "The helicopter will drop you here and your partner *Gay es Gay Neun* team here."

Looking at the map, the teams could see they were being dropped about 10 kilometers from the target on opposite sides. The objective was to move towards the camp in a radio-coordinated approach, surround and assault the bad guys, who would be GSG-9 role-players. It was a fairly simple task: work up an op plan first, then do logistics, load up rucksacks and check weapons, eat dinner, then move to a field outside the base.

At the appointed time, two dark-green Federal Border Guard Bell 212 helos swooped in to pick up the teams. They flew west towards the Hürtgenwald, a dense forest that most famously hosted one of WWII's worst battles.

Once again, west with the night. About twenty minutes into the flight, the birds broke left and right. Daylight was gone and the waning twilight permitted only faint glimpses of the landscape sliding quickly underneath them. The bird came over some trees, flared, sat down in a field long enough to let the team roll out and then it was gone. It was dark. Actually it was black except for the scattering of stars in the sky overhead. The team went into a security perimeter at the edge of the field and the map came out.

The first thing Russ, the intelligence sergeant, said was, "They put us down in the wrong spot."

Nick's response, "I hope the damn Germans are lost too."

Russ shot an azimuth and moved the team to the first road. Reaching it, two men went left, two went right. Ten minutes late they converged again. "We're here," said Nick, pointing at a spot on the map and proving his expert recon skills. "I found a road sign." OK, maybe not so expert, but directions are always good when you're looking for something.

Now with coordinates, Russ announced, "They only put us 10 clicks [kilometers] off our original landing zone. Let's get going." The march began and through the night the team moved—first quickly, then slowly, deliberately and quietly to the assembly point. Morning would be on them soon, so a short break was taken and then, at the appointed hour, radio contact was made with the GSG-9 teams.

"We're ready, you ready?"

"We're ready and moving, call us when you're in assault position."

"Roger."

Silence. Moving stealthily forward, half a league, half a league onward. Expecting an ambush at any time, moving tactically towards a known enemy position is like leaning into a punch. You hope you're the only one that knows you are there.

Russ halts the team with a hand signal. "We're here."

"Ready?"

"Ready."

"We're moving."

"Roger, *Vorwarts.*"

The teams would not converge directly opposite each other, but more like an open clamshell, giving the bad guys an open door to escape. Another GSG-9 team was in position to act as the blocking force—the anvil.

The team walked slowly forward. The grass was wet, lessening the noise of movement somewhat. Before long, the Americans could glimpse the slate-green uniforms of the GSG-9 troopers on their flank, their German paratrooper helmets reminiscent of another era. The Germans would later say that the Americans were harder to detect, that they moved differently, that their uniforms blended into the forest better. That, and a coat of dirt from rolling in the road helped immensely.

Suddenly came the rip of machine-gun fire and the radio crackled, "Action front!" The Germans were in contact. The Americans swung left to close the door and the firefight broke down into a free for all.

The bad guys had covered their front with a MG1, the modern version of the MG42, a machine gun that sounded like a bedsheet being ripped when it fired. At 1,200 rounds per minute it was scary fast shooting.

It was clear that the terrorists had been waiting—it was an exercise after all—but the teams managed to sweep through and round the five bad guys up. They were subdued and secured before the observer called "End Ex."

Then came another helo ride back to base, where a shower and change of clothing made everyone ready for the evening. A night of beer and schnapps followed, with Americans and Germans exchanging stories and uniforms, often with back slapping and wishes for future cooperation, and only a little food.

The next morning, GSG-9 wings were presented and the team was off for home, back to Berlin for some down time before the next good deal.

But the fires to the East were still burning.

Tehran, November 4, 1979

The morning started out quietly at the US Embassy in Tehran, but quickly turned into what would be a 444-day nightmare for the United States. Radical Iranians had planned to demonstrate in front of the large American diplomatic compound in order to air their grievances against the "Great Satan" as they referred to the USA. But, instead, the siege morphed into an all-out assault as hundreds of students stormed over the walls and seized 66 Americans as their hostages. Ostensibly, their complaint against the United States was that Iran's former leader, Shah Mohammad Reza Pahlavi, had been allowed to seek medical care in the US. Some diplomats believed the students were protesting the direction the revolution was taking and wanted to marginalize the moderates to the benefit of the clerics.[2] The event shook the US Government and military as the new provisional government of the Islamic Republic of Iran seemingly could not or deliberately would not do anything to resolve the issue.

The Iranian revolution started in the fall of 1977 with sporadic demonstrations by opponents of the Pahlavi regime. Shortly after the ousting of the shah in January 1979 and his departure from Iran, Ayatollah Ruhollah Khomeini returned to the country to take control. Within days, Khomeini's people were in charge of the government and trying to consolidate their position at the expense of the moderates. Despite the United States' best efforts to work with the new government, including warning them of Iraq's imminent intention to attack Iran, the radicals wanted nothing to do with the United States. When Carter gave in to pressure and allowed the shah to seek medical treatment in the United States, the storm broke loose.

Khomeini denounced Carter's decision and the United States, while at the same time criticizing moderates and secularists in his own government. Radical students, thus encouraged, stormed the US Embassy while the remaining moderates within Khomeini's government quickly resigned. Khomeini cleverly used the incident to complete his vision and establish a hard-line Islamic theocracy.[3]

President Jimmy Carter had few options. Only several months before, the Iranian Foreign Minister had resolved a similar incident with his personal intervention. It initially seemed that might be the case with this takeover, but it soon became clear that the minister's power had been usurped by the radicals. The rhetoric became much more ominous as the radicals' leaders threatened to kill all the hostages should the US intervene. When the crisis began to drag on, Carter choose economic sanctions over military action, but the hostages remained in their new "prison," the US Embassy compound in central Tehran.

While diplomatic measures were underway, the military immediately began contingency planning for a rescue mission. The task would be Herculean as the hostages were in hostile territory far from the United States. Only once before had such a difficult mission been attempted, when American forces tried to rescue POWs from a North Vietnamese prison at Son Tay in November 1972. That mission had been conducted by helicopter assault from bases in neighboring Thailand and required massive resources to undertake.[4] The Iran mission offered a much more difficult problem because Tehran lay far beyond the range of any available helicopter and the target was in the middle of a large, potentially hostile city.

Initially, EUCOM placed several military units on alert, including the 1/509th Parachute Infantry Regiment in Vicenza, Italy, for an emergency rescue, but the order was quickly rescinded as it became clear the mission was too complex for a simple solution. The national assets would be called upon to execute the operation.

The Detachment had been exposed to the Iran issue already. Earlier, as Iran spiraled into the revolutionary abyss in 1978, EUCOM tasked the unit to prepare for a potential deployment to protect, remove, or destroy sensitive US assets located within the soon-to-be Islamic republic. This mission did not go forward and the Detachment wasn't deployed. However, its familiarity with the target country ensured it would be involved in the rescue mission planning, which commenced after November 4, 1979.

When President Carter outlined his goals for the mission, it was clear that he wanted to proceed with the least intrusive option:

> We want it to be quick, incisive, surgical, no loss of American lives, not involve any other country, minimal suffering of the Iranian people themselves, to increase their reliance on imports, sure of success and unpredictable.[5]

The military's plan would be extremely complex, but first information was required to prepare for the operation. Although some Agency officers could possibly enter the Iran, few were trained to collect the tactical intelligence needed or support the mission when it began.

By 1979, the CIA's Directorate of Operations (DO), the team of men and women used overseas primarily to recruit agents, collect intelligence, and perform other clandestine tasks, was a shadow of its former self. Total personnel reductions of nearly 40% under the short tutelage of Director James Schlesinger, appointed by President Nixon, and then by President Carter's CIA director, Admiral Stansfield Turner, had decimated and demoralized the Agency. These actions bookended the Senate's Church Committee investigation and hearings that exposed operations and struck at the very core of the DO and the Agency as a whole. Those events, coupled with the seizure of the Embassy, left the CIA with few if any assets on the ground in Tehran or the country of Iran. The Agency was not operationally prepared to assist, but beyond that problem lay a distrust of the military. It would later become apparent that the CIA was withholding specific information that, if revealed, could have endangered those few assets it did have.

At the Pentagon, General James B. Vaught was selected to head up the mission's Joint Task Force. The planning phase, Operation RICE BOWL, began with a study of the mission requirements and selection of the forces needed. As the commander and the senior NCO of one of the only two certified US counterterrorism units, Colonel Olchovik and SGM Raker went back to the Pentagon to participate in the initial consultations with Special Operations Division for what would be called Joint Task Force 79 (JTF 79). Its top secret mission statement was simply stated but belied how difficult its goal would be:

> MISSION: Joint Task Force conducts Operations to rescue U.S. personnel held hostage in the American Embassy Compound, Tehran, Iran.[6]

The plan would be even more complex because Americans were being held in two locations—the Embassy Chancery compound and the Iranian Ministry of Foreign Affairs (MFA). It was also apparent the CIA would not provide adequate intelligence support. A CIA liaison officer told Raker at the time that the Agency was in contact with only one of its assets and they were unsure who actually was controlling him.[7]

DOD planners came to the conclusion that it would have to fill the deficit of ground intelligence assets itself. After scouring the DOD databases for Iranian-born military members, the search was expanded to consider other available assets. The fact that the Army would likely be doing much of its own intel work on the ground forced planners to look inward. Since the Detachment was already in the conversation, Olchovik was tasked to conduct the advanced reconnaissance of the targets. This was because the Det was the US military's only dual-capability unit having counterterrorism and unconventional warfare as its primary missions, and had the trained men to take on the job.

Then came the second mission for the Det. As the consultations progressed, Colonel Charlie Beckwith, who had remained at Fort Bragg with his unit, announced that SFOD-Delta could handle only the assault of the Embassy compound. He would need all of his 90 men to conduct that operation, which required the breaching of the compound's walls and the search of a number of buildings, all while securing the outside perimeter to counter any Iranian security force response. Delta simply did not have the manpower to take on the second target. As soon as those words were spoken Olchovik immediately pronounced: "We can handle it."[8]

With that, Detachment "A" would not only be involved in collecting the intelligence necessary for planning and assisting the assault forces' infiltration into Tehran, it would also rescue the three Americans at the Foreign Ministry. It would be a very busy winter.[9]

The US Chargé d'affaires Bruce Laingen and two other embassy officers, Victor Tomseth and Mike Howland, were being detained at the Foreign Ministry where they had had an appointment when the Embassy compound was stormed. Now they were "guests" of the Foreign Minister, who declined to let them depart.

Back in Berlin, SGM Raker began planning for the mission. Because of its location and the visibility of American military in the city, all preparations were conducted with operational security in mind. The first decision was that all training and exercise commitments would be unchanged and the teams participating would be kept intact. That meant the mission personnel would be chosen from the remaining, uncommitted teams. But before that challenge was undertaken, there was the question of who would go on the advance reconnaissance mission.

MG and Scotty

The man called the "Mad German" (MG) by his comrades was worried. He had been precipitously called back to Berlin from Berchtesgaden where he had been conducting alpine ski training with his team. He thought the recall must have something to do with his antics of the previous two days. He and Don, another unit member, had crashed a religious retreat of military wives that had been arranged by a general's wife.

It seemed like a good idea at the time. When the two soldiers found the meeting hall of the Hotel McNair set up for the event, the women had not yet arrived. The hotel was one of several US Armed

Forces recreation centers (AFRC) set up for the troops in southern Germany following WWII. It was also a haunt for Detachment members who came down from the mountain after a hard day of ski training on the slopes. It was a more "target rich" environment than the sedate *Gasthof Vorderbrand* on the mountain. They volunteered to serve drinks and Don secretly spiked the group's punch with a bottle of vodka that he smuggled into the event. Unfortunately, the ladies noticed that not only were they getting tipsy but the two young men serving them were notably unstable. The hotel manager unceremoniously banned them from the McNair and all other AFRC hotels in Berchtesgaden.

The next day, the ban was confirmed to be in effect when a waitress refused them a beer at another AFRC hotel. They then had to resort to German locales to quench their thirst.

Now it was day three and MG was winging his way back to Berlin wondering what his reception would be and a little curious as to why his partner in crime, Don, had not been recalled with him.

Coming out of the terminal, he was surprised to see SGM Raker waiting for him. MG sheepishly climbed into the car and waited for an ass chewing.

"So, how was ski training?" Raker asked.

Thinking he was being led into an ambush, he warily replied "Fine."

Then came something unexpected: no ass chewing.

"We're going to take a trip. You have enough time to repack your bags."

Raker had chosen MG and four other men from the unit to go to Frankfurt for a meeting. He revealed nothing about the nature of the trip, but it was fairly easy to surmise it was related to the US Embassy seizure. The men were taken to a secure facility and CIA officers subjected them to an intense set of interviews and reviews of their backgrounds.

The five had been chosen to meet the Agency's simple criteria, which was to select two men who could enter Iran with foreign documentation and survive scrutiny by hostile security forces. There was no time to train a candidate; they had to be able to support a foreign persona now. Raker had sixty good men to choose from and in the end chose soldiers who could be quickly prepared for the mission.

When the interviews were over, MG and John "Scotty" McEwan were selected; they would travel into Iran. The two could not be more different. Scotty was a wildly gregarious character who lived on the ragged edge of all that was prudent. MG on the other had a serious, calculating personality. He had two years on the ground in Vietnam in a Ranger company, served as a Ranger instructor, and was a high-altitude mountain rescue team member. Where MG sought out adrenaline, Scotty sought out fun. In military situations that translated to wanting to have MG at your "six" protecting your backside, while having Scotty out in front of you where you could keep him in sight. Now they would be dependent on each other on a very dangerous mission.

They were given lightly backstopped identities and cover stories with passports in new names. Before they left the facility, both were required to sign a secrecy agreement.

The situation in Tehran had disrupted the US's ability to collect information and the seizure of the Embassy by radicals presented a problem that was new and unexpected for the intelligence community. The military required precise information on the layout of the city, the US Embassy compound, and the MFA. This was tactical information that the CIA did not normally collect. Additionally, the State Department did not maintain detailed construction data on American facilities abroad at that time, so it did not exist. What was needed was classic targeting intelligence, all the information to plan a raid that would get the assault forces in and the hostages out safely. Moreover, the information was needed immediately.

In later years, this type of mission would be called "advance force operations" or AFO, but in 1979 it was simply an advance reconnaissance of the objective. What did the target look like, who was defending it, what enemy forces could come to the defenders' aid, and of course, where were the hostages located? There were many more questions that needed answering and the military commanders needed them sooner rather than later. Satellites could collect high-resolution imagery of the buildings and streets, but only a personal reconnaissance could show the ground truth. Special Forces training produced the kind of soldier needed to do the job and former Major Richard Meadows was one.

Meadows had been a highly decorated SF trooper and officer, and was now retired. He would infiltrate Iran and be on the ground when and if the mission went forward. Although Meadows had unparalleled combat experience, he was not trained in clandestine operations and he was not prepared to take this mission on alone.[10] That said, he had the courage to volunteer or, more accurately, insist that he be inside Tehran. He would be assisted by "Fred," an Iranian-born USAF sergeant who would act as his interpreter. But "Fred" was not trained for "clan work" either and that was where the Detachment's operators came in. Both MG and Scotty had the experience and, like most of the Detachment's operators, they were well suited for a task that went beyond collecting intelligence information; they had to be experts in special operations as well. There simply was no other unit in the US military or the intelligence community with personnel who could conduct that kind of mission.

Meadows, Scotty, and MG would also meet the assault force and get them to the targets. When the time came, the reception committee, code-named "Esquire" with Meadows in charge, would meet the force outside Tehran and bring them into the city. But that part of the plan had not yet been developed. Much work had to be done to determine exactly how to get into Tehran, into the building, and back out again with the hostages.

As the planning progressed, [Redacted], the Rangers, and the aviation component of the mission assembled and began to practice in the southwestern United States. The Detachment would conduct its training in Germany and join the main force later. There would be many changes to the assault force's configuration along the way, determined either by the intelligence received or more importantly the technical issues surrounding how the force would be inserted into the country.

It was also decided to rename the operation. Whereas RICE BOWL was deliberately chosen to imply an Asian target, the military wanted something more aggressive for the actual mission. The planners chose Operation EAGLE CLAW.

As MG and Scotty prepared for their first trip into Iran they pored over the available data on the two target sites, as well as everything they could find on the city itself. Street maps were studied to pick routes to any of the possible evacuation points the assault force would be required to use, including the main airport, parks, and stadiums. Bob Meadows had arrived in Frankfurt and began his work to put together a rudimentary cover. Luckily he had some good friends in the UK who helped backstop his legend. The men would travel into Tehran separately. They would stay in different hotels: Scotty at the Intercontinental, and MG at the Park. Journalists and businessmen favored the "Intercon," while the Park was hosting many of the new regime's elite.

It was late March 1980 before the team was given the go-ahead to fly out. Scotty and MG departed in early April from Frankfurt. Several days before their flight, they met one more time with a liaison officer from EUCOM, a USMC major, at a hotel near the airport. After reviewing the intelligence requirements, contact procedures, and emergency plans, the major told them there was one last bit of paperwork to be signed: a statement of understanding that the US Government would deny their activities if they were arrested or captured.

Both men were incredulous at the prospect of being hung out to dry by their government, but it was MG who now chose to be funny. As he handed the signed papers back to the liaison officer, MG told the officer, "You know we signed with a disappearing ink pen the Agency gave us."

MG later happily remembered, "You should have seen the look on the Jarhead's face."

Scotty and MG had authentic foreign passports, just in alias names. It was decided that the first step before they traveled would be to get valid visas from the Iranian Embassy in different countries, rather than count on obtaining one on arrival in Tehran. When MG arrived at the embassy, he found that a group of Iranian student protesters had occupied the lobby of the embassy and their protests were causing a disturbance. The Iranian diplomats were very uncomfortable with the students' presence, so MG decided he would ask a lot of questions about the protestors. His plan worked. The consul spent little time checking on his documents and after asking a few perfunctory questions, approved his visa. Then MG returned to Frankfurt with his new visa.

At the Pentagon, the overall operations plan came together. It was decided that the assault force would be transported by C-130 airplanes to a refuel site known as Desert One where the men would transfer to RH-53 helicopters flown in from the aircraft carrier USS *Nimitz*. They would continue on by helicopter alone to a laager site outside Tehran called Desert Two.[11] There the reception committee, Meadows, MG, and Scotty—along with three Iranian-Americans recruited to be translators and drivers—would meet them and transport the assault force into the city and directly to their targets.[12]

The Agency assigned one of its contractors to arrange the logistics on the ground. "Bob Plan" had served with both the OSS and the CIA and, following his retirement, he worked as a contract officer. He had the language and area knowledge to work in Iran and traveled there to acquire trucks and a Mercedes sedan, make sure they were operable, and find a warehouse to hide them in. The Agency also managed to bring in a HF radio transceiver that would be needed during the rescue phase of the mission itself. Bob succeeded, acquiring a warehouse on the southern edge of the city where he stored the vehicles and other equipment that would be needed by Meadows' reception committee.[13] The Mercedes would be crucial for the collection of necessary intelligence.

Once in country, MG and Scotty worked separately, coming together only occasionally at the Intercontinental in secluded, brief meetings to discuss what they had seen and what still needed to be covered. Along with details about Iranian security and the layout of the buildings and surrounding area, the two Berliners had to cover the primary and alternate routes from the warehouse to the targets and exfil points, as well as the route out to the location where they would meet the assault force.

Scotty covered the MFA in detail, surreptitiously taking pictures of the building, its entry points, and the security surrounding it. The team made 12 separate trips around the MFA and the Embassy and, at one point, Scotty entered the building, ostensibly to get forms for the export of Iranian goods, and was able to get a look at the interior layout of the ground floor. At the same time, MG was scouting the routes and collecting information on the security procedures at both sites. The planners wanted to know what defensive measures the forces would face during the initial assault and what backup the Iranians had available nearby. MG also shot videos of the Embassy, MFA and surrounding areas—the combination of photos, video, and maps reinforced the oral reports they would give back in Europe. It was the best intelligence the planners got.[14]

While the men spent a lot of time walking the city, the Mercedes was used to run the routes. It was important to understand timing, traffic patterns, and where navigation might be difficult at night; all things not easily seen while on foot.

The team departed separately from Iran one week after they arrived. Because of the tradecraft they employed, Scotty and MG were very confident they had not been linked together by the security forces. Returning to Frankfurt, each man was debriefed in detail while photographs were developed and maps annotated. All the information would be disseminated to the planners and the assault forces.

The Ground Force Prepares

Until General Vaught stood in front of the assembled JTF in an Egyptian aircraft hangar on April 23, 1980 and announced that President Carter had given his "Go," the plan was just that, a plan. It had yet to be approved by DOD and it had not been presented to the National Command Authority. This fact was important for a dual-mission unit like Det "A." While a pure CT unit could focus exclusively on the Iran mission, the Detachment had continuous obligations that came with its UW mission. One of those obligations was to support USAREUR's exercises, one of which was already on the calendar and would not go away.[15]

In the 1970s the Cold War was still on the minds of policy makers and the military. Massive exercises like REFORGER (Return of Forces to Germany) rehearsed the Allied plan to counter any Warsaw Pact aggression. In the special operations world, this contingency was practiced during FTX FLINTLOCK. Special operations forces from the US and other nations would jump, swim, and walk into simulated targets in Europe. It was a huge undertaking from a planning and logistics standpoint and one in which the Detachment traditionally played a large role.

But none of the men cared about that requirement once the Iran mission was known. Here was a mission reminiscent of Son Tay and no one wanted to miss out. No one spoke of risk or danger even though it was clearly a risky and dangerous undertaking. If it hadn't been, no one would have clamored to go, just the opposite.

In the spring of 1980, one half of the unit's "A" Teams were committed to FLINTLOCK, just when the commander and SGM needed to be able to look at every team member it had for possible deployment. Significantly, Teams One, Three, and Five were dedicated to the exercise that would take place in southern Germany in 1980 and, to avoid raising any suspicions, the SGM decided he would not make any changes to the roster.

The sole task other than FLINTLOCK that could pull members was the intelligence collection mission, for which MG and Scotty were already committed. Members of the Foreign Ministry assault element would be selected from members of the remaining teams: Teams Two, Four and Six.

This caused significant consternation among those who were tasked to support FLINTLOCK, especially as it became more and more apparent that EAGLE CLAW would actually happen. For once, no one wanted to participate in a four-week exercise and total immersion in Bavarian and Swabian culture. The dilemma was further exacerbated by the simple fact that the odd number teams had some of the most experienced personnel. Membership of Team One was almost wholly predicated on Vietnam service and most of the team had not only been SF in Vietnam, but in the Special Operations groups like Command and Control North (CCN). Team Five was also one of the better teams and had coalesced into a younger version of Team One with a highly effective team sergeant and team members. Team Three, the SCUBA team, also had strong members who wanted in on the Iran mission. It finally came down to the fact that the Det leadership knew the exercise was a sure thing, but they didn't know if the Iran contingency members would ever leave the city, never mind actually go to Iran.

With many factors up in the air it became a difficult task to select a team for possible Iran deployment. Both Teams Two and Four had lost one man to the advance team and Team Six was short due to recent rotations out of the unit. Early in the internal planning cycle it became apparent that the team which would be sent down range would be an ad hoc element put together from whoever was available. How would the team be selected?

Who would command the element was the easiest call, since Army leadership decided that Colonel Olchovik would lead the Detachment "A" effort. Early on, it was decided that there would be no medics on the team, due to constraints on the number of personnel who could go forward and the presence of medical personnel within other ground elements. This further restricted potential membership in the Det's Iran effort by about six, the two medics from Teams Two, Four, and Six now effectively out of the running. Probably one of the most important decisions on team composition was that of who would be the assault force senior NCO. The detachment had no shortage of strong leaders in this area, especially in the master sergeant and sergeant first class ranks. For Raker and Olchovik it was imperative that this NCO would be one who could efficiently mold this element into an effective team and train it to go forward. The criteria came down to a soldier with least one, if not more Southeast Asia tours under their belts and with special project experience as well. Team One's "Corky" Shelton was chosen as the assault force team sergeant.

For the rest of the team, different members were selected in diverse ways.[16] A two-week CQB course and shoot-off competition was held with the top finishers being assured of potential Iran team slots. The only problem was that the top two finishers in this contest, Sergeants "Styk" and Jon, were both from Team Five, which, because of FLINTLOCK, put them out of the running. When they were excluded, the number three finisher from Team Six, Stu, an engineer, was chosen as one of the members who would leave Berlin for Iran.

The final assemblage was diverse. Nine men would eventually make the mission and they included one member from Team One, "Corky" Shelton the lead NCO, two members from Teams Four and Six and three from Team Two. By specialty, most of the team members were weapons sergeants along with only two engineers. Of these, two had not served in Vietnam, but every member was a volunteer.

Although men had been selected, the mission timeline was extremely vague; no one knew when actual deployment might take place. This necessitated everything to be readied quickly. All the equipment was off-the-shelf from Det "A" or Berlin Brigade supplies and the training schedule was, at best, fluid. The advantage the new element had was that all the skills needed for success were ones in which the element members were very proficient: moving, shooting, communicating, breaching, room clearing, rappelling, and driving were second nature to all of them.

In early March, members of the element were assembled in the Detachment's conference room and informed of their selection. From that point onward that room would be the planning area for the rescue. Their mission was outlined: the successful liberation of the three Embassy staff from the Iranian Foreign Ministry and movement to the soccer stadium near the US Embassy where they would meet the [Redacted] main contingent for exfiltration. The three men had been held at the Foreign Ministry since November 4; their conditions of confinement were significantly different from those at the Embassy, but they were prisoners nonetheless. The team members were also informed that they did not have to worry about how they would get into Iran or Tehran, or for that matter how they would get out of the country. Their focus should only be on cracking the Foreign Ministry nut.

The first decision that had to be made was how to actually get the three Americans out of the Foreign Ministry (which was conveniently located across the street from a police station), and then to the soccer stadium where they would link up with the hostages from the Embassy. The entire group would then be picked up by helicopter to Manzariyeh air base, which was to be seized by a Ranger company. The question of the hostages' location was solved very simply. US Chargé Laingen was able to send letters and talk on the telephone, both with local diplomats in Tehran and with the State Department in Washington DC since they had only been "detained" and not taken hostage. He and his two comrades managed to send very good details about the room they were in as well as the security situation in the areas near them. After exploring options of storming the building by air and rappelling from the roof, the team's final plan was also the simplest.

The team would drive up to the Foreign Ministry, get out of the vehicle, walk into the building and take the hostages out. The feeling at the time was that the element of surprise would give the team enough of an advantage to get to the hostages before their captors could react or have a significant advantage in firepower. If the team didn't achieve surprise, their estimation was that they would be screwed anyway. Early into the planning process a crate arrived from the US that contained a detailed mock-up of the target area surrounding the Foreign Ministry.

But until MG and Scotty were debriefed, there was a dearth of information on the physical layout of the MFA and the activity around it. To effectively plan its mission, the team needed to know how many people worked in the building, how many security officers were on site, and how they secured the facility. They also needed information on how many men were assigned to the police station across the street and how they were armed.

The lack of intel support could be attributed to two primary factors, distance and separation. Any classified information going to Berlin had to be telexed to the Berlin Headquarters or sent by courier. Throughout the planning phase most of the information came from Detachment leadership after each trip made to the Pentagon or Patch Barracks in Stuttgart, the location of SOTFE. In the days prior to digital secure communications, that meant long transmission times or a reluctance to send information through personnel who were not authorized to see it, even if they had the proper security clearances. The rescue mission planning was classified at the very highest level.

The second factor was that the Detachment was located far from the other participants. For operational security reasons, it was decided that the Det would not participate in any of the full rehearsals with the other units. The majority of the Det's men only met their teammates from other units when they arrived in Egypt, less than a week before launching into Iran.

These factors contributed to a large extent to the disjointed situation in which the team members found themselves. The intelligence information received from the advance team helped enormously, and the unit was able to prepare and train prior to arriving in Egypt but they were largely unaware of the other units' plans. Although this isolation would not materially affect the unit's performance, it was a factor that would be highlighted in the Holloway Commission report after the failure of the mission.[17]

Within this isolated environment the unit worked each day, and later and later into the night. First, the team had to formulate a way to get the three Americans out of the Foreign Ministry and to the stadium. Corky Shelton led this effort while the commander and SGM Raker were devoting much of their time in Stuttgart and the US working with other unit leaders and planners. By early April, the force received the first reports from the advance team and knew the ground situation a little better. Scotty and MG had obtained good information on the MFA's layout, local security forces, and the surrounding area. It was enough to make a plan. About the same time, the CIA unexpectedly came up with a large amount of intelligence on the Embassy compound that they attributed to a Pakistani cook who worked at the Embassy and had recently left Iran.[18] The Agency had little new information on the MFA, but communications from the diplomats held there had already enabled the team to pinpoint their location. That intelligence as well as the information collected by Scotty and MG were critical to the Detachment's final operational plan.

About April 10, the teams participating in FLINTLOCK regretfully departed Berlin, leaving behind the force preparing for an uncertain mission launch. Despite last-minute pleas to the SGM, there were no changes to the roster. Those men not on the mission would hear about the mission's outcome along with the general public through news reports in southern Germany on the morning of April 25.

The team decided that the assault on the Foreign Ministry would be straightforward and direct. The team would approach in their vehicle and stop adjacent to a gate on the side of the Foreign Ministry nearest to where the hostages were held. Two men would approach the lightly guarded gate as if to ask directions and then neutralize the guards with sound-suppressed pistols. Then four men, led by Colonel Olchovik, would follow and enter the building on foot. They would secure the hostages on the third floor. If necessary, breaching charges would be carried for use on secured entry points. Two men would stay with the vehicles as a security element to put fire onto the nearby police building and into any response force as necessary. This contingency was necessary because the Iranian Army Officers' Club was across the street from the MFA and there was a building at the end of the street that housed elements of the National Police. Two threats, two men to counter them—no problem.

The entire plan relied on surprise, speed, and violence of action. Once the hostages were secured, the team would get out of the building and head off across town to the soccer stadium where they would link up with the main force and the Embassy hostages for a helicopter exfil to the airport. The plan was simple and also contingent on the fact that they would not be met by a large force guarding the Ministry. Nine men with small arms would not want to encounter a larger, better equipped force. One of the few pieces of good news the Berliners got before departing the city was that Iranian security forces at the MFA were few in number, inexperienced, and lightly armed. They also knew the exact location inside the MFA where hostages were detained.

For everyone who was aware of the mission, waiting was the hardest part. At the end of each duty day, after the team members planned, rehearsed, fine-tuned their tasks, and worked on their equipment, they would either return to their barracks rooms or to their residences not knowing when or even if the mission would go ahead. Many leaders, from the National Command Authority (NCA) on down, were betting the mission would not happen. Many felt that President Carter would never approve the operation and that the plan was just a contingency in case the "students" started killing the hostages.

As April progressed, issues within Iran itself seemed to be coming to a head with more talk of trials or tribunals for the hostages coming from the Revolutionary leadership. Each day in the Detachment the team would depart for the evening and joke about how many minutes of sleep they would get that night.

Then, late in the second week of April 1980, Colonel Olchovik returned from Washington after meeting with General Vaught, the JTF commander. He assembled what remained of the unit in the third-floor hallway for an announcement. He and Raker came up the stairs, stood in front of the group, and announced that the Iran team would be going forward to their jump-off point. The mission was a "Go"—at least in part. The element didn't know if they would be going to Iran, but they were sure as hell leaving Berlin. One or two adult beverages may have been consumed that evening in the "Speak Easy" bar across the street from the Det's home at Andrews Barracks.

CJCS had only approved the final plan in early April. On April 12, the JTF commander was instructed to prepare for deployment forward. The planners determined the mission needed to take place before May as the increasing heat would affect helicopter performance. Additionally, the flight plan required eight hours of darkness. The nights were currently only nine hours and getting shorter. D-Day was set for April 24 and the execute order was issued on April 17, 1980, which triggered the move forward to Egypt.

On April 19, the Detachment's Iran team drove to the US Air Force base at Tempelhof airport. As the team moved though the city traffic in the Det's civilian vans, each member went through mental checklists ensuring that he had each item needed. While most were sure that they had forgotten some essential item, in most cases they probably hadn't. The list was short: weapons, ammunition, more weapons and ammunition, and a blade. Each member had either a Walther MPK or an M-16 with as many loaded magazines as he could carry; at least one pistol, a suppressed Hi-Standard HDM .22 caliber pistol as well as at least one knife. The Detachment also carried special "lock eating" tools—the product of some engineer's twisted mind. The devices looked like a flare pistol and used a stream of burning thermite to cut through hardened steel locks and hinges in seconds—quite useful for opening recalcitrant doors.

The team didn't plan to carry big rucksacks or a lot of food or water, they were prepared for one night's work in Tehran and little else.

Arriving at Tempelhof, the team waited in the military lounge for their ride. It would be a C-130 aircraft that would take them all the way to Egypt; the same aircraft would transport them to Iran. When the Hercules arrived, the crew got off and went into the terminal to file their flight plan and get some coffee as the Detachment's men moved to the aircraft. Depositing their gear on the tailgate of the aircraft the team members loitered near the front of the bird. Then on the spur of the moment, someone decided to gather the team for a photograph to mark the occasion. The photo shows nine men in front of the camouflaged aircraft. They are of various ages with haircuts that don't look quite military and dressed in olive-green coveralls. Although most are smiling, they may have had something else on their minds.

The Second Insert

Between April 17 and 19, MG and Scotty returned individually to Iran. Their job had changed from collecting intelligence and preparing for the mission to receiving the assault forces and moving them to the targets: the Embassy compound and the MFA. The stakes were much higher as they now had the responsibility for getting 100 men into the city without being detected. They were joined by Dick Meadows during this, the execution phase of the mission. Meadows would stay at the Arya-Sheraton.

MG had to first obtain another visa to return to Tehran. This time he went to the Iranian Embassy in Geneva, Switzerland. Arriving at 0900 and presenting his paperwork, he proceeded to cool his heels for three hours. At noon, seeing the Embassy was preparing to close for lunch, MG decided it was time for "Hermann," his evil twin, to show up. He knocked on the glass of the visa office until a different official showed up and demanded to know why he had been ignored for so long. The Iranian apologized and said that MG had been forgotten and scurried off to get the documents. He returned in short order with a properly stamped passport. MG had the feeling the Iranians were thoroughly checking his background, but the fact that it withstood their scrutiny gave him confidence to travel.

Once back in Tehran, they had five days to recheck all the sites and travel the routes to make sure their plans would still work. Meadows got up to speed on the routes to the laager site (Desert Two) from town and the routes to the Embassy compound as he would lead the main force to their target. Scotty and MG force-fed Meadows as much information as he could absorb.

One small mistake nearly upset their plan.

MG was driving the route towards the Embassy with Scotty in the front seat. Meadows was in the back taking the scenery in. Scotty had previously walked, not driven, this particular route while Dick and MG took a drive out to Desert Two and the warehouse. As they drove, Scotty was giving directions and told MG to turn a corner. MG suddenly realized he was in a bus and taxi lane, but the barriers prevented him from leaving it. The only breaks in the barriers were at intersections. MG inched forward in traffic hoping to reach the next intersection but it was taking an interminable amount of time. As the minutes ticked by, MG was not feeling very positive about the situation. Finally, the intersection came into view but his relief was very short lived, as several groups of Iranian policemen were standing on every corner of the intersection. A quick count of about 20 cops made them realize that this might not be their day. They briefly regained hope that they would escape their scrutiny when a car in front of them, which was also in the wrong lane, was waved on by the closest cop.

That relief did not last long as they were waved over to the curb. MG rolled down his window and the cop demanded in broken English to see his driver's license and passport. Confidently, he reached behind the seat, searching for the familiar feel of his leather briefcase that contained all his documents. All he came up with was Meadows' legs and, slightly irritated, MG asked him to pass the case forward. While waiting for him to hand the case over, MG looked into the mirror and noticed Meadows' expression had changed from his usually very confident look to suddenly very worried. Meadows spoke in a hushed voice so the cop would not be able to hear, whispering that he moved the briefcase to the trunk in order to have more room in the back seat.

Still unsure why that would be much of a problem, MG told Meadows that he would hop out and retrieve it from the trunk. In a barely audible voice Meadows followed up with, "Be careful, the radio is unconcealed in the trunk. The case is on top on the right side."

MG now knew that he would have to play the role of his life for the next few minutes or Raker's prediction of him hanging from a lamppost in Tehran if caught would come true. MG's response to Raker had been "*Unkraut vergeht nicht*" (I'm hard to kill). Now he would find out for sure.

While getting out of the car, MG's evil twin took over once more and he let the cop have it. Speaking mostly in German with a smattering of broken English, his voice got louder and louder to the point of almost shouting. Knowing that the officer had about 19 other cops to back him up, MG did not push too hard. The policeman reciprocated as he looked right in MG's face with such disdain that MG expected to be slugged any minute. His eyes did not leave MG's face and that was exactly what MG needed him to do. With a fast hand movement that would have made Houdini proud, MG opened the trunk just enough to pull out the briefcase and prevented the police from casting a detailed look into the trunk. While this intermezzo took place, another, more senior cop stepped up to the vehicle and told the first cop to step back on the sidewalk.

It seemed he felt embarrassed that the younger cop had raised so much commotion and felt the need to intercede. The veteran cop took the situation in hand and, sensing the change in the situation, MG immediately calmed down and became submissive to the new authority. The new policeman said that driving in this lane was a minor traffic offense and a traffic citation would be issued, which could be paid before departing Iran. They all apologized profusely. With the violation in hand and Scotty shouting out the lowered side window, "Khomeini is great!" with a raised fist for emphasis, they departed the area as quickly as possible.

While Meadows was mostly silent and breathing deep with relief, MG continued to vent by chewing Scotty's ass for the unnecessary screw up. Meadows knew that his actions, although small and unintended, had almost caused the mission to end right there and then. He apologized in his own way, by stating that when they were stopped, he literally froze and was unable to think properly. He sheepishly admitted his only solution was to shoot his way out of the situation—fortunately, there were no weapons available and far too many cops. Meadows commended MG on his training for such situations. MG responded: "There's always more than one way to skin a cat."[19]

A day before the mission was to begin, Meadows had to solve a small problem at the warehouse. A work crew had dug a cable trench along the street that blocked the building's doors. He solved the problem by paying a work crew of young men to fill it in so the trucks could get out.

He worried the ditch was a deliberate effort to block the warehouse, but then realized the ditch blocked more doors than just his.

The team was satisfied with their preparations and, on April 24, the three Iranian drivers were picked up and brought to the warehouse. Meadows and the drivers piled into the trucks and started out. The drivers knew the route only to the edge of the city where they would pick up MG and Scotty. Thereafter, only the three Americans knew the entire route out of the city and their final destination for that night.

Scotty and MG left their hotels about the same time and linked up, MG picking Scotty up as he drove the Mercedes. They headed to the city's southern district and parked the car near where they were to meet the trucks and waited. When Meadows and his convoy approached, MG hopped in the cab of the second, and Scotty into the cab of the third truck for the drive to the rendezvous point (RV) where they were to wait for the arrival of the assault force. The three trucks headed southeast out of town for about an hour until they turned off the main road and went cross-country on a rough desert track.

MG later remembered the driver of his truck smoked so much that he was forced to keep his head outside the window to avoid being overcome by the fumes. The driver did have terminal cancer, which was the reason he had volunteered to go on the mission in the first place. MG was sure he would be next to get the disease.

Finally, the trucks arrived near the RV location and were parked in a concealed fold of the hillside. The drivers remained with their vehicles, while Meadows, Scotty, and MG climbed the hill with their equipment to the plateau above them. After a nearly hour-long trek, they crested the edge of the plateau and began to set up.

This was the laager site known as Desert Two. Once the assault force, the [Redacted] and Detachment operators, arrived at Desert One by C-130 and transferred to the refueled helicopters from the USS *Nimitz*, they would fly to Desert Two and then move by truck into Tehran to their respective targets. The three Americans of the advance team would guide them first to the trucks and then into town.

Meadows set up the SATCOM radio and tested it briefly before turning it off. He would turn it back on just before the C-130s launched from Egypt. He then told MG and Scotty that it would be a while before the assault elements arrived. MG said he would go to sleep and to wake him up when they were inbound. Meadows was a bit non-plussed saying excitedly, "We're making history here, we're part of a big historical event." MG rolled over and went to sleep.

The plateau was an ideal landing zone for the helicopters and, because it was slightly lower in the center, the helicopters could not be seen from below. From the top of the hill it was only a few minutes' flight into the city. The plateau was quiet, the night sky replete with a blanket of stars and the Milky Way twinkling above. To the south, the heavens were not as calm.

From Egypt to Desert One

The Det team arrived in Egypt in the early evening of April 19, landing at Wadi Kena, a former Russian airbase with its attendant bunkers and hangars. It reeked of burned and burning kerosene. Colonel Beckwith greeted Colonel Olchovik and his team with a beer. The team members were shown to their assigned area and told to stow their gear and to get chow in the main hangar where the entire force was gathered. The main area was large and covered. As team members filed in they saw well over a hundred other men from a variety of military services milling around. Each unit had set up shop in their own section of the hangar. Placed around the hangar there were barrels filled with ice containing cold beverages. Each of the Berliners grabbed some food and something to drink, in some cases meeting old friends who had wound up in other SpecOps units. The unit members were brought up to speed on the mission, most of the participating units were in Egypt and a few more entities would soon arrive. Everyone was waiting for the elusive "word" as to whether the mission would be a go or not. Even at this point in Egypt with most of the current SpecOps community in attendance, there was still healthy speculation about whether the President would give the final go-ahead. As everyone was in Egypt, it was felt that a decision would have to be made soon. The units could only be on the ground here for so long before either the Russians spotted them from space—during certain periods of the day, everyone had to be inside while the Russian satellite flew over. HUMINT or SIGINT would probably reveal the Americans' presence eventually as well. Further, with so many Special Forces assets absent from their home stations, it would not take an analyst or even a journalist long to figure out that there was something afoot. Despite all the precautions taken, each day spent on the ground in Egypt added to the mission's OPSEC vulnerability.

As soon as they got settled, the Det's leadership went to work with other unit commanders to iron out the final details. Since the unit had not been involved in mission rehearsals and had only leadership-level involvement in planning there was a lot to do.

The gathered forces were impressive and many old friends found each other. A Ranger company—C Company, 1st Battalion, 75th Ranger Regiment—showed up, its commander Captain David Grange had attended Ranger school with the Det "A" Team's radio operator, "OC." Grange was taken aback when he saw OC's long hair and asked when he had joined the CIA![20]

While each element went over final details, the Det team conferred with their guardian angel, the AC-130H "Spectre" crew that would fly overhead to provide covering fire. The officers' club and the Police building were discussed as potential threats, especially as the Police were known to have at least two Cadillac Gage V-100 armored cars. The Spectre pilot said "Not to worry," he could hit "a bug in the butt" if need be. It was comforting to know the firepower would be above them.[21]

The final intelligence reports from the team on the ground were integrated into the plan while everyone impatiently awaited the "Go" order. Finally, two days before the actual launch, word came down, but not the word anyone wanted.

Corky Shelton brought the two engineers, Brad and Stu, together and sat them down; both knew that it was not likely to be good news. Over the past days, the conversation had been about weight, specifically that there was too much for the aircraft. The Berliners had been told to worry about their portion of the mission and not to concern themselves with the larger mission; the larger mission was now going to intrude.

The basic plan was still the same: fixed-wing assets (C-130s) would depart Egypt carrying the ground elements and land at a site called Desert One. There they would marry up with rotary-wing assets from the Navy, RH-53Ds, one of the few active birds that could make the long-distance flight into Iran. The birds would launch from the USS *Nimitz* in the Gulf. Because the helicopters couldn't refuel in flight, they would be required to land and take on fuel before proceeding on to Desert Two, where they would RON and then move out the next night to Tehran to complete the mission.

Overall confidence in the Navy helos and their Marine pilots was not very high. The helos had maintenance issues and the pilots had not successfully completed a practice run of the mission profile. Simply put, the commanders weren't sure that the Navy birds would all still start after arriving at Desert Two or the next night for the exfiltration of the two assault teams out of Tehran to complete the mission. The lack of confidence led the senior leadership on the ground in Egypt to pare down the overall mission weight to accommodate a smaller number of helos that would be expected to make the whole two-day evolution. Everyone expected two to three of the helicopters to fail.

This resulted in the Det "A" Team being whittled down to seven persons going forward from Desert One and the two engineers would not be among that number. Instead, they would be part of the road team at the first landing site. The Berliners were divided up into two teams, those in the assault element and two in the road team. The separation would happen after Desert One, when the two engineers would return with the C-130s to Egypt and the rest of the team would go forward to Desert Two.

The Detachment's job at the Foreign Ministry would be carried out differently than at the Embassy. Whereas Delta planned on going in full bore with an all-out assault to quickly take out the defenders, Olchovik's final plan, though daring, would be relatively low key. Olchovik's final plan, though daring, was low key. The team's VW van would stop on the street adjacent to the gate. Two men, map in hand, would approach the guards as if to ask a question and then eliminate them with suppressed pistols. The team would then extract the Americans and head off to the RV point to meet up with the other troopers for the helo exfiltration to the airport. Breaching tools would be carried to open any locked gates or doors met along the way. It was a simple plan that would rely on surprise, speed, and violence of action for its success.

Later that day all the men were asked to gather in the main hangar for an announcement. When everyone saw General Vaught standing on a makeshift stage to address them, they knew they were going to Iran.

There was one final twist to the planning. Someone, probably a staff officer, decided that it would be a good idea to parachute two men into Desert One the night before the main force arrived to act as pathfinders and to provide intelligence on the local situation. It would be a High Altitude-Low Opening (HALO) free-fall drop and naturally, Brad and Stu volunteered for the mission, this despite the fact that neither was HALO qualified. "No matter," Stu thought, "a quick training session and a prayer and all would be good." Providentially perhaps, a more senior officer got wind of the plan's existence and strangled it in the crib after only a few hours of life.

On April 24 all of the men assembled to hear a last brief by General Vaught and then moved to the aircraft. The hostages had been taken on November 4 and now the US was going to get them back. The Det "A" Team would again split up, the assault element would go on one of the first birds, while Stu and Brad would arrive at Desert One on one of the fuel birds.

When they heard that they would be spending the trip riding on a fuel bladder on an aircraft overloaded by about 10,000 pounds beyond its wartime max weight, they were less than thrilled. En route to Iran, all the aircraft stopped in Oman for fuel. While sitting on the runway in Oman, their aircraft was waiting to takeoff when another nearly collided with it. Everyone laughed nervously and silently thanked God that they had averted a potential disaster before they even arrived in Tehran.

The scene at Desert One could only be described as chaotic.

The road team was on the first bird in and immediately deployed to provide security for the landing site. A perhaps overzealous Ranger decided that a truck racing through the area could best be stopped with a LAW rocket. Unfortunately, the truck turned out to be a fuel tanker and exploded. Its driver bailed out of the burning vehicle and made Olympic time to escape in a following vehicle. Then a bus filled with Iranian peasants, students, and other travelers rolled onto the scene and was detained by the road team. A hulking Ranger with a M-60 machine gun stood guard over the terrified passengers.

It was originally envisioned that the fixed-wing aircraft (the C-130s) were to park on one side of the unpaved road with the rotary-wing birds on the other side. Instead of an orderly fuel and personnel transfer point, the planes were parked at odd angles off the road, without much order and certainly not the clean lines envisioned by the planners.

On top of this, the Iranians on the bus watched all that unfolded as the fuel truck, still burning with flames reaching 60 feet in the air, fully illuminated the scene. It was a very dicey moment.

While Stu and Brad were with the road team, the MFA assault team waited behind their aircraft. They had unloaded the camouflage netting that would be used to conceal the helicopters at the laager site; personal gear came off last. As the helicopters were refueled, most of the pilots insisted that their passengers offload.

There was a lot of waiting. There needed to be at least six operational helos to go forward and what was thought to be the sixth operational rotary-wing asset wouldn't arrive until nearly 0300 local. If all the helos left at that moment, they would arrive at the laager site in broad daylight. The feeling among many of those present was that at least one or two Iranians might notice six US Navy RH-53s flying in formation over their country.

Through the early morning hours, the RH-53s were way behind schedule as they struggled through a *Haboob*—a huge dust storm—and the loss of two of the birds. One sat down in the desert and was abandoned because of a mechanical failure while another turned back to the aircraft carrier after becoming lost. At Desert One, the men were unaware they were already down to six birds and the departure time for the night flight to the next stop had already passed.

Nevertheless, the operators gathered their gear and awaited orders to load. When the final Navy bird set down there were six operational helos ready to move forward, exactly the number needed for mission continuation. But that quickly fell apart, when the pilot announced the last bird wasn't mission capable. Now there were only five helos and six was the hard number needed to go forward. The leadership group on the ground, Air Force Colonel James Kyle, Army Colonels Beckwith and Olchovik, and Marine Lieutenant Colonel Ed Sieffert came together to discuss the deteriorating situation. While the conclave was going on, the operators continued to load and check their gear. They would get another order once the meeting was concluded.

The situation was confused and the scattered disposition of the aircraft compounded the problem. Men were in scattered pockets around the C-130s waiting as the helos that showed up were fueled and made ready for loading for the onward flight. Orders had to be literally run by couriers between the different knots of soldiers and aircrew. Soon after the arrival of the final helicopter, instruction was passed to load, but that order was given before the leadership group had decided the fate of the mission.

Then it came, the order filtered out to unload the helos and reload the C-130s. It was a surprise for most and simply a shock to many. The leaders had met, discussed the situation and spoken to Washington and the President. The decision had been made in concert with the NCA: the mission would be scrubbed for at least that night.

For most on the ground, the reason for the postponement was not clear and everyone felt the air go out of their sails—the disappointment was palpable. The men moved their gear back to fixed-wing aircraft and boarded the camouflaged birds to leave. One final hurdle had to be overcome, it was necessary to move the now non-critical rotary-wing craft so the C-130s could head back to Egypt, but at least they would be lighter now that the majority of the fuel they carried had been pumped into the tanks of the "53"s.

This stage was relatively easy for the Detachment men; they only had their weapons, ammo and themselves to get onto the aircraft, whereas the other outfit had ladders and heavy breaching charges to load. As the helicopters began to move out of the way, most of the assault force operators were standing clear of the aircraft and watched the disaster unfolded. A RH-53 was given the signal to lift off and shift position.

As its engines increased power, the dust kicked up by the helo's rotor wash obscured all vision. Inside the aircraft, the pilot lost all his reference points. The helicopter slid out of its hover position and slowly drifted into a C-130 parked to its front.

A huge shower of sparks kicked up as the rotors tore into the airplane just behind the cockpit. For many, the first sign of trouble was the sound, a loud "whump" that reverberated through the area. Some would later say that it sounded like the area was taking mortar fire.

After the collision, disorder reigned for several minutes. Everyone had been complaining about standing outside in the cold night, but now they were thankful the pilot had made them get off the aircraft. Ironically, the only pilot that hadn't insisted was the pilot of the aircraft that was struck, but most of the men were able to exit the aircraft and calmly moved away from the danger. Many of the operators assisted the aircrew who had been injured off the two birds. Two soldiers would later receive Soldier's Medals for their bravery, entering the burning C-130 to pull injured crewmen out of the inferno.

The C-130s immediately began to taxi away from the flames, leaving some of the assault force to wonder if they were being left behind. Corky and OC were standing together wondering what was going to happen next. Corky said something about being stuck in Iran and began to calculate how much ammunition they had if it came to a shootout. Corky looked at OC and in his best bad imitation of Butch Cassidy said, "Those 'MFs' are in a lot of trouble." The tension evaporated.

By this time the commander decided that the area had to be cleared immediately. The C-130 set up to reload and, after a final check for missing personnel was made, started to move for take-off. There was no attempt to destroy the helicopters left at the site, despite the fact that weapons, explosives, money, and documents were left on board. It was a fateful decision.

With the last plane sitting at the end of the strip preparing for take-off, Brad Cooper realized there might be an issue—the crew apparently didn't realize there were still men on the ground as no headcount had been taken. Cooper directed a Ranger to drive his bike in front of the airplane so he could signal the pilot to hold in place. Some frantic arm waving got the pilot to bring his engines back to an idle. Cooper went to the back of the plane and met the Air Force loadmaster and told him others would be streaming in. They did and the plane went from having a few passengers to about forty when it lifted off.

Now sure the last man had been accounted for, the final C-130 took off. The excitement wasn't over, however, as the plane slammed into a low sand wall as it was lifting off. Although the plane continued to climb, rumors swirled through the aircraft that they would have to ditch in the water, but thankfully it was able to continue and made the trip to Oman without further problem.

The wounded were discharged and the aircraft again took off for Egypt. Whereas the aircraft had been filled with the painful sounds of the wounded before, now they were shrouded in quiet. Just the constant drone of the four engines reminded them they were in the air. Air Force crew, Marines, and Army were intermingled on the flight back, no one spoke a word.

As the aircraft landed back at the base, the men filed quietly off the aircraft and into the main hangar. General Vaught met them and once again spoke to the assemblage of mentally and physically exhausted troopers. This time he had a much different message—he thanked them for their efforts but signaled the mission had failed. When Beckwith spoke he was overcome with emotion and his full frustration and anger was vented on the troops. He would later apologize, but it signified the stress and forlorn hope the entire contingent was experiencing.

About the same time, two boxes were delivered from some British airman who were present at the base. They had put two and two together and decided to send some cold beer over to the men with a note. It said simply: "To you all, from us all, for having the guts to try."[22]

For the next two days, the Berliners loitered around the Egyptian base talking to their comrades, but still not really saying all that much. They were really just waiting for a ride back to the city. The other units split off and flew back to Florida and Ft Bragg. The Marines went back to their bases. The Berliners had the shortest commute, and would head back to Ramstein, Germany in one flight leg with a C-141. There they waited for another airplane to take them home. After several hours, a C-130 landed and the pilot and crew got off to meet their passengers. The pilot was a one-star Air Force general and his co-pilot a full colonel, while the enlisted crewmen were all senior master sergeants. It seemed the squadron's entire senior leadership volunteered to fly the team home that night.

As the plane droned through the sky, Brad was on the ramp smoking a cigarette, sitting on a box. A crewman came back to make small talk and asked him what the brightly painted red box was for. Brad looked at him with a deadpan expression and calmly said "Explosives." The crewman decided it was a bad idea for Brad to sit in that particular spot and smoke.

The flight back to the city was otherwise quiet and the men landed at Tempelhof in the middle of night, which was unusual as the airfield was normally closed. The Air Force made an exception. The unit's XO, Major Wise, was waiting for the team and everyone loaded into the same vans that had brought them to the airfield just 10 days earlier. There was a cooler of beer and everyone popped one open for the ride home. Back at the unit, they stowed weapons and inventoried equipment, figuring out just exactly what had been inadvertently left in the Iranian desert. The Iran team were greeted with questions from those who had stayed behind, but not too many and in hushed tones.

Two days later, the team met with Colonel Olchovik and were debriefed. They were given a week off and most spent the next several days in various states of inebriation, trying to get the smell of burning flesh out of their nostrils.

Desert Two and Escape

The "Esquire" team was on top of their plateau waiting to receive the helos, fully unaware of the disaster at Desert One, 270 miles away. They just knew the mission was way behind schedule.

Finally, a call came through on the radio but reception was poor and all the men heard was that the mission was postponed, not that it had been called off. They packed up their gear, headed back to Tehran, and parked the trucks in the warehouse before splitting up and returning to their hotels and some welcome rest. They were prepared to repeat the routine the following night, but were unaware that they were in extreme danger. Now, they were really on their own.

The next morning, MG was up and getting ready for the day ahead. He turned on his shortwave travel radio and was listening to *Deutsche Welle*, the German overseas news channel. Remembering the moment very clearly years later, he said "I almost cut my throat shaving when I heard that President Carter had announced the failure of the rescue mission that morning. I knew we all were in serious trouble."

The broadcast was quickly translated into Farsi and transmitted out over Iran's airwaves. All hell broke loose in Tehran. Thousands poured into the streets as the Great Satan's defeat was announced, in spite of the fact that no one had known Americans were anywhere near Iran before Carter's announcement. The situation was now potentially deadly for the team, as it would only be a matter of time before the local security forces put together a picture of what had happened and, worse yet, recovered papers from the site that detailed the plan. That information included the location of the warehouse and radio call sign cards that showed a reception team was inside the country. MG did not know the extent of the compromise but assumed the worse and realized they would have to get out of the country soon.

MG got his gear together but left it in his room and went to find Meadows at the Arya-Sheraton. He emerged from his hotel to find the streets filling quickly with men shouting slogans, fists raised to the sky. He decided to walk and moved out along the crowded streets. At times, he was caught up in the crowds and found himself the subject of some very hostile stares until he too raised his fist and shouted along with them.

It was a tense hour to walk the route and he felt only slightly safer once he was inside the Sheraton. Scotty was already there, sitting with Meadows in a secluded part of the hotel. There were many journalists and other foreigners nervously listening to the crowds outside, who showed no special interest in the hotel. The Iranians had never interfered with them before and seemed to see this particular group of foreigners as harmless. It would be the Iranian Revolutionary Guards who would begin searching for the Americans when and if they put the clues together. For the moment, they were safe.

The team was dismayed. They had been abandoned without any notification of the mission cancellation or the President's announcement. Now they would have to make it out on their own. Staying calm and rational was key to success and this was where their training played a big role. The team had several escape options, some worse than others like an overland trek to the Turkish border, but only one quick way out. That was to leave the way they had come in, through the airport. MG counseled against an immediate departure—rushing for the airport might bring more attention than waiting for a couple of days.

As the advance team prepared to get out of the country, a Pentagon staffer with no regard for security gave a "deep background" interview to a journalist the day after the mission was aborted. The briefing detailed the mission plan and the existence of the team in Tehran. *The Washington Post* and the English-language *Tehran Times* picked the story up and ran it, putting the team in an even more dangerous position.[23]

So they waited. They made flight reservations to depart three days later and waited some more. The drivers and Fred (Meadows' assistant) made their own way out; as Iranian nationals, they had more options and needed to stay away from "foreigners." The operators were locked into a course of action that could end badly at any moment.[24]

On April 29, the three Americans made their way to the airport. They had booked themselves onto one of the few remaining international connections out of Tehran, an Air France flight that departed in the evening. It was already on the tarmac when they got to the airport. MG could see the tail sticking up above the terminal as they approached the airport, its red, white, and blue logo offering sanctuary. But first they had to clear customs and immigrations procedures and no one knew what to expect. As it happened, the procedure was easy—except for one small glitch. Customs searched MG's suitcase and found several blocks of Iranian stamps with the Shah's picture that he had purchased as a souvenir. The officials wanted to know why MG had stamps depicting a man they considered a very bad criminal "who deserved hanging." MG told them he hoped the Shah would be hung as it would increase the stamps' value. That comment met with the officials' approval. He was waved on without any more questions.

MG and Scotty made their way through the maze of stations and were sitting in the departure lounge when they glimpsed Meadows step into the room. Suddenly, he was hauled back into the clearance hall by a man in uniform—he had tried to skip an empty desk but its occupant returned just in time to see and pull him back for questioning. Naturally, Meadows had raised suspicions by skipping the desk and was thoroughly interrogated by the authorities, but his cover withstood the review. In the meantime, MG and Scotty died a thousand deaths waiting for Meadows to come back, not knowing why he had been singled out. They knew they weren't going anywhere as five or six "students" with Kalashnikovs were stalking the departure lounge.

Once the discrepancy had been cleared up, Meadows was allowed to proceed and, after everyone's blood pressure returned to normal, the exit went like clockwork. The three boarded their flight and sat expectantly until the pilot made his preflight announcement and the plane pushed back from its parking position. Looking out the windows, the men imagined what might have happened if the mission had come off. They would have been departing on a USAF C-141 from an airfield across the city under very different circumstances.

As the plane's engines started, the whine of the jets only added to the anxiety, but it taxied to the end of the runway and immediately turned onto the departure runway and lifted off. They were out of danger but the three sat silently in their seats until the pilot announced they had crossed the Iranian frontier. Cognac was immediately broken out and together they toasted their freedom.

SNOW BIRD/STORM CLOUD

Days after Operation EAGLE CLAW was aborted, planning began anew for a second rescue attempt. President Carter, despite his disappointment with the failure of the first operation, was determined to get the hostages back. And while diplomacy was taking place, the military was gearing up for the next attempt.

For the next round Navy helicopters were out, as were Marine pilots.[25] Air Force transports and Army rotary-wing assets would be the ones to bring force to bear. The ground force would involve the same players, but plussed up to the point where the mission profile was no longer a "humanitarian" effort—it would be a rescue mission with attitude if it came off. It didn't, but there is value in looking at what was done because it points to the future of Special Operations.

The Detachment's target remained the same: the MFA. The Det's element was enlarged and carried more firepower, as did the other forces involved. Initially, the planners struggled with locating the hostages as they were dispersed across Iran immediately after April 25.

The three Americans in the MFA, Laingen, Tomseth and Howland, had not been moved so the Detachment could count on that certainty. Teams One, Three, and Five were selected for the mission this time—nothing else would interfere. There was some grumbling from Team Four whose commander tried to argue that it was better prepared than Team Five. Captain Feudo and MSG Krajicek reviewed the record with the command group, citing recent training events and the results of the CQB shoot-off in March and the issue was quickly resolved—Team Five would go.

The approach this time was completely different than the previous plan. Whereas EAGLE CLAW relied on stealth and surprise, what was now called Operation SNOW BIRD would rely on violence.

The Detachment's participation was code-named Operation STORM CLOUD, which fit the plan well. It would be a helicopter assault on the MFA with two teams providing security on the ground while one team stormed into the MFA to rescue the three Americans. Training resumed but at an intensity not previously seen in the Detachment. Many thousands of rounds were fired on the ranges, while assault training and immediate action drills were practiced in as many different locations as possible. The so-called "Doughboy City" in Berlin's southern Lichterfelde-Süd district played host to a lot of nighttime training as it was too close to the Wall and easily watched by East German guards during the day. An abandoned industrial facility in the center of Berlin was also used, causing a great deal of consternation to Berliners who tried to make sense of all the smoke and grenade simulators disturbing their daily routines.

While the building team relied on Walther MPKs, Remington 870Ps, and pistols for the inside work, the security teams went for M-16s and medium machine guns, in this case the Heckler & Koch HK-21. The HK-21 was a good weapon that could deliver a very damaging quantity of 7.62mm firepower quickly and accurately onto most any target. It had one minor flaw—it tended to jam when hot. The gunners compensated by carrying not only spare barrels, but a quart spray bottle of gun oil to relieve the problem. Each man's basic load of ammunition was impressive: the building team carried around 25 magazines per man, while the security teams were at 30 mags per man. Each machine gunner carried over a thousand rounds of linked 7.62mm ammunition that included a mix of standard ball, armor-piercing incendiary, and tracer rounds. Two hundred additional rounds were carried at the ready with the remainder on each gunner's back. Two M72 Light Anti-tank Rockets (LAW), two Claymore mines, as well concussion and smoke grenades completed the load. They were loaded for the proverbial bear.

A degree of irreverence permeated the training. All team members had olive drab t-shirts with the logo "The Empire Strikes Back" stenciled on them. An even larger stencil was made that would have been used to spray paint the same logo onto the MFA building in the middle of the assault. An American flag stolen from the Berlin Brigade headquarters would have replaced the Iranian flag outside the MFA.

The unit was now out of the intelligence-collection business. There were other activities underway by national assets to determine where the hostages were located as well as to conduct disruptive and diversionary attacks on the Iranian command and control infrastructure. If the mission did take place, it would not be "humanitarian," it would be punitive.

In October 1980, Col O told the force that they were going back to the States for further training and rehearsals. One last practice run was scheduled and, secretly, the force was assembled at a secure landing zone at Rose Range. Just after dusk, three UH-1H "Hueys" flew into the LZ and the teams climbed on, Team Three was in the lead bird, Team One in the second, and Team Five in the last. The flight lifted off and headed for Doughboy City. Flying a fairly direct course into the range facility, the birds did an assault landing on a road adjacent to one of the largest buildings. The security teams poured off the birds and set up in their blocking positions, while the building team raced to its objective. It was a full-on assault with few subtleties. Anything that came into view was considered hostile and "taken out." Team One ran up the stairwell leaving a small security element at each level until it reached the third floor, gathered the hostages and turned around picking up its security as it returned to the ground level and back into the street. Once the building team and their "precious cargo" were onboard, the security teams ran to their respective helos and loaded. The birds took off and then the assault was repeated. Col O and the SGM watched closely from different vantage points making sure all went as desired before they called it a night. The helos flew back to Tempelhof while the teams conducted a "hot wash" to review and critique the practice. It was the best preparation anyone could hope for before getting back to the States.

The time in Berlin was not all spent on the mission. Seeing the unit need somewhere to burn off its excess adrenaline, the XO, Bob Wise, coached the unit's football team to the Brigade championship. While the unit had mixed luck with its soccer team, especially at the hands of the Germans, its American football team was a different story. The Brigade's teams were normally made up of young men in their early twenties, while the average age of the Det's team was closer to thirty, a bunch of (comparatively) old grizzled men. One of the opposing players commented, "What did they do, let those guys out of prison?"

That might have been one of the more positive interactions the unit had with people from the other units. Between exercises, shooting, and city operations, twenty guys found time to practice and play. It paid off when the unit won the trophy early that fall and a raucous, if somewhat besotted celebration followed to the tune of Queen's *We are the Champions*. Then, it was back to work.

Florida

While the unit's actions on the objective were being practiced in Berlin, planners in the Pentagon were working out the method of inserting the teams. The solution for some involved bigger helicopters, while the Detachment literally got the little birds. The venerable OH-6 Cayuse helicopter, the military version of the Hughes 500, was nicknamed "Little Bird" and looked much like an olive-drab, flying egg. Its fuselage was actually one of the safest designs ever achieved for an aircraft. In a crash, even though its tail and rotor blades would break off, its egg-like shape absorbed the shock of impact and protected the occupants. Still, the Detachment was taken back a bit when told that 12 Little Birds would ferry them into the objective area.

The entire Berlin force was flown by C-141 to Hurlburt Field in the Florida panhandle for rehearsals. The MFA assault element was increased from nine to 23 men. Col O would still command the ground element, while SGM Raker would fly in the Command and Control (C2) aircraft overhead. A number of the Detachment's support staff came back to assist in the training along with two extra men from each team—about 50 men in total.

There the Detachment met the crews who would fly them in. It was a new, provisional outfit equipped with OH-6 helicopters pulled from National Guard stocks.[26] The pilots were from the 101st Airborne Division and were all very experienced. Importantly, they were qualified to fly with night vision googles (NVG)—an entirely new methodology for the time.

The first briefings centered on how the birds would fly into and out of the targets, loading and unloading, as well as emergency procedures. Some birds would carry three assaulters, some only two. The real catch was that only one crewman would be on the bird, the pilot. One assaulter would sit in the co-pilot's position, the rest rode in the back. Daytime flights were made to allow the assaulters to determine the best load plan and where to locate their weapons. The tail security team wanted its machine guns to face the police station on infiltration to facilitate engaging any hostile threat that might come from that location, for example.

Practice mission profiles were flown during daylight and the pilots familiarized the assaulters with enough "stick time" to be dangerous, the theory being that if the pilot was wounded, the front-seat assaulter could help get the bird on the ground. Of course, there was no chance of that ever happening at night, in a hostile environment, with anything less than ten hours of practice. That said, most could keep the birds on the straight and level without too much problem. It was the transition to hover and landing that would kill everyone on board.

Then came night flying with all the birds in close formation. The pilots flew with NVGs while the team members stared into the darkness as the birds went through their routes. Lit only by very small side markers the OH-6s were all but invisible and even in close formation, only the occasional main rotor blade of another bird would be sensed as it swished by just beyond the rotor tips of the observer's bird. It was a relief to end the flights as crews and assaulters would be mentally drained after even a one-hour flight.

For the mission, the OH-6s would be loaded onto a C5A Galaxy with their rotors folded up in transport position and the whole package flown into an airfield that would be seized by the Rangers. The Little Birds were to be wheeled off the ramp and put back together quickly, loaded, and launched for the rescue. Simultaneously, the main force would be doing the same thing with its UH-60 Blackhawks. The assembly procedure was practiced multiple times until the crews and support personnel were able to make each aircraft flight-worthy in several minutes. The assaulters always wanted to touch the "Jesus Bolt" that held the main rotor in place, just to make sure it was good and tight before the pilot cranked his bird up.

Gunnery practice was also big on the program and ranges were acquired and set up for the helos to practice assault landings coupled with a live fire. Anything dangerous is best done in small practice steps before the full Monty is applied. That was the case in this instance as well. Static offloads and firing came first, followed by single bird and section landings before the entire flight was practiced. The pilots quite enjoyed the experience of landing 12 birds with 24 weapons firing live ammo out their port doors. Surprisingly, no one was shot out of the sky.

Only one mishap occurred when a wind gust caught the tail rotor of one of the birds and it spun out of formation. Luckily, the bird spun up and away from the others and the pilot was able to recover and set the bird down in a field.

A final weapons practice was run at night, which was most impressive as every weapon was loaded with tracers. The guns opened up as each section settled in to land and continued until all the birds were down. There was little attempt to conserve ammunition. The result was a horizontal wall of flame that reached from the birds to the ground and tore up everything in it path. The targets placed in the field were shredded by the machine guns, flopping over backwards as the bullets cut them in half. There were more than a few 40mm rounds pumped out of grenade launchers—using training practice rounds to avoid shrapnel damage to the birds. There was a short intermission to let the smoke drift off and to reload the aircraft. Then the routine was repeated as the birds lifted off to return to base.

The final practice runs were done at Camp Rudder on Eglin Air Force Base, the location of the Florida phase of Army Ranger training. The headquarters building, a concrete-block, three-story barracks, was eerily similar to the Iranian MFA and would be the target of the assault. The landings were practiced again by section and then with the complete package until everyone was satisfied with the landings and placement. After that, the teams practiced off-loads and taking up their positions while the building team did its thing of retrieving the hostages and reloading the birds.

The daytime practices took the better part of several days until the force was ready for nighttime runs. Short flights preceded the longer until the full mission flight profile was practiced.

On the night of November 23/24, 1980, a full-scale exercise of the mission took place. The Det loaded its helicopters after a simulated unload and assembly of the OH-6s. The birds flew a nearly two-hour-long mission that simulated the extreme flight duration. Taking off from Hurlburt, the birds flew out over the swamps of Florida, while the assaulters sat back and tried to enjoy the flight. Further up in the sky, AC-130 gunships covered the approach to the target while a C2 aircraft provided control. For the actual mission, the AC-130 gunships would lay down preplanned 105mm gunfire before the assault to eliminate a number of known or suspected Iranian military positions, including the Ministry of Defense. Having "Spectre" overhead with all its firepower was a comforting thought when flying into what could well be a hornet's nest.

The pilots signaled their final approach and sat down on the road with the teams running to their designated security positions at the ends of the road. The building team breached the gate and entered the MFA and within minutes the "hostages" were loaded onto the birds. The commander spoke the withdrawal code-word and everyone folded back to their birds by section and the flight took off and ran for home. It went well the first time and it seemed like the plan might actually work. Unbeknownst to the Detachment members, that night the entire SNOW BIRD force had practiced in dispersed locations across the United States. The operations order was code-named STORM CLOUD.

It's All Over but the Shouting

By late 1980, the Iranian hostage drama had become a political football and it became clear the mission would not go forward. With Reagan's election, signals were sent that the hostages would be released and SNOW BIRD/STORM CLOUD was put into mothballs.[27] The Task Force broke up and the Detachment returned to Germany shortly before Christmas 1980. Everyone was ready, but the release of the hostages on Inauguration Day, January 20, 1981, canceled the need for any operation for good.

Several days before the men flew back to Germany, General Vaught visited the unit, which was still at Hurlburt Field. He had made a whirlwind tour of all the different elements that were involved and this was his last stop before heading back to Washington and the Pentagon. The helicopter crews were tinkering with their aircraft on the flight-line and the men from Berlin were sitting in the grass cleaning their weapons. Despite their disappointment over the mission being scrubbed, it was a glorious, sunny day. Vaught was talking with Colonel Olchovik as he walked over. There was a bit of small talk with each man and then he spoke to the whole group to thank them for their work. He said it was "at least, good training." No one could fault his logic, but suicidal or crazy as it may sound, each man just wanted the mission to go.

As the two officers walked away, Jim let the bolt of his HK-21 slam forward and said, "That's all she wrote then."

"J. J." Morrison summed it up best: "It would have been glorious."

The Detachment and its soldiers who participated received a JCS Letter of Commendation for its part in the mission. It was classified top secret and has not seen the light of day since it was filed away in the S-2's safe.

CHAPTER VI

THE FINAL DAYS (1981–1984)

Das dicke Ende kommt noch![1]

The failure in Iran was a very disappointing turn of events. It was not a failure of will as mechanical issues forced the first mission to abort, while political developments at the highest levels ensured the second attempt never happened. While the end result can now be seen as perhaps for the best in that no more lives were lost and the hostages all came home—the overwhelming feeling in the unit as the time was that an opportunity to demonstrate Det "A's" (and Special Forces') direct-action capabilities had been missed. The unit went back to its normal cycle of operations. While the Holloway Commission was dissecting the failure in the desert and pondering changes for the special operations community as a whole, the Det returned to plans and preparations for World War III.

In the wake of Colonel Olchovik's departure in early 1981, Lieutenant Colonel Darrell Katz took command of the 39th SFD. During his pre-arrival preparations, Katz noted that the unit's priority was still the traditional UW mission under OPLAN 4304, while the CT mission was its secondary tasking. USAREUR had recently given guidance that CT training should not exceed 25% of the unit's training effort.[2] In reality, the unit was still focusing on the CT mission and that led to a degradation of the unit's urban UW skills. There were significant numbers of noncommissioned officers (NCOs) in the unit either on their second or third tour in Detachment "A," as well as perhaps a dozen NCOs of

German or Eastern European origin. That was a solid foundation, a cadre of men in the unit to conduct and support meaningful UW and stay-behind training and operations. It simply was not being done at the proper level.

Katz knew he had to get the Det to focus on its most important mission. At the time, the 39th's most significant UW training was supporting the annual FTX FLINTLOCK. About 25 men deployed each year to role-play the organization of a UW support structure. To run the operations, an asset control group would set up in southern Germany with a commander, usually a senior NCO, directing all the operational cells though a non-technical communications system, i.e. dead drops, brief encounters, and personal meets in secluded locations. The cells ran operations such as E&E networks for "downed" pilots and collect intelligence on the "aggressor" forces. Others posed as "G" chiefs for the teams from the 10th SFG at Bad Tölz or the States who participated in the exercise. Some of the cells did the occasional unsanctioned "sabotage" mission against enemy encampments when things got slow. All of this was done in civilian clothing using contrived documentation in the "enemy's" territory. Along with avoiding the US Army's aggressor force patrols and counterintelligence elements, the cell members had to avoid scrutiny from the West Germans who were playing the role of enemy internal security forces and the locals who were naturally suspicious of anything that looked out of place. The men worked among the civilian populace, stayed in small hotels or with families, drove local cars, and became part of the community—not an easy task. In Berlin, one could disappear into the millions of inhabitants; not so in southern Germany where everyone was curious about their neighbors and strangers alike. It was a good test for techniques and procedures, but not as intense as the real thing. In war, there would be no "get out of jail" cards and few second chances.

In the early 1980s, the emphasis in the US Army was on winning a future conventional land battle against the Soviet hordes in Europe. Vietnam was a bad memory and UW was still the stepchild in the military's arsenal, right behind counterinsurgency and peacekeeping operations. All were contrary to the "American way of war," which remained predisposed to firepower, heavy maneuver forces, and the annihilation of the enemy.

It's a Question of Time

The Supreme Allied Commander, General Bernard "Bernie" Rogers, visited the unit to receive a formal mission briefing in July 1981.[3] After listening intently to the presentation, Rogers said that his highest wartime priority for the unit was strategic intelligence collection and reporting on the Soviets, not UW. If war should come, he wanted to know when and where the Warsaw Pact units and equipment were moving, preferably as it was happening. That task was to be the Detachment's new priority mission. Katz sent a memo to the commander of SOTFE summarizing the visit and the CINC's comments. Almost a year later SOTFE issued specific guidance placing emphasis on "Strategic Intelligence Collection and Target Acquisition" (SICTA). Accordingly, that became the focus of the Detachment's training. Even before the guidance came back, the unit began to plan and train for what some called strategic reconnaissance, relying heavily on the experiences and methodologies of the British SAS who had been doing this for some time.[4]

Rogers said intelligence in the first 24 hours of a war would be critical for a successful defense of Europe and asked Katz to plan accordingly. He summed up his needs succinctly, "Buy me time, Colonel, any time at all."

But, even then, he agreed to the unit's original paradigm of four teams outside the Wall and two teams inside. If war came, the two inside teams would still sabotage the critical infrastructure to delay a Soviet take-over of West Berlin, while the four "outside" teams would carry the tools essential to destroy targets. Sabotage would, however, alert the Soviets and East Germans to the presence of a SF team, making that mission a secondary task.

It was time for the unit to adjust. CT skills developed and honed would not be forgotten, just de-emphasized as preparation for UW again took the driver's seat. This meant that every operator in the 39th had to be proficient in the conduct of SICTA and special operations unique to an urban environment, while keeping up his skills to neutralize terrorists.

Before Rogers departed, he asked about the unit's cover and its operational security (OPSEC). Roger's wanted to know what measures were being taken to protect the details of the Detachment's mission and the identities of its personnel from the Soviets. Katz admitted the unit did not have a DA-approved cover plan and this fact hurt its OPSEC.

Rogers just said "Fix it."

How to fix it was a difficult problem for which the CINC offered no solution, but knowing Rogers was serious, Lieutenant Colonel Katz asked for a Department of the Army OPSEC review that would have far-reaching implications for the unit.

Moving On Again

In the meantime, the Detachment was tasked to participate in USEUCOM's Return of Forces to Germany (REFORGER) exercise, code-named CARBINE FORTRESS. Unlike the FLINTLOCK exercise, REFORGER was huge and involved thousands of NATO troops and German security forces. The local populace was also more aware due to the massive numbers of troops and equipment involved. FLINTLOCK was low key by comparison.

The unit sent Teams One and Five, plus radio operators from other teams, the S-3 NCO, and a communications truck with three radio operators. The teams organized into three-man cells and deployed throughout the exercise area to clandestinely collect intelligence on the "aggressor" forces. The operations section established a Forward Operating Base (FOB) that was co-located with the VII Corps G-2 section on Storck Barracks at Illesheim, Germany.

The cells moved into their operational areas (AO) and began to send in intelligence reports on the locations and activities of the enemy. Each cell member lived and operated separately, passing reports through dead letter drops and brief encounters. Rarely did the cell members come together in public. Meetings were done only when absolutely necessary and then usually carried out on an isolated trail deep in the forest or at night on the edge of a factory complex. These security precautions were necessary to keep the cell members safe, although it slowed communications somewhat. But there was always one person who didn't pay attention in school.

The exercise was unfolding well until mid-September when one of the cells was rolled up by the German police. It seemed their compromise was due to a combination of factors: suspicious-looking non-Germans who spoke good German, late night comings and goings together, and too much money spent in the local bars, which prompted the locals to report them to the *Polizei*. It was careless behavior by three soldiers who, thinking they were in a friendly country, completely underestimated the true security environment. The officers suspected the three of being terrorists, which they were, just not the garden-variety RAF bad guys they usually came across. The *Polizei*, being ever efficient, thought the prudent thing would be to arrest and interrogate them at the local station.

Captain Gene Piaseki, a Team Leader and the Detachment's field commander for the exercise, was forced to go to the police station. After he showed his exercise credentials to the officer in charge (which were then verified by the corps G-2), Piaseki went home but the wayward cell members were treated to an overnight stay at the jail to remind them of their error.

The next morning, the VII Corps G-2 HUMINT (human intelligence) officer and Piaseki were summoned to the exercise headquarters. A Canadian brigadier general, an American major general and representatives of their staffs were waiting for them. When they entered the room the Canadian's first comment was: "Who the hell are you and where the hell are you from?" Piaseki told him who he was and his unit of assignment. The Canadian then cleared the room of everyone but himself, the American general, the VII Corps representative and Piaseki. The first thing the general said was that the men who had been arrested were out of the exercise and to return to Berlin immediately. After a salute, the two chagrined officers left as fast as they possibly could. The cell went back to Berlin while the remainder continued with the exercise. Piaseki met with all the cell leaders to explain what happened and remind them take the exercise seriously. Even if the environment was friendly, the cells' primary job was to perform without being noticed. The rest of the men understood that well and no further incidents took place. Thereafter, the leader of the cell that had been arrested was known as "Agent Orange" for the short time he remained with the unit.

Despite the embarrassment, General William J. Livsey, the VII Corps commander, praised the Detachment's overall performance and said it was the only reliable source of intelligence that allowed his forces to meet the aggressor.

USA vs England: Once More Into the Breach

In 1983, a four-man cell was again dispatched to England for the third running of RED SAILS, or what was now known as the "USA–England Terrorism Games." The Detachment used the urban exercise to employ all their technical tradecraft skills in a scenario that required a lot of street smarts to succeed.

The Detachment's element comprised Howie, Mike, Mark, and Pat. Knowing the British would use all means to defeat the team, Lieutenant Colonel Katz authorized a pre-exercise reconnaissance visit to Southampton where the exercise would again take place. In November 1982, Mike and Howie traveled to the UK to do what any good terror team would—prepare for the mission by doing an advance reconnaissance of the area and determining their cover, i.e. an ostensible reason to be in the area. Coming up with a plausible cover story for four military-age men traveling without wives or girlfriends is a tricky prospect. To add to the difficulty, as one local put it: "Southampton was not a tourist spot." With insufficient time to organize a truly professional cover, the only option was for each man to create his own legend and for the four of them to avoid public contact. They would use impersonal methods of communication, like dead drops and brush passes, saving face-to-face meetings for critical discussions and then only in secluded spots.

What Southampton had in abundance was its connections to the sea. Mike was able to establish himself as a student of maritime history. With a forged letter of introduction in hand, he was able to access the archives of the University of Southampton to research the *Mayflower* voyage. Along with the university card, he gathered "pocket litter" such as association memberships in his cover name and joined a local Cypriot sports club. He then started to make inroads into the local Greek Cypriot community and joined a night club, which would provide places to avoid police scrutiny when the team returned. The documents would also help the men to avoid the hotels where the British exercise directors told them to rent rooms. Howie had another plan. He had served on exchange with the British SAS for a year and still had some close chums from the unit, including a regimental sergeant major who had retired to Southampton. Howie arranged to use the RSM's residence as a safehouse while maintaining the MI6-assigned hotel downtown. Likewise, Mike was able to rent a room at a small public inn using his contrived student identification. Along with the alternate lodging sites that would serve as safehouses, they set up a non-technical communications system of dead drops, personal meeting sites, cache locations, and surveillance detection routes that the entire team would use during the course of the exercise.

They also joined an "after hours" club, purchasing four membership cards in throwaway alias names valid for the duration of the exercise. The police wouldn't go into the clubs during the exercise because there was a cover charge, exactly why it was a good place for meetings. After casing Southampton and the target, a tank farm complex, Howie and Mike returned to Berlin and briefed the other two team members. Mark and Pat—the cell's demolitions specialists—analyzed the tank farm to determine the best way to destroy it. In the coming weeks leading up to the deployment, they rehearsed cover stories, contact plans, and their escape and evasion plan.

Once in England, everyone checked into their assigned hotel. Mike and Howie kept their separate bed down sites for later in the exercise when they would need to drop out of sight. The exercise kicked off with Mike meeting a MI6 case officer who passed over the team's clandestine tasks. Over the course of the exercise the team would be required to make a key (a fairly difficult task during the heydays of IRA activity, as key making was closely controlled), emplace explosives in a cache, conduct a reconnaissance of the target site, write up cache reports, take pictures of the Southampton police station, and finally conduct an attack on the tank farm, all the while evading capture.

As in the previous exercises, the men were subjected to periodic shakedowns to see if they would compromise themselves. On the third evening, a detective banged on Mike's hotel door, badged him, and stated that he wanted to search his room for drugs. After finding nothing, he questioned Mike on his cover story. When the interview was finished, the police seemed unsure if he was part of the team. The others were also rousted in their sleep under the same guise and their cover stories held up.

To avoid being trapped, the team had organized itself to conduct tasks individually and to stay in contact through dead drops and announcements posted on bulletin boards. With the surveillance of the target having been completed before the deployment, by the time the target was to be hit, the Brits were no closer to rolling up the men than they had been on Day One.

Towards the end of the exercise, Mark and Pat uncovered the cache of inert C-4 explosive and linked up with Howie and Mike at a preselected pub in the countryside. They then proceeded to a rally point near the fenced tank farm. The two engineers (Pat and Mark) cut through the fence, emplaced the charges on the tank's valves in the middle of the farm, set the timers and then retreated to the waiting vehicle. This time, the Brits ensured they documented the attack by having a section of Special Boat Service (SBS) operators film it from the top of one of the huge tanks.

After the attack, the team drove towards the ferry dock which would take them to the Isle of Wight, their notional escape plan, but encountered a police roadblock en route. A police officer manning the checkpoint told them that a group of four men fitting the team's description had beaten and robbed an elderly woman. When asked where they were headed, one of the team mistakenly said, "We're headed for the Isle of Man." That slip—the Isle of Man was 600 kilometers in the opposite direction—meant it was end of exercise. They were pulled from the car, handcuffed, and taken to the police station, where they were stripped, searched, and interrogated. Despite having been awake for 48 hours, the interrogation report gave a good account of their responses under duress. The mission and exercise completed, the team was then taken to MI6's fortress headquarters for their exercise debriefing. By all accounts they were treated royally with breakfast in a room decorated in colonial style and plied with single malt Scotch and Cohiba cigars during a debriefing attended by "Mick" the local SIS chief, the police commissioner, the MI5 surveillance team leader, and SBS commander.

It was for good reason that the Detachment was invited more than once to participate in RED SAILS again. The British were impressed by the team's tradecraft skills and appreciated the challenge presented to their CT units. The debrief and dinner that evening were not completely devoted to extolling the virtues of the opposition, however, and a few laughs were elicited at the expense of others, including police surveillance techniques reminiscent of the movie *The Pink Panther*.

The Queen and the President were toasted and the night's drinking continued.

The DCI Comes to Town

In March 1983, William F. Casey, then Director of the CIA visited the unit to introduce an advanced tradecraft course. It was not the first time the Agency had been in Berlin to instruct members of the Detachment, far from it. Since 1960, active and retired CIA operations officers had been conducting training. The DCI wanted to visit the unit his officers helped train for so many years. The training provided by the Agency was geared to reinforce the existing program and to update parts that needed refinement. As often happened with guests who visited and trained in the city, many of the instructors spoke no German and had little clue on how to navigate the city's oft-intimidating transportation system. Off and on one of the instructors would call into the unit and explain that he had become disoriented and needed directions. Asked where he was, the response was often "the corner of *Umleitung* and *Einbahnstraße*" (detour and one-way street), which made it difficult to provide good directions. Somehow, the instructors always managed to find their way back.

While the CIA gave the Detachment training, the Detachment was training other special operations units who sent their teams for what was appropriately called "City Training." Additionally, ODAs from the 5th and 10th SFGs also came to the city for the two-week crash course in urban UW operations, which concentrated on urban guerrilla warfare. Tradecraft subjects such as non-technical communications and surveillance were covered, as was target analysis (TA). TA was the one subject that always caused problems because the "operators" from the States had a tendency to be heavy handed in their methods. When visiting a facility they tended to ask directly where its Achilles' heel was located and how to break it, rather than use more subtle lines of questioning. This approach tended to alert the security manager that his facility might be in harm's way. Both units had guys more suited for shooting things in the head than working to arrange their demise by subtler, i.e. clandestine, means. They also had the same problem the Agency did with street names. Two keys to success were language ability—at least a basic knowledge—and a cultural awareness of the surrounding environment, things always mastered by Special Forces for their missions.

Training was only the first step in the process of making an operator. Practice was the second, and practice in the actual operational area was even more important. The Detachment's operators were getting fully back into their urban UW mode when a request for assistance came to the unit from US Army's 766th Military Intelligence Detachment. The 766th was responsible for counterintelligence and counterespionage operations in the city and they needed the 39th to conduct surveillance on an East German who had recently escaped to the West. He had been taken in and interviewed by the Joint Allied Refugee Operations Center–Berlin (JAROC-B), but his answers and demeanor made his hosts question his genuineness as a refugee. The 766th wanted his movements and activities watched, but didn't have the manpower to get the full coverage they required. Team One got the mission and was given a profile on the subject that included his name, photograph, and where to find him, but little else. A meeting in the team room sorted out the plan. The entire team would be on the streets working a classic discreet surveillance with four to six men on foot to tail the suspect and the rest as back-ups in two VW buses. The team communicated by radios outfitted with "clan kits" so they weren't visible to other pedestrians.

The 766th hadn't provided much information on why the man needed to be watched other than his motivations for coming across the border seemed doubtful. That meant he could be anything from mentally unstable to an agent provocateur. If he was a school-trained intelligence officer, he would know not to make contact with his assets or friends so early in his new life, but one could never tell. Additionally, the East German MfS and Soviet KGB officers could cross the inter-city border fairly easily to meet assets, so this man's motivations seemed even more puzzling.

The team hit the street very early the following morning to pick up the subject and were rewarded with an early and positive identification. In a compact, busy city of three million souls, it's not an easy proposition to conduct surveillance. Contending with multiple transportation systems, changing population profiles, and different landscapes is a challenge for a team that doesn't want to stand out. The team members had to look like they belonged in each environment they visited, so they had extra hats and coats stashed in the vehicles for quick disguise changes when the team rotated its surveillants.

Throughout the day, from morning until evening when they "put the subject to bed," the team stayed on their quarry and put together a surveillance report describing the subject's activities, addresses visited, and behavior. The report was illustrated with photographs of the man entering and leaving stores and offices and anyone the team observed in contact with him. The routine was repeated for several days with no discernible routine emerging, but each day starting and ending like the first. When the 766th said enough, the team quit the detail and filed a final report, sat back and waited.

Like previous tasks or chance encounters reported to the 766th, the report went in, but little came back as far as an explanation or determination. In all likelihood, the man was subjected to additional questioning about his activities in the city. It would have been interesting to see his reaction of feigned or actual surprise and hear what determination his interrogators made, but, as is usually the case, the results of an intelligence operation remain unknown to all but a few. This was one of those instances.

Kicking Doors

Despite the reemphasis on the wartime mission, the threat of terrorism was still prevalent and the unit could not relax its guard. Since the mid-1970s, Berlin had been living what the United States would experience after 9/11—a surge of security preparedness, but without the patriotic fervor. Heavily armed German police with submachine guns and dogs patrolled the airport and every other likely terrorist target. Elements of the Red Army Faction, the successor to the Bader-Meinhof gang, were active in the city, where they had a sizable support group of young men who had fled to Berlin to avoid being drafted into the army.[5] There were also many women in the group. The women were by no means lesser terrorists and were often more ruthless than their male counterparts.

Teams continued with their CT training in the city and at the SOT facility at Fort Bragg, NC. One team had the unenviable opportunity to make a long-range infiltration from Berlin to Fort Bragg, a first in Detachment history. The team used a MC-130 for a non-stop flight back to the US that required three aerial refueling operations. Parachuting onto St Mere-Eglise DZ, the team made its way to the Mott Lake facility where they spent the next two weeks. While many of the hard skills training the unit needed for the CT mission could be accomplished in Berlin or West Germany, SOT provided an all-in-one solution that was not easily duplicated in the city. Aircraft assets, demolitions and shooting ranges, and classrooms were all located in one isolated spot far from unwanted observers.

At the same time, the unit was acquiring new equipment for both missions that included improved ballistic vests, helmets and assault shields for the CT mission, along with special munitions and explosives from the Natick and Naval Surface Weapons laboratories. The Detachment's venerable Walther MPK submachine gun had been replaced by the Heckler & Koch MP5, which fired from a closed bolt and was more accurate, but marginally less reliable.[6]

Nevertheless, the skills needed to do the CT mission began to dull. With the emphasis back on UW operations, the 39th had less time to exercise the "hard skills." This was a consequence of the choice to be excellent at one skill rather than just good at two. Despite the reemphasis on UW, Lieutenant Colonel Katz later remembered that the USAREUR and SOCEUR staffs were more interested in CT operations and provided little guidance on the unit's wartime mission.

Zum Teufelsberg

Teufelsberg was an artificial hill in the north central section of Berlin on the edge of the Grunewald Forest. About 350 feet in height, it was built from much of the rubble that came from the Allied bombings of Berlin. Built atop the ruins of one of the Nazis' chemical warfare laboratories, it was the highest point not only in Berlin, but much of the surrounding countryside. In the early 1960s, it was quickly identified as the ideal location for a signals collection site. The Americans built a facility atop the mountain manned by civilian and military intercept operators from the National Security Agency (NSA), its British counterpart, Government Communications Headquarters (GCHQ), and the Army Security Agency (ASA).

It was one of the best intercept locations signal collectors could wish for. It was also considered a possible target for terrorists and Warsaw Pact special operations forces. In early 1983, the Detachment was asked to conduct a test exercise against "T-Berg" to test its security. Team One was tasked and began its planning by conducting a reconnaissance of the area. The forest near the facility was used on a routine basis by civilian trekkers, so this first step was relatively easy. Nighttime visits were then made to get closer to the fence lines to determine possible weak points. The only unusual event that occurred during this phase was when one of the surveillants thought he had been spotted by a guard. Staring through the darkness into a pair of eyes not 10 meters away, the surveillant pulled his knife when the "guard" suddenly rushed toward him. Only when the eyes flew over his head did he realize he was being attacked by an owl. Luckily, the owl did not report the intruder.

After two weeks of preparation, the team was ready to move in. The plan was to drive into the unrestricted forest area near the facility in civilian vehicles and move by foot up the mountain to the secure perimeter. Several locations in the fence line were determined to be blind spots where the guards could not observe activity on the outside. Additionally, the guards did not patrol outside the perimeter, which was another weakness.

On the night of the attack, twelve men in two vehicles drove into the forest and parked in one of the conveniently provided lots for daytime visitors. The lots were dark, secluded and the team could quickly exit and get into the forest before a chance police patrol might happen by. Normally, the team would have been carrying their newly acquired MP5SD suppressed submachine guns, but they didn't function with blank ammunition, so standard MPKs and MP5s were the weapons of the day.

By sheer happenstance, things got interesting when a green and white Berlin police van rolled into the parking area. Most of the unit's men were in the forest and concealed from view as the two police officers dismounted and walked up to the vehicle to check things out. The lone remaining soldier was sitting at the wheel of the truck with his pistol on the seat when the officer asked him what he was doing. Using the steadiest, calmest German he could muster, "Mark" informed the policemen they had stumbled into a military exercise and flashing his identification, informed them they were his prisoners. The officers would have laughed except that they sensed they were in a bad position when some of the element stepped out of the brush with their weapons at the ready. The officers were reassured that they weren't in danger and left under guard while the section carried on with its mission.

The element continued up the hill, quietly this time, until they were next to the fence. That obstacle was quickly breached with wire cutters and cloth to muffle the noise. And then both sections were through the fence. The main assault element had no specific objective; the point was merely to demonstrate the facility could be penetrated. Once inside, the gate guards were "neutralized" from inside and the entrance to the facility was breached with sufficient noise to announce the team's success.

Despite looking like a hard target, in reality it wasn't to any determined attacker, a point made clear by the test.

An after-action report illustrated with surveillance photographs, lines and drawings, and commentary outlined the facility's security shortfalls. The successful penetration of the main facility served to back up the written word as gospel. Once again, the method of using the criminal to show how best to secure the bank worked and the Berlin command took many of the recommended measures to protect the site. However, another survey conducted two years hence would demonstrate the same vulnerabilities.

The Raven Comes Home to Roost

The OPSEC survey requested by Lieutenant Colonel Katz was finished in late 1982. The findings were predictable, but its effect was completely unforeseen. As with many units, OPSEC was a burdensome distraction in Detachment A. From its inception, there had never been an officially approved unit cover statement, which resulted in a different legend being told or used by each Detachment member. During Katz's first visit to SOTFE as commander, he was again advised of the command's concern that the Detachment lacked an official cover plan and the OPSEC problems resulting from its dependence on the Berlin Brigade for support.

The Detachment's minimal cover had been eroded by many years of using the same procedures put in place at its inception in the 1950s. Exposure to German civilians in the USAB housing section, conducting the unit's budget transactions through the Berlin Command's finance office, or routing operational traffic through the G-3 had exposed methods, capabilities, and identities to other Americans, military and civilian alike, as well as many local nationals (Germans) who had no need to know.

The unit and higher commands did not initially address the issue as a high priority, but that changed when the unit's OPSEC was further compromised in a *Newsweek* magazine article. The article profiled Major Dick Meadows' long career in Special Forces and his part in the Iran mission. It also mentioned that two soldiers from a "Special Forces unit in Berlin" had participated.[7] The leak was caused by someone outside the Detachment, very possibly Meadows himself, and it would be hard to put the genie back in the bottle.

As a result, Katz visited the Special Operations Division (ODSO) at the Pentagon and US Army Intelligence and Security Command's (INSCOM) cover support detachment at Fort Meade in August 1982 to request an analysis of the unit's OPSEC vulnerabilities, and to get recommendations on how to fix the problem. His priorities were to get the unit's financial records out of Berlin, an office largely staffed with German civilians, and to establish an approved, back-stopped unit cover. Approximately four months later, Army Lieutenant Colonel "Chip" and Major "Dale" visited Berlin. They were from ODSO, but specifically they belonged to a sub-element known by its code name: "Yellow Fruit," which had been established in June 1982 by the ODSO chief, an Army colonel, to provide operational security and counterintelligence support to classified special operations and intelligence elements.[8] This element would oversee the survey of the 39th SFD/Detachment "A."

The study was completed by military and civilian agencies and determined the following:

1. The Detachment was a high intelligence collection priority for the Soviets.
2. System weaknesses had likely been exploited by the skilled Soviet and East German intelligence services.
3. As long as all the personnel assigned to Detachment "A" had a Special Forces background the Soviets would not be deceived as to the nature of the unit.[9]

The official conclusion was that it would be necessary to make the Soviets work harder at targeting the unit and cause them to dedicate additional resources to the effort. However, simply leaving the Detachment in place with an approved cover and taking the records out of Berlin would not accomplish the desired effect. It was recommended that Detachment "A" be inactivated and a new unit located at a different installation be activated. With that, the other shoe dropped. The plan was not infallible. It probably wouldn't fool the Soviets but it would reduce the unit's profile and force them to work harder to collect intelligence on the unit and its activities.

To make this effort work, no soldier who had previously been assigned to Det "A" could serve in the new unit. All personnel processing and financial support would be handled in the continental United States (CONUS). The Army's Personnel Command (PERSCOM) had committed to ensuring qualified men would be available and that they would receive language training en route. The Yellow Fruit officers coordinated this concept with the key activities at Department of the Army, INSCOM, EUCOM and USAREUR, but moving ahead was contingent on Berlin's ability to provide a facility for the new unit and on whether they could support an official unit cover with plausible deniability. Lieutenant Colonel Katz briefed the concept to Brigadier General Leroy N. Suddath, commander of US Army Berlin, who committed to funding the refurbishment of a building in Roosevelt Barracks. That is where the new, yet unnamed, unit would be housed.[10]

Once the USCOB's approval was given and the supporting units were on board, the commanding general of 1st Special Operations Command, Brigadier General Joe Lutz was briefed during a visit he made to Berlin in early 1983. The project went as planned for about a year. A number of soldiers were identified and programmed for language training, while a small advance party arrived to monitor construction at the new facility.

Preparing for the End

Lieutenant Colonel Katz had to break the news of the unit's demise to its members. It happened in November 1983, as the unit was preparing for the annual FLINTLOCK exercise. Katz called everyone together and explained that the unit would be inactivated; another unit would take over the Detachment's mission, but no details were given.

While two teams departed for the exercise, the rest of the unit was relegated to preparing to shut down. When the teams returned from West Germany, the unit was no longer considered operational for the wartime mission. It stayed on CT standby until June 1984, when that responsibility was also passed to the successor unit.[11]

In the meantime, there was one last mission to be done.

Operation ODESSA (May–June 1984)

In May 1984, the unit's deactivation began. All training had ceased, the team rooms were being taken apart, files were being reviewed, and equipment was being prepared for inventory and turn in. One day during this routine Petras was ordered to report to Lieutenant Colonel Katz. It was not a common thing for individual team members, unless they were the Team Leader or team sergeant, to be summoned to the commander's office. Although odd, Petras didn't give it much thought as he descended down the stairs to the first floor. When he reported to the commander he saw two other men, outsiders. Katz introduced them by name and mentioned they were investigators from the Berlin police and German Customs. Pausing for a moment, he added they were looking for someone who could speak Russian and German.

Any anxiety Petras had quickly turned to relief. Katz knew Petras had been born in Germany and spoke German as his first language and he was also a recent graduate of the Defense Language Institute where he had spent a year studying Russian. Born to a German mother and a Lithuanian father, Petras was comfortable in both cultures. The investigators were satisfied and after some small talk arranged to meet later in the week. A few days later he met again with the two investigators at police headquarters in the Tempelhof district. They briefed Petras on the case they were working on and gave him the files to review.

The case involved a major criminal gang that was being investigated for its smuggling of drugs, weapons, documents and other items of value into the city. The group was being investigated by a joint Berlin police/ Customs narcotics investigations unit (*Gemeinsame Ermittlungsgruppe Rauschgift* or GER) which had been working the case for some time.

Operation ODESSA, as it came to be known, would be the Detachment's last mission in the city. Approximately two dozen operators were involved in a major surveillance operation against a criminal smuggling ring.

The joint unit, or GER, had a general idea of how this group was bringing contraband into the city but did not have enough information to justify an arrest. It was known that one or more of the group would leave the city periodically and after a week or two would make their way back to the city with the smuggled goods. It was the goal of law enforcement to apprehend them as they re-entered the city.

Berlin at that time, enclosed as it was by kilometers of concrete and barbed wire, was an island with only three land routes that connected the city through the Communist East to the West. There was a northern, western, and southern corridor whereby people and goods could move by rail or vehicle. East and West German border checkpoints were set up at both ends of each corridor and customs police rode the trains.

With the amount of traffic exiting and entering the city the GER knew it was near impossible to be perpetually vigilant for one or two smugglers among the thousands of people and vehicles that moved along these six avenues daily. If, however, the authorities could determine when members of the group left the city, they calculated they could maintain a higher state of vigilance in the short term until they returned.

The GER knew who the principals were: two Russians, a Ukrainian, and a Lithuanian. The file they had on each man was limited to personal information. In order to determine when their next run to the west would be they needed to get closer to the group. Infiltrating this tight-knit circle was not an option. Penetration operations take a long time and the level of criminal activity did not justify that sort of effort. But it was thought that simple observation and overhearing bits of conversation might be of some help. An idea was explored to have someone get at least near the periphery of this group. But that person needed to be fluent in German and able to understand Russian; an asset the narcotics unit did not have.

The GER knew the addresses of these men but had no information on their daily habits. It was assumed they had no steady work. Petras was initially given a simple assignment. The investigators gave him a list of bars, restaurants, and casinos thought to be frequented by members of the group and asked to "hang out" to see what could be picked up. The original concept was for Petras to discover if anyone of the group actually showed up in any of these places. If they did, he would focus on those establishments and just observe and listen. He was told to report in once a week.

Petras spent the next few weeks, dusk to dawn, working his way through the list of some nice, some not so nice places. A few had knuckle draggers out front who simply said "Privat" and motioned him away. After weeks of no sightings it was pretty clear that this approach relied too much on chance. At the next meeting, he asked what specific information they were looking for if and when they ever got close to these men. It was at that meeting that the police said they needed to determine when their suspects left the city in order to beef up checkpoints in anticipation for their return. Petras considered that for a moment and suggested that perhaps a 24/7 surveillance of the group from the time they left their residences would tell them exactly what their habits were. They answered that they didn't have the resources for such an operation. To which Petras replied, "But I do."

Soon after Petras started working with the GER, Katz was reassigned and command went to Major Terry Griswold. Now Petras went straight back to the Detachment to meet with Major Griswold and pitch this new mission concept to him. It would take at least 20 unit members as well as surveillance and communications equipment to run the operation and it would have an impact on the effort to close the unit down. On the other hand surveillance and countersurveillance were fundamental skills for everyone in the Detachment. It was essential for the success of many urban operations the men were expected to conduct under the unit's war plan. The Det's operators were a perfect fit.

Major Griswold was very receptive to the mission and together they worked out some details as to what the Detachment would provide in terms of logistics and manpower and what was required from the law enforcement partners. After a subsequent meeting with the GER where they hammered out each other's responsibilities, "the Griz" gave Petras the go-ahead to develop an OPLAN. But OPLANs need a name and as one of the smugglers came from Odessa, Operation ODESSA was born.

In May of 1984 there weren't many men left in the unit. With the help of the few remaining members of Team Five, Petras put together a quick operation order and briefed the 20 or so operators assigned to the mission. The mission was to pinpoint the exact time any or all of the suspected smugglers left the city of Berlin. The concept for the operation was to conduct a round-the-clock surveillance against all four of the suspected ring members.

It was planned in two phases. The first phase was a static surveillance of three known residences and one place of business, a private club located on the Olivaer Platz just off the Kurfurstendamm, to establish any patterns of their comings and goings. Soon after they started, two of the sites were scratched from the list because they were unproductive.

The second phase would incorporate mobile and foot surveillance of the gang's movements to establish any other criminal activities and to photograph and identify any other contacts. Once the team started, the Detachment's photo lab was kept busy round the clock developing film and enlarging photos (the old-fashioned way).

Unlike what is often portrayed in films, discreet static surveillance is not a car parked across the street with two guys sipping coffee. Facilities and props are needed. In this regard the Berlin police were extremely resourceful and cooperative in providing the necessary access. In one case the Germans ran through their personnel files and found that one of their officers lived across the street from one of the targets. It was suitable for surveillance. The officer moved out that day and left it to the team for as long as it was needed.

Another target location was a large apartment building complex in a commercial part of the city that sat across from a large, new, postwar hotel. The hotel windows were mirrored and the effect prevented anyone from seeing inside. The first step was to get the manager's cooperation. When he arrived at work one morning, two officers displayed their *Kriminalpolizei* disks. He quietly led them to another room and asked how he could be of service. They asked him for a room on the fourth floor facing the street, in the middle of the building. The manager simply nodded his head, asked how long the room was needed and if they wanted any services while the room was occupied. They told him no services were necessary and thanked him. No more questions asked.

The third location was more of a challenge. The leader of the group ("Mr. Big") lived on a very quiet, residential street. In fact, he lived around the corner from Petras, who could see Mr. Big's apartment building from his balcony. Down the street from his building was a large grassy area that faced the street. The space served as a parking area at the rear of a house further back on the lot. With the permission of the owners, the police produced a small camper and parked it on the lot. The challenge there was rotating the shifts in and out of the trailer without anyone noticing. Once positioned, the watchers quickly became the target of every kid in the neighborhood who spent their time after school inspecting this new addition to their neighborhood. The men at the Tactical Operations Center (TOC) had to listen to transmissions about children trying to peer inside and attempting to get in.

The police had the perfect solution for the TOC as well. There was a communications center in the city which controlled and monitored all law enforcement radio communications. It also had a huge map of the city on one wall which became very useful for tracking movement and guiding the Det's guys through the city. The staff set up some space to establish the team's operations center. The Americans were a bit of a curiosity to the regular residents as they didn't know what organization or agency the strangers represented and were even more baffled by their knowledge of the city and the German language. The police had a good crew and a very good relationship was developed.

The ODESSA team established cells for each of the four locations and worked out their individual execution of the plan and logistics. In short order, they were all in position and everyone settled into a routine. It only took a few days for a pattern to emerge. Two of the four sites had no activity at all while "Mr. Big" would leave his driveway every day around 0900 hours. About fifteen minutes later he would arrive at the apartment building across from the hotel. He would stay there all day until about 1800 hours then return to his flat. He made no deviations or stops along the way. It was decided to shut down surveillance at the two sites where there was no activity to focus on "Mr. Big" and the apartment complex across from the hotel.

From the hotel, the team determined that "Boris," one of the gang members, was living in an apartment with his girlfriend, "Natasha." Because of the size of the complex they could not determine which of the people entering or leaving the building had any connection with the ring, so the team photographed everyone entering and leaving. The police found this very useful and were able to identify other known persons of interest. On some days "Mr. Big," "Boris," and others would come out onto the street to smoke and chat. Once in a while they would stroll around the block while half a dozen Detachment members lurked about. This habitual activity continued for about ten days.

Then one morning the routine suddenly changed. An urgent transmission from the camper came over the radio. "Mr. Big" had left his apartment at the usual time but sped away in the opposite direction of his usual route, all the while accelerating until he was out of sight. This maneuver caught the mobile units off guard. They quickly scrambled in an attempt to regain contact but they were unsuccessful. In the TOC, the team studied the area on the map and tried to determine whether this was an innocent case of being late for an appointment or a deliberate effort to draw out potential surveillance. A little while later the team at the hotel reported his arrival at "Natasha's" apartment. That incident put the ODESSA team on high alert.

Later in the day, "Mr. Big" and "Boris" emerged from the apartment and took a longer than usual and circuitous route around the neighborhood. This led the team to believe that the targets were purposely trying to detect surveillance in a prelude to some other activity. The team did a quick evaluation of their actions up to that point and considered what was needed to go forward. A few team members on foot surveillance felt they could no longer continue without being "burned" and were switched out. Another vehicle was brought in. Collectively, the team was on edge and prepared to react to any sudden or abrupt actions of the targets.

They didn't have to wait long. Towards evening "Mr. Big" and "Boris" left the apartment together, got into separate cars on a side street and drove out to the four-lane street between the hotel and the apartment building. They both turned onto the street in the same direction and stopped at the traffic signal. The team had four tail vehicles on station, which was enough to follow one of the cars, but not both. When the light turned green "Boris" made an immediate U-turn and sped off in the opposite direction. "Mr. Big" raced off through the intersection. Only one of the vehicles was in position to follow "Boris" and its crew made an on-the-spot decision to do so. Petras ordered the remaining teams to split up in order to follow both vehicles.

In the TOC the team and the GER agents were all on their feet, eyes on the map. Both targets were moving through the city seemingly randomly and the surveillance teams were doing their best to keep up. The targets were expected to make their way towards one of the three border crossings in the most western parts of the city, but instead, they stayed in the inner city. "Mr. Big" was working his way towards Charlottenburg. This erratic car chase only lasted about half an hour although it seemed much longer to those involved.

Eventually, they lost contact with both targets. After taking some time to review the last reported sightings, one of the GER agents observed that "Mr. Big" was last seen very near Berliner Zoo, the site of Berlin's main train station. A quick call to the station confirmed that a train headed for West Germany had left within 30 minutes of the last sighting.

"Mr. Big's" car didn't reappear at his residence and there was no activity at "Natasha's" location. After some discussion with the task force, the team concluded that one or both targets had probably left the city. If that was the case, it was now in the hands of the German joint task force. After a couple days, the men shut down the Det's part of the operation and went back to the miserable task of deactivating the unit.

A few weeks later the two detectives from the task force contacted Petras to inform him that the ringleader had been stopped at one of the checkpoints entering Berlin and arrested for attempting to smuggle drugs and weapons into the city. It was good news and it was good to hear that the Detachment's part of the operation had been successful. Petras asked that a letter of recognition be sent out for every Detachment member that participated, and the police agreed. It was a gratifying conclusion for the men who participated in their last operation in Berlin.

Back at the Ranch[12]

After Lieutenant Colonel Katz departed the unit, Major Terry A. Griswold took charge; he would be the last commander of the unit.[13] By early fall, Sergeant Major Terry Swafford departed and MSG Gil Turcotte filled in as acting SGM.

It was now up to Griswold and Turcotte to ensure an orderly reassignment of personnel and closure. Turcotte realized that a unit without a mission would lead to serious training problems for the men, so he devised a military stakes course to make sure everyone was up on the skills necessary for a successful transition back to a "regular" SF unit. This meant that the men would not only be required to maintain a high degree of physical fitness, but would be required to perform a series of tasks taken from the skill qualification test manuals for Special Forces soldiers. Each team had to negotiate the course together as a unit and could not begin a station task until all team members were present. It turned out to be an excellent competition, but also one that was pointedly final in the history of the Detachment.

At the same time, Griswold and MSG LeRoy F. Miller, the unit's S-1, arranged for a personnel specialist from Fort Bragg to travel to the city to discuss each and every soldier's reassignment. Their reassignment desires were met for the most part, but everyone was naturally still disappointed at having to leave Berlin and the Detachment.

Turcotte and Griswold were the next to go (on December 7, 1984) and MSG Glen Watson assumed the duties as senior NCO. The final days were spent clearing the building to ensure no classified materials were left behind.

On December 16, 1984, Gene Piaseki, the senior officer during the unit's last ten days, gave the Chief of Staff of the Berlin Brigade a final situation report prior to leaving the city. Piaseki later remembered it as a very sad duty to case the colors and shut the doors.

Postscriptum

In 2014, in a tribute to Detachment "A" Berlin Brigade (aka 39th SFD) in the US Army Special Operations Command's journal *Veritas*, the reasons for the unit's inactivation were explained thus: "by late 1983, changes in Allied and Soviet military demographics across Europe negated the requirement for the Detachment's unique capabilities and skills and the unit was deactivated [sic] in December 1984."[14]

Even thirty years later, the unit's existence was still cloaked with disinformation.

CHAPTER VII

THE NEW KID ON THE BLOCK (1984)

Lieutenant Colonel Mercer "Mac" Dorsey was selected for battalion command in 1983. An officer with experience in infantry units in Vietnam and Berlin, Mac had served in Detachment "A" as a Team Leader in the mid-1970s. He had hoped to take command of 1st Battalion, 10th SFG at Bad Tölz, but a telephone call from 1st Special Operations Command (SOCOM) changed that. Instead of Bad Tölz, Dorsey was offered SF Berlin. Dorsey was a bit disappointed as he had already served in the city, but accepted the posting. The assignment would turn out to be something quite different than he anticipated.

Dorsey was briefed at the Pentagon on the new unit and the process that was unfolding. He was told that concerns about the Detachment's security profile had led to an OPSEC review and the decision to shut the unit down. The missions had not gone away, and as the 10th SFG was not in position to take them on, it was decided to build up a new Special Forces unit and position it overseas, under cover, in a manner that would allow it to conduct its peacetime training and prepare for its wartime mission.

The question the Pentagon needed to answer was: what kind of unit and how would it be set up? At the Pentagon's Special Operations Office (ODSO), Colonel Roger Seymour and Major Corky Hilton had mulled over a number of different ideas. One idea was to set up a new unit in West Germany and have its operators travel to Berlin periodically on temporary duty (TDY) to prepare for their wartime mission. This plan was rejected because, in a crisis, travel could quickly be shut down and cut most of the unit off from its operational area. Additionally, the episodic travel of 72 operators (the envisioned size of the new unit) in and out of the city would have created a bad OPSEC signature and require a huge budget for travel and per diem costs. That kind of cash was not available.

Another proposal was to station singleton operators in the city who would live on their own and operate as an underground network even before the balloon went up. That idea was good in principle, but the mechanisms required to provide each man with good documentation, pay, and provide cover support would have been even more difficult to sustain or manage.

The chosen solution was not the most elegant nor was it perfect, but it was manageable and could be accomplished quickly. A new outfit would be stationed in Berlin as a lodger unit, not directly assigned to the Berlin Brigade. The Pentagon would support the unit's financial, administrative, and special logistical requirements through a series of classified cutouts that obscured the "spec-ops" relationship. The Berlin Brigade would be responsible for routine logistical and general services support, and provide housing.

The unit would be known as US Army Physical Security Support Element—Berlin (PSSE-B), ostensibly a Military Police (MP) unit tasked to analyze the security of and conduct vulnerability surveys of US Government facilities to protect them from a terrorist or an enemy special forces attack. That cover legend would explain its status and activities and its need to conduct intensive tactical training. A copy of that detailed (but unclassified) mission statement was taken to the Berlin Brigade legal office for a technically perfect translation into German— this placed the cover story right where it needed to go and soon it was well disseminated in the community and probably to the KGB and MfS.

Major William "Bill" Davis, late of the 5th SFG, would be the unit's first XO. He went first to the Pentagon to put together the unit's unclassified and classified modified tables of organization and equipment (MTO&E). The unclassified document provided the background for the unit's MP cover mission and its equipment, while the secret document provided the manning and means for the wartime mission. Davis would later relate that he thought there was a lot of pressure to make the activation of the unit happen fast, even though it was an extremely complicated and unique project. It may well have been a first to develop the concept and then organize, man, equip and position a classified special forces unit directly into an overseas operational area. Davis arrived in Berlin in November 1983 and began his work.

Mac Dorsey would be PSSE-B's first commander.[1] Dorsey arrived in Berlin in April 1984 and was surprised to find Detachment A's inactivation behind schedule. While Davis and the initial cadre of the unit were beginning to set up the new headquarters in a renovated building at Roosevelt Barracks, across town, Dorsey took custody of the classified operational files from the old unit. Most of the Detachment's equipment was returned to CONUS, but its special weapons and equipment were secretly shuttled to the new unit as quietly as possible.

Yellow Fruit Hits the Fan

In December 1983, the cover plan faltered when the principal "Yellow Fruit" officers, "Chip" and "Dale" decided they had a golden-egg-laying goose on their hands. Their secret unit was so secret that they apparently felt they could spend money on unauthorized travel and equipment purchases without being caught. They even brought their wives along for sightseeing tours on the Army's dime. After a colleague reported the illegalities to ODSO's chief, Colonel "Longshank," an internal investigation cleared them of any wrongdoing. The colleague didn't let the issue slip away, however, and went up the chain to complain to officers outside ODSO. This time the Army took charge and brought in the FBI to help with the investigation.

Chip and Dale were formally charged with offenses, including fraud, in relation to their duties managing "Yellow Fruit." Along with the two officers, a number of other personnel were also investigated and charged, including "Longshank," the chief of ODSO. The magnitude and scope of the investigation essentially brought much of the support required for PSSE-B's implementation plan to a halt. Despite the fact that Yellow

Fruit was a Pentagon element within ODSO and had no command and control functions over PSSE-B or any other unit, the resulting "guilt by association" would affect many units and their operations for several years.

Fortunately, the cover support element was already in place and functional. The major impact was a loss of support at PERSCOM and soon, some former Det "A" members were being assigned to PSSE-B, a direct contradiction to the OPSEC plan. Throughout the transition, the prime movers in US Army Berlin and at USAREUR were entirely supportive, but SOTFE considered it an "Army" project and did not want to get involved. That left things to develop on an uncharted course and a number of errors were made that damaged the new unit's cover from the beginning.[2]

One of the first OPSEC mistakes occurred with two of the Detachment's old vehicles. The trucks had been turned into the motor pool and repainted. With the same logbooks showing the Detachment to be the previous owner, they were assigned directly to PSSE-B, leaving a connection that was visible to the lowliest German mechanic. Far more serious was the transfer of about ten men from the old unit directly to the new. No matter what explanation was given for the transfer, this showed a direct link between the two units.[3] At the same time, Detachment operators were conducting cross-training of PSSE-B personnel and, although discretion was used, the linkage could be observed by the Brigade's range personnel and occasionally by Berlin police officers on nearby firing lines. After the last of the Det "A" personnel left Berlin, PSSE-B's profile was too similar to be deceptive.

Dorsey's motto would become, "If you stick to the lie, tell it repeatedly, eventually they will believe it." This worked on a general day-to-day level, but the Soviets and East Germans presumably realized a switch had been made fairly quickly. But, as the saying goes, when you have broken eggs, you make an omelet.

Behind the cover story, PSSE-B's missions were exactly the same as the Detachment's; they were to conduct operations under OPLAN 4304 and CONPLAN 0300. Like his predecessor, Dorsey's first trip was to meet the Commander, US Army Europe, General Glenn Otis, to discuss the missions in detail. Otis confirmed the priority mission of reporting on Soviet operations for a minimum of 24 hours at the outbreak of hostilities. The teams would have to be in position on the main Warsaw Pact routes to collect and transmit that intelligence as soon as hostilities began. That would be no easy task.

The next stop was to discuss targeting, which was what Dorsey found most troubling. Although Berlin had its own set of targets, they had never been coordinated with USEUCOM. That meant that the Air Force was planning on taking out some of the same targets the Detachment had been tasked to destroy. Dorsey began the process of deconfliction. The Detachment would have first strike priority on designated key targets near Berlin in the first days of the war; the Air Force would only carry out raids if further destruction was required. This targeting approach ensured two things: first, the teams knew they would not be on the receiving end of an F-111 strike—friendly fire isn't—and second, the targets would be worth the effort to get to and not something that could be repaired quickly.

Meanwhile, the search for new personnel was rapidly expanding. Soldiers were being recruited, but not in the usual manner. Selection teams traveled across the States to conduct interviews of the men whose records had been screened for the assignment. The basic criteria were similar to that used for the old Detachment: SF qualification in one or more of the required specialties, excellent evaluation reports, qualification in German or an eastern European language, and a TS clearance. But the selectees were not able to volunteer. They were chosen and once selected, their records were pulled from the mainstream personnel system into a restricted system: the Department of the Army Special Roster (DASR) for classified personnel actions.

Naturally, Fort Bragg was one of the interview locations. A typical interview went more or less like this:

Senior JFK Center SERE instructor Master Sergeant Don Neill came into the committee's office on Fort Bragg's Smoke Bomb Hill and called for Jim, one of the junior instructors there. Neill handed him a note and said, "You have an interview at 1700 this afternoon at the location in the note. Go in civilian clothes and be on time."

The "invitation" came out of the blue. Jim didn't have any fore-warning or idea of what it was about other than a vague feeling that it was for one of the special units. Dave, one of the other instructors who overheard the conversation said, "I know what it is. You're being considered for [a named special unit]. I gave them your info." Jim still didn't know what to expect.

Showing up at the hotel (within the four-minute window), Jim went to the room number on the note as instructed. The door was opened and Jim ushered into the room where two obvious army intelligence types produced their shiny credentials. They then went through a secur-ity brief that specified anything discussed from that moment on was classified and not to be discussed with anyone. The usual death threats and incarceration warnings were given and the brief continued. Jim was told he had been recommended and his record reviewed for a special assignment. No details, no job title, just the broad fuzzy outline of a mystery were presented. They reviewed his qualifications to make sure what was recorded was correct: SF weapons sergeant, operations and intelligence qualified, cross-trained as a medic with German language scores of 3 plus across the board. Check. TS clearance, no bad behavior (of note), and a picket fence medical profile.[4] Check. So far, so good.

Then came the offer, "Will you accept an assignment to Berlin?"

And the qualifier, "No, it isn't Detachment 'A.' It's a new unit and the details are classified."

Jim was surprised, first, to hear it wasn't the "special unit" he thought it might be and second, that there was something in Berlin besides the Detachment.

"What happened to the Det?" was his first question.

"It's been disbanded."

"What's the new unit and what's its mission?"

"We can't really answer that."

Then, clearly remembering that age-old advice never to volunteer for anything, especially a "good deal," he did just that.

Another candidate had a slightly different experience. After his initial interview, Carl was asked if he had any distinguishing scars, body marks, or tattoos of a military nature. He described his various scars and told them about a tattoo on his right buttock. The interviewers consulted amongst themselves and decided that a tattoo in that location shouldn't be a problem but asked him to describe it. Carl had received this personal symbol in Bangkok Chinatown at "Papa-san's Professional Tattoo Parlor." It was a Playboy bunny logo with a green beret. It was Carl's "Hare on My Ass" for those times when he was challenged with the proverbial, "you don't have a hair on your ass." It was always good for a free drink.

When the two heard the tattoo depicted a green beret, they were shocked and appalled as only intel types could be. They told Carl it had to be removed before he reported to the unit. Naïvely, he had visions of sex with Russian female spies and other related fantasies. Carl thought, "Why else would a tattoo on my ass, of all places, have to be removed if I were not to be in compromising positions that would expose my buttocks?"

A few weeks later Carl arrived in West Berlin and was dropped at his quarters to rest. The next day his sponsor picked him up to begin his in-processing. When he saw his sponsor's forearms decorated with every military tattoo imaginable, Carl's fantasies of being seduced by a Russian spy evaporated.

CHAPTER VIII

UNTIL THE FALL (1984–1990)

"If you can wait and not be tired by waiting…"
   Rudyard Kipling

The men of the new unit came trickling in, slowly at first, then in a wave that would rapidly fill the ranks. The unit was to be based in a renovated three-story building on Roosevelt Barracks near the Steglitz district of Berlin, several kilometers from the old unit's location. As the facility hadn't yet been completed, a set of offices in a neighboring building was commandeered. Major Bill Davis was the first of the command section to arrive and oversaw the construction and preparations for the move in. As unit facilities went, Building 817 was a great improvement with larger team rooms and staff offices, a work-out area, a dedicated arms room and weapons cleaning facility, and, unusually, storage for the unit's basic load of munitions.

Each team room was protected by a vault door and soundproofed to prevent eavesdropping, while the building was periodically swept for electronic "bugs" by specialist "pest control" teams. Once construction was completed, the building was quickly occupied with men, equipment, and files. All the classified files from the 39th SFD were transferred to the new unit and mission planning resumed.

Physical Security Support Element—Berlin's (PSSE-B) unclassified organization looked like that of a specialized MP company, but its classified organization looked much like that of the old Detachment "A." It also had six "A" Teams, but its support staff was much larger.[1]

Because its financial and administrative functions were carried out in-house, a support center was created with a number of specialists in each field. The S-3 and S-2 offices were also enlarged to five men and combined into the operations center. In terms of staff, the unit's size approximated that of a standard SF battalion. As the unit was organized, it was decided not to use the word "team" and, as a result, the six "A" Teams were designated "sections" numbered P-17, P-23, P-34, P-43, P-52, and P-61. It was hoped that this numbering system would throw off the enemy analysts if they tried to figure out the unit's organizational structure.

As part of the cover plan, the unit's staff wore uniforms in their often daily interaction with the Berlin Brigade. Along with the commander, the S-3 and S-2 spent a lot time at Clay Compound (Brigade Headquarters) and suffered the indignity of having to wear MP branch insignia. Bruce Hoover later commented that it was "was a deplorable, sacrificial act of humility" to have the MP's crossed pistols on his fatigues. It was necessary for the greater good or at least to convince unit personnel that they were doing all they could to support the legend. Sometimes the enlisted men who had to wear uniforms pushed to the ragged edge as when PSSE's S-3 NCO was stopped on the wide stairwell of the former Luftwaffe headquarters that now served as Brigade headquarters. Brigadier General Tom Griffen was climbing up to his office as "Thomas" was going down. Realizing he could not disappear or turn and run, Thomas continued his descent to face the general. Griffen stopped on the stairs as Thomas greeted him and asked "Sergeant, what unit do you belong to?" With the expectation of an ass-chewing Thomas responded, "PSSE, sir." The general looked him up and down, seemingly noting every detail, from the pressed fatigues to the polished German paratrooper boots, and shook his head. Then he sighed and said, "You might want to tighten up that haircut, soldier," and continued up the stairs.

The rest of the unit, the men on the teams, were still trying to fit into Berlin's culture. In the 1960s and 1970s, American jeans were never seen in Berlin, while in the 1980s, they were prolific. Nevertheless, the men were required to dress (mostly) in more suitable attire, to approximate what a blue-collar worker might wear, rather than a teenager. The fashion trends of the 1980s in Berlin were as fascinating as those of London in the 1970s. Tall Mohawks, rat tails, spiked hair, orange and purple hair, pierced ears on males, and bizarre and colorful clothing were all the rage. Everyone had a tan in winter, acquired from the ubiquitous, seemingly nuclear-powered tanning salons that prematurely aged the skin of most German women to the consistency of a pork-rind. Then there was the biker look of leather pants and jackets that the Harley crew fell in love with, while "man purses" were strapped to their wrists and often concealed a snub-nose revolver (the chosen caliber was usually .38 Plus P) or a Walther PPK. Although unit members were obligated to emulate the contemporary German look—some failed miserably, unable to mask the proverbial American GI appearance and persona.

Mission First

The commander of all US Army Special Forces, Major General Joseph Lutz, decided it was time to visit Berlin in the early fall of 1984 and flew into Europe from Fort Bragg. Despite the cover concerns, the general was received and briefed, but only after a few special arrangements were made. Lutz first visited Bad Tölz and the 10th SFG in southern Germany before heading to Ramstein Air Base where he got a ride on an USAF liaison flight and arrived incognito at Tempelhof airfield. For the next two days, the Detachment and PSSE-B entertained the general, briefed him on the transition, and gave "dog and pony shows"—essentially capability demonstrations—all the while concealing his presence from strangers. One night, after the general had visited the new unit's facilities, he was taken in a blacked-out van to an isolated parking area in the Grunewald where he was "passed" to another vehicle and taken to the other unit. The general was told that it was necessary for him to see how the inter-unit communication plan worked. The final exchange was done outside the Brigade headquarters on Clay Compound. The PSSE van came in one guarded gate and the Detachment's truck came in another—the general was walked to a meet point and handed off to the other unit's escorts. When Lutz commented that the exchange seemed just as secure as meeting in the forest, he was told that Soviet intelligence officers watched the outside gates of all US military compounds and could connect the dots if they saw the two vehicles together. General Lutz was probably never quite sure if he was being BS'd or not.

In 1984, the fledgling PSSE-B took over the nearly three decades of planning and preparation done by its predecessor and reapplied it to the problem of unconventional warfare. The problem remained the same—how to enable six teams to successfully conduct operations behind enemy lines long enough to satisfy the theater commander's thirst for intelligence and mayhem. Lieutenant Colonel Mercer "Mac" Dorsey arrived in April to take command of the unit and received his marching orders from General Glenn Otis, CINCUSAREUR. The unit began to work on the premise that providing intelligence to the European Command in the opening days of a conflict was the priority followed by destroying key targets in and around Berlin. To complete the unit's activation, Special Operations Command Europe (SOCEUR) sent a classified message in the early fall that gave the unit a classified designation: the 410th Special Forces Detachment.[2]

Preparing for the Cold War mission was just as difficult as it had been for the old unit. Target selection was more focused than in previous plans. The teams were assigned fewer (often only one), but difficult targets, like the hardened headquarters bunkers of the Soviet Forces in Germany at Zossen-Wünsdorf or the East German National Defense bunker northeast of Werneuchen, as well as other sites that might survive air strikes. But, the first priority was to prepare for the SICTA—strategic intelligence collection and target acquisition—mission. The basic tenet of SICTA was to have American eyes on the ground observing enemy activities and sending timely, actionable information back to the theater commander by secure radio communications systems.

SICTA was a new name for an old mission, a task that SF kept in its bag of tricks, but one that was very much unloved. The major reason it was disliked was that it entailed sitting in a "hide site" deep behind enemy lines for days at a time. And, although both the old and the new unit planned on spending time in the enemy's backyard, the prospect of sitting in a hole in the ground was less appealing than conducting direct-action or guerrilla operations. That said, SICTA was the CINC's priority mission and thus it was the unit's.

Getting over the Wall was the major problem for the teams. Solutions similar to those developed in the Detachment were still considered viable. The key to crossing was choosing a spot that was isolated, both at the Wall itself and beyond. A team would have to get over, through, or under the Wall and get as far away from it as quickly and quietly as possible. Another option was commandeering the Berlin Aviation Detachment's six "Huey" helicopters. The helicopters would have provided a quick one-way trip into enemy territory with the pilot either returning to base or abandoning his bird in an East German swamp and joining the team on its adventures. Just how much attention that would focus on the team was another consideration.

Once over the Wall, the teams would move to preplanned locations near major routes that the Russians and East Germans would use to send their troops forward to the front. That meant PSSE-B was ideally located to place teams along the rail and road networks around Berlin at the very onset of hostilities. The unit also began to conduct field training in West Germany in conjunction with the annual REFORGER and FLINTLOCK exercises to refine its tactics and techniques.

The Ratline

In the late summer of 1984, P-17 was the first fully manned and operational team and deployed on the annual FLINTLOCK exercise in southwest Germany. The main exercise had several smaller pieces, one of which was known as "Fleet Deer," a somewhat clever euphemism for an escape and evasion (E&E) exercise. P-17 was dispatched to Stuttgart to work with the SOCEUR planners before the exercise began. During the exercise, it and a second section were tasked to emplace caches along the E&E lanes in southwest Germany. The caches contained food and water for "downed" pilots who had to evade their way through enemy territory. Before the exercise, participants were given an E&E plan, like they would have if they were flying a combat mission. They had to memorize the details and would then be dropped off and pushed out into the forest to begin the exercise. The first part was the hardest for the pilots, as they had to figure out where they were located, then make their way to the cache site, which also served as a contact point where they were to meet an agent of the underground, role-played by the men from Berlin.

Comically, SOCEUR was trying to save money and gave PSSE a couple of Chrysler "K" cars with US Forces Europe license plates to drive, so two German-speaking, long-haired, civilian-clothed soldiers, Karl and Dave, were sent out to surreptitiously emplace the caches. A good deal of countersurveillance was used to avoid both suspicious police and young, curious Germans who might want to discover the contents of the hidden packages.

Once the exercise kicked off, the team members operated as the "underground" running the E&E "ratlines." This required them to live incognito amongst the local population—after dumping the "K" cars for German vehicles. They employed local citizens as the "auxiliary," many of whom had supported the exercise for years and provided safe-houses, vehicles, and role-players. Most of the pilots made it through the network without incident, but the team had fun with the new SOCEUR commanding general, a Marine, who went through the system as an evader. He spent more time blindfolded and tied up in the trunk of vehicles than most, all so he could better appreciate the experience.

Bureaucracy

Along with preparation for the wartime mission, every section member was required to complete the unit's operator training course (OTC) to prepare for the CT mission using task, conditions, and standards (TCS) adopted from other units and Det "A." Each section then trained to the collective standards before being tested on both individual skills and team skills, culminating with each four-man assault team running through a final exercise. Once all the elements were successfully evaluated, the unit fielded 12 assault teams and six sniper/observer teams. The unit was ready for its precision direct-action missions.

As the year 1984 closed, the new unit struggled with organization and operational issues. Terrorism was still a threat in Europe and that mission still pulled at other priorities. More visits took place, as it seemed Berlin was a good stop on every general's itinerary. One afternoon, some of the unit's men were working in the building when SGM "Mac" walked in the front door with a stranger wearing cowboy boots and a football team jacket. Naturally inquisitive, one of the guys yelled out, "Hey Sergeant Major, who's the cowboy?" At the same time one of the others whispered, "Oh shit, that's General Downing." Someone had forgotten to inform the troops that the new commander of 1st Special Operations Command was visiting.

1985 also began with a notification that the unit would undergo an Inspector General review of the unit's operations, especially its finances. It was a result of the "Yellow Fruit" investigations that had been initiated in 1984. Every unit remotely associated with Yellow Fruit was subjected to an "IG" that seemed predisposed to finding wrongdoing.

In the United States, several officers and enlisted men were charged with fraud and a number of units had been thoroughly investigated. Despite little evidence of systemic malfeasance, several other units had their operations temporarily suspended. When the IG arrived in Berlin, they seemed like sharks following the scent of blood, agitated and ready to tear apart any wounded prey they encountered.

One of the investigating officers was so full of himself that, when confronted with a keypad cypher lock at the front door of the unit, he declared he could unlock it merely by looking at the wear on the buttons. He failed.

Bill Davis, PSSE-B's executive officer, was ready for the inquiry. The unit's special accounting and procurement procedures were completely spotless according to one of the IG team members. "It almost seemed like they were disappointed," Davis reflected later, "but the unit was totally correct in all its activities." It was a bullet dodged not by luck but because the staff and sections had done their homework and followed regulations. That covered all the areas the IG was interested in and, where there were no regulations to follow, procedures were instituted to prevent problems. The IG thought that was an unusually prudent step for a small unit. The staff saw it as ensuring they stayed safely in the game.

Always a Bridesmaid...

Despite the commander's best intentions, real-world terrorism kept interfering with preparations for the theoretical wartime mission.

In June 1985, Trans World Airlines Flight 847 with 139 passengers and eight crew was hijacked just after it departed Athens en route to Rome. The hijackers, two Lebanese members of Hizb'allah who had smuggled pistols and grenades onto the airplane, forced the pilot to divert first to Beirut where 19 passengers were released in exchange for fuel, and then to Algiers on June 14.

While the plane was on the ground at Algiers, SOCEUR staff sent an alert notification to Berlin and PSSE-B went into launch mode. Because the alert reached the unit during a duty day, no time was lost assembling the unit. With the exception of two teams that were training in the city, everyone was already in place. Well within two hours, the unit had uploaded the alert vehicles and three teams—two assault and one sniper—were standing by to move to Tempelhof airfield.

Teams went into planning mode and reviewed the schematics for the B727-200 and its seating configuration. An emergency assault plan and several proposed deliberate assault plans were developed while the force waited for a launch signal. The commander and XO were at the Brigade headquarters, so it was the S-3, Captain Phil Tuttle who initially had overall command while a section leader took charge of preparing the assault force to roll out.

Just after the commander returned to the unit, a second message came in informing the unit to stand by, as the aircraft had departed Algiers for an unknown destination. This would turn out to be Beirut airport, a denied area surrounded by thousands of Shi'a militiamen with guns—a location where it would be impossible to launch a rescue. Everyone knew the mission would go nowhere once that happened. Although the unit would stay on standby for the next 48 hours, the incident was eventually resolved through negotiations. Although US Navy sailor Robert

Stethem was murdered, a quick rescue operation that would not result in the deaths of the passengers and crew was out of the question, because the plane was parked at Beirut's airport and the passengers hidden at an unknown location deep inside the city.

Impossible Mission II

Shortly after TWA 847 came the *Achille Lauro* incident in October 1985. The MS *Achille Lauro,* an ill-starred luxury liner, was seized by four Palestinian Liberation Front (PLF) terrorists as it departed Alexandria, Egypt en route to Israel. The PLF men had actually screwed up their operation. They had originally planned to attack a target once they got to Ashdod. Instead, a crew member stumbled into the hijackers' room as they were cleaning their weapons and the Palestinians felt they had no other option but to seize the ship. They were stuck with their decision and had to come up with an improvised plan. In the ensuing hours, the terrorists irrationally decided to kill a disabled American Jew, Leon Klinghoffer, and dump his body overboard.

[Redacted]

The point was moot, however. Yasser Arafat and the Palestinian Liberation Organization (PLO) leadership realized the operation was detrimental to their cause and sought to negotiate their way out of it.[3] With the liner sitting in Egyptian waters just off the coast near Port Said, a solution was found by the Egyptians. In return for the release of the passengers, the Egyptian government promised the hijackers safe passage.[4]

The hijacking ended, but the terrorists' odyssey was not over. Despite demands by the governments of Italy, Israel, and the US for their extradition, the terrorists were allowed to leave the country on an EgyptAir flight to Tunis. Upon hearing the news, President Ronald Reagan agreed to his staff's suggestion to intercept the plane and force it to land and capture the terrorists. Despite the possible foreign policy complications, the White House seized on the opportunity to act firmly in the face of terrorism, something that had eluded the US since the Tehran Embassy seizure.[5]

Aircraft were launched from the aircraft carrier USS *Saratoga,* the command ship of the Sixth Fleet in the Mediterranean, and EgyptAir

Flight 2843 was intercepted and successfully diverted to the joint Italian-US Air Base at Sigonella.

When the aircraft was on the ground, Navy operators quickly surrounded the airplane. MG Stiner, his staff and other operators returned from Akrotiri shortly thereafter and moved in as well, but the Italians one-upped the Americans and surrounded them with 300 armed soldiers and police. It was a stand-off until high-level negotiations and an order from the JCS permitted Stiner to defuse the situation.

Where was PSSE-B during this incident? In a militarily parallel universe, SOCEUR had again alerted the unit for a possible deployment to Sigonella. Section P-17 was alerted and ten men from that element and Mac Dorsey, the commander, flew forward to Rhein-Main Air Base and then to a forward base in another country where they were placed into isolation. The team was told to prepare to "break the terrorists out" of their Italian jail. Somewhat incredulously, the team started their planning, which was interrupted when the mission changed to "escorting" the terrorists from the jail to an American military aircraft that would be waiting at Sigonella. The team wasn't sure if they were going to be breaking down the doors themselves or getting a hand-off from another group that somehow had gotten control of the terrorists. Because of that, the operation never solidified into a plan and no further information was given the team. After several days, the team was told to pack up and go home. The whole exercise seemed to be a contingency operation that someone in SOCEUR dreamed up, but could never push forward. It could have just as easily come from someone in the White House. They never were told from whom the order came. It was just as well; removing the terrorists from sovereign Italian territory without the host government's permission would have been dicey—as another group of Americans would later find out.[6]

Dark Days at the Mission

The new unit continued operations with the US Military Liaison Mission (USMLM) as the Detachment had done. The gains outweighed the OPSEC risks and a handful of PSSE's NCOs were attached to the

Mission and went over the border to run tours in East Germany. A lot of new Soviet equipment, including the improved T-64B tank and the new SU-25 "Frogfoot" close support aircraft, appeared for the very first time in the GSFG arsenal around that time and, as they had since 1949, the tours were looking for new Soviet toys to photograph and document. Working with the Mission gave the unit access to the latest intelligence on Warsaw Pact OB and its equipment. While some of the unit's men were assigned to the MLM as drivers, everyone else was learning how to identify Soviet and East German units based on their assigned vehicles. Paul S created a training course which included a new school of study called "Tarpology." It entailed learning how to identify a vehicle by—for example—seeing nothing more than a tank's track guide with the rest of the 60-ton monster hidden under a tarp. It was minutia that would pay off in the field, and it was based on the extensive work Paul and several other men of the unit did to put the training together.[7]

The previous year had been a difficult one for the Allied missions; a French tour officer was killed when his vehicle was rammed by a Soviet truck. The next one was also bad. On March 24, 1985, the Americans lost one of their own when Major Arthur "Nick" Nicholson was shot and killed by a Soviet guard at Ludwigslust, East Germany. None of PSSE's men were present during that incident, but it served to remind everyone of the dangers of dealing with the Soviets and the bravery of the MLM crews. Nicholson was walking outside his vehicle near some empty tank sheds, when the young guard shot him without warning or provocation. For over three hours, the Soviets denied Major Nicholson any form of assistance and kept his driver in the car under armed guard. It was a cold and calculated murder, which the Soviets tried to blame on American missteps. The incident would color the MLM's activities from then on.

Still, there were occasional bits of good news such as when the Mission provided concrete evidence of Soviet readiness and tactical capabilities that was of interest to Allied commanders in West Germany. Some of the information captured by the PSSE men included photographic coverage of major river-crossing exercises, photos of the first Soviet SS-21 (short-range ballistic missile) brigade, and the new T-80 tank.

In one misadventure, a Soviet missile transporter-launcher chased the MLM vehicle permitting the vehicle's capabilities to be filmed and its top speed calculated.

The most important aspect of the tour experience was to scout the area for future operations. The Soviets often commented that they believed the MLM personnel were intent on emplacing small nuclear weapons all across East Germany. Their paranoia was probably based on too much propaganda and, although it was a reasonable idea, no "nukes" were ever left unattended.

Shortly after Major Nicholson was killed, a PSSE sergeant photographed two Soviet officers on the other side of the Wall. The high-definition photographs were blown up and the commander took them back to the States for a conference at the Pentagon. He passed the pictures around with crosshairs marked on each head without a comment. The intent was clear and many agreed with the idea, but no one was willing to let loose the "dogs of revenge."

Living the Cover—the Regional Survey Team

Through the CT alerts, exercises, and preparation for World War III, the men of PSSE-B also conducted their cover mission, which was to conduct vulnerability surveys to "enhance the security of government facilities overseas." Ostensibly, the unit had been stood up just for this task and it had to deliver a product to actually maintain the story. Initially, the unit concentrated on US diplomatic facilities. That included embassies and consulates in Europe, Africa, and the Middle East, but the tasking soon expanded to special weapons storage sites and command facilities like the Supreme Allied Forces Europe (SHAPE) bunker in Mons, Belgium.

Several of the unit's soldiers had been part of survey teams with SF in Panama and other locations. Miguel was one, and he brought many of the basic formats and procedures that would be used for the program.

The unit fielded regional survey teams (RST) to do the work and one of the first visits was to the US Embassy in N'djamena, Chad led by Virgil and Karl. As each team gained experience, the number of visits multiplied exponentially with one "veteran" leading new surveyors to show them the ropes. The trips were resource intensive; a typical survey started with a visit by a two- or three-man team to a site where they would spend three to five days collecting data, photographs, and plans. Then the material would be assembled into a usable product—four identical copies of properly annotated and geographically oriented maps, photos of every building, fence, door and window from all possible angles, plus blueprints, diagrams, and amplifying descriptions. It was the kind of material that would be invaluable for a crisis incident, but was an enormous workload on the team that put it together.

Where the security surveys of diplomatic facilities were tedious, vulnerability surveys offered a bit of interesting change. A typical task was to assess the security of the many special weapons storage sites across Europe. P-43 was given the mission to check several locations, the first being a depot in Holland. Several of the men had not been on a survey before, so everyone went to the first location to familiarize themselves with the routine and then split up to finish the other sites, which were in Germany.

In Holland, the sight of eight young men in two big silver-gray Mercedes sedans with German plates arriving in the tiny village was enough for the local populace to slam the shutters of their homes shut and clear the children off the streets. The Dutch seemed to think the German army had invaded. An old man ventured out, asked the team leader who they were and sounded the all clear when he found out the strangers were Americans. What happened next was reminiscent of a scene from *The Wizard of Oz*—everyone slowly crept out of their houses to say hello. The team didn't speak German for the rest of the visit.

The first day at the weapons site was spent checking the outside perimeter from a safe distance to get a feel for how well the location was guarded and to see what normal procedures looked like. The next step was to make contact with the site commander and explain the survey process. After a tour inside the facility, an unannounced alert was conducted to let the team observe response times and procedures.

Many sites were guarded with a combined force: local Dutch troops outside and American MPs on the inside of the perimeter. These were American weapons after all. In the event of an incident, whether real or training, Dutch troops from a nearby base would respond to reinforce the site. But, as with many sites, the security forces often used methods that became routine and thus predictable to an outside observer. In this case, the responders used the same road to approach the site every time, a weakness that could be easily picked up and exploited by an attacker.

After several days, the team was able to make suggestions to improve the technical aspects of security and critique the tactical plans of the guard force. The defenders were shown how a Soviet *Spetsnaz* attack might look compared to that of a less sophisticated terrorist group. Most importantly, the PSSE team offered alternatives to the MP's standard by-the-book operating procedures. It was a methodology the unit carried over from its earliest days: think like the bad guy and look for ways to defeat rigid behavior and techniques.

Travel was the most rewarding aspect of the mission, as it entailed free visits to many exotic locations, hours on the site and then, often, some time off in the country. But, as with any military endeavor, the best-laid plans always seemed to go awry. Carl got thrown out of SHAPE by a MP colonel who hadn't received the news that a long-haired, civilian-clothed master sergeant was there to survey "his" bunker. After the colonel was informed by officers who outranked him that Carl was indeed an invited guest, he changed his tune and provided first-class support.

In Zambia, another PSSE surveyor was almost shot by a policeman who challenged his presence in a quiet residential neighborhood. The policeman appeared out of nowhere while "Jim" was standing in the street photographing the US Ambassador's residence. The police corporal made for a comical sight because his FN FAL rifle dwarfed him in size, but it was loaded with real bullets and he appeared to know how to use it. Besides, he was backed up by another policeman a few yards away. It was 1985, during the Apartheid days of South Africa and apparently the exiles who occupied the African National Congress' headquarters across the street were wary of white men who looked like South African commandos on their doorstep. Talking fast, Jim explained his presence all the while offering cigarettes and compliments on the diminutive corporal's uniform and superior watchfulness, thus proving discretion is indeed the better part of valor.

Despite the enjoyable experiences that came from conducting vulnerability surveys across Europe, the Middle East, and Africa, the mission was an onerous burden. The rough rule of thumb is that the workload to support an organization's cover should never require more than about 20 to 30 percent of the total, leaving at least 70 percent of their time to do the real work.[8] RST activities consumed about 60 percent of a section's time. While occupied with the surveys, every other mission suffered.

A Wilderness of Mirrors

Quietly, the unit turned its sights back onto the urban UW mission. While CT and SICTA operations could be practiced on the ranges and in the field, the city of Berlin offered the perfect environment for practicing the clandestine tradecraft necessary to survive as an underground organization. In September 1985, the unit ran its first, full urban UW exercise. It was designed to test communication methods between the deployed teams and the unit headquarters. Somewhat ambitiously, it tasked teams to send and receive all their messages using non-technical means, i.e. dead letter drops and brief encounters. Communications done in this fashion are time consuming; a message passed in one direction, from headquarters to team for example, can take several days to reach the last man in the chain if all the proper signals and countersurveillance methods are used. The messages were encrypted using improvised methods—book codes and key phrases—rather than an "approved" system that might not be available in wartime. The teams had to collect and report on specific targets to the headquarters element, which then gave each team a different target to raid or destroy for the exercise's culmination. The exercise was compressed into eight days and forced everyone to move quickly to accomplish all the tasks required. When it was completed, all the participants had a much better idea of the challenges they would face if the balloon did go up. One lesson learned was that trying to time an operation through a non-tech communications system was extremely difficult because many things could delay the transmission or receipt of messages. Technical advancements were also beginning to impact the unit's methodologies as a surveillance exercise conducted shortly thereafter illustrated.

In November, a British Army special operations intelligence company came to Berlin to work on their surveillance methods.[9] PSSE was tasked to provide "rabbits" for an exercise. The rabbits were given time windows to visit specific locations and told they should merely pretend to case the sites for some clandestine purpose. The sites included train stations, city government buildings, and specific stores. The rabbits went out and visited the sites after conducting countersurveillance runs, but oddly, no surveillance was detected.

Coming back together after four days of wandering through the city, the rabbits met with a lone representative of the British unit who laid out several dozen photographs and said his outfit had come up with around twenty suspects. They had taken hundreds of photographs of the people who passed by and through comparison and elimination identified all those individuals who had visited more than one of the designated sites. He explained that they had set up remote-controlled cameras in cars or motorcycle saddlebags near all the sites the rabbits had visited, which explained why no surveillance had been detected. Several of the unit's "rabbits" were snared in the process. It showed everyone another surveillance trap to avoid.

New arrivals to Berlin were met and introduced to the unit in several ways, but one of the cleverest was that devised by P-61. When the section was notified that it had a new man arriving, they decided an initiation was in order. It would be a quick plunge into Berlin that tested the newbie's language abilities and coolness under stressful conditions. He was, for obscure reasons, code-named "Tozan" and was first met by "Greg," a team member he had never met. Greg had Tozan's photo and met him at Tegel airport as he disembarked. After picking up his luggage, Tozan followed Greg to a waiting car where he was told to follow the driver's instructions. Greg stayed behind. The next man took Tozan to a nearby U-Bahn station and told him to take a train to another station. There, he would be met by someone wearing a specific item of clothing.

The driver did not say another word to him except to tell him to leave his luggage in the vehicle. In this way, Tozan spent the rest of the day "getting to know the city" and meeting all the members of the team (save the one man who knew him) in one fashion or another. Throughout the day, he encountered strange things and people that were calculated to gauge his reactions. En route to one rendezvous point in a bad part of the city, he was intercepted by a drug pusher trying to sell him hashish. The dealer was actually one of his future section mates, but Tozan didn't pick up on the offer. Another meet was in a coed sauna where the clientele were required to strip off all their clothes. His final stop was in a "dive" bar in Kreuzberg—a hang out for anarchists and other strange characters. "Brad" was dressed in an outrageous mix of clothing to blend in with the regular clientele, but his costume ended up being tame next to one unforgettable patron—a large, bald-headed man wearing a pink tutu and combat boots. After successfully meeting Brad, it was off to a more sedate locale where Tozan was finally greeted by "Gator," the one man in the section who knew him. The rest of the section rejoined the party to give the newbie his official welcome over a stein of beer.

Wach am Rhine[10]

In the fall of 1985, several sections again deployed on FLINTLOCK, this time to conduct a SICTA or strategic reconnaissance (SR) missions. P-17 was one of the three tasked teams and went into isolation to prepare for the exercise. They were to "infiltrate" into the operational area, establish a hide position and report on train movements at a point along the Rhine River. They developed their operational concept and prepared equipment that, in addition to rucks with the normal load, was augmented with construction tools to build their hide site: shovels, picks, and rolls of chicken wire. The team sergeant's rucksack was the lightest at 110 pounds, the heaviest weighed in around 150 pounds. Once ready, they presented the typical SF brief-back to the commander and again to General Otis. The general seemed impressed if only for the fact the men could carry so much junk on their backs.

The team launched on the exercise from the base at Heidelberg, West Germany and traveled overland via a euphemistically named "C-2½ ton" truck to a drop-off point that had been chosen to simulate a DZ. The team jumped off their road-bound "airplane" and crashed into the forest to hump cross-county on foot. Ten kilometers later, they approached their surveillance site and went about selecting and building a hide site where they would live, observe, count, and report the trains moving on the railway that ran along the river. Communications was done via satellite radio and digital burst transmission from another location site far from the hide site. The combination of encrypted messages, short air time, and a narrow transmission beam, made intercept and direction finding of tactical satellite communications by the enemy very difficult.

For most of the exercise the men were steeped in boredom with few or in many cases nothing to report as the exercise planners had not arranged for anything to be on the roads. The major entertainment for one team was encountering a German *Forstmeister* who enlisted their help to spot and count the wild animals in his forest who he seemed to know by name. The final count was worth a good Swabian meal and beer at the conclusion of the exercise.

In general, the guidance from SOCEUR was to "observe and report"—generally, a waste of some highly trained, highly paid assets—and the teams that participated came away with the same assessment. Instead of a true unconventional warfare mission intended to build a resistance movement behind Soviet lines, the unit was relegated to an essentially passive role. Assuming the team survived its initial mission, only then would it embark on the direct-action phase and attack designated targets, support the recovery of downed pilots, or conduct UW operations. The planners at SOCEUR, however, never got that far with the planning. Everyone, from the four-star general in charge of European Command to the lowest private, concentrated on one premise only—stopping the Soviets as they rolled through the Fulda Gap. The few SF men dedicated to the longer fight behind the lines were but a small appendix to the main plan.

"This is Iron Man. I have control!"

The two earlier alerts and rollouts prepared the unit for its next endeavor, an exercise designed to test the unit's capabilities for its CT mission. In

February 1986, the unit was again notified and called to action. The staff duty NCO activated the unit's pager alert system and every member of the unit received the alert signal to return to unit.[11] Observers from SOCEUR showed up unannounced to watch the unit's preparations and its movement phase.

The men arrived and assembled in their team rooms, while the team leaders and sergeants went straight to the S-3 for an initial briefing. The special action force (SAF) was to be ready to move to Tempelhof no later than two hours after the alert order had been received. The initial information was that an USAF C-141B aircraft had been commandeered by an unknown number of "terrorists" and was sitting on the ramp at Sembach Air Force Base.

Three sections, P-17, P-34, and P-43, plus the command group and staff were designated for the fly-away. The rest of the unit assisted with the load-out. The teams prepared their gear, drew weapons and were ready in short order. A basic load of ammunition was loaded directly from the basement bunker, while the high explosives had to come from the Brigade bunkers—that was the most time-consuming task to be accomplished and, by the time those materials arrived, the SAF was completely uploaded. Two trucks carried equipment, while two buses carried the troops. Well within the time limit, everything and everyone was staged for movement. The convoy rolled out of Roosevelt Barracks and headed to the airfield with an MP escort clearing the route.

It was not the best of travel days. First, a civilian motorcyclist was left in the dust nursing his wounds after losing a battle with one of the big Mercedes trucks. Second, the Air Force loadmaster loaded the aircraft incorrectly, putting the heavy truck on last, which made the plane tail-heavy. That forced the pilot to battle the aircraft, which wallowed rather than flew all the way to the next destination. The loadmaster was fired on the spot when the plane landed. But before that happened, as the plane was landing, a second aircraft taxied across the main runway and forced the pilot to put down short and hard. Luckily, the result was only a broken landing gear. The SAF was just happy to have made it to their first destination alive and, having survived, they assembled in a hangar to prepare for their mission.

The exercise, code-named "Ellipse Bravo," was another certification for PSSE. The unit was to be tested in their proficiency to take down a simulated CT target, in this case a hijacked USAF airplane. The C-141 differed greatly from a civilian airliner. There were no window exits because the wings were placed high over the cargo compartment and only three doors. The clamshell tail ramp could not be used for entry because the controls were inside the plane. The only good news was that C-141s did not have emergency slides to interfere with ladders and its doors were lower to the ground than on a commercial jet.

GSG-9 had also been invited but would only practice on the aircraft, which they hadn't seen before. PSSE-B had flown on the plane often enough but never practiced assaults on it, so both units spent hours getting familiar with the aircraft and trying different entry techniques. The Germans liked fast, mobile approaches and once they were familiar with the aircraft, set up for a full practice assault.

True to form, they used a *Blitzkrieg* approach with their assaulters hanging out the doors of VW buses and riding on the special roof racks of their Mercedes sedans. While a *Bundesgrenzschutz* helicopter hovered in front of the target to distract the terrorists, the vehicles raced up to the plane. As GSG-9's snipers covered the few, small windows, the force assaulted the plane. But precious time was lost in the dismount and setting of ladders for their entry and the vehicles were seen driving towards the airplane by the "terrorists." Once the assault was over, the observers assessed that it had been compromised before the doors were breached. Lessons were learned on both sides and good operational methodologies were exchanged.

After GSG-9's practicing was done, the Berliners retired to the hangars to prepare for the test. To judge PSSE's performance, several observers waited inside the plane with about twenty airmen acting as terrorists and hostages. Outside on the tarmac, an officer was observing the action, along with an Air Force general and more SOCEUR observers. PSSE's SAF waited in the hangar until dark. The launch time arrived and the SAF loaded onto two USAF Special Operations Squadron MH-53 helicopters and were given a short tour of the countryside to simulate an infiltration into the airfield. Dropped off out of earshot of the target aircraft, the force then made its way to the objective.

First, sniper teams were posted to cover the cockpit and exits. Then the assault team, led by "Iron Man" Bill Davis, conducted a stealthy approach on foot towards the tail of the aircraft. The teams set up ladders to enter all the doors. On command, a small, electrically fired explosive charge would be set off in front of the cockpit to start the assault and hopefully disorient the terrorists temporarily.

With "Iron Man" calling the play, the teams reported back and then the explosive was set off with a click of the switch. The snipers were only able to see and report that bad guys were on the flight deck; they were unable to engage, so the assault teams knew they had to take out the "terrorists" themselves. The doors were opened and the men swarmed the aircraft, quickly securing the cargo hold and the flight deck. The action was over in seconds and the team began pulling passengers off the plane to safety.

The observers were happy. The teams had moved into position without being seen or heard and the assault was executed with speed and precision; it was judged a "positive resolution" of the incident. Malvesty and his SGM gave the unit a "thumbs up." Just over one year after its activation, PSSE was declared proficient to conduct CT operations. Shortly thereafter, the unit began exchange training with Delta, sending several four-man teams to train and work side-by-side with the national force.

Another alert was called several weeks later, but it was a local situation. The on-call sections were isolated in their team rooms and fed intelligence about a "hostage situation at a Berlin airport." Finally, late in the day, the SAF was moved to the US military airfield at Templehof where they practiced taking down a Pan Am Boeing B727. When darkness fell, the force was moved across town to Tegel airport, the primary commercial airfield in the French sector of the city. There they learned they were part of an exercise to take back the airplane and resolve the hostage situation. Sniper teams from P-52 were placed to observe activity in the aircraft and warn if the situation appeared to be deteriorating to the point where an emergency assault might be necessary.

As with the Sembach exercise, the assault force approached the airplane straight from the rear where they couldn't be seen from the plane. A four-man team from P-34 set up on the front entry door with ladders placed against the plane and two four-man teams climbed onto the port-side wing to go in through the two window emergency exits. The assault sections from P-43 supported them by placing and holding the ladders on the fuselage and at the wing roots. They would provide back-up if there were any casualties.

In front, the team climbed the ladders to await the signal. Once the door was pulled open, the first man in would clear the immediate area and turn into the first-class section of the plane, while the second would clear the flight deck. The third and fourth assaulters would support the first two men. The men on the wings would punch open the emergency exits and flood the passenger compartment to the rear and front.

When the execute order came, the doors and windows were breached by hand and the teams quickly flooded the aircraft. According to the observers, the "terrorists" were "shot" and most of the good guys—assaulters and hostages—survived. At the rear of the plane, a support team opened the B727's tail stair to get the hostages off the plane and screened to ensure no terrorists were among them.

Some thirty military personnel from Berlin Brigade role-played for the exercise with several SOCEUR observers and the Brigade commander hiding among them. After the exercise concluded, everyone climbed back on board for a quick "hot wash" of the exercise.

Although it was easy to claim success after each of these exercises, it was clear the unit was up to accomplishing the mission. It had mastered the technical aspects of CT operations on a number of different targets, excellent marksmanship was second nature, as were the more esoteric skills of explosive breaching and entry work. Teamwork and good planning, along with stealth, speed, and violence of action, increased the probabilities of success in precision strike operations and the unit had that in spades.

After this exercise, however, only one thing mattered to the men. They went home to bed.

Warning Order

It was very early in the morning of April 5, 1986 when James felt a short tremor that shook the bed he was lying in. About the same time a muffled "whomp" reached the building. Both together signaled something was not right and he realized there had been some sort of explosion. He rolled out of bed and looked out of the apartment window in the Friedenau section of Berlin. There was nothing for a while and then came the alternating high-low sirens of the emergency service vehicles. There were many and they sounded to be some distance away, not close enough to worry or to go see what the commotion was about. He went back to bed.

The next morning, he rolled into work with the local radio station chattering away. A bomb had ripped through a local discotheque, La Belle, killing two people and wounding about two hundred more. The commentators were saying it was terrorism. Inside the PSSE's building, everyone was listening to news reports and waiting for the latest from Bill, the S-2. As the unit's senior intelligence NCO, he was connected with all the right players to get the latest information. As of yet there was nothing.

La Belle was a favorite hangout for young GIs from the infantry regiment who liked drinking, dancing, and fast times. One of the two people killed was a soldier, many others were wounded. The motive seemed obvious, less so the identity of the perpetrators.

There was nothing for the unit to do, so activities continued as scheduled. A couple of teams went to the range to shoot, one went downtown to do "city training," which usually meant casing of operational sites, surveillance training, or reconnaissance along the Wall. The rest were in planning for upcoming exercises. It would have been a routine day, but in the back of everyone's mind was the bombing.

Several days later, Bill shared that signal intercepts indicated the bombing was "state-sponsored" and Libya was the backer. The Libyan People's Bureau, their so-called equivalent of an embassy, was located in East Berlin. If the bombing was a Libyan operation, it probably originated from their offices across the Wall. It was probably the same MO that "Carlos the Jackal" had used when he bombed the French Cultural Center in Berlin years before. Carlos smuggled 25 kilos of plastic explosives across the border with help of his assistants and then detonated them to punish the French.[12] The Libyans had apparently decided to use similar tactics to punish the Americans after several naval confrontations in the Gulf of Sidra.

Immediately, discussions in the unit centered on extracting some sort of pay-back. "What about a snatch operation?" someone suggested. And so began the planning. Teams could easily access the East on "official duty." What happened after that was the question. For several days the plan was tossed about, but specific targets could never be determined.

While the specifics were being debated, maps were consulted, knives were sharpened, and gear sorted. Each man constantly adjusted his gear, moving pouches from here to there, stuffing who knows how many magazines into each to test capacity, and then pulling them out rapidly to see how quickly they could be swapped with an empty one from his weapon. It was a ritual played out before every operation until the operator was satisfied or at least happy with the interim result.

No "launch" order was received, but the wheels kept turning nevertheless, and the team leaders kept badgering the commander about whether or not the operation should be proposed to higher. Wisely perhaps, he waited and monitored the heated conversation going on between the commandant of Berlin and the CINCEUR. Something else was afoot, he cautioned. Abducting just any Libyan diplomat might prove counterproductive. Moreover, the East Germans might object if they determined the Americans had been up to no good in their sector of the city.

On April 15, ten days after the incident, 18 F-111 bombers, 24 A-6 Intruders and F/A-18 Hornets took off from the United Kingdom and US Navy aircraft carriers off the coast of Libya. Over Tripoli and Benghazi, the aircraft bombed Libyan military facilities in retaliation for Muammar Gaddafi's affront to America. For the planners in the Pentagon, strategic bombing was established as the method of choice in dealing with terrorist incidents and Operation EL DORADO CANYON was its name.

In Berlin, the plans were shelved and the teams went back to their "normal" routines. Once again, terrorism's ugly head had risen and diverted the unit's attention from its wartime mission of UW. More than that, it showed that CT was becoming the new norm. Unfortunately for the teams, terrorism reinforced the necessity of the RST mission, which was still pulling resources and required inordinate amounts of paperwork and administration. Shortly after the US bombing of Libya, it was decided an inspection of NATO weapons storage sites in Greece might be a good idea. The trip was a tense time for the team members as they knew they had to protect themselves as well as conduct the surveys. Since the killing of the CIA's chief of station, Richard Welch, in 1975, the terrorist group 17 November had made Greece a dangerous place for American diplomats and military personnel. The men were never more serious about tradecraft and situational awareness than when moving around the country and while at their hotel. Comparatively, the weapons facilities were pretty safe places.

Bulldog

Mac Dorsey departed in August 1986 and was replaced by Lieutenant Colonel Jack "Bulldog" Moroney. A different sort of commander, Moroney once said he was just "a soldier in officer's clothing." He was, as his moniker suggests, a bulldog of a man—short and stocky with a neck like an ox. He was tenacious and had a temper you did not want to test first-hand. He was a stickler for details, but didn't waste time with in-depth explanations; his meetings were short and to the point. At the weekly operations meeting, section commanders were allowed about three minutes to present their training plan using briefing slides. He'd look at the schedule and ask pertinent questions on why and how the training was to be done. God help anyone who read to him verbatim off the paper or didn't have a succinct answer. Most importantly, he got things done for the unit and the men.

One of the first complaints to reach his ears was the burdensome requirements of the RST program. Within weeks, he arranged for the program to be shifted to a dedicated cell at USEUCOM in Stuttgart. The sections cleaned up and finished their remaining reports and then happily jettisoned all their remaining binders and document protectors. It was time to go back to real training.

Major Davis was still XO and, for the moment, SAF ground commander. Dorsey had relinquished the role in deference to "Iron Man's" composure under stress. Bulldog observed the SAF training and operations for several weeks and then took command. No one doubted his ability to control things. During a later exercise, the S-3 Bruce Hoover told the XO, "You know he doesn't need us around at all; he just tolerates junior officers as a way to prepare them for future assignments."

He also directed a reorganization of the unit to better conduct its CT mission. Four sections—P-23, 34, 43, and 61—were designated as assault teams, each with two four-man elements. The other two sections, P-17 and 52, became dedicated sniper/observer teams. This permitted each group to concentrate their training on one expertise and facilitated command and control.

Bulldog would invariably appear at training locations to quietly observe from a distance. He usually didn't interfere or ask questions and if he remained quiet it was a good sign. If he grabbed the team leader by the neck and disappeared around the corner, you knew something was wrong.

One of Bulldog's first contributions was to get the logisticians back in the States to supply the unit with much-needed new equipment. The shipments would include state-of-the art night vision devices, new rifles and optics, along with better body armor and assault uniforms. It required some typical "Bulldog" persuasion skills including one man being drug over his desk by the lapels of his uniform to make a point about ballistic armor. No one was badly hurt in the process though there were a few bruised egos. Moroney somehow knew he would never be promoted and did his best to make sure the promotion boards understood his position. His usual comment was: "I have no delusions of making general. The only way I'll wear a star is if I work at Texaco when I retire."

He also improved coordination with the Agency, which in turn provided the unit with access to equipment unavailable through military channels, including technical surveillance gear that gave the sniper teams the ability to see things much further away than standard optics. Both mission capabilities were enhanced by joint cooperation.

Bill Davis departed the XO position and returned to the States in the late 1986 to take a battalion command. He was followed by Major Steve

Philbrick, a warrior-scholar with a healthy disregard for convention. Although some wondered about Philbrick's proclivities when he chose "Hangman" as his code name, he was adept at keeping the unit running smoothly while Bulldog chewed heads off. He acquired another nickname—"Huey Lewis"—as he bore a striking resemblance to the singer. And, despite his seemingly complacent outlook on life, Steve did not suffer fools lightly. He just wouldn't call them that to their face, unlike Bulldog, who did.

Cracks in the Curtain

The 1980s were a tough decade for the Soviets. They were fighting a difficult insurgency in Afghanistan that would prove intractable by mid-decade. Poland was struggling with civil unrest started by the Solidarity union strikes, which threatened to encourage like-minded groups in other Warsaw Pact countries. At one point in late 1980, the Soviets proposed intervening with Warsaw Pact troops in Poland to "crush the anti-socialist opposition."[13] The Polish leadership warned Moscow that the introduction of Soviet troops might cause a disaster, but if the East Germans came over the border it could lead to war. Communist or not, Germans were disliked in Poland.

The Soviet Union's foreign policies of the 1970s, especially its drive to achieve military superiority over the United States, had failed. Its attempt to force accommodation by the West had resulted in confrontation, especially in the Third World. Because of this, NATO still believed the Soviet military planned a rapid and massive conventional offensive to achieve a quick victory if war came, and responded with its own military expansion.

After the deaths of Soviet leaders Leonid Brezhnev in 1982, Yuri Andropov in 1984, and Konstantin Chernenko in 1985, Mikhail Gorbachev took the reins of power.

Across the Atlantic, President Ronald Reagan was pushing his tough policies against the Soviet Union, while Gorbachev began to reassess Soviet power and the way his country dealt with other nations. Gorbachev called it "new thinking" and his leadership signaled a possible relaxation in the Cold War tensions that had gripped Europe since 1946. Gorbachev planned a sea-change in policy that gave priority to the "pursuit of cooperation with the West over the search for unilateral [military] advantage."[14] But others within the Soviet Union, especially the military, were not ready to accept this new way of thinking.

Despite the seeming thaw, in the mid-1980s, NATO remained skeptical of rapprochement with the Soviet Union. The SACEUR General Rogers continued planning the defense of Western Europe as before. That said, the planning for war centered on conventional forces and scant attention was paid to Special Forces. SF was only a small cog in the huge machine that was the European Command and NATO. The only guidance SF Berlin had was that in the event of war they were to "buy time."

Reagan's visit to Berlin on June 12, 1987 reemphasized the city's importance as the "Outpost of Freedom" in the Cold War, and the unit went to standby alert in case someone tried to disrupt the event. After several hours of oiling guns, sharpening knives, and twiddling of thumbs, the teams stood down and everyone filtered out to the Wall and Tempelhof airport to hear the President speak.

His call for Gorbachev to "tear down this Wall" was seen by some as a call for peaceful change, while others worried it was a provocation. The Soviet economy was severely impacted by the pressure of a continued arms race, while Afghanistan was a strain on the army. Soviet military doctrine had rejected Brezhnev's doctrine of an assured supremacy threatening the West to one of possessing the military sufficiency to collectively defend the Warsaw Pact. The immediate threat of war in Europe seemed very far away.

Kicking Doors

In the late fall of 1987, Bulldog devised an exercise for the entire SAF. Two teams were designated as role-players and set up a complex of three buildings for a hostage scenario. Three other teams were alerted and went through the load-out procedure before they received a brief on the target. Ostensibly, the target was inside East Germany and the initial vehicle movement was done with teams hidden inside closed trucks. They were taken to a drop-off point where the cross-country walk began. How an actual border crossing was to be done was not addressed, but everyone instantly assumed the exercise was a rehearsal for an actual mission to recover someone or something.

It was pitch black as the teams assembled on the ground and began their movement through the heavily forested area to the edge of an abandoned factory compound. There, four assault ladders were set up for the teams to climb over two sets of brick walls into the compound. Once inside the team leaders briefly coordinated their movement and the force separated to move into position.

The movement phase had already taken an hour from the drop-off point and the second phase required another 30 minutes for everyone to get to the launch points that overlooked the buildings. The general configuration of the target buildings was known, but little else was. The interior layout, the location of any hostages, exactly how many bad guys there were and what defenses they had in place, were all unknowns. It was not the ideal scenario; there were too many variables for anyone to be comfortable.

One building was reportedly secured with a metal grate and padlock. There was only one entry and something was inside that needed to be recovered. That would happen last, after the immediate threats were eliminated and the living "precious cargo" recovered. Two teams set up to enter the buildings with the third in security. "Hangman" had the troops in position and quietly spoke the codewords into his radio that handed command over to "Bulldog."

It was quiet. Gas lights flickered in the buildings and an occasional laugh or loud word could be heard from within. Outside, the only noise was a whisper of wind through the pine trees. The radio came to life. It was Bulldog, giving the codeword for the assault teams to report their readiness. One by one they came back, "Thunder, roger," "Hammer, roger," until all were accounted for. Bulldog came back, "I have command, stand by." Everyone leaned forward waiting for the next transmission, and when it came—"Execute! Execute! Execute!"—they launched.

Doors were breached, and windows broken as teams flooded the buildings tossing flash-bang grenades and searching through the rooms with infra-red lights and night vision goggles for their prey. The bad guys had prepared well. Team Thunder hit one door and "Mac," the point man, stepped into the building only to be greeted with the flash of an explosive charge. A booby trap made from an electrically detonated grenade simulator went off, throwing him to the ground. Protected as he was by his helmet, heavy Nomex overalls, and ceramic "chicken-plate" armor, he was luckily not hurt. Nevertheless, scorch marks on his uniform attested to the proximity of the blast. The remainder of the team stepped over Mac and continued on, "eliminating" the two hostiles in that building. There were no hostages. After quickly securing the bad guys and searching for additional explosives, Team Thunder backed out of their target and secured the perimeter around Hammer's objective. Gunfire and grenades continued to echo from within. Adding to the din was a voice cursing up a storm in a combination of anger and pain. A flash-bang had gone off, spewing its flaming sub-charges, one of which landed between the thighs of a restrained hostage, burning him badly. In the confusion, a medic was attending to him as the last of the bad guys were subdued.

Then began the last phase. Team Blast attached a thermite torch to the steel grate of the final target and fired it. In a blinding flash, the flame cut through the hardened steel of the lock and the grate was pulled open. Entering the building, the team found a long box that looked vaguely like a Soviet surface-to-air missile (SAM) shipping container. They grabbed the box and joined the queue outside. All the teams moved out as they had come in, moving with freed hostages, one in a litter, and the prize box. This time a fence was cut and the party, now nearly forty men, moved into the forest to the pick-up point. Trucks were loaded and everyone returned to base, except for two medics and their burn patient who earned a trip to the US Army Berlin hospital.

Back at the unit, the teams climbed off the trucks, returned their equipment to lockers, and did a preliminary cleaning of weapons as Bulldog gave his evaluation. Generally he was pleased, although he thought the SAF would have suffered some significant casualties. The bad guys assessed they had been surprised and that the raid would have worked. Everyone agreed it was a difficult problem to solve. Everything said and done, the men speculated what the colonel had in his back pocket—was it just a fly-away exercise or preparation for a special mission for God and country? As it turned out, he just wanted to test his unit's ability to deal with an unclear situation—the *in extremis* solution that called for action in extremely difficult conditions. It was the scenario that would sometimes be faced by forward-based SF units.

Where the Ellipse Bravo exercise had certified PSSE to conduct CT operations, Moroney wanted to push the envelope with an exercise that was ambiguous and, because no rehearsals were conducted, required excellent teamwork, improvization and flexibility. There were the usual bruises and a few burns, but overall it was a good test.

Planning for War, Again

Having passed the colonel's diabolical scheme in the forest, it was time for another exercise. This one was more taxing cerebrally as it required a relook of the primary mission. Despite the overt signs that the Warsaw Pact was embracing detente, Moroney believed the possibility of a general war in Europe remained real. He directed all the teams to return to their war plans and conduct an extensive reevaluation using the so-called CASMAP outline. The "Command Area Study and Mission Analysis Program" was a total immersion planning tool used by SF teams to prepare for their operations. Much of the work was already complete, being in the operational area was advantageous after all, but the Bulldog instructed each team to prepare a brief-back to demonstrate they understood their mission and had a feasible plan for getting it done.

Each team settled into their team rooms for the duration, breaking down their existing plans into digestible parts for review and revision. The rooms were off-limits to all but the members and, for once, the building was quiet during the day. Two- and three-man cells would slip out from time to time to check details of the city or take a closer look at sections of the Wall. When things got boring, the men would try to spook the East German guards to time their response and observe routines with vehicles and dogs. At the same time, they had to avoid getting shot or arrested by the West Germans who frowned on such incitement.

The latest OB data and overhead imagery was obtained through the S-2 to complete the packages. When all was completed, the teams rehearsed their briefing and tried to shoot holes in the plan's logic. The last thing anyone wanted was to not be ready for the commander's post-brief interrogation. Throughout the day, the clank of weights from the gym downstairs would echo through the hallways. It was Bulldog, often the only man to use the facility during work hours. He heaved the equivalent of a small Volkswagen around as a way of working off frustration. It also signaled the troops that he was in the building.

Each team was given a date for the brief-back once they declared they were ready. Bulldog showed up without any staff officers to act as witnesses, so the men relaxed somewhat. And the briefings began with scratch-built models, some with Rube Goldberg-like mechanical demonstrations, that were supplemented by maps and photographs to illustrate the most important phase—breaking out of the city and getting to the operational area.

The two city teams had a relatively easier task to plan, while the over-the-Wall teams had to demonstrate a plan that was feasible and not suicidal. Stealth and route selection were all important, so stealing small airplanes or riding out of the city on horseback were not acceptable ideas. More than one team had to fine-tune or completely change plans the colonel didn't like. Once he gave his approval, the teams put the plans away and only returned to them for periodic review and change.

The unit's so-called "City Exercise" that practiced the "4304" mission continued on an annual basis for the entire unit and, on a smaller scale, several times a year for individual sections. In addition, each section's communicators deployed to West Germany to practice technical communications (HF and SATCOM). "Bulldog" mandated that everyone be capable of sending and receiving Morse code at 15 words per minute, which meant a lot of time was spent wearing headphones in the unit's learning center.

The exercises themselves were often boring and psychologically wearying—a good test of a man's resolve. With each team broken into three or four cells, the men would go days without physical contact as they ran through their assignments.

The exercises had evolved to include multiple teams (sections) and culminated in a series of combat actions that were coordinated through non-tech and technical communication systems. Teams conducted snatches of "enemy" officers or intercepts of couriers on the streets of Berlin—all of which were worth the tedium leading up to the execution of the task. The entire unit was incorporated into the exercises, including the support center personnel who were used to run safehouses and emplace caches. This required the staff to go through intensive training, a unique requirement that finance and supply specialists would otherwise never experience. The scenarios were based on the CASMAP identified requirements; one of the exercises concentrated on surveillance and countersurveillance in a hostile city that was done without technical communications methods. The basic scenario was based on a sudden outbreak of hostilities and was kicked off with a non-pager/non-telephone alert at 0300. It was a scary prospect to knock on doors at that time of morning because most everyone in the unit was a bit paranoid and heavily armed. Luckily, no one was shot.

Unexpected finds were sometimes the catalyst for a plan change, sometimes not. Section P-34 made an interesting discovery in the forest near the southern end of the Wannsee, not far from the so-called "Freedom Bridge" (*Glienecke Brücke*).[15] Gary found an old cistern system that had served Berlin University and which had been completely destroyed during the war. It was in the woods and underbrush about 75 meters from the Wall. A manhole cover concealed the entrance, but it still had a steel ladder that descended into the earth. The team decided to see if it could be cleared out and worked on it for about a month, digging inside the tunnel at night to see if it might lead to the other side in the GDR. They never reached the end and it became a little too dangerous since there were occasional passersby. One night Gary and Mike were down bringing up buckets of rubble to dump in the bushes outside the entrance. As Mike moved the cover off and started to come out of the tunnel, he spotted a German standing close by with a dog that started to bark. The gentleman, thinking the two bedraggled men had just escaped from the East, said *"Hallo, Heißen Sie willkommen in West Berlin!"* (Welcome to West Berlin). Their presence discovered, they gave the man a story about treasure hunting and disappeared, never to return.

Fly Away

No matter how important the wartime mission was, the CT mission always came back to assert itself in the unit's activities. The staff at SOCEUR never ceased putting together more and more intricate tests of the unit's CT capabilities. The exercises occurred on at least a twice-yearly basis, grew larger and more complex, and usually involved more than one unit. On one hand, the threat of terrorism was high and CT operations required practice. On the other, they were easier to organize, much shorter in duration, and had a higher profile than UW exercises. In short, they were much more interesting for the generals to watch! Most took place at the Royal Air Force base at RAF Wentworth either as the target or staging area and often included USAF helicopters out of RAF Bentwaters. Practice sessions with the rotary types often included aerial refueling, fast roping, and door gunner exercises over the English Channel.

The first fly-away exercise took place in the spring of 1988. The unit was called in at zero-dark 30 and, in the morning, the force moved out to Tempelhof. Loaded onto a C-130, they flew to England and the next day were flown back into West Germany on MH-53 "Pave Low" helicopters to a military training area where a camp had been set up with tents and a shed for the command center.

The usual pre-mission prep began. Bulldog was wound up, as he always was and overseeing just about everything oversee-able. Someone told him to get some rest in the early afternoon since things weren't going to happen until that night, but being a hyper-energetic commander, he said he couldn't or wouldn't. He was somewhat reminiscent of a Tasmanian devil with his whirlwind of activity, albeit one that could bench-press a small car. Everyone kept out of his way and got on with the work.

The target was a two-story, free-standing building that sat among several others along a street. The teams were briefed that a group of six terrorists were holding probably fewer than ten hostages. With no way to break in from an abutting building, sewer, basement, or tunnel, the only way in was an approach from outside; that meant through the doors or windows.

While two teams (eight men) stood by in case an emergency assault had to be launched, sniper/observer teams were put into place. They began to report back to the command center by radio on activities inside and providing information that would help the full assault force get to the target.

When the force finally got the word to approach the target, they went forward with three four-man assault teams. One would enter through a second-floor window on a side of the building away from the terrorists, while the other two would use breaching charges to blow through the ground-floor side and front doors. With all the teams in position, Bulldog took control and counted down to execute the assault. With his command of "Execute! Execute! Execute!" the charges went off. One team went through the shredded front door and the second-floor team broke through the window.

Then a call came over the radio. The side door breach had failed. The third team abandoned their planned entry point and entered through the front door in order to get to their assigned area. The ladder team took the second floor to "kill" the bad guys and secure the hostages. The whole operation took about 90 seconds.

Once the building was secure a "hot wash" was conducted to review the exercise. The failed breach turned out to be the result of a cross bar on the door which held the metal door in place and caused much of the blast to vent sideways. When it went off, the Number One man who was holding a blast shield was thrown back about 15 feet. His ceramic blast shield was shattered and he was peppered with shrapnel that caused superficial wounds in his lower legs. Even exercises could be dangerous.

Bulldog has left the Building

Colonel Moroney departed in March 1988 and was replaced by "Obie." His arrival was a wake-up call for the unit. Moroney's style of leadership (and stepping on of toes) had made some enemies and some believed

"Obie" had been sent as a counterpoint. Despite the fact that he had previously served with Detachment "A" as a Team Leader in 1974, he seemed out of his depth. His qualifications were first questioned when he saw the unit's arms room and asked: "Why are there so many guns?" The fact that every man in the unit had at least three assigned weapons—assault rifles, submachine guns, sniper rifles, as well as pistols—was Moroney's doing. The new commander didn't grasp the need for a variety of weapons to match the range of missions the unit was asked to accomplish. His demeanor and inexperience made him one of the least liked commanders and the target of many wisecracks. It would be through the force of his XO, staff, and the men alone, that the unit would carry on. The XO would again take over as SAF commander as "Obie" seemed oddly detached from the unit's activities. He was often physically absent from training he should have been present for, giving weak excuses like: "It's raining." It fell to the XO, the S-3 section, and the SGM to ensure things ran as they should, with "Hangman," the XO, as de facto commander. To many in the unit it seemed evident that "Obie" was there to shut the unit down. There could be no other rational explanation for his arrival.

One Last Shot

The unit participated in what would be its final Ellipse Bravo in 1989. It turned out to be a classic case that illustrated the gulf that often exists between a staff's ideas and reality. The exercise took place in Scotland and an advance element deployed via MH-53 helicopter from an airbase in West Germany across the English Channel to put "eyes on target." The rest of the force was to follow three days later.

Things started to go bad when the advance element landed and were told they were conducting a cross-country march to the Forward Operating Base (FOB) near the target, led by a "trusted agent" from 1st Battalion 10th SFG. The element consisted not only of a sniper/observer team (P-52), but also the Tactical Operations Center (TOC)—an S-3 operations officer and a communications support package that was carrying much of its SATCOM equipment in large hard cases. The later explanation was that the exercise scenario depicted a "denied area," and the target would not have been accessible other than on foot. They just forgot to mention that detail and the advance team expected motor transport.

After a long, hard "hump" through kilometers of sheep fields and over dry stone walls, the group reached the FOB, an old farm house. There the element linked up with a technical team from another agency who would assist with observation of the target. A field TOC was set up and observers were deployed forward to overwatch the target, an old dormitory building.

They did this for several days before the remainder of the force deployed forward on two MH-53s. The Channel crossing was not uneventful; one of the birds, with "Hangman" the SAF commander onboard, suffered a component failure and almost ditched in the sea. Luckily, it made the coast safely and landed in a football field. There the entire force was loaded onto the remaining helicopter to complete the flight.

The force was ready, having been told what to expect by the advance team. It was properly prepared with rucksacks (rather than the usual equipment bags) and came off the birds and went straight into its cross-country trek to the FOB. After a day of preparation, rehearsals, and briefings, the assault on the target was launched the following night. It lasted the better part of 30 minutes to account for all the "enemy" and "hostages" and to prepare for evacuation from the area. Once the objective was secured, two telephone poles were cut down with explosives to make room for the choppers and a tactical exfiltration pulled the entire force out. The helos flew to a point near an airbase where they began to loiter—circling in the air—as a Ranger company conducted a combat assault to secure the airfield below. It was a plan reminiscent of Iran. Once the airfield was secured, the MH-53s landed and the SAF transferred to a C-130 transport for their long ride home.

And the Wall Came Tumbling Down

The cracks in the Soviet system became more apparent in the late 1980s. Few understood the implications of what was happening and no one expected the Wall to fall.[16] Nevertheless, trying to flee from East Germany was still a dangerous decision; the last fatality happened in March 1989, when Winfried Freudenberg was killed as he attempted to escape to West Berlin in a homemade hot air balloon.

The events that led to the fall could be traced to Mikhail Gorbachov's policy changes four years earlier. They were meant to make the Soviet Union more competitive with the West, not end its occupation of East Germany. But he unwittingly unleashed forces that would dismantle the Warsaw Pact and force massive shifts in power in the East.

During the late evening of November 9, 1989, no one was more surprised than Bill Billingslea when he received a telephone call from Brigade headquarters informing him the border was open. Bill was PSSE's "CQ" or Charge of Quarters, with responsibility for the security of the facility and ensuring alert messages got to the unit leadership quickly. No one was sure what was happening at the Wall, just that people were coming across from East to West in their thousands.

It was a flood that would change the bipolar politics of Europe completely. For the moment, it was a celebration; the hangover would come later.

For Special Forces Berlin, one thing was clear: an old paradigm would soon be swept away.

Within weeks, the mission of US Forces in Europe changed. With the "main enemy" removed from the equation, the utility of unconventional warfare and the missions of special operations forces were questioned. PSSE would become one of the first casualties.

For the unit to remain operational, PSSE's true status would have to be declared to the West German federal authorities once it took full control of West Berlin. USAREUR intended to pull all clandestine units (SF and military intelligence) out of the city and then decide which should be reinserted, with the German government's permission.

The unit was instructed to prepare a decision briefing for the CINCEUR. Two senior NCOs traveled to Stuttgart to put together the argument to save the unit. After three days of intense work with the SOCEUR staff, the results were presented to Brigadier General James T. Scott, the SOCEUR commander. Scott was to brief the CINCEUR, but never made it that far, possibly because the CINC was on his way out the door and was followed by a new commander who was not a fan of SF Berlin. But it could well have been the USAREUR commander who ensured the proposal to save the unit was strangled in its infancy. He was not a supporter of Special Forces as an organization in any event.

The unit's clandestine status and complicated support system, as well as its location, contributed to its demise. Eliminating the unit would save money; a first step in the peace dividend that came with winning the Cold War. Furthermore, it had competition [Redacted] and other special mission units saw PSSE as an anachronism. The UW mission in East Germany, being no longer required, would disappear, while 1st Battalion, 10th SFG at Bad Tölz would officially take over the CT mission as part of the Theater CINC's In Extremis Force (CIF) in 1990.[17]

But, before the lights were turned off and the doors closed, PSSE's skills were needed for one more mission.

JAROC—A Final Task

Among the streaming throngs of East Germans coming to West Berlin through the newly opened frontier, there were a number of persons of interest to Western intelligence agencies. The first stop for refugees— even before they applied for West German assistance—was the Joint Allied Refugee Operations Center in Berlin. During the Cold War, it was manned with language-qualified interviewers from all three Western powers. The refugees were debriefed as to military service, information on infrastructure, etc.

With the opening of the borders, JAROC was flooded with refugees and a call went out for additional language-qualified personnel to assist with level one screening. The unit responded by sending its best linguists to help with the interview process.

The men were provided a basic screening checklist and interviewed refugees for several weeks after the Wall fell. Specific "priority inform-ation requirements" keyed the interviewers to look for certain kinds of people. If there were any hits from that list, they would take the packet back to the actual JAROC employees who would make a decision on secondary screening. If there were none, the paperwork was stamped and the refugee was sent to the next processing step.

Although the intent of many refugees was only to get the required paperwork stamped so they could get the 100 marks the West German government had promised, the procedure marked a important historical transition. East Germany had experienced a total collapse of its infrastructure and the [former West] German government was obligated to take care of the refugees who had been left without a social net. To continue their lives the refugees had to go through the process and become "westernized" to live in their new home: Germany. It was no longer East or West, it was just Germany.

One of the unit's interviewers, "Dave," remembered debriefing a former NVA tank company commander who had been stationed at a nuclear power facility. He described the rise of unrest in the GDR and how the facility first increased its defensive posture. Their tanks were pulled off the site and replaced with armored cars. Later, all armored vehicles were removed and they were left with just light vehicles and weapons. He was sent to secondary, where the analysts were able to piece together the GDR's disintegrating command and defense system.

Another encounter was with a husband and wife. He had been a lieutenant colonel in the NVA, but stated that he had retired. JAROC's screening criteria were constantly changing as to the period of interest. Before the fall of the Wall, the interviews would go back to at least a decade of military service, later it was just the last two years, and finally, only the last two weeks. The officer was outside the stated scope of interest and Dave was ready to let them move to the next step in processing when he happened to ask the wife what she did. It turned out that she had been a personal secretary to a general on the main staff. It was interesting to watch the husband as the wife started to cough up information and he tried to stop her from talking. He was reminded that he had voluntarily come to the West and had to decide where his allegiances would lie. He rolled pretty quickly. Both went to secondary. It turned out that she had every business and home phone number for everyone in the NVA general headquarters. The JAROC folks were most happy. They were just as happy with the former commander of all East German Army training; he had brought all the East German Army's instructional materials to the interview. As these mirrored Soviet training methods, they were quite useful to the Allies.

Dave remembered another rough-looking guy who, based on his BIC pen tattoos, had obviously been in prison. The man leaned over at one point and asked Dave if he would have to talk with "them?" "Which them?" Dave asked. The guy looked around conspiratorially, leaned in and said "the Allies." Dave felt like his conversational *Berlinerisch* was pretty good at that point.

The British and Americans were quite serious about the work, but the French had other ideas. They sat in the background until a pretty, young German girl showed up. They took those interviews and returned to their coffee and cigarettes once they were finished chatting up the woman. Our dear French allies.

The intelligence screening was important for the Allies, but that process was overshadowed by something larger, the stories of the people themselves. Many were poignant reminders of a failed system, others were just human failings.

Bud, another of the interviewers from the unit, had one memorable day filled with such stories. He showed up at the processing facility at 0700 hours as usual and took his position at a table facing a huge hall full of chairs filled with expectant refugees. One of his first applicants was an old lady who came forward and sat down at the desk with eight stacks of paperwork.

He asked her who the files were for. The woman replied that one was hers and others were for the seven elderly men sitting in a row behind her, each physically and mentally handicapped. Their care facility near the Polish border had closed and the staff disappeared. The lady was a nurse there and had been caring for them. After several weeks alone in the facility, she had managed to contact a facility in West Germany that would take the men. She wanted to get them there. She took a letter from the top file and showed it to Bud; it was from the hospice. Bud went to get some help from the German social workers. They skipped the intelligence questions.

Later, a little old man showed up and handed Bud his paperwork. Bud asked all the questions until finally he asked "Have you had contact with *Stasi*."

The man said, "Oh yes, I was arrested." Bud asked "Why?"

The man responded quietly that he was arrested for being an American spy and had spent the last 13 years in jail. He had recently walked out the prison. Bud went and got the big boys. They came to escort the man off to a backroom. A couple of hours later they told Bud that the tale was true. As soon as they had confirmed the story, the man was put into the "take good care of this guy" category.

Late in the evening he got one of the last refugees for the day. A young girl, perhaps nineteen, from East Berlin and, as Bud described her, hotter than the major's playboy-wife, but not too smart. She had a thick Berlin accent and the French would be pissed for going home early had they found out. She answered all the questions and, yes, she had been arrested for "anti-socialist behavior" like everyone else. "Why did you come across?" Bud asked. "Well," she responded dreamily, "all my friends did, so I guess I had to." Bud shook his head and moved her on in the process. He went home upset; the girl had no concept of the important things happening around her, he thought. He didn't get over it until he talked to his wife. She said that the girl getting out of the East and being given a chance was really what the whole program was about. The East German people's world had been turned upside down.

The Curtain Falls

The Wall went down without a shot and the face of Europe changed. While the Berlin Brigade itself would remain until July 6, 1994, PSSE was officially disbanded on August 15, 1990 thus ending the history of a unique and critically important Special Forces mission. The unit's former commander, Sid Shachnow officiated at the small ceremony that took place.[18]

US Special Forces were present in Berlin for a span of 34 years and contributed greatly to the end of the Soviet domination of Eastern Europe. The principal Warsaw Pact commanders were aware of its existence and respected its capabilities—it was one more deterrent that prevented a Cold War from going hot.

When the doors finally closed, the "Green Berets" who served in Berlin went back to the Special Forces Groups in the States and elsewhere to continue their careers. Like their predecessors in Detachment "A," many of its men would fill important leadership roles throughout the Army, in Special Forces and Special Operations into the 21st century and long after 9/11.

It was a proud unit that disappeared quietly into the night.

Postcriptum II

In 2014, US Army Special Operations Command tweeted out an official announcement:

> On this day in USASOC History, 16 April, 1984, the Physical Security Support Element was activated in Berlin, West Germany. This support element replaced Detachment A (39th Special Forces Operational Detachment).[19]

A CASUALTY OF PEACE

It has been over 25 years since the Berlin Wall fell and the Iron Curtain was drawn open. With that event came an expectation of peace. It was believed the time had come for much of the United States' military in Europe to be reduced. In 1994, the Berlin Brigade was disbanded. Following a final Allied celebratory parade, the *Bundeswehr* was once again able to march down the streets of the German capital.

Several years earlier, few had noted the departure of Special Forces Berlin after nearly 35 years of service. It left as it had arrived, quietly and without fanfare. Throughout its existence, this small band of men was poised to execute a mission that held small promise of success. They were aware of the odds against them and the threat posed by the Warsaw Pact forces stationed just kilometers away. Despite that, no one wavered in their commitment to face and deter the Soviet war machine.

The preceding pages describe two Special Forces units that served as part of the Allied effort to deter Soviet expansion during the Cold War. Despite the commonality of their organization and missions, the OPSEC issues that precipitated the inactivation of Detachment "A" ensured there could not be a direct lineage between the two. In fact the US Army Center for Military History has no record of Physical Security Support Element-Berlin or the 410th SFD.[1]

Det "A" and PSSE-B shared a history and heritage much like that of the Office of Strategic Services and its successor, Special Forces. The first unit is inextricably connected to the second: they were both Special

Forces in Berlin and shared more than the tradition of Chicken Friday. They had the same missions against the same enemies—the Warsaw Pact and terrorists—just at different times.

Above and beyond their two primary missions, the men proved their adaptability to meet new demands as they emerged. Providing vulnerability assessments was one of the first of those requirements, then came counterterrorism and finally, the regional survey team mission. In between came ad hoc taskings: surveilling hostile intelligence agents or criminal enterprises, terrorism ordnance surveys, and the training of police. The unit's leaders never felt constrained to remain within the limits of the stated missions, rather they sought out opportunities to show the intangible qualities of the men who served there—the versatility and flexibility to accomplish anything, anywhere, any time. In this they succeeded.

But, just as the units had commonalities, both suffered a few fundamental problems.

The Detachment's lack of an approved cover mechanism and the resulting operational security problems led to its inactivation. The security environment that existed in 1956 was quite different than the one that existed in 1982. For one, the Soviet and East German security services were most concerned with their own internal security in 1956 and did not expend extensive resources collecting intelligence on their enemy's order of battle. However, as they fully consolidated control over their countries, their focus moved increasingly outward. Additionally, American journalists, spurred by incidents during Vietnam, became increasingly willing to report on classified military operations and programs, as Jack Anderson did when he exposed the second Iran rescue mission in August 1980.[2]

But having an "approved cover" was not an airtight method to keep the KGB, MfS, and news organizations at bay. It was just a starting point. The measures put in place to protect the security of PSSE-B did help the unit to better conceal its activities. Most people were convinced that PSSE *only* conducted security surveys and vulnerability assessments. That part of the cover plan did provide a modicum of security.

The CT mission was both an opportunity and a problem. The training and operations were challenging but there was a tendency to emphasize the hard skills of direct action—shooting, breaching, assault operations—over the more esoteric tradecraft required for the wartime UW mission. There were several reasons for this. First, the chances of actually conducting a CT mission were greater than World War III breaking out. The leadership realized this and worked to ensure the assault force could meet the exacting requirements needed for success. That demanded specialized equipment and very intense training.

Second, there is immediate gratification and measurable performance criteria associated with conducting direct-action missions, be it an airplane takedown, raid, prisoner snatch, or a long-range sniper shot. That gratification was less evident in "practicing the clandestine tradecraft necessary to survive as an underground organization."[3]

As the Detachment disappeared in 1984, PSSE-B showed up on the scene. Because both units spent a lot of time on ranges honing their combative skills, the two units looked suspiciously similar. Berlin police officers, who used some of the nearby ranges, undoubtedly realized there was more than just a superficial connection between the old and the new. Likewise, the hostile intelligence services on the other side of the Wall understood that if it looks and quacks like a duck, it probably is a duck.

In December of 1989, Major General Sid Shachnow, who commanded the Det "A" in the mid-1970s, returned to become the US Commander of Berlin. Shortly after the Wall fell, the chief of the KGB's *Rezidentura* in Berlin-Karlshorst, General "George Dulenko" visited Sid's home along with the Soviet commander of GSFG. Shachnow took the opportunity to ask Dulenko if the KGB knew anything about US Special Forces in Berlin. Dulenko confirmed that they were aware of the unit and said they had estimated its strength at 500 men.[4] Whether that number, a 400% increase of the unit's actual strength, was based on flawed information or a Soviet tendency to inflate their enemy's size is unknown. The appendix that follows shows how the East German *Stasi* and, by extension, Russian KGB viewed their American target on the other side of Wall over the years.

But OPSEC and the cover plans were only meant to protect the unit up to the moment of war. Once war began, the enemy would have to find 100 dangerous men scattered among several million people. That was where individual and team training and preparation would be key to survival. The foundation of any special operations unit is dependent on the quality of its personnel. To get qualified men (or women), a vigorous and effective assessment and selection (A&S) of each person must be conducted to the standards established for each unit's particular requirements. That was done with both units but, as with A&S programs in all special operations unit, there were a few soldiers who passed through the initial program but did not adapt to the demands of the job. The unaccustomed freedom found working under a quasi-civilian cover, along with long hair, "civies" (civilian clothing), alcohol during duty hours, operating as a singleton, and living among the local populace, proved to be the downfall of more than a few army commandos. For that reason, a unit must have a probationary period that is stated and understood from the outset and enforced for those that can't adapt or fit in.

Language and cultural knowledge were extremely important skills that each and every soldier assigned to either unit had to master, unless they were a native-born German. Living a cover required more than adopting the dress and hairstyle of a local; each man had to be able to play the role his legend described. Conversely, a soldier's refusal to abandon chewing tobacco because he once saw a German do it (and who probably never did it again) was both denial and admission that he couldn't adjust to a new environment.

Both units went to extraordinary lengths to give the men the necessary skills in language, as well as cultural and area knowledge. Even then, speaking a foreign language fluently is no guarantee a man or woman can carry out the mission; some just can't adapt to a different culture.

Careful screening was required of everyone before assignment to ensure they had the conspiratorial behavioral skills and demeanor of a clandestine operator to survive as part of an urban underground, as well as work in the field. Determination, adaptability, flexibility, and innovation were equally important for the individual operator. The soldiers needed to succeed as team members, but also have the stamina to work for long periods as a singleton on their own in an difficult environment.

In war, the men would rely on their wits, training, language skills, and individual cover identities to protect them. The majority of men assigned to the units were equal to the task of the UW mission. Most could be documented and pass themselves off as a German or a foreign national, although the documentation process itself was too slow.[5] As a result, some of the unit members "generated" their own German identification documents that just might have gotten them past a Soviet, if not a German checkpoint. For those lacking professionally produced false documentation, it was better than nothing.

Though the soldiers could accomplish both missions, a small number were only well suited for the direct-action (CT) mission. All were proficient in their specialties—some extraordinarily so—but a few would not have been able to pass as anything other than American. These men should have been screened and excluded from the assignment both for their own, as well as their teammates' sakes. Maturity and experience were also important—several soldiers who lacked those attributes proved themselves unable to act inconspicuously. They were unceremoniously sent out of Berlin.

The other and most important question to consider is whether or not the units could have accomplished their wartime mission. The question is speculative as war never came and could be argued ad nauseam since a negative is hard to prove. What can be said is that the UW mission would have been extremely difficult.

The unconventional warfare mission for both units was to be executed just before, or on the outbreak of a general war in Europe. The foundation on which the plan rested was based on the experiences of the OSS in World War II and its UW operations in France, Italy, and Yugoslavia, all locations where receptive, mostly cooperative, and—critically—experienced underground and resistance forces were already conducting combat operations.

Many planners believed the same thing would be possible in Eastern Europe. The CIA's experiences in the 1950s in Albania, Ukraine, and Poland showed that UW was not feasible in the Soviet satellites during peacetime. The Agency's Operation ROLLBACK took George Kennan's idea of containment and turned it into counterforce program intended to physically undermine the Soviet Union. It did not work for two reasons: first, the Soviets and their satellite states had perfected a near-total internal security state, and second, Soviet penetrations of Western intelligence by men like Kim Philby had reduced the chances of success to near zero. Most of the agents parachuted into Eastern Europe were quickly, if not immediately captured and executed. Despite this, many senior US military and intelligence officers expected UW operations would succeed during wartime. That was based on an assumption that the fog of war would disrupt internal controls and encourage resistance.

Chaos would reign in the initial days of a conflict, which theoretically would have permitted teams to penetrate enemy territory. Given warning, the Berlin Brigade could have mounted a limited defense of the city and, as combat raged around the borders, SF Berlin would have been able to cross over to conduct its direct-action and/or strategic reconnaissance missions, while the in-city teams would have caused grief for the attacking forces.

A higher chance of success might have been achieved had all six teams remained in the city to conduct urban UW. The follow-on mission of linking up with resistance forces and conducting guerrilla warfare outside the city of Berlin proper would have been much more difficult. This was because a capable resistance force did not exist in East Germany and no one can know how long it might have taken to establish one.

The CIA's Role

Declassified documents show the Agency's willingness to support the military for UW was waning in early 1960s.[6] While that organization promised to provide contact information on resistance organizations at war's onset, by 1965 the CIA had likely ceased or lost contact with any clandestine organizations in the Soviet Bloc. In other words, American Special Forces teams would have been obligated to establish and build a resistance organization from scratch—an extremely difficult proposition in the total police state that defined East Germany and the rest of Eastern Europe.

In East Germany, without an existing resistance force and in the presence of many thousands of enemy rear-echelon security troops, American Special Forces teams would have faced a difficult environment in which to wage a war. In fact, their chances of survival might have been better further East, in countries where greater resistance potential existed. While it is possible that indigenous East German opposition to the Soviets would have emerged later in a conflict, it is doubtful that it would have been useful to the Americans when most needed: at the onset of hostilities.

By the early 1980s, conditions in the Warsaw Pact began to change. The populations of the Soviet satellites were beginning to tire of their Communist masters and, as the populace became restive, the political scene also changed. This would lead to the destruction of the Soviet monolith through passive resistance, government mismanagement and mistakes, not war.[7] In Poland, a trade union called Solidarity and activists associated with the Nikolai and Reformed churches in Leipzig, East Germany led the way in discrediting the Communist governments through non-violent means. The rest of Eastern Europe would follow suit and the Warsaw Pact would fold without conflict.

Issues of Command, Control, and Oversight

Throughout the history of SF Berlin there was a lack of coordination between the field and the headquarters' planning staffs. Neither Det "A" or PSSE suffered from too much command oversight, quite the contrary. Although annual evaluations were accomplished through UW field exercises (and later CT exercises) minimal intrusion came from the special operations staff at USEUCOM.[8] Both the Detachment and the later "Element" ran their operations more or less unfettered by their higher headquarters. To an even greater extent, the US Army Berlin headquarters' involvement was less invasive. Besides occasional briefings and capability demonstrations to the commanding general, the headquarters' primary concern, other than knowing what targets it would destroy in the opening stages of a future conflict, was that the unit would literally go off the reservation and unilaterally start a war.

One reason in particular led to this situation—there was little or no expertise in urban UW operations in the US military. Nearly all the subject matter experts on urban UW and how it was to be executed were assigned to the unit and almost every aspect of how the work was to be done was devised from within. Similarly, the tasks, conditions, and standards for CT operations developed by Det "A" and PSSE were adopted by USEUCOM for use with the CINC's In Extremis Forces (CIF). The flip-side of this coin meant that little in the way of operational guidance and targeting support was or could be provided from higher echelons—what was received was often the result of questions the units themselves had initiated. Deconfliction of targets was done by the units' S-2 and S-3 staffs with SOTFE/SOCEUR directly, from the bottom to the top. It should have been done the other way around, starting at the headquarters level before the targets were ever assigned.

A secondary reason for the units' isolation was the extreme level of secrecy and compartmentation that surrounded their existence and operations. With classified operations, normal coordination and cooperation was difficult except with those organizations working on a similar security level, such as the USMLM, military intelligence detachments, and the CIA. The stringent security requirements restricted contact to a degree that made it hard to maintain productive relationships. It must be said that, to a degree, some of this was self-imposed to keep the "un-indoctrinated" at arm's length. In this, the units were successful, although that often deterred some useful relationships. It also ensured that few outsiders knew or understood the true potential of either unit. The units' location in Berlin made them even more remote, both literally and figuratively, from Army leadership at the Pentagon.

The Legacy

After the Wall fell, the fate of SF Berlin was quickly decided. A highly specialized tool in an army that was becoming smaller was found unnecessary, much like the OSS after World War II.

At the time, no other US military unit possessed both a robust direct-action capability (a combination of the CT mission and basic

UW skills) and a unilateral US clandestine special operations capability. Both the Detachment and PSSE were hybrid organizations, the only such unit(s) in the US military that integrated urban special operations, intelligence, direct action, and UW stay-behind operations skills in one package, not to mention its cover RST mission. Nevertheless, although it was extremely well trained and prepared, its role was weighed against other available assets when the time came to make choices.[9]

The reconnaissance operation, which the Detachment had carried out in Tehran, was a key capability that is rarely (rightly so) discussed— the clandestine special operations intelligence and operations support capability. The small advance force assembled for Tehran collected the key tactical intelligence for the raid and assembled the necessary support to infiltrate the city and conduct the mission. It was completely successful in its activities from start to finish—never being detected by the Iranian security services. This mission devolved to other units created specifically for this task. They still exist and continue to accomplish their missions. This too is an important legacy of Operation EAGLE CLAW. All of these "special mission" units are based in the United States, closer to the flagpole and with security profiles that are easier to manage.

The unit's primary mission of clandestine unconventional warfare was never well understood by outsiders. After 1990, few military or political leaders thought a conventional war in Europe remained probable and with that perception of a diminished threat, the services of SF Berlin were no longer required. It was one of the "dividends" of the new peace. And with that, a key capability was lost.

Following the demise of the Warsaw Pact, US Special Forces entered a new period. The Cold War was over and the Army Special Forces continued its focus on missions begun in Vietnam: foreign internal defense and development (FID) and counterinsurgency operations (COIN) in "Third World" countries around the world. These missions were easy to justify on the policy side of the Pentagon and in the White House. Even in the 1990s, Special Operations Forces were regarded with skepticism by the conventional leadership at the Joint Staff. The result was that Special Forces was given politically low-risk missions like FID and COIN, while more sensitive operations like UW and CT were off the table.[10]

Meanwhile, Unconventional Warfare was largely forgotten. Although it was still listed as a mission for SF, training to support guerrilla warfare faded from the scene as a priority. It would not return until shortly after 9/11, when teams were deployed into northern Afghanistan to defeat the Taliban. But even then, with the return of a "functioning" government in Kabul and the need to train the Afghan security forces, the mission quickly changed to FID and COIN.

Recent events in Syria, Ukraine, and other exotic locales have shown that there is a place for UW as a tool of strategic policy. While the CIA has often been regarded as the organization of choice for implementing such strategies, it doesn't have the capability to support long-duration missions, nor does it have the well-trained soldiers who can conduct these operations in the field over the long haul like those of SF Berlin. Those the Agency does have, are all veterans of the military.

The Commander of US Army Special Operations Command, MG Charlie Cleveland, recently noted that there is:

> a key capability gap to conduct "high-end" UW ... where resistance movements are just beginning and operating clandestinely, the occupying power is highly capable, limited safe havens exist, and where the degree of risk is exceptionally high.

Through the efforts of Cleveland and the USASOC staff, UW is beginning to be reemphasized as a key SF mission. Given the nature of the threats that loom on the horizon, all instruments of power must be available for consideration. The reemergence of unconventional warfare is long overdue.

IN THE SIGHTS OF THE ENEMY

Berlin was a wonderful city for a spy to work in, particularly if you were a member of the Warsaw Pact. When the Wall was built, it became more difficult for Western countries to conduct espionage in East Berlin and East Germany. West Berlin, however, was a relatively easy place for the Warsaw Pact intelligence services to work, because of its unguarded transport connections with the East. To the Allies, the KGB and MfS were known as "Hostile Intelligence Services" or "HOIS" in military parlance. The acronym found its way onto all manner of posters that warned the regular soldiers of the Berlin Brigade and EUCOM about the threat just beyond the safety of their barracks walls. Because of the threat, there was an all-pervasive feeling of paranoia in the Brigade that spies were everywhere. The ubiquitous OPSEC posters warned against "loose lips" and not to trust the telephone.

The East German Ministry for State Security (MfS) or *Stasi*'s main intelligence directorate, the *Hauptverwaltung Aufklärung* (HVA) and its other elements, tried to penetrate NATO and collect intelligence on its organization and plans to defend Europe.[1] Over the course of its history, the MfS was able to recruit around 30,000 assets in the West. The Soviets had a large KGB base in the Karlshorst section of East Berlin, from which they sent agents into West Berlin. While the KGB primarily sought intelligence of political and military value, the *Stasi* also collected information on people and organizations critical of the GDR and its government.

Berlin was full of intelligence targets for the Warsaw Pact: the US, British, and French occupation forces, Berlin's security and police, and its government and political organizations, were all of interest, but a few were more interesting than others. The Communists were extremely interested in Allied code materials so they could read "the mail," as well as specifics on intelligence agencies and certain military units. The US Army Security Agency (ASA), later known as Field Station Berlin (FSB), was a priority because of its communications-monitoring capabilities. The Allied Military Liaison Missions (MLM) were another; the Soviets wanted nothing more than to interfere and make their valuable work in East Germany difficult. There were other interests: the CIA (the KGB's "main enemy") and the 766th Military Intelligence Detachment. Naturally, Special Forces in Berlin was a prime intelligence target because of the threat they posed to Warsaw Pact war plans.

The KGB and MfS often worked together to recruit agents who could provide them with the information they wanted and although Allied soldiers were prized, German nationals who had access to lesser-quality information were also recruited. Cleaning crews in the USMLM's Potsdam House were East Germans and, if left unsupervised, tried to steal any piece of paper they could get their hands on. Telephone books, unit rosters, and housing lists provided by Germans in the Berlin Brigade headquarters gave basic details that were the foundation for more detailed collection and often provided leads for the recruitment of soldiers. Over the years, several successful recruitments resulted in the penetration of FSB and the Berlin Brigade that resulted in the compromise of classified operational files and planning documents. That fact, coupled with recruitments that took place in West Germany, gave the Russians in the 1980s a fairly clear picture of the Allied plan for the defense of Europe. At the time it was assumed that most of Detachment "A's" personnel were known to the Russians, as were those of Physical Security Support Element–Berlin (PSSE-B). Both units' mission plans were classified at the top secret level and accessible by a very restricted number of people outside the unit. That said, Special Forces' mission in general was known—only the specifics of what targets and how they would be attacked would have been unknown.

On New Year's Day 1980, during the USMLM's celebration at their Potsdam House residence, Army General Yevgeni Ivanovski, the commander of Soviet Forces in Germany singled out the Detachment's commander, Colonel Olchovik, and asked, "Colonel, are your men going to kidnap me tonight?" It was clear that Ivanovski knew and understood the threat Detachment "A" posed.

Both the KGB and MfS repeatedly attempted to photograph unit members for their files and, for this reason, both units avoided any kind of publicity that would reveal identities. On several occasions, intelligence officers were dispatched from East Berlin to take photographs of the US military facilities that housed the units. It seemed as if it was an exercise for the Soviet school for spies because many were quite inept. Photography at Andrews Barracks was difficult because of its size and the number of soldiers working at the location. Identifying Detachment members was difficult, although attempts were probably made. At Roosevelt Barracks, PSSE's home base, it was a different story.

One day in 1985, a man was standing across the street from the main entry of Roosevelt Barracks, blatantly shooting pictures of everyone who drove through the gate, using nothing to conceal his actions or camera. While he was absorbed in his photography, two German policemen came running down the street on their morning jog. Seeing the photographer and quickly surmising he was up to no good, the policemen strong-armed the man and shoved him across the street and into the guard house. Forced to produce his identification, the man pulled out his Soviet passport and tried to claim immunity from arrest.[2] The guard called PSSE and within a few minutes several men showed up to investigate.

One of the men, a Russian linguist, interrogated the photographer. While the Soviet was distracted, the others photographed his document-ation and pocket litter. The information was passed to the 766th MI and the man was escorted to Checkpoint Charlie by the police where he was sent home without his film. Although he failed the exam, there may have been others who were more successful.

A Closer Look

To better understand what "HOIS" knew about the two units, it was necessary to go into their files. Unfortunately, the short period of friendliness that occurred with the Russians after the Wall came down is over and they are no longer cooperating with the West. Getting any of their documents was not possible. Luckily, the files of the *Stasi* are now in the hands of the unified German government with the "Federal Commission for the Records of the Security Services of the former German Democratic Republic" or BStU for short. Knowing the *Stasi* would likely have had more success against the units—essentially working on their own turf—a request for a search of the millions of files in their hands was made. Their initial response was encouraging but daunting. They had files, 260 to be exact, but these files comprised around 100,000 pages of material to search through. They said it would take time and it did. Six months went by, then eight. Then one day the postman delivered a thick package of over 500 MfS documents that a BStU employee had culled from the stacks of records. It was the first batch of what would prove to be an interesting set of revelations that would change the thinking on what the "enemy" knew about Detachment "A" and PSSE.

What became immediately obvious was that the East Germans had a very clear idea of the size, location, function, and capabilities of US forces in Berlin—up to a point. Holdings describing the 6th Infantry Regiment were reasonably complete, including diagrams and maps of McNair Barracks that outlined specifically where units were billeted, tables of assigned equipment, and training regimens. A document from 1971 assessed the combat capabilities of the infantry regiment as fair and the quality of the personnel as poor, an accurate reflection of the state of the US Army at the end of the Vietnam War, but not the Detachment.[3] Line and block charts accurately depicted the organization of the entire Berlin Brigade, to include a description of the brigade staff and its functions.[4] Another document dated 1984 gave a complete run-down of the 6th Infantry's training and exercises for the year 1981 by battalion and company.[5] The MfS's agents in West Berlin apparently scored a few successes.

MfS documents concerning the United States' intelligence structure in the Federal Republic of Germany (West Germany) and Berlin (West) were also accurate but reflected information that was openly available, including telephone directories of the period. In fact, one MfS chart was attached to a copy of the official US Mission Berlin directory of units and key personnel, and shows the East Germans were easily able to get copies of unclassified documents and translate them.[6]

Thereafter, the view gets fuzzy. One MfS chart dated 1979 shows "probable" US intelligence units in Berlin, in other words units that were assessed to have intelligence-related duties, but not confirmed as such. Among these were a number of technical and electronic security units and Detachment "A" with the remark that "according to information from 1975, Russian language courses were taught at the unit and its members are reportedly continuously traveling the roads between West Berlin and West Germany." It appears the MfS was getting a few spot reports on the unit's activities, but not enough to make sense of them.[7]

The earliest mention of the unit was dated 1975 (remember the unit had been stationed in Berlin since 1956) and it stated that "Detachment 'A' was probably (*vermutlich*) a sub-element of the 10th Special Forces in Bad Tölz." No other data was provided. Another detailed report on Detachment "A" was dated November 1982 and comprised five pages of a standard East German intelligence order of battle work sheets.

The report assessed that:

> Detachment "A," stationed on Andrews Barracks in Lichterfelde, West Berlin, belonged under 10th SFG and its known missions were:
>
> - Combat, sabotage and diversion operations against military and civilian targets,
> - Investigation of anonymous telephonic bomb threats,
> - Search of buildings and installations for explosives,
> - Regular control and search of vehicles belonging to high ranking officers for explosives,
> - Preparation and training of the three infantry regiments in scout swimmer tactics in West Germany.
>
> In the past, the unit has practiced sabotage operations against military targets, such as bridges, in West Berlin. The members of the unit wore both civilian and uniform during operations.
>
> According to information received thus far, the personnel of the Detachment work closely with the radio intercept battalion, Field Station Berlin (FSB),

formerly known as the Army Security Agency. Elements of FSB are also stationed at Andrews Barracks and operated, among other things, the Teufelsberg radio intercept station.[8]

The report also listed former commanders of Detachment "A" including "Sidney Shachnow," "Moran McKenzie" [sic], "J. L. Dalia," "Olchoviks" [sic], "Katz," and acting commander "Robert W. Wise." One additional commander was named for 1973, but the entry was incorrect, naming a Team Leader who was no longer with the unit at that time. No other unit personnel were named in the report.[9]

By 1982, the MfS had a picture of the unit's mission that was generally correct, but still incomplete. The report erroneously listed the unit's standard weapons as the M16A1 rifle and M1911A1 pistol, while giving its strength as 80–100 men, closer to the actual strength than the Russian estimate (500 men) given General Shachnow circa 1990.[10]

The MfS apparently had only a rudimentary understanding of the unit's wartime mission: "sabotage and diversion," but little else. Further, while listing several terrorism-related tasks, the counterterrorism and VIP protection missions seem to have escaped the analysts' attention completely.

A large number of the formerly top secret documents provided by BStU were directives signed by MfS Chief Colonel-General Erich Mielke concerning the "imperialist" Allied Military Liaison Missions (MLM). As early as 1955, the documents reveal the East Germans' angst over the possibility that the MLMs were subverting their citizens, recruiting intelligence sources, stealing secrets and details about how the *Stasi* tried to protect its assets.[11]

Among the reports found in the archives was one that tied Detachment "A" to the USMLM. As described earlier, Detachment men had been detailed to the Mission not only to assist tour officers in their duties, but also to collect information about the operational area their team would be working in should war break out. The report is a *Stasi* action plan from June 1985 that details its intent to approach and recruit "Justin," a member of the USMLM. "Justin" was an American born of German parents and spoke flawless German. He was also a member of the training cadre who showed new members of the MLM how to drive the

Mission's vehicles and, most importantly, how to elude the Soviets and East Germans while on tour in "Indian Country."

The plan outlines goals to be achieved by officers working with so-called "unofficial collaborators"—*IMs* as they were known inside *Stasi*—working inside the USMLM.[12] This would indicate that the *Stasi* had recruited individuals, in all probability German nationals, who had access to the Mission or were employed by USMLM—most likely at its facility in Potsdam, East Germany.[13] Their job was to watch "Justin" and provide details that would lead to his being approached and convinced to work for the East Germans or compromised into spying for them. The 1985 plan was accompanied by a report of results achieved, dated January 1986, that indicated the operation was still proceeding.

Of specific interest, was the *Stasi's* belief that "Justin" was a member of Detachment "A" who was working with the USMLM. He was not, but the *Stasi's* mistake begs a question: how did they make that assessment? In all likelihood, it came from one of the *IMs* that had close contact with him. "Justin" did train some of the Detachment men on the nuances of the Mission's cars when they were detailed to drive for the MLM. This contact may have been observed by an *IM* and interpreted incorrectly.

This mistake aside, that assessment provides the most detailed information of what the East Germans knew and didn't know about the Detachment. First, as late as 1986, the *Stasi* was not aware the Detachment had closed its doors two years earlier. Second, a much clearer picture of the unit's mission was available to them after 1982.

After stating that "according to available information, 'Justin' is a member of Detachment 'A,'" both the 1985 and 1986 documents detail the unit's mission:

> Detachment "A" is an Army special unit that, as a sub-unit of 10th Special Forces Group, is concealed within the Berlin Brigade. It is a special reconnaissance and combat unit detailed for operations in the enemy rear areas, especially diversionary missions.
>
> The 10th SFG in Bad Tölz is specifically oriented for operations in the territories of the European Socialist [ed: Warsaw Pact] countries, while Detachment "A" is oriented on self-reliant operations in the adversary's rear areas. The individual "Kommandos" of the Detachment are specialists in diversionary and subversive warfare.

Detachment "A" has often supported the USMLM in the past with cadre who primarily served as drivers during operations.[14]

No other MfS documents concerning the Detachment exist after January 1986 and it is doubtful new information would have come to light that would have changed their assessment. Importantly, the MfS seems to have determined the unit's mission through its assumed association with 10th SFG rather than analysis of the Det's operations themselves, as no documentation has come to light describing them. Only bits of the unit's counterterrorism duties were alluded to, and even these are more in the VIP protective services realm than actual CT operations. The real surprise is that, contrary to contemporary expectations, the *Stasi* appears not to have known the names of the unit's personnel and no details on personalities, other than the mention of several commanders' names, has come to light.

Perhaps the Soviets were more thorough in this regard, as it was they who manned Checkpoint Alpha at Helmstedt and Checkpoint Bravo at Drewitz-Dreilinden on the *Autobahn* between West Germany and West Berlin. The Russian soldiers meticulously copied the details of each traveler's "Flag Orders," which included their name, rank, identification number, and nationality—but not their unit. The Russians may have had everyone's names, but would probably not have been capable of correlating names to units.

The most threatening detail the East Germans possessed was the exact location of the unit's headquarters. With that information, they and or the Soviets could have conducted a surprise attack to eliminate the core of the unit. Again the probability of that happening without any advance warning would have been very low.

What of PSSE-B? The new unit's assumption in 1985 and after was that it had been compromised to the enemy from the beginning—at least that it was known to be the successor unit of Detachment "A." That assumption may have given the East Germans too much credit.

One document, dated October 7, 1985, details information about the PSSE-B that originated from a *Stasi IM* source.[15] The file suggests the *IM* had access to personnel of the German 6941st Labor Service Guard Battalion whose headquarters was on Roosevelt Barracks, where

PSSE-B's building was also located.[16] It begins with the general statement that:

> Since around April/May 1984, a US secret intelligence agency exists [on Roosevelt Barracks]. In July 1985, the following sign was observed on the entry to the organization's building:
> Berlin Brigade
> Physical Element

A second report (September 1985) would later change the name to: "Security Supply Element." It was only correctly rendered in a later report as: "Physical Security Support Element Berlin."[17]

Name aside, the MfS reporting noted that until May 1985 around 20–40 men between 25 and 45 years old were working at the facility, but that around 100 men belonged to the agency in July 1985. This would reflect the steady increase of assigned soldiers to the unit, although in actuality the strength of the unit had reached 100 by the fall of 1984.

The IM also reported the construction of the building accurately:

> Building 817 was renovated before the unit was stationed there. Protective grates were installed over the windows and some were closed up so that the neighboring buildings could not see in. There are two entrances, but only the one on the right is used. Antennas have been installed on the roof of the building.
>
> In the period of 1984/1985, the LS Guard Battalion was instructed that the building housed a secret intelligence agency and the LS Guards were to "act correctly in their encounters with the members of the unit; the unit members were not to be watched nor bothered. The building was not to be entered." For their part, the LS Guards called the men of the facility "spooks" and "bandits."
>
> During a four-week observation period, it was observed that the building was occupied day and night. The employees of the facility wore civilian clothing, but the exact nature of their duties cannot be determined at this time.

Additional spot reports concerning military and civilian visitors, delivery of furniture, training of men in sport clothing, and vehicles of the Berlin Brigade, Military Police, and Tempelhof airport at the location, make it clear that the MfS had fairly consistent observation on the building itself, but was no closer to determining the occupants' mission two years after the establishment of PSSE-B.

Circa 1986, a report surfaced that outlined a MfS collection tasking. The tasking was to determine the status of eight US military men who were assigned to Roosevelt Barracks. The tasking outlined that the eight had been assigned to Berlin before and had returned. No other details were provided. This was one of the few indications that the East Germans were following personnel closely. As of yet, no additional information has come to light on this tasking and whether it might have anything to do with the few soldiers who served in both units, Detachment "A" and PSSE-B.[18]

By 1987, the political situation in East Germany and the Warsaw Pact had been profoundly altered. The MfS was more and more focused on internal issues and one can only wonder whether its focus on the external threat was diminished.

None of the information outlined in this appendix would indicate what might have happened had war come to Europe. With hindsight, it seems estimates of what the enemy knew of Special Force Berlin was less than feared. The Russians and the East Germans knew there was a unit, at least between 1973 and 1985, that intended to cause them harm. It is unclear what exactly they knew about PSSE-B. Plans revealed after the fall of the Wall show the Warsaw Pact intended to destroy Berlin Brigade quickly at the outset of hostilities. Much of their plans relied on knowing where the enemy would be located when the balloon went up. But the men of both units did not intend to stay where the enemy thought them to be.

That said, the actions of a few men in carrying out their wartime mission behind the lines in East Germany would have relied as much on skill and luck as anything else. It seems clear, however, that had the Soviets and East Germans missed their quarry at either Andrews or Roosevelt Barracks, their work to find and neutralize the men of Special Forces Berlin would have been cut out for them.

LEADERSHIP

Detachment A

Commanders

Maltese, Edward V.	May 1956–1957
XO: Barton, FNU	1956–1958
Croft, Bliss Henry	1957–1958 (Acting)
Piernick, Roman T.	1958–1961
XO: Croft, Bliss Henry "Crafty"	–1959
XO: Patton, Frederick C.	1959–1962
Mahan, Francis L.	1962–1964
XO: McManus, Dick	1963–1964
Johnson, James	1964–1967
XO:	
McDaniel, Burl	1967–1969
XO:	
O'Malley, Robert	1969–1972
XO: Karow, Pete	
Shachnow, Sidney	1972–1974
XO: Langston, John W.	1973–
McKenzie, Moran A. "Moon"	1975–
XO: Langston, John W.	–1975
Rau, Raymond	1976
XO: Katz, Darryl	1976
XO: Fergusen, Luke	1976
XO: Dahlia, Jeffrey	1976–1977

Olchovik, Stanley	1976–1981
XO: Wise, Robert W.	1977–
Katz, Darryl	1981–1984
XO: Wise, Robert W.	–1982
XO: McGoey, Kevin	1982–1983
XO: Griswold, Terry	1984
Piaseki, Gene	Dec 1984 (Officer in Charge)

Unit Sergeants Major

Lynch, Marshall	1956
Galvin, Frank R.	1957–1960
Leal, Carlos	1960–1963
Pilkington, Carl E., Sr.	1963–1966
Schlegel, Darryle	1967–1969
Kriculi, Tony	1970–1972
Smith, D. A.	1973–1975
Kullek, Hilmar	1975 (Invalided/Accident)
Fulp, Jack—S4	1975–1976 (Acting)
Raker, Jeffrey	1976–1981
Swafford, Terry	1981–1984
Turcotte, Gilbert	1984 (Acting)

PSSE-B

Commanders

Dorsey, Mercer	1984–1986
XO: Davis, William "Iron Man"	
Moroney, Jack "Bulldog	1986–1988
XO: Davis, William "Iron Man"	
XO: Philbrick, Steve "Hangman"	
Obie	1988–1990
XO: Philbrick, Steve "Hangman"	
Philbrick, Steve	1990 (Acting)

Unit Sergeants Major

McKeon, Bill	1984–1985
Robblee, Don	1985–1990

SPECIAL FORCES BERLIN, 1956–1990

Fall 1955	USCOB requests SF to conduct operations to destroy strategic targets around Berlin.
November 1955	CINCUSAREUR concurs and authorizes assignment of six teams and staff to 6th Infantry Regiment.
May 1955	CINCUSAREUR authorizes use of SF in USCOB defense plans. SOTFE to direct UW operations thereafter.
June/July 1956	A modified SF company departs Bad Tölz, Germany for Berlin and is administratively assigned under Headquarters and Service Battalion (HSB), 7781st Army Unit (AU).
August 1, 1956	Special Forces Berlin officially activated in classified orders.
September 1, 1956	Under the cover name of Security Platoon, Regimental Headquarters, 6th Infantry Regiment, the unit moves into McNair Barracks, West Berlin (Building 1000B).
1958	HSB, 7781 AU is renamed Headquarters and Headquarters Company (HHC), US Army Garrison Berlin.

April 1958	The "Security Platoon" is renamed Detachment "A" and assigned to HHC, US Army Garrison. It moves to Andrews Barracks (Building 904, Section II).
August 12–13, 1961	East Germany begins construction of the Berlin Wall.
April 1962	Unit is separated from US Army Garrison and is renamed Detachment "A," Berlin Brigade.
August 27, 1965	The 39th Special Forces Detachment, 1st Special Forces formally constituted in classified orders. (USAREUR General Orders Number 263).
September 1, 1965	The 39th SFD is formally activated in Berlin. "Detachment A" remains the unit's cover name until its inactivation in 1984.
November 4, 1979	US Embassy in Tehran overrun by Iranian "students."
November 9, 1979– January 21, 1981	Operation RICE BOWL/EAGLE CLAW/ SNOW BIRD.
April 24/25, 1980	Operation EAGLE CLAW executed.
April 16, 1984	Physical Security Support Element–Berlin (PSSE-B) is activated.
October 1, 1984	Inactivation of 39th Special Forces Detachment (USAREUR Perm Order 58-22).
December 16, 1984	Detachment "A" cases its colors.
December 1984	PSSE-B is designated as 410th Special Forces Detachment (Airborne).
November 9, 1989	The Wall falls.
August 15, 1990	Inactivation of PSSE-B.

IRAN MISSION, 1979–1981

November 4, 1979	US Embassy in Tehran occupied.
o/a November 8	Colonel Olchovik and SGM Raker travel back to CONUS.
December 1979– February 1980	Operation RICE BOWL planning.
February 1980	"Bob" acquires vehicles and warehouse.
March 24	Clearance for the advance team given.
March 25	Invisible ink in Frankfurt.
March 17–28	Close Quarter Battle course.
April 6	Advance team makes its first trip into Tehran.
April 12	18 Detachment men travel to Zone for FLINTLOCK.
April 15–May 22	Asset Control Group FTX FLINTLOCK "Schwarzes Pferd."
April 17	Advance team, plus Meadows, returns to Tehran.
April 19	Detachment's assault force leaves Berlin.
April 23	Carter gives "Go" for mission.
April 24/25	Operation EAGLE CLAW.
April 28/29	Advance team exfils Tehran.
May	Preparation for second mission begins.
Mid–May	Iranian drivers leave country.
June	"Fred" exfils Iran.

November 12, 1980– December 21, 1981	Operation SNOW BIRD/STORM CLOUD.
January 8, 1981	JCS Letter of Commendation to Detachment "A."
January 20	President Reagan assumes office. Five minutes later the hostages are released.

ABBREVIATIONS
AND ACRONYMS

0300	Contingency plan for Counterterrorism (CONPLAN 0300)
4304	Operational Plan for Unconventional Warfare (OPLAN 4304)
A&S	Assessment and Selection
ADM	Atomic Demolitions Munition (US)
AFO	Advance Force Operations (US)
AFF	Army Field Forces (US)
AO	Area of Operations
ASA	Army Security Agency
ATP	Army Training Program (US)
BAOR	British Army of the Rhine (UK)
BBde	Berlin Brigade (US)
BE	Brief Encounter
BGS	*Bundesgrenzschutz*—Federal Border Guards (FRG)
BND	*Bundesnachrichtendienst*—Federal Intelligence Service (FRG)
BOB	Berlin Operations Base (US)
BSC	British Security Coordination (UK)
BStU	Federal Commission for the Records of the Security Services of the former GDR (FRG)
CIA	Central Intelligence Agency (US)
CID	Criminal Investigations Division

CIG	Central Intelligence Group (US)
CIF	CINC's In Extremis Force (US)
CINC	Commander in Chief (US)
CINCEUR	Commander in Chief Europe (US)
CQB	Close Quarter Battle
CoC	Change of Command
COIN	Counterinsurgency Operations
COMSOTFE	Commander, Support Operations Task Force Europe
CONUS	Continental United States (the 48 states)
CPU	Car Pick-up
CT	Counterterrorism
DA	Department of the Army
DD	Dead Drop aka Dead Letter Drop (DLD)
DOD	Department of Defense (US)
DZ	Drop Zone
E&E	Escape & Evasion
EG	East German
FECOM	Far East Command (USA)
FID	Foreign Internal Defense and Development (USA)
FOB	Forward Operating Base
FRG	Federal Republic of Germany—*Bundesrepublik Deutschland,* BRD
GCHQ	General Communications Headquarters (UK)
G	Guerrilla
GDR	German Democratic Republic—*Deutsche Demokratische Republik,* DDR
G-Force	Guerrilla Force (USA)
GI	Government Issue, also a US Army soldier (US)
Green Beret	A felt hat worn by Special Forces soldiers
Grepo	*Grenzpolizei*—Border Police (GDR)
GRU	Main Intelligence Department, Army General Staff (USSR)
GSFG	Group of Soviet Forces Germany (USSR)
GSG-9	*Grenzschutzgruppe 9*—Federal Border Guard Unit (FRG)

GW	Guerrilla Warfare
HF	High Frequency
Huey	Bell Utility Helicopter (UH-1)
HVA	*Hauptverwaltung Aufklärung*—Main Intelligence Office, MfS (GDR)
IM	*Inoffizielle Mitarbeiter*—Unofficial Collaborator (GDR)
JCS	Joint Chiefs of Staff (US)
JSOC	Joint Special Operations Command
JTF	Joint Task Force
KGB	Committee for State Security (USSR)
KSK	*Kampfschwimmerkompanie*—Combat Swimmer Company (FRG)
LZ	Landing Zone
MfS	*Ministerium für Staatssicherheit*—Ministry of State Security (GDR)
MI5	Military Intelligence, Section 5 aka The Security Service (UK)
MI6	Military Intelligence, Section 6 aka Secret Intelligence Service (UK)
MLM	Military Liaison Mission
MP	Military Police
MPK	*Maschinenpistole Kurz*—submachine gun, short
MTO&E	Modified Table of Organization and Equipment (US)
"Nark"	East German Mobile Surveillance Team
NCA	National Command Authority (US)
NCO	Non-Commissioned Officer
NSA	National Security Agency
NVA	*Nationale Volksarmee*—National People's Army (GDR)
OCPW	Office of the Chief of Psychological Warfare
ODA	Operational Detachment Alpha—US Army Special Forces "A Team"
OG	Operational Group (US)
OGA	"Other Government Agency"—the CIA (US)
OP	Observation Point
OPSEC	Operations Security

OSS	Office of Strategic Services (US)
OTP	One Time Pad—a single-use, unbreakable encryption system.
P-38	Either a Walther 9mm pistol, a GI can opener, or an aircraft—all good tools
PERSCOM	US Army Personnel Command
PM	Personal Meeting aka Personal Meeting Point (PMP)
POW	Prisoner of War
PW	Psychological Warfare
RAF	*Rote Armee Fraktion* (Red Army Faction)—German terror group
RDF	Radio Direction Finding
REDCOM	Readiness Command (US)
REFORGER	Return of Forces to Germany—USAREUR's major annual exercise (US)
RIAS	Radio in the American Sector
RIF	Reduction in Force
RV	Rendezvous Point
SADM	Special Atomic Demolitions Munitions (US)
SAF	Special Action Force (US)
SAS	Special Air Service (UK)
SAT	Special Action Team (US)
SATCOM	Satellite Communications
SBS	Special Boat Service (UK)
SCUBA	Self Contained Underwater Breathing Apparatus
SDR	Surveillance Detection Route
SEAL	Sea, Air, Land—US Navy Special Warfare teams
SEK	*Sondereinsatzkommando*—Police Special Operations Command (FRG)
SF	Special Forces—US Army Special Forces
SHAPE	Supreme Headquarters Allied Powers Europe (NATO)
SICTA	Strategic Intelligence Collection and Target Acquisition
SIS	Secret Intelligence Service aka MI6 (UK)
SMG	Submachine Gun
SMLM	Soviet Military Liaison Mission

SOCEUR	Special Operations Command Europe (US)
SOE	Special Operations Executive (UK)
SOF	Special Operations Forces (US)
SOT	Special Operations Training (US)
SOTFE	Support Operations Task Force Europe (US)
SR	Strategic Reconnaissance
SSU	Strategic Services Unit (US)
Spetznaz	Special Purpose Forces (USSR)
Stasi	Nickname of the East German Ministry of State Security (GDR)
TO&E	Table of Organization and Equipment (US)
USAB	US Army Berlin
USAREUR	US Army Europe
USASOC	US Army Special Operations Command
USCOB	US Commander of Berlin
USEUCOM	US European Command
USSOCOM	US Special Operations Command
USMLM	US Military Liaison Mission to Group of Soviet Forces Germany
UW	Unconventional Warfare
UWO	Underwater Operations—Combat Diver Operations (US)
UWOA	Unconventional Warfare Operational Area (US)
VoPo	*Volkspolizei*—People's Police (GDR)
VS	*Verfassungsschutz*—Office for the Protection of the Constitution (FRG)
WPID	Warsaw Pact Identification

NOTES

Chapter I: The Origins of Special Forces

1   David Murphy, Sergei Kondrashev, George Bailey, *Battleground Berlin: CIA vs KGB in the Cold War* (New Haven: Yale University Press, 1997), 167.

2   Figures on the number of people arrested and killed varied greatly depending on the source. The initial Russian estimate was 84 wounded or killed and 700 arrested, while early (1966) West German estimates stated that over 500 were killed, 106 executed, 1,300 injured, and over 5,000 arrested.

3   Central Intelligence Agency, *On the Front Lines of the Cold War: Documents on the Intelligence War in Berlin, 1946 to 1961*, Part III: June 1953 [document online] edited by Donald P. Steury, available at https://www.cia.gov/library/center-for-the-study-of-intelligence/csi-publications/books-and-monographs/on-the-front-lines-of-the-cold-war-documents-on-the-intelligence-war-in-berlin-1946-to-1961.

4   Colonel Aaron Bank, letter to John F. Kennedy Special Warfare Center (USAJFKSWC). With the reactivation of the Ranger battalions beginning in 1974, the Ranger companies were removed from SF's lineage.

5   CIA, "Early History of the CIA" [document online], accessed at www.cia.gov, January 2003.

6   Thomas F. Troy, *Wild Bill and Intrepid: Donovan, Stephenson and the Origin of CIA* (New Haven: Yale University Press, 1996), 77–92. Troy assigns no small amount of credit for the organization to Canadian William Stephenson, Chief of British Security Coordination (BSC) in the US.

7   *US Army Field Manual 31-20, Special Forces Group*, Headquarters, Department of the Army (Washington, DC: GPO, 1955).

8   These included secret intelligence, counterespionage, and paramilitary activities. Office of the Historian, US Department of State, "Foreign Relations of The United States, 1945–1950: Emergence of the Intelligence Establishment"

[document online] available at http://history.state.gov/historicaldocuments/frus1945-50Intel/ch7.

9   Major General George V. Strong, "Comments on Memo from the COI re: Organization of Guerrilla Warfare Command," 23 June 1942, Record Group 319, Army Intelligence, 370.64, Box 874, National Archives.

10 National Security Council Directive on Office of Special Projects, NSC 10/2, June 18, 1948.

11 Larry Cable, *Conflict of Myths: The Development of American Counterinsurgency Doctrine and the Vietnam War* (New York: New York University Press, 1986), 29. In actuality, USMAPG Commander Admiral James Van Fleet crafted a military assistance plan that used US advisory expertise to its best effect and made the Greeks fight their own counterinsurgency campaign.

12 Peter Grose, *Operation Rollback: America's Secret War Behind the Iron Curtain* (Boston: Houghton Mifflin, 2000), 2.

13 Truman locked up the Clifford-Elsy Memo because, although he felt it useful for his own policy thinking, it was too explosive to release to the public. Kennan's telegram, on the other hand, was rewritten and published under a pseudonym in 1947 as "The Sources of Soviet Conduct." It did create a sensation and a firestorm of debate.

14 Arthur H. Paddock, Jr., *US Army Special Warfare: Its Origins: Psychological and Unconventional Warfare, 1941–1952* (Washington DC: National Defense University Press, 1982), 88. Paddock's exhaustive work is the best and most complete history on the origins of US Army Special Forces.

15 Ibid, 89.

16 Ibid, 120. SF's antiguerrilla warfare or counterinsurgency operations responsibility would be developed later with the beginnings of the Vietnam conflict.

17 Aaron Bank, *From OSS to Green Berets: The Birth of Special Forces* (Novato: Presidio Press, 1986), 159–161.

18 Paddock, *US Army Special Warfare*, 107. The CIA had long insisted that it must be the sole agency to conduct organized foreign clandestine operations.

19 Public Law 597, "An Act to provide for the enlistment of aliens in the Regular Army," 2nd Session, 81st Congress.

20 Paddock, *US Army Special Warfare*, 123.

21 Ibid, 131.

22 Ibid, 127.

23 The original "A" Detachment was called an FA team. An FB team (equivalent to the current Operational Detachment Bravo (ODB) or Company Headquarters, commanded six FA teams. An FC team or OD Charlie (Battalion Headquarters) was designed to command and control FA and FB teams including Guerrilla Warfare (GW) area commands operating in a single country.

24 This was later changed to six ODAs per company because of manpower restrictions.

25 Bank, *From OSS to Green Berets*, 161.

26 The 10th was officially activated on June 20, 1952. The 77th followed on September 25, 1953.

27 Bank, *From OSS to Green Berets*, 169. These requirements remain generally the same today.

28 The Jedburghs were three-man teams infiltrated into enemy-held territory to assist local resistance forces. The OGs were larger units, usually 20 or more men, designed to assist guerrilla units and conduct combat operations.

29 Curtis Peebles, *Twilight Warriors: Covert Air Operations Against the USSR* (Annapolis: Naval Institute Press, 2013), 175.

30 Bank, *From OSS to Green Berets*, 185. Of course, the observers came from the OCPW, the only source of such expertise in the US Army.

31 "Smoke Jumping" is the art of intentionally and, hopefully, safely parachuting into heavy forest as practiced by National Forest Service to fight fires in remote areas.

32 President Roosevelt preferred an occupation plan that divided Germany into zones that met in Berlin, however Prime Minister Churchill wanted the Russians to have an incentive to continue their offensive into German territory and his plan was approved by the European Advisory Commission where the occupation borders were decided and accepted by the Soviets. Lord Strang, *Home and Abroad* (London: Andre Deutsch, 1956), 213–215; and Gerhard Weinburg, "Some Myths of World War II," *The Journal of Military History* (Vol 75, No 3, Lexington: The Society for Military History, July 2011), 709.

33 The Allies felt a neutral, unified Germany would end up with the same fate as Poland, i.e. under Soviet subjugation. Federal Republic of Germany Chancellor Konrad Adenauer was also reluctant to follow this offer.

34 Ostermann, Christian F., "The United States, the East German Uprising of 1953, and the Limits of Rollback," The Cold War International History Project, Working Paper No. 11, Christian F. Ostermann, Series Editor (Washington D.C., Woodrow Wilson International Center for Scholars, 1994,) 5.

35 Ibid, 8.

36 National Security Council 158, "United States Objectives and Actions to Exploit the Unrest in the Satellite States," June 29, 1953. The PSB consisted of the deputies of the State and Defense Departments and the CIA Director and was to coordinate and plan for psychological operations; the Operations Coordinating Board (OCB) later absorbed its responsibilities.

37 The most formidable obstacle to the success of such operations, both in peacetime as well as war, would be the oppressive security conditions that existed in the Soviet-controlled areas.

38 Michael Boll, "By Blood, Not Ballots: German Unification Communist Style," *Parameters* (Spring 1994), 67.

39 Some reports indicate the Soviet Army had as many as 80 divisions at its disposal. See: Historical Section, Supreme Headquarters Allied Powers Europe, "The New

Approach: 1953–1956, NATO Report 3340/11-3/s/11/76" (Brussels: SHAPE, 1976), 18–20.

40 The British and French occasionally deployed small SOF elements to Berlin but none were permanently assigned to the city.

41 Headquarters, US Army Europe, *The U.S. Army in Berlin, 1945–1961*, AG TS 2-102 (Heidelberg: USAREUR, 1963), 54–55; declassified December 11, 2000. While the deployment of Special Forces units fell under the responsibilities of USAREUR, command and control of operations was the responsibility of the commander in chief, US European Command (CINCEUR).

Chapter II: The Formative Years (1956–1971)

1 Their departure was covered in the 10th SFG Yearbook for 1952–1956 with a curious note that stated "orders were received in January 1956 reducing the strength of the unit and many members returned to the States in June." The announcement of the soldiers' return home was most probably made to cover their departure from Bad Tölz and true destination: Berlin.

2 The basic selection criteria was similar to that of the OSS: a willingness to perform hazardous duty, language ability, area familiarity, physical conditioning, specialized skill training, and a character assessment that looked at a candidate's good judgement and stability. See OSS, *Operational Groups Field Manual* [secret—declassified 12/3/2013] (Washington DC: OSS, 1944) and Aaron Bank, *From OSS to Green Berets: The Birth of Special Forces* (Novato: Presidio Press, 1986).

3 One of these NCOs, Sergeant Paul Vukovich, took part in the first SF qualification course in late 1952.

4 Unlike standard SF ODAs, the Detachment did not have team executive officers in its organization.

5 The key was to be able to pass cursory checks, at least until your accent gave away your or your language teacher's origin. Most Americans in the unit were able to carry on non-technical conversations and instruct classes in their specialties.

6 By the 1980s, that ratio was more like 10% foreign-born soldiers to 90% native-born American, as few of the Lodge Act program soldiers remained in service and fewer still had managed to escape from the Soviet-occupied areas.

7 Harry Bertrand, telephone interview December 12, 2014.

8 The 7781st was a service battalion that provided the US Army Berlin Command with administrative and combat support. McNair Barracks was a former Telefunken factory complex in Berlin-Zehlendorf seized by the Americans to house troops after the war. Maltese set up shop on the top floor of building 1001B, which housed the 6th Infantry's regimental headquarters.

9 Later, when the soldiers were permitted to drive the *Autobahn* route, they would be subjected to the military's bureaucracy. The MPs checked the elapsed time and

mileage on the vehicle to make sure the driver had neither exceeded the speed limit nor taken an unauthorized joy ride off the main road, which was entirely possible. The Allied command was concerned that some enterprising soldiers would take detours to smuggle East Germans out of the country.

10 Jim Wilde, interviews, March/April 2014.

11 This was especially true in the late 1960s and into the 1970s, when the two most popular reps were Mrs Billye Drake Alexander and Miss Palmer, in which case flowers and cards worked well.

12 In 1956–1959, there were fewer than 800 fully qualified SF soldiers spread around the globe.

13 Prior to 1959, each team had a radio operator (MOS 051, later 05B) and a radio repairman (MOS 296). The team structure was modified in early 1959, when the radio repairman was deleted and a second radio operator was added. Radio operators were able to operate several different types of long-range radios, send and receive Morse code at least 20 words per minute (wpm); some could manage over 30 wpm. Many were capable of receiving an encrypted message and simultaneously transcribing it into clear text using a one-time code pad and memorized trigraph. The other team members were required to send and receive Morse at a minimum of 10 wpm.

14 US Army Berlin, Berlin Command, History Division, Historical Report Files, 1951–60, Annual Reports 1955–56 to 1958–1959, Box 44, Entry 012, Records Group 549, Declassified, National Archives and Records Agency (NARA), College Park, MD.

15 In 1961, the Allies planned on around 16,000 *Bereitschaftspolizei* and *Schutzpolizei* (uniformed police) as part of their defense plan. Against that small force, the East Germans could muster around 50,000 paramilitary police and defense forces in addition to their regular army formations.

16 Hilmar Kullek, emails with author, March–December 2014.

17 Philip Broadbent, Sabine Hake, *Berlin Divided City, 1945–1989* (Oxford: Berghahn Books, 2013), 157.

18 Karl Wheeler Soper, "Appendix C: The Warsaw Pact," Ihor Gawdiak (ed.), *Czechoslovakia: A Country Study* (Washington DC: Federal Research Division, Library of Congress, 1987).

19 US Congress, Office of Technology Assessment, "New Technology for NATO: Implementing Follow-On Force Attack," OTA-ISC-309 (Washington DC: US Government Printing Office, June 1987), 56.

20 Following the end of the Berlin Airlift in 1949, the US forces in the city were designated Berlin Command, then US Army Garrison Berlin, and finally US Army Berlin in 1961. The combat arms units (infantry and armor) were grouped into the Berlin Brigade from 1961 until its inactivation in 1994.

21 By the mid-1960s, SOTFE would designate the Detachment's targets outside the city, leaving the Berlin commander responsible only for peacetime administrative control of the unit.

22 The Air Force's Air Resupply and Communications Service and specialized Troop Carrier Squadrons supported UW operations in Europe up to the 1960s.

23 SOTFE, a sub-element of US European Command, was initially based in Paris in 1956. Its staff wrote unconventional warfare plans to support the plans of commander in chief, US European Command (CINCEUR). The first SOTFE UW plan was COMSOTFE OPLAN 57-1, which supported the CINCEUR's OPLAN 100-7 for the defense of Europe. The CINCEUR plan detailed how every unit in the European Theater would react to a Soviet attack across the border, while the separate SOTFE plan detailed how Special Forces would support the mission behind enemy lines. The plans were updated and periodically rewritten to reflect changes on both sides of the border, to include alliances. Later, when the main war plan was CINCEUR PLAN 4102; SOTFE's OPLAN 4304 was the basis on which subordinate units, like SF Berlin, would plan their unconventional operations. SF Detachment Berlin was also responsible to support Commander USAB's Plan for the Defense of Berlin. See also: Eugene Piaseki, "Reminiscences of Detachment A, Berlin 1982–1984," *Veritas* (Vol 2, No 3, 2006).

24 The groups comprised Teams One and Two, Five and Six, and Three and Four respectively. Detachment "A" would use this configuration until 1975 when it changed back to six individual teams.

25 HQ, USAREUR, *The U.S. Army in Berlin, 1945–1961*, AG TS 2-102, USAREUR GC/28/62, 56; declassified August 11, 2000.

26 Ibid, 70, 54.

27 In the most optimistic scenario, the Det "A" commander and staff could have relocated to the wartime EUCOM/SOTFE headquarters in France or, later, the UK prior to the outbreak of hostilities.

28 SF used the acronym CARVE to analyze targets: Criticality, Accessibility, Recuperability, Vulnerability, and Effect. Later another R would be added for Recognizability—the operator had to be able to identify the critical component for the attack to be effective.

29 Associated Press, "Officer Says He Was Held By Reds," *Harrisburg Telegraph* (Harrisburg, PA, April 17, 1946).

30 Douglas Selvage, "Khrushchev's November 1958 Berlin Ultimatum: New Evidence from the Polish Archives," *Cold War International History Project* (Bulletin 11, Washington DC: Woodrow Wilson International Center for Scholars, Winter 1998).

31 The radio station Radio in the American Sector, or "RIAS" as it was popularly known, was of special interest for the Russians and East Germans because of its popularity and influence in Eastern Germany. The Communist leaders of East Germany felt it was a primary contributor to the workers' uprising of 1953.

32 The *Wachregiment "Felix Dzerzhinsky"* (Guard Regiment) was the MfS's paramilitary arm. Officially, it was not part of the armed forces and was stationed inside

Berlin in contravention to the Four-Power Agreement's prohibition against GDR forces in the city. It was named after the founder of the *Cheka,* the Soviet secret police, in 1967. It grew from 1,500 in 1956 to 10,000 men in 1989.

33 The CIA's planning for stay-behind operations is described in detail in the CIA-cleared memoir of William Colby, *Honorable Men: My Life in the CIA* (New York: Simon & Schuster, 1978).

34 CIA, "AEDEPOT" and "CADROWN" [declassified documents online], Special Collection FOIA ERR, available at foia.cia.gov and "Lexicon" [document online], available at http://www.archives.gov/iwg/declassified-records/rg-263-cia-records/second-release-subject-files.html.

35 The CIA defined Eastern Europe as the following countries: Balkans, Greece, Czechoslovakia, Baltic States, Poland, Hungary, Germany, Austria, Switzerland, and the USSR.

36 CIA/OPC, Strategic War Plan in Support of the Joint Emergency War Plan [declassified document online], Foreign relations of the United States, 1950–1955, Document 61, available at https://history.state.gov/historicaldocuments/frus1950-55Intel/d61.

37 CIA/OPC, "Project LCPROWL" [declassified document online], available at http://www.foia.cia.gov/sites/default/files/document_conversions/1705143/LCPROWL%20%20%20%20VOL.%201_0036.pdf.

38 CIA, "WUDEPOT" [declassified document online], available at http://www.foia.cia.gov/sites/default/files/document_conversions/1705143/AEDEPOT%20%20%20VOL.%202_0022.pdf.

39 These would be replaced with weapons of European origin, as the unit was able to obtain them. In 1963, three unit members, Captain Lunde, Sergeant Jaworski and Sergeant Kullek, went to the Walther arms factory at Ulm and obtained the company's latest submachine gun, the 9mm Machinenpistol Kurz "MPK." It was used until 1983, when it was replaced with the H&K MP5.

40 Sterile equipment is unmarked and untraceable to its origin. Although Sten guns were "British," they were not in the current inventory of any European army and P-38s were used on both sides of the Wall.

41 None of the locations were compromised during the emplacement process. Throughout the existence of the Detachment, the sites were periodically checked by the S-2 to ensure they had not been discovered. Several cache containers were retrieved in the 1970s for testing. The material inside was still "serviceable," e.g. usable. In 1990, the caches were successfully recovered.

42 This plan had the same weakness as the cache plan—finding the vault key at headquarters with the Russians coming over the walls could have been problematic and explosives probably would have come into play. Before the fund was returned to the US Government in 1986, the numismatic value was assessed to be "priceless" because of the condition and extreme rarity of many of the coins, especially the Russian rubles. When the coins were taken to Tempelhof airport for their

return to the States, many of the unit members who escorted the coins that day contemplated theft and a subsequent life in the tropics.

43 Training was derived from manuals like the OSS, *Secret Intelligence Field Manual* [top secret—declassified 2013] (Washington DC: OSS, 1944). See also Hank Crumpton, *The Art of Intelligence: Lessons from a Life in the CIA's Clandestine Service* (NY: Penguin, 2012), for his take on the art of tradecraft.

44 Andrew Molnar et al, *Human Factors Considerations of Undergrounds in Insurgencies*, DA Pamphlet 550-104 (Washington DC: Special Operations Research Office, 1965), 102.

45 Contrast this with casing in the 21st century. Today an intelligence officer can use open-source Internet tools like Google Earth and a web browser to find almost all the information needed to case a site. Personal visits are still necessary in order to see the "lay of the land" that cannot (yet) be well depicted in the virtual world. Even so, security is just as important when using the Internet. Virtually visiting a site or subject too often on the internet can be just as revealing to a hostile security service as loitering outside the physical target.

46 Kim Kendle, email to author, April 21, 2014.

47 As opposed to information provided to the Agency's Berlin Operational Base, which would rarely acknowledge receipt of a tip and never comment on the results of their investigation.

48 Although I'd like to take credit for this description, others have used it before me. See, for example Roger Hilsman, *American Guerrilla* (McLean: Brassey's, 1990), 58.

49 Bob Olson, email to author, December 19, 2014.

50 The Detachment kept Berlin Brigade in the dark about the specifics of its operations. The West German government was never informed.

51 The RS-6 was replaced first by the AN/PRC-74 and then the British RACAL TRA-931. The available AN/GRC-109 had several large, heavy components and its range was not as good as the PRC-74.

52 A modified long wire antenna could also be hung inside the room, but the radio's transmitting power was often attenuated by the building's construction, especially if metal reinforcement was used in the walls.

53 Mike Kelly, email to author, April 2, 2014.

54 The exercises were first named for the year as in Field Tactical Exercise 58-2, and then given code names like HIGH POINT in 1962, and SEA RULER in 1963.

55 The Aggressors were called "Circle Trigon" forces. Their name and symbol, a green triangle inside a circle, was used for training after WWII and referred to any foreign enemy. The Army created an in-depth but fictitious Order of Battle and a role-playing manual for this force called *Handbook on Aggressor Military Forces* and noted that "the country, peoples and forces described are entirely fictitious. Any resemblance to existing countries or forces is inadvertent and coincidental."—FM 30-102, Headquarters, Department of the Army, Washington DC, 1959.

56 Jim Wilde, interview with author, March 12, 2014.

57 The other was Henrik Lunde, a Norwegian.

58 Adam Klys, interview August 18, 2014.

59 This was one of the most classified programs in the military until well into the early 1990s. It was recently detailed in *Foreign Policy* magazine and a later SADM device is exhibited at the National Museum of Nuclear Science and History in Albuquerque. The Navy Underwater Demolitions Teams (UDT), the forerunners of the SEALs, also had the mission primarily for maritime and littoral area targets. See: http://www.foreignpolicy.com/articles/2014/01/29/the_littlest_boy_cold_war_backpack_nuke.

60 Col Gerald Brown and Major James Glock, "Employment of ADMs," *Military Review* (Vol LXII, No 11). (November 1982), 33–37. See also COMSOTFE OPLAN 1-56, Annex F that detailed the planning for use of ADMs by SF in European UW operations, NARA, RG 349.

61 Harry Brown, email to author, December 9, 2013.

62 [Redacted]

63 Pronounced "bay-zette," the BZ was East Berlin's center-left daily newspaper.

64 Jim Wilde, interview with author, March 12, 2014.

65 The border separating West Berlin from East Germany proper was already closed off, as it was between the GDR and the FRG.

66 USCINCEUR, Special Plan Number 300-1, Country Cold War Plans, Berlin [declassified NARA file online], Available at http://research.archives.gov/description/6036651.

67 John F. Kennedy, Speech on the Berlin Crisis, July 25, 1961 [document online], available at http://usa.usembassy.de/etexts/speeches/rhetoric/jfkberli.htm.

68 Headquarters, Berlin Brigade, BB-OPLAN-1, Nov 1962, Tab H; BB-OPLAN 3-11; and BC OPLAN 2—Unilateral Plan (TS) For Detachment "A" [declassified, NARA files], available online at http://media.nara.gov/research/1961-berlin-crisis/36093-3-1-1/36093-3-1-1.pdf.

69 On August 17, 1961, Secretary of the Army Elvis J. Stahr Jr. announced an extension of the tours of all Army personnel in Germany. Hermann Halterman, interview with author, June 12, 2014.

70 Any soldier with a "TS" clearance was required to have special permission to travel in the East Bloc and (prior to circa 1965) could not drive the *Autobahn* in East Germany between Helmstedt and Berlin (West).

71 "Leg" is the airborne soldier's least derisive name for a non-airborne person, place, thing, or unit.

72 Kim Kendle, email to author, April 21, 2014.

73 Excepting the CIA's non-official cover officers or NOCs, who had the appropriate cover to work inside the Soviet Bloc.

74 The Huebner/Malinin Agreement of 1947 set out the conditions for the US and the Soviet MLMs. The British and French had their own reciprocal agreements with the USSR.

75 The MLM mission was one of the reasons for conducting the extremely thorough Warsaw Pact Identification (WPID) training, the other was the unit's wartime SR mission.

76 The SAS also participated in the MLM "tours" for the same reasons albeit on a smaller scale. Ken Conner, *Ghost Force: Secret History of the SAS*, (London, Weidenfield Military, 1998), 283–301.

77 ASA was later known as Field Station Berlin.

78 *SS-Oberst-Gruppenführer* was the equivalent rank of a four-star general officer.

79 The materials were actually equipment destined for use by ASA. John Blevins, email to author March 31, 2014.

80 Christopher Andrew, *The World Was Going Our Way* (New York: Basic Books, 2005), 40; Hal Brands, *Latin America's Cold War: An International History* [Dissertation] (Austin: University of Texas, 2009), 37.

81 Technically, war was never declared, but with nearly 3.5 million men serving there between 1960 and 1973, 550,000 in 1968 alone, the point is moot.

82 The Mudslow list was a manual of often outdated weaponry, tools, and explosive items available for acquisition through special channels. The availability and usefulness of special weapons and materials improved as military's special warfare laboratories expanded their research capabilities in the 1980s.

Chapter III: A New Mission and a Midlife Crisis (1972–1976)

1 Wilde served in the Det 1957–1963 as a radio operator and then went to OCS.

2 Shachnow would retire as a major general after having commanded all of Special Forces and serving as the US Commander of Berlin.

3 This despite a traditional history that idolized unconventional commanders like Francis Marion, Nathanael Greene, and John Singleton Mosby; modern "special operations forces" were marginalized in the US Army until 9/11.

4 This changed with the creation of the Special Forces Officer Branch in 1987. Career Management Field 18 (Special Operations) was created for SF NCOs and warrant officers in 1984.

5 East German military commanders were thinking along the same lines in their planning for an attack on West Berlin and might have deployed their special operations forces in the opposite direction.

6 Shachnow asserts in his book, *Hope and Honor*, that the Detachment never again ventured underground. Perhaps "officially," but his was neither the first nor the last time the unit went under the city's streets. It was, however, the only time they were caught in the act. When he departed Berlin, the reprimand did not make it into his official file and he ended his career as a major general.

7 The KSK refused to use the Emerson and called it a "death rig."

8 SCUBA—Self-Contained Underwater Breathing Apparatus. The SCUBA badge would later be replaced with the Special Operations Diver Badge.

9   Det "A" was the first US military unit to utilize the Dräger system until the LAR V was evaluated and purchased by the Navy and distributed first to the SEALs and then to US Special Operations Forces in the mid-1980s.

10 "Haus" later commanded the Special Forces Underwater Operations School at Key West, Florida. He left Team Two in June 1974 to attend the Infantry Advanced Course at Fort Benning.

11 All the teams were technically "stay-behind," Teams Three and Four just didn't need to move as far.

12 Karrin Hanshew, *Terror and Democracy in West Germany* (Cambridge: Cambridge University Press, 2012), 112. The Libyans used its diplomatic mission in East Berlin to stage their attack on the *La Belle* nightclub in 1986. The MfS was most likely aware of Libya's plan days before the attack was carried out.

13 GSG-9 was created on September 26, 1972 by order of the German Ministry of the Interior.

14 Although the military is not prevented from law enforcement duties or from supporting civilian police forces within the United States, their use is limited by the Posse Comitatus Act of 1878—Title 18, US Code, Section 1385.

15 In fact, at the highest levels DOD regarded terrorism as "not up to the standard of [its] definition of war, and therefore not worthy of [its] attention." General Pete Schoomaker quoted in Richard H Schultz, Jr., "Nine reasons why we never sent our Special Operations Forces after al Qaeda before 9/11," *The Weekly Standard* (Vol 9, No 19, January 26, 2004,).

16 Rod Lenahan, *Crippled Eagle: A Historical Perspective of US Special Operations, 1976–1996* (Charleston: Narwhal Press, 1998), 5–17.

17 The Son Tay raid took place during the Vietnam War in November 1970. See Benjamin Schemmer, *The Raid* (New York: Harper & Row, 1976).

18 SOT was later known as the Special Forces Advanced Recon and Target Exploitation Course (SFARTEC).

19 See Eugene Piaseki, "Reminiscences of Detachment A, Berlin 1982–1984," *Veritas* (Vol 2, No 3, 2006).

20 This section is based on many discussions with Mac Dorsey and Darrell Katz in 2014.

Chapter IV: The Pros from Dover (1976–1981)

1   Ivanovski to Olchovik at Potsdam House, December 1978. Ivanovski (also Evgenii Ivanovskii) was the commander of Soviet Forces in Germany.

2   Fulp was the unit supply sergeant and had just been promoted to the top NCO rank. He had to fill in temporarily as unit sergeant major when D. A. Smith departed earlier in the year.

3   Literally "Lone Warrior course," usually translated as Ranger or Commando school.

4   The German Paratrooper song. Raker and Roelle established an individual and unit friendship that endured many years.

5   As the unit's reputation later grew under Olchovik's tenure, accolades from as high up the chain as the Joint Chiefs of Staff convinced General Adams that "he" had made the right choice.

6   1933 was the year Hitler assumed power as Chancellor and dictator of Germany.

7   There were other ways to ensure each man met the unit's goals and stayed qualified to conduct operations.

8   Soraya Ansari, a PFLP terrorist involved with the LH181 hijacking, was reportedly shot several times with a .357 during the GSG-9 raid that freed the hostages on board the aircraft. Colonel Wegener was the only officer who carried that caliber handgun.

9   Operation *Zauberfeuer* (Fire Magic).

10 The men of SEK were usually anti-Communist and, sometimes, to the extreme right politically. At the same time, it had to be remembered they would have been among the first arrests made by East German state security when war came. Predictably, the *Stasi* tried to infiltrate the West Berlin police to collect intelligence on the government and the Allies and, as such, a certain amount of healthy suspicion was required for every relationship, including civilian girlfriends.

11 *Mist* is German for crap.

12 It didn't matter as the SGM already knew from the arms room custodian; he would have been more upset if they had not been unarmed.

13 *Mobiles Einsatzkommando* (mobile operations command): the police surveillance and sniper unit that usually worked with SEK.

14 An abbreviated version of the incident can be seen in the USMLM Annual Report for 1980, Section II-46, Available at: http://www.coldwarspies.com/resources/uh1980.pdf (declassified 2006).

15 Internal SAS training document, undated, circa 1976.

16 The Detachment was the first of what would later be known as the CINC's In Extremis Force or CIF.

17 Charlie Beckwith, [Redacted].

18 Interestingly, a second character showed up in 1981 to look at the Detachment's training and facilities. Navy Commander Richard Marcinko, who worked in the Pentagon as a planner for the Iran hostage rescue mission, came to Berlin to gather tactics and ideas for the newly created SEAL Team 6 that he was to command.

19 The SAS was aware there were American SF "A" Teams operating in Berlin. Ken Conner, *Ghost Force: Secret History of the SAS*, (London, Weidenfeld Military, 1998), 295.

20 The son of Field Marshal Erwin Rommel, the "Desert Fox" of WWII North Africa fame.

21 "We Defy"—the motto of the Special Operations Training cadre.

22 Hopefully, with less ammunition as the Dutch Marine Commandos expended several thousand rounds of ammunition to kill six terrorists with 111 bullets.

23 The Special Projects Team was set up for CT operations in 1975. Training was done internally by the Counter-Revolutionary Warfare Wing and its alert team was called "Pagoda Troop."

Chapter V: Appointment in Tehran

1 Command and Control North, part of Studies and Observation Group (SOG), consisted of small teams that conducted reconnaissance missions in enemy-held territory. Nick was a CCN Recon Team member.

2 Bruce Laingen, "The Iran Hostage Crisis: Moments in U.S. Diplomatic History" [article online], available at http://adst.org/2012/10/the-iran-hostage-crisis-part-i/.

3 Kai Bird, *The Good Spy: The Life and Death of Robert Ames* (New York: Crown Publishers, 2013), 229.

4 The Son Tay raid failed to bring back the POWs, but was successful in sending a message to the North Vietnamese government. The treatment of the POWs by their captors immediately improved. The raiders killed approximately 300 enemy soldiers during the assault, some possibly Chinese advisors. All the US forces returned home without serious injury.

5 Jimmy Carter quoted in Rose McDermott, "The Iranian Hostage Rescue Mission," *Risk-Taking in International Politics: Prospect Theory in American Foreign Policy* (Ann Arbor: University of Michigan Press, 1998). 71.

6 COMJTF OPLAN: "Rescue of American Hostages From AMEMB Iran" [declassified document online], available at http://www.dod.mil/pubs/foi/International_security_affairs/iranian_hostage_crisis/536.pdf. (Washington DC: Headquarters Joint Task Force, February 26, 1980), 1A29.

7 That officer, Howard Bane, [Redacted] the Dalai Lama's escape from Tibet into India in 1959. See also: John Roberts and Elizabeth Roberts, *Freeing Tibet: 50 Years of Struggle, Resilience, and Hope* (New York: AMACOM, 2009), xii, 66, 73.

8 Stanley Olchovik, "Desert One and Operation Eagle Claw," interview in *Special Forces: The First Fifty Years* (Tampa: Faircount LLC for the Special Forces Association, 2002).

9 Stanley Olchovik, "Desert One and Operation Eagle Claw," interview in *Special Forces: The First Fifty Years*, (Tampa: Faircount LLC for the Special Forces Association, 2002).

10 Dick Meadows was a member of the assault force during the 1972 Son Tay POW rescue mission in North Vietnam.

11 "Laager" is a military term for a defended encampment that originated with the Boers in South Africa.

12 "Fred," who would assist Meadows initially, was instructed to "go to ground" inside Iran before the actual mission. He stayed with friendly contacts in the country and then returned to the US several weeks after the mission abort.

13 Michael Smith, *Killer Elite* (New York: St Martins Press, 2006), 10. Plan's activities may have been run by CIA Ops Officer Howard Bane. See also Alan Parker, "Interview with James Earl Parker, Part II" [blog], *Toronto Sun* (December 6, 2013).

14 Rod Lenahan, *Crippled Eagle: A Historical Perspective of U.S. Special Operations, 1976–1990* (Charleston: Narwal Press, 1998), 98.

15 CINCUSAREUR was not fully briefed on the Detachment's involvement in the Iran mission until late March 1980. See Rod Lenahan, *Crippled Eagle*, 93.

16 Colonel Olchovik asked MG to review the names he and the SGM had chosen for the mission and to give his opinion about their suitability for the mission. When it became known that he had the boss's ear, every man promised MG the world if he would mention their name.

17 Holloway Commission Report [document online], available at http://nsarchive. gwu.edu/NSAEBB/NSAEBB63/doc8.pdf.

18 The Agency more likely chose not to reveal the information they had until they were sure the mission would proceed in order to protect the real asset. The "Pakistani cook" was probably a cover story.

19 MG never did pay the ticket and it sits in his "war room" at home.

20 Grange retired as a major general in 1999.

21 The AC-130 was armed with a M102 105mm howitzer, a 40mm Bofors canon, and two Vulcan 20mm canon, each capable of extremely accurate, pinpoint fire.

22 James Kyle, *The Guts to Try: The Untold Story of the Iran Hostage Rescue Mission by the On-scene Desert Commander* (New York: Orion Crown, 1990), 7.

23 When MG got back to the States, he personally delivered a copy of the newspaper to the JTF J-2's desk and demanded, "Who the hell is the idiot that tried to get us killed?" It is assumed the staff officer was quickly hidden from the team.

24 Fred was already outside Tehran staying with his family up country.

25 According to Meadows, during the five rehearsals for the first mission, only once did the pilots execute the plan partially correct. The other times Meadows was forced to break noise and light discipline in order to guide them in to the target LZ. In another event, MG spoke with the USMC command pilot at the Pentagon to brief him on the best suitable HLZs, possible obstacles and other danger areas. After the brief, complete with pictures and locations of all wires in the immediate area that he and Scotty had taken, MG said, "You're not going to let us hang, are you?" The Marine responded, "I promise you we will get you out, no matter what." He was the pilot of the bird that turned back to the *Nimitz*.

26 This provisional unit would later coalesce into the officially designated 160th Special Operations Aviation Regiment and an even more secretive element that will remain nameless. Fred J. Pushies, *Night Stalkers: 160th Special Operations Aviation Regiment (Airborne)* (St Paul: Zenith Press, 2005), 15.

27 An additional factor for the cancellation was its compromise by journalist Jack Anderson. In the fall of 1980, Anderson announced the military was preparing for

a second mission. His announcement may have alerted the Iranians as there were indications the mission would have met serious resistance.

Chapter VI: The Final Days (1981–1984)

1   "The worst is yet to come!"—the motto of the 1st Special Service Force.
2   [Redacted].
3   The Supreme Allied Commander Europe (SACEUR) simultaneously held the position of USCINCEUR and was responsible for all Allied contingency and war planning in the European theater. No one called him "Bernie" to his face.
4   The British Army refers to this mission as Intelligence, Surveillance, Target Acquisition, and Reconnaissance (ISTAR), which is conducted in the "deep battlespace" far behind enemy lines.
5   As inhabitants of an occupied city, West Berliners were not subjected to be drafted into the *Bundeswehr*. That was not the case in East Berlin, the capital of the GDR, where all males could be conscripted for service in the NVA.
6   When the unit tested the MPK in the 1960s, one of the key factors for its adoption was its reliability under severe field conditions. The MP5 was not as comfortable with mud and dirt as its simpler "cousin."
7   David C. Martin, "Inside the Rescue Mission: The Point Man in Iran," *Newsweek* (Vol C, No 2, July 12, 1982).
8   DCSOPS-ODSO was a sub-element of the Army's Deputy Chief of Staff for Operations (DCSOPS). See Michael Smith, *Killer Elite* (New York: St Martins Press), 325. "Yellow Fruit" was an independent, classified CI element within ODSO and did not have any formal command or control over operational units. Its primary purpose was to advise units on their cover and operational security plans. The names of the ODSO officers involved have been voluntarily redacted.
9   Lieutenant Colonel Darrell Katz, interview September 18, 2014.
10   Funding for the building, as well as its logistics and maintenance, were paid by the Berlin city government, the same as for all Allied facilities in Berlin. However, the German government was unaware of the purpose the building would serve.
11   The official inactivation of 39th Special Forces Detachment is recorded as October 1, 1984 by the US Army Center for Military History. On December 16, 1984, Detachment A cased its colors and locked its doors.
12   This section is drawn from an article by Eugene Piaseki with his permission, "Reminiscences of Detachment A, Berlin 1982–1984," *Veritas* (Vol 2, No 3, 2006).
13   CSM Jeff Raker email, April 13, 2015.
14   "Newest Additions to USASOC Memorial Plaza," *Veritas: Journal of Army Special Operations History* (Vol 10, No 1, 2014). According to the US Army CMH the proper term is "inactivated" rather than "deactivated."

Chapter VII: The New Kid on the Block (1984)

1 Dorsey was in fact Commander, Special Forces Berlin and responsible for both units.
2 The "Yellow Fruit" investigation would have consequences for a number of other special elements that it supported, including those that were called "Special Mission Units" or SMUs. See Alan Strait, *The Dilemma of Covert Action*, monograph (Carlisle Barracks, US Army War College, 1989), 27.
3 The only mitigating factor in this process was that the men were not processed into the Berlin Brigade as members of Detachment "A."
4 A "picket fence" meant all ones (111111) on a soldier's medical profile, i.e. no medical restrictions or conditions.

Chapter VIII: Until the Fall (1984–1990)

1 PSSE's sections had 12 men rather than the old unit's 11, and included an executive officer position filled by an SF 180A warrant officer (WO). When the TL (captain) position was vacant, the WO would command the team.
2 Interview with Mac Dorsey, April 2015. SOTFE was redesignated as Special Operations Command Europe (SOCEUR) on November 1, 1983.
3 Michael Bohn, *The Achille Lauro Hijacking: Lessons in the Politics and Prejudice of Terrorism* (Dulles: Potomac Books, 2014), 8.
4 Ibid, 21. The Egyptian Foreign Minister wanted assurance from the Italian, German, British, and US ambassadors that they would not "give chase." The Americans and British refused that demand.
5 Ibid, 35.
6 Rachel Donadio, "Italy Convicts 23 Americans for CIA Renditions," *New York Times* (November 4, 2009).
7 Among them Sergeants Brad, "der Hop," Rick, and Barney were instrumental in this project from beginning to end.
8 OSS, *Secret Intelligence Field Manual* [top secret—declassified 2013] (Washington DC: OSS, 1944), 11–14.
9 It was a classified unit organized to conduct undercover surveillance against suspected members of terrorist organizations in Northern Ireland and elsewhere in support of UK Special Air Service (SAS) COIN operations.
10 Watch on the Rhine River.
11 This was the same system the Detachment used to alert its personnel. Acquired circa 1976, the system was turned over to the new unit in 1984. The OPSEC implications were considered negligible, as similar devices were used throughout the Berlin Command.
12 It was later determined he had help from East German intelligence, specifically Stasis's *Abteilung* XXII (Department 22). *Abt XXII* was ostensibly a counterterrorist unit; in reality, it sponsored terrorist operations against NATO countries in Western Europe.
13 Mark Kramer, "The Soviet Union, the Warsaw Pact, and the Polish Crisis of 1980–1981," in Lee Trepanier (ed.), *The Solidarity Movement and Perspectives*

on the Last Decade of the Cold War (Kraków: Krakowskie Towarzystwo Eduk, 2010), 43.

14   David Holloway, "Gorbachev's New Thinking," *Foreign Affairs* (Vol 68, No 1, 1988).

15   So-called because many exchanges of spies had taken place there. It was also called "Bridge of Spies" and "Unity Bridge" by the East German government.

16   Mary Elise Sarotte, *The Collapse: The Accidental Opening of the Berlin Wall* (New York: Basic Books, 2014), xx.

17   Some sources say 1/10 SFG picked up the CT mission in 1984; the full 0300 tasking was given to the unit in 1990 after PSSE-B was inactivated.

18   Major General Shachnow was US Commander of Berlin at the time.

19   #usasoc, message posted April 16, 2014. Fort Bragg: US Army Special Operations Command.

Epilogue: A Casualty of Peace

1   The US Army's Center for Military History files at Fort McNair in Washington DC hold only eight pages of documents on the 39th SFD, the first dated 1965; the National Archives have only the Brigade war plans that refer to the unit.

2   Jack Anderson, "Iran invasion plan reported, denied," syndicated column (August 16, 1980).

3   Stejskal, 347.

4   Shachnow, *Hope and Honor*, 376 and interview with author, January 24, 2015.

5   The production process from initial paperwork to document in hand required about six months under normal circumstances. In an emergency, they could be produced quicker.

6   The CIA's declassified files on these programs are held by the National Archives and can be found at Records of the Central Intelligence Agency (Record Group 263) [document online] available at http://www.archives.gov/iwg/declassified-records/rg-263-cia-records/second-release-subject-files.html. Internet.

7   Sarotte, *The Collapse*, op cit, xxvi.

8   First SOTFE and after 1984, SOCEUR.

9   By 1989, the unit's mission as the CIC's In Extremis Force was completely turned over to 1/10 SFG.

10   Richard H. Shultz Jr., "Showstoppers: Nine reasons why we never sent our Special Operations Forces after al Qaeda before 9/11," *The Weekly Standard* (January 26, 2004, Vol. 9, No. 19).

Appendix A: In the Sights of the Enemy

1   Other "elements" included the *Hauptabteilung* I [Main Department I] (Surveillance and Security of the NVA), HA II (Counterespionage), and HA VIII (Observation and Investigation of the Military Liaison Missions).

2 Technically, as a member of the occupation forces, he could not be arrested or held.

3 MfS Hauptabteilung (HA) I *"Hinweise zum Kampfwert der Infanterieeinheiten West Berlin,"* dated 10.12.1971, BStU File Nr 3430.

4 MfS HA I Report, BStU File Nr 16897.

5 MfS HA I Report, dated 16.1.1984, Nr 54/86, BStU File Nr17667.

6 MfS HA II, BStU File Nr 37449.

7 MfS HA II *"Auskunft über vorliegenden Erkenntnisse zu US Geheimdienststellen in Berlin (West)"* dated 12.4.78, BStU File Nr 37493.

8 The belief that the units worked together "intensively" may stem from the fact that they were stationed on Andrews Barracks in two separate sections of the same building. In reality, contact was limited to personal relationships only.

9 MfS HA I Report *"Information über die in den McNair, Andrews, und Turner Barracks stationierten Kampf- und Unterstützungseinheiten der US Berlin Brigade,"* dated 10.03.1983, BStU File Nr.3552.

10 MfS HA I Report, BStU File Nr. 3552. Shachnow's encounter was discussed in the Epilogue.

11 DDR State Secretary for Security, Instruction Nr. 8/55, dated 2.3.1955, GVS PA II/50/55, BStU File 003112.

12 *Inoffizielle Mitarbeiter (IM)* were recruited assets who accomplished specific tasks for their assigned *Stasi* intelligence officer, often without pay.

13 The Potsdam House was the "official" venue for the Mission's liaison activities with the Soviets. It was maintained and cleaned by a host of East Germans and Soviet workers who were known to be either KGB or MfS employees.

14 MfS HA VIII, Abt 5, Referat 1 Reports, 06.2.85 and 27.1.86, BStU File No. 7274.

15 MfS HA I Report, *"US Geheimdienststelle—Roosevelt Barracks,"* dated 7.8.1985 and 23.12.1985, BStU File Nr. 17624.

16 The Labor Service Guard battalions were made up of German men hired to provide security for US installations in Germany and West Berlin. The 6941st had 850 men in five companies and guarded all 32 US facilities in West Berlin, including Roosevelt Barracks.

17 This was the designation on the sign originally posted in April 1984; the *IM* apparently had trouble copying the name correctly.

18 Rick Hendrik, telephone interview July 25, 2015.

SOURCES

Interviews

"Aristide"	Email exchanges 2012–2015
Baty, Dave	Interview 2012; email exchange November 2014
Bertrand, Harry	Telephone interview, December 12, 2014
Billingslea, Bill	Interview, email exchanges September 2014–January 2015
Blevens, John	Email exchanges March/April 2014
Brokhausen, Nick	Interview, email exchanges 2014–2015
Brown, Harry	Email exchanges, December 2013–February 2015
Bruce, Ron	Email exchanges November 2014
Charest, Bob	Interview, email exchanges 2012–2015
Cleveland, LTG Charlie	Discussions June 2015
Davis, Bill	Interviews, 2014–2015
Dorsey, Mac	Interview, email exchanges 2012–2105
Duchow, Roy	Telephone interview, email exchange December 2014
Farr, Grayal	Email exchanges November 2014
Fontana, Gerald	Email exchanges November 2014–February 2015
Franquet, Carl	Email exchange November 2014
Gazdzik, Joe	Email exchanges November/December 2014

Gould, Pete	Email exchange February 2014
Halterman, Hermann	Interview with author June 12, 2014
Hendrick, Rick	Interviews, email exchanges 2014–2015
Hoover, Bruce	Interview, email exchanges April 2015
Hopkins, Robert	Discussions 1977–2015, email exchanges 2014
Katz, Darrell	Telephone interview, email exchanges
Kelly, Mike	Email to author April 2, 2014
Kendle, Kim	Email exchanges February 2014–February 2015
Klys, Adam	Telephone interview August 18, 2014; email exchanges 2013–2015
Kreuscher, Rolf	Email exchanges February 2014; interview April 11, 2014
Kullek, Hilmar	Emails to author March–December 2014
Linnane, Mike	Email exchange April 2014
McLeod, George	Email exchanges December 2014–January 2015
MacRae, Al	Interview, email exchanges 2012–2015
"MG"	Interview April 2014; emails 2013–2015
Mulieri, Mike	Interview January 2014; email exchanges 2014–2015
Niedringhaus, Larry	Email exchanges November 2014–May 2015
O'Callaghan, Jim	Telephone interview, email exchanges February–April 2015
O'Neill, Stuart	Written notes, discussions, email exchanges 1977–2015
Odom, Bud	Email exchanges 2014–2015
Olson, Bob	Email to author December 19, 2014
"Petras"	Email exchanges 2014
Piaseki, Eugene	Email exchanges September 2014
Philbrick, Steve	Interview, email exchanges April/May 2015
Picknell, Robert	Email exchange November 2014
Piusz, Paul	Email exchanges March 2014
Raker, CSM Jeffrey	Interview June 13, 2014; emails 2012–2015
Renta, Juan	Interview February 2014; email exchanges

Roberts, Jonathan	Discussions, email exchanges 1976–2015
Schreiber, Bob	Interview 2012; email exchange April 2012–May 2015
Scheckler, Ron	Interview, email exchanges, January–May 2015
"Scotty"	Interview 1982 (Presidio of Monterey), 1983–1984 (Fort Bragg)
Shachnow, MG Sid	Interview June 13, 2014; emails 2014–2015
Sherman, Roger	Email exchanges April/May 2012
Snow, Doug	Email exchanges 2012–2014
Stephens, Mike	Email exchanges 2013–2015
Turcotte, Gil	Telephone interview September 2014
Wallace, Robert	Email exchange February 2012
Warriner, Dennis	Email exchanges December 2013–February 2015
Wilde, Jim	Interviews March/April 2014
Williams, Sid	Interview, email exchanges April–October 2014

Official Documents and Publications

Central Intelligence Agency, "*AEDEPOT*" and "*CADROWN*" [declassified documents online], Special Collection FOIA ERR, available at foia.cia.gov.

Central Intelligence Agency, *Early History of the CIA* [document online], accessed at www.cia.gov, January 2003.

Central Intelligence Agency, *Lexicon* [document online], available at http://www.archives.gov/iwg/declassified-records/rg-263-cia-records/second-release-subject-files.html.

Central Intelligence Agency, "*WUDEPOT*" [declassified document online], available at http://www.foia.cia.gov/sites/default/files/document_conversions/1705143/AEDEPOT%20%20%20VOL.%202_0022.pdf.

Central Intelligence Agency/OPC, "*Project LCPROWL*" [declassified document online], available at http://www.foia.cia.gov/sites/default/files/document_conversions/1705143/LCPROWL%20%20%20%20VOL.%201_0036.pdf.

COMSOTFE, *OPLAN 1-56, Annex F, ADM Operations*, NARA, RG 349, declassified August 11, 2000.

Headquarters, Berlin Brigade, *BB-OPLAN-1, Nov 1962, Tab H; BB-OPLAN 3-11* [declassified, NARA files], available online at http://media.nara.gov/research/1961-berlin-crisis/36093-3-1-1/36093-3-1-1.pdf.

Headquarters, Berlin Brigade, *BC OPLAN 2—Unilateral Plan (TS) For Detachment "A"* [declassified, NARA files], available online at http://media.nara.gov/research/1961-berlin-crisis/36093-3-1-1/36093-3-1-1.pdf.

Headquarters, Department of the Army, *US Army Field Manual 31-20: Special Forces Operations*, Washington, DC: GPO, 1955.

Headquarters, Joint Task Force, *COMJTF OPLAN: Rescue of American Hostages from AMEMB Iran*, Washington DC: HQJTF, February 26, 1980. Declassified.

Headquarters, US Army Europe, *The U.S. Army in Berlin, 1945–1961*, AG TS 2-102, Heidelberg: USAREUR, 1963; declassified December 11, 2000.

Historical Section, Supreme Headquarters Allied Powers Europe, *The New Approach: 1953–1956, NATO Report 3340/11-3/s/11/76*, Brussels: SHAPE, 1976.

Holloway Commission Report [document online], available at http://nsarchive.gwu.edu/NSAEBB/NSAEBB63/doc8.pdf.

Molnar, Andrew, et al, *Human Factors Considerations of Undergrounds in Insurgencies*, DA Pamphlet 550-104, Washington DC: Special Operations Research Office, 1965.

National Security Council 158, *United States Objectives and Actions to Exploit the Unrest in the Satellite States*, June 29, 1953.

National Security Council Directive on Office of Special Projects, NSC 10/2, June 18, 1948.

Office of Strategic Services, *Operational Groups Field Manual* [secret—declassified March 12, 2013] Washington DC: OSS, 1944.

Office of Strategic Services, *Secret Intelligence Field Manual* [top secret—declassified 2013], Washington DC: OSS, 1944.

Office of the Historian, US Department of State, *Foreign Relations of the United States, 1945–1950: Emergence Of The Intelligence Establishment* [document online], available at http://history.state.gov/historicaldocuments/ frus1945-50Intel/ch7.

Soper, Karl Wheeler, "Appendix C: The Warsaw Pact," in Ihor Gawdiak (ed.), *Czechoslovakia: A Country Study*, Washington DC: Federal Research Division, Library of Congress, 1987.

Special Air Service, *Close Quarter Battle* [internal training document], undated, circa 1976.

Strong, Major General George V., *Comments on Memo from the COI re: Organization of Guerrilla Warfare Command*, June 23, 1942, Record Group 319, Army Intelligence, 370.64, Box 874, National Archives.

US Congress, Office of Technology Assessment, *New Technology for NATO: Implementing Follow-on Force Attack,* OTA-ISC-309, Washington, DC: US Government Printing Office, June 1987.

US Army Berlin, Berlin Command, History Division, Historical Report Files, 1951–60, Annual Reports 1955–56 to 1958–1959, Box 44, Entry 012, Records Group 549, declassified, National Archives and Records Agency (NARA), College Park, MD.

USCINCEUR, *Special Plan Number 300-1, Country Cold War Plans, Berlin.* [declassified NARA file online], available at http://research.archives.gov/description/6036651.

US Congress, Public Law 597, "An Act to provide for the enlistment of aliens in the Regular Army" aka "The Lodge Act," 2nd Session, 81st Congress.

USMLM, *Annual Report for 1980*, Section II-46 (declassified 2006), available at: www.coldwarspies.com/resources/uh1980.pdf.

BIBLIOGRAPHY

Anon, *List of All US Nuclear Weapons* [document online], available at http://nuclearweaponarchive.org/Usa/Weapons/Allbombs.html.

Andrew, Christopher, *The World Was Going Our Way*, New York: Basic Books, 2005.

Associated Press, "Officer Says He Was Held By Reds," *Harrisburg Telegraph* (Harrisburg, PA), April 17, 1946.

Bank, Aaron, *From OSS to Green Berets: The Birth of Special Forces*, Novato: Presidio Press, 1986.

Bank, Colonel Aaron, letter to John F. Kennedy Special Warfare Center (USAJFKSWC).

Bird, Kai, *The Good Spy: The Life and Death of Robert Ames*, New York: Crown Publishers, 2013.

Bohn, Michael, *The Achille Lauro Hijacking: Lessons in the Politics and Prejudice of Terrorism*, Dulles: Potomac Books, 2014.

Boll, Michael, "By Blood, Not Ballots: German Unification Communist Style," *Parameters* (Spring 1994), 66–77.

Brands, Hal, "Latin America's Cold War: An International History," [Dissertation], Austin: University of Texas, 2009.

Brown, Colonel Gerald, and Major James Glock, "Employment of ADMs," *Military Review* (Vol LXII, No 11, November 1982), 33–37.

Cable, Larry, *Conflict of Myths: The Development of American Counterinsurgency Doctrine and the Vietnam War*, New York: New York University Press, 1986.

Colby, William, *Honorable Men: My Life in the CIA*, New York: Simon & Schuster, 1978.

Conner, Ken, *Ghost Force: Secret History of the SAS*, London, Weidenfield Military, 1998.

Crumpton, Hank, *The Art of Intelligence: Lessons from a Life in the CIA's Clandestine Service*, NY: Penguin, 2012.

Donadio, Rachel, "Italy Convicts 23 Americans for C.I.A. Renditions," *New York Times* (November 4, 2009).

Grose, Peter, *Operation Rollback: America's Secret War Behind the Iron Curtain*, Boston: Houghton Mifflin, 2000.

Hanshew, Karrin, *Terror and Democracy in West Germany*, Cambridge: Cambridge University Press, 2012.

Holloway, David, "Gorbachev's New Thinking," *Foreign Affairs* (Vol 68, No 1, 1988).

Kennedy, John F., Speech on the Berlin Crisis, July 25, 1961 [document online], available at http://usa.usembassy.de/etexts/speeches/rhetoric/jfkberli.htm.

Kramer, Mark, "The Soviet Union, the Warsaw Pact, and the Polish Crisis of 1980–1981," in Lee Trepanier (ed), *The Solidarity Movement and Perspectives on the Last Decade of the Cold War*, Kraków: Krakowskie Towarzystwo Eduk, 2010.

Kyle, James, *The Guts to Try: The Untold Story of the Iran Hostage Rescue Mission by the On-scene Desert Commander*, New York: Orion Crown, 1990.

Laingen, Bruce, "The Iran Hostage Crisis: Moments in U.S. Diplomatic History" [article online], available at http://adst.org/2012/10/the-iran-hostage-crisis-part-i/, Internet.

Lenahan, Rod, *Crippled Eagle: A Historical Perspective of U.S. Special Operations, 1976–1990*, Charleston: Narwal Press, 1998.

McDermott, Rose, "The Iranian Hostage Rescue Mission," in *Risk-Taking in International Politics: Prospect Theory in American Foreign Policy*, Ann Arbor: University of Michigan Press, 1998.

Olchovik, Stanley, "Desert One and Operation Eagle Claw," interview in *Special Forces: The First Fifty Years*, Tampa: Faircount LLC for the Special Forces Association, 2002.

Paddock, Arthur H., Jr., *US Army Special Warfare: Its Origins: Psychological and Unconventional Warfare, 1941–1952*, Washington, DC: National Defense University Press, 1982.

Parker, Alan, "Interview with James Earl Parker, Part II" [blog], *Toronto Sun* (December 6, 2013).

Peebles, Curtis, *Twilight Warriors: Covert Air Operations Against the USSR*, Annapolis: Naval Institute Press, 2013.

Piaseki, Eugene, "Reminiscences of Detachment A, Berlin 1982–1984," *Veritas* (Vol 2, No 3, 2006).

Pushies, Fred J., *Night Stalkers: 160th Special Operations Aviation Regiment (Airborne)*, St Paul: Zenith Press, 2005.

Rawnsley, Adam and David Brown, "The Littlest Boy" [article online], *Foreign Policy* (January 29, 2014), available at: http://www.foreignpolicy.com/articles/2014/01/29/the_littlest_boy_cold_war_backpack_nuke.

Roberts, John & Elizabeth Roberts, *Freeing Tibet: 50 Years of Struggle, Resilience, and Hope*, New York: AMACOM, 2009.

Roger Hilsman, *American Guerrilla*, McLean: Brassey's, 1990.

Sarotte, Mary Elise, *The Collapse: The Accidental Opening of the Berlin Wall*, New York: Basic Books, 2014.

Schemmer, Benjamin, *The Raid*, New York: Harper & Row, 1976.

Schoomaker, General Pete, quoted in Richard H Schultz, Jr., "Nine reasons why we never sent our Special Operations Forces after al Qaeda before 9/11," *The Weekly Standard* (January 26, 2004, Vol 9, No 19).

Selvage, Douglas, "Khrushchev's November 1958 Berlin Ultimatum: New Evidence from the Polish Archives," *Cold War International History Project*, Bulletin 11, Washington DC: Woodrow Wilson International Center for Scholars, winter 1998.

Smith, Michael, *Killer Elite*, New York: St Martin's Press, 2006.

Strait, Alan, "The Dilemma of Covert Action," monograph, Carlisle Barracks, US Army War College, 1989.

Troy, Thomas F., *Wild Bill and Intrepid: Donovan, Stephenson and the Origin of CIA*, New Haven: Yale University Press, 1996).

INDEX

6th Infantry Regiment, 18, 21, 66, 99, 102, 105, 283, 292, 304

10th Special Forces Group (Airborne), 3, 11–12, 14, 18, 26, 48, 54, 56, 74–75, 80, 83, 85, 88, 195, 203, 220, 229, 262, 265, 284, 286–287, 304

11th Airborne Division, 50–51

39th Special Forces Detachment, x, xiii, 104, 194, 209, 219, 227, 269, 293, 315, 317

77th Special Forces Group (Airborne), 21, 303

410th Special Forces Detachment, x, 230, 270, 293

582nd Air Resupply Group, 12

766th Military Intelligence Detachment, 41, 203–204, 281

7781st Army Unit, 20, 292, 304

Achille Lauro, 235, 316

Advance Force Operations (AFO), 158,

Alpine skiing, 83, 156

Army Field Forces (AFF), 12

Army Security Agency (ASA), 71–72, 206, 281, 310

Astalos, Peter, 50–51

Atomic Demolitions Munitions (ADM), 5559, 309, 322, 324

Autobahn, 20, 66, 112, 122, 128, 287, 304, 309

Bad Tölz *also* Flint Kaserne, 18, 37, 47, 54, 59, 80, 147, 220, 292

Bane, Howard, 155, 313–314

Bank, Aaron, 3, 8, 301–302, 304

barracks, Andrews, 21, 31, 66–67, 71 92, 131, 135, 169, 282, 284–285, 289, 293, 318; McNair, 20, 31, 283, 292, 304, 318; Patch (Stuttgart), 137, 166; Roosevelt, 31, 210, 222, 227, 245, 282, 287–289, 318; Storck (Illesheim), 197; Turner, 31, 318

Barnett, Pappy, 42

Baty, Dave, 266–268

Beckwith, Charlie, 95, 132, 155, 174, 179, 181, 312

Berliner Aussenring, 27, PLATE 3

Berchtesgaden, 83, 105, 156, 157

Berlin Brigade, vii, 19, 23, 27, 36, 39, 62–64, 68, 73, 78, 99–104, 114–115, 128, 165, 187–188, 208, 218–219, 221, 223, 228–229, 234, 245, 248, 264, 268, 270, 275, 280–281, 283, 286, 288–289, 305, 308–309, 316, 318

Berlin Command, 16, 18, 21, 208, 304–305

Berlin Wall, the building of, 28, 61–64, 280; OPLAN STRANGLE *also* plans for destruction of, 64, 289; evolution of, 107–108; crossing points, 108, 196, 231, 258; surveillance of, 109, 186, 249, 257; fall of, 254, 263–266, 268, 270, 272, 277, 317

Bertrand, Harry, 304, 20

Birmingham (UK), 123

Billingslea, Bill, 264

Bluebird Fund, 37

"Blue Light," 95–96

"Bob Plan," 161, 294

Brandt, Willy, 59–61

Braughton, Ron "Ninja," 124–127, PLATE 18, PLATE 19

Brenerhaven, 47, 65, 67

Bristol (UK), 123

British Army of the Rhine (BAOR), 51

British Security Coordination (BSC), 301

Brokhausen, Richard, "Nick," 106–107, 116, 128, 139–142

Brown, Harry, 30, 309, PLATE 4

Bruce, Ron, 87

BStU, Federal Commission for the Records of the Security Services of the former GDR, 283, 285, 318

Buchenwald (East Germany), 122

Bundesgrenzschutz (BGS) *also* *Grenzschutzgruppe 9* (GSG-9), 94–95, 97, 110–113, 132, 144, 148–152

Bundeswehr, 49, 113, 270, 315

cache *also* Mission Support Site (MSS), 35–39, 58, 85, 88–89, 91, 126, 200–201, 231–232, 259, 307

Central Intelligence Agency (CIA), xiii, 5–7; Berlin Operations Base (BOB), 31, 40; Global War Plan for Clandestine Operations, 33; National Security Council Directive 10/2 (NSC 10/2), 7, 10, 302; Office of Policy Coordination (OPC), 7, 307;

role in Iran rescue mission, 154–155, 161, 167; role in UW, 6–10; Strategic Services Unit (SSU), 4; training provided by, 74, 107, 202–203

Checkpoint Charlie, 40, 63, 70, 282

CINC's In Extremis Force (CIF), 265, 277, 312, 317

Clay, Lucius D., 63,

Clay Compound, 37, 228–229

Cleveland, Charlie, xiv, 279

Clifford, Clark, 6

Close Quarter Battle (CQB), 114, 128–129, 130, 164, 186

Collins, J. Lawton, 7

CONPLAN 0300 *also* Contingency Plan for Counterterrorism, 98, 223, 317

Counterterrorism, vii, x, xvi, 61, 94, 97, 113, 116, 149, 155, 271, 285, 287

Croft, Bliss, 29, 290

Davis, Bill "Ironman," vii, 221–222, 227, 233, 244, 247, 251–252, 291

Detachment A, Berlin Brigade, *also* "Det A," the Detachment, activation of, 16–17, 292, 293; as 39th SFD, x, 293; ADM, 56–59, inactivation of, 21, 211, 219, 222, 230, 270–271, 293, 315; wartime mission and training, x–xi, 15–16, 26–28, 31, 35, 44, 48–49, 64, 70, 74, 80, 82, 98, 100, 194–196, 203, 210, 223, 258, 283, 306; CT mission *and* training, 93–96, 98, 127, 144–146, 194, 204–205, 210; organization of, 18, 75, *see also* Strategic Intelligence Collection and Target Acquisition

Donovan, William "Wild Bill," 3–4, 11, 301

Dorsey, Mercer "Mac," 98, 220, 222–224, 230, 236, 251, 291, 311, 316

"Dulenko," George, 272

Duty Train, 20, 55, 65, 104, 147

EAGLE CLAW, 159, 163, 185–186, 278, 293, 294, 313

East Berlin, 23, 38, 40, 61, 63–64, 68, 70, 77, 82, 249, 268, 280, 282, 309, 311, 315
Eisenhower, Dwight, 6, and "New Look" strategy, 55
Ellipse Bravo, 246, 257, 262
Elsey, George, 6
Escape & Evasion (E&E), 3, 12, 47–48 76, 195, 200, 231–232
"Esquire," 159, 182

Fallschirmjäger, 49, 102
"Fall X," 32
Far East Command (FECOM), 8–9
Federal Bureau of Investigation (FBI), 94, 97–98, 111, 129, 222
Fedor, Howard "Howie," 149, 199–202, PLATE 19, PLATE 22
Fertig, Wendell, 4, 8
Flint Kaserne *also* Bad Tölz, 18, 47, 80
FLINTLOCK, 83, 162–164, 167, 195, 197, 210, 231, 243, 294,
Frankfurt a.M., 56, 65, 147–148, 157, 160, 162, 294
Franquet, Carl, 225–226, 230
Fürstenfeldbruck, 54

Gazdzik, Joe, 92
Gemeinsame Ermittlungsgruppe Rauschgift (GER), 211–218
General Communications Headquarters (GCHQ), 206
Glienecke Bridge, 122, 259
Grechko, Andrei, 2
Grenzpolizei also Grepo, 38, 65, 108
Grunewald, 21, 35, 38, 47, 206, 229
Group of Soviet Forces Germany (GSFG), 17, 119, 121, 237, 272

Halterman, Hermann D., 63–64, 309, PLATE 5
Harrison, William E., 18
Hauptverwaltung Aufklärung (HVA), 280

Heilbronn, 56
Helmstedt, 20, 147, 287, 309
Hendrick, Rick, 122, 123, PLATE 22, PLATE 26
Hennessy, John, 95
Hizb'allah, 234
Hoover, Bruce, 228, 252, PLATE 31
Hopkins, Robert, 316

IRA, Irish Republican Army, Provisional IRA, 110, 123, 127, 129, 136, 200,
Iran, vi, 146, 152–156, 158–192, 194, 208, 263, 271, 278, 293–295, 312–315, 317

Joint Chiefs of Staff (JCS), 5, 10, 14, 62, 95–96, 169, 193, 236, 295, 312
Joint Allied Refuge Operations Center (JAROC), 203, 265–266
Joint Task Force 79 (JTF 79), 79, 155, 162, 168–169, 313–314
JTF 7X, 95

Kampfschwimmerkompanie (KSK), 85–87, 91, 310
Katz, Darrell, 98, 194–199, 206, 208–213, 218, 285, 290–291, 311, 315
Kelly, Mike, 48
Kendle, Kim, 40–41, 66–67, 308–309
Kennan, George, xi, 5–6, 264; and Long Telegram, 302
Kennedy, John F., 61–63, 309, 325
KGB, 73, 204, 221, 271–272, 280–282, 301, 318,
Khrushchev, Nikita, 30–31, 61, 306
Kingston, Robert C., 95–96
Klys, Adam, 54, 309, PLATE 5
Kreuscher, Rolf, 35–38, 82
Kullek, Hilmar, 39, 291, 305, 307, 320

Lengreis, 83
Lichterfelde-West (West Berlin), 66, 147

Lodge Act, *also* Public Law 597, 9, 19, 22, 29, 50, 79, 104, 135, 304, 323
London (UK), 123, 139, 229
Ludwigslust (East Germany), 237
Lutz, Joseph, 210, 229–230

Mackmull, Jack V. 96
McClure, Robert, 6–9, 11
McEwan, John "Scotty," 156–162, 166–167, 170–174, 183, 185, 314
McNair Barracks, 20, 31, 283, 292, 304, 318
"Mad German" *also* "MG," 156–163, 166–167, 170–174, 183–185, 314
Maltese, Edward "Malt," 18–20, 26, 29, 290, 304
Marcinko, Richard, 312
Maschinenpistole Kurz (MPK) *see* Weapons: Walther MPK
Meadows, Richard "Dick," 158–161, 170–174, 183–185, 208–209, 294, 313–314
MI5, *also* Military Intelligence, Section 5 (aka The Security Service), 124, 142, 202
MI6, *see* SIS, 123–127, 139, 141–142, 200, 202
Mittenwald, 83
Military Liaison Missions (general), 68, 281, 285, 317, *see* US Military Liaison Mission (USMLM)
Ministry for State Security (MfS), *also* "Stasi," 32, 41, 68, 73, 108, 119–120, 268, 272, 280, 283, 285, 287; *Abteilung* XXII, 94, 316; *Hauptverwaltung Aufklärung* (HVA), 280; *Inoffizielle Mitarbeiter, 286, 318*; "Nark," 119
Mott Lake, 96, 142, 205
Mulieri, Mike, 112, 199–201, PLATE 18
Murnau, 75

National Command Authority (NCA), 168, 179

Nationale Volksarmee (NVA), 23, 32, 119, 266, 315
National Security Agency (NSA), 206
National Security Council Directive 10/2 (NSC 10/2), 7, 302
Neubiberg, 54
Nicholson, Arthur "Nick," 237–238
Niedringhaus, Larry, 86–87, 109
North Atlantic Treaty Organization (NATO), xi, xii, xiv, 14–15, 23, 25–26, 30, 49, 69, 83, 93, 197, 251, 253–254, 280, 304–305, 316

O'Neill, Stuart, 164, 175, 177–178, PLATE 24
ODESSA, Operation, 211–216
Odom, Bud, 267–268
Olchovik, Stanley "Col O," 101–104, 131, 139, 145–146, 148, 155–156, 164, 167–168, 174, 176, 179, 182, 187–189, 193–194, 282, 285, 291, 294, 311–314, PLATE 24
Operational Detachment Alpha (ODA), *also* "A" Team, 10, 88, 95, 148, 203, 302, 304
OPLAN 4304, *also* Operational Plan for Unconventional Warfare, 98, 194, 223, 258, 283, 306
OPSEC, *also* operational security, 66, 175, 196–197, 208–210, 220–221, 223, 236, 270, 272, 278, 280, 316
Otis, Glen, 223–224, 230, 243
Osborne, Ralph, 59

Pace, Frank, Jr., 7
Palestinian Liberation Organization (PLO) *also* Palestine Liberation Front (PLF), 235
Pan American Airlines, *also* Pan Am, 133–134, 247
Parks Range, *also* "Doughboy City," 116–117, 131, 140
Patch Barracks, *also* Stuttgart, 56, 137–138, 144, 166–167, 231, 251, 264

Patrick, Richard "Rick," 91, 106
PERSCOM, 210, 223
"Petras," 211–218
Philbrick, Steve, PLATE 32
Piaseki, Eugene, 218, 291, 306, 315
Picknell, Robert, 86
Piernick, Roman, 29, 47, 56, 59, 79, 290
Piusz, Paul "Pauli," 115
Physical Security Support Element—
 Berlin (PSSE-B), 221, 293; activation
 of, 222; as 410th SFD, 230; alerts,
 234, 236; classification of, 281; cover
 plan and mission, 223, 238; first
 commander, 222; counterterrorism,
 223, 232, 234, 317, 244–246, 247,
 257, 260; missions and planning, 220,
 223–224, 227, 230–231, 244, 250,
 257–259, 264–265, regional survey
 team, 238–241, organization of,
 227–228, inactivation of, 268, 293,
 see also Strategic Intelligence Collection
 and Target Acquisition, urban
 unconventional warfare, 241, 258
Potsdam (East Germany), 68, 91,
 120–123, 147, 281, 286, 311, 318
Project "Under," 35
Psychological Warfare (PW), 6, 7, 9, 11,
Psychological Warfare Center (PWC)
Public Law 597 *also* Lodge Act *also*
 10-8-12 Club, 9, 19, 22, 29, 50, 79,
 104, 135, 304, 323

Radio Free Europe (RFE) *also* Radio in
 the American Sector (RIAS), 2, 28, 306
Raker, Jeffrey, 101–104, 110, 115,
 155–157, 164, 167–168, 171, 189,
 291, 294, 311, 315, PLATE 24
Ramstein Air Base, 144, 181, 229
Rangers, 3, 5, 8, 159, 177
Rau, Raymond, 100–101, 103, 290
RED SAILS, 124, 139, 199, 202
REDCOM, 95
REFORGER, 162, 197, 231

Renta, Juan, 87, 93
Rhein-Main Air Base, 236
RICE BOWL, 155, 159, 293–294
Ridgeway, Matthew B., 8–9
Roberts, Jonathan, 118, 148, 164,
 PLATE 18, PLATE 22
Rogers, Bernard "Bernie," 137–138,
 196–197, 254
ROLLBACK, Operation, 274,
 302–303
Roosevelt Barracks, 31, 210, 222, 227,
 245, 282, 287–289, 318
Rote Armee Fraktion (RAF), *also* Bader-
 Meinhof Gang, 94, 137, 205

Sankt Augustin/Hangelar 110, 148
Scheckler, Ron, 91–92, PLATE 18
Security Platoon, x, 21, 23, 292–293
SCUBA, *see* Underwater Operations
SEAL, SEAL Team, 83, 85, 95, 309,
 311–312
Secret Intelligence Service (SIS),
 123–127, 139, 141–142, 200, 202
Sections, 228, 252; P-17, 231, 236, 243,
 245, PLATE 24, PLATE 27 ; P-23,
 PLATE 29, P-34, 245, 247, 259,
 PLATE 26, 245; P-43, 239, 245, 248;
 PLATE 30, P-52, 247, 262, PLATE
 30, P-61, 242
Sembach Air Base, 245
Semyonov, Vladimir, 2
Shachnow, Sid, 78–80, 82–83, 97, 99,
 268, 272, 285, 290, 310, 317–318,
 PLATE 32
Shelton, "Corky," 164, 167, 175, 180
SIS, *see* Secret Intelligence Service
SNOW BIRD, 185–186, 192, 293, 295
Sondereinsatzkommando (SEK), 113–115,
 118, 312
Southampton (UK), 123–124, 139,
 199–201
Special Action Force (SAF), 129
Special Action Team (SAT), 129, 148

Special Air Service (SAS), 52, 123, 129, 130, 132, 136, 144, 146, 148–149, 196, 200, 310, 316
Special Atomic Demolitions Munitions (SADM), 55, 309
Special Boat Service (SBS), 201–202
Special Forces (SF), creation, 2, 8, 301–302; organization, 8, 10; missions, 10, 15, 26, 74, 278, 281, 304; training, 11–12, 158, 203
special mission unit (SMU), vi, xii, xiv, 133, 265, 278, 316
Special Operations Command Europe (SOCEUR), 206, 230–232, 234, 236, 244–246, 248, 260, 264, 277, 316–317
Special Operations Forces (SOF), vi, 16–17, 26, 304
Special Operations Training (SOT), 96, 142–143, 205, 311
Spetsnaz, Russian Special Operations Forces, 15, 240
Stalin, Joseph, 5, 13
STRANGLE, OPLAN, 64
Stiner, Carl, 236
STORM CLOUD, 185–186, 192, 295
Strategic Intelligence Collection and Target Acquisition (SICTA), 196, 230–231, 241, 243
Strategic Services Unit (SSU), 4
Stuttgart also Patch Barracks, 56, 137, 138, 144, 166–167, 231, 251, 264
"Styk," 105, 118, 142, 148, 168
Support Operations Task Force Europe (SOTFE), 16, 17, 26–27, 33, 49, 51, 96–98, 124, 144, 146, 186, 196, 208, 223, 277, 292, 305–306, 309, 316–317
Supreme Allied Commander (SACEUR), 25, 254, 315
Supreme Headquarters Allied Powers Europe (SHAPE), 15, 137, 238, 240

Taylor, Maxwell, 7–8
Teams, 19; Team One, 137, 149, 163–164, 188, 203, 206, PLATE 21; Team Two, 49, 51, 84–88, 164, 311; Team Three, 89, 90–91, 98, 163, 188, PLATE 12, PLATE 18, PLATE 22; Team Four, 89, 184; Team Five, 56, 59, 105, 115–116, 137–138, 147, 149, 163–164, 186, 188, 214, PLATE 4, PLATE 14, PLATE 17, PLATE 19; Team Six, 105, 163–164
Tegel, 32, 133, 242, 247
Tehran, 147, 152–156, 158–162, 165, 169–171, 173, 176–177, 182–184, 235, 278, 293–294, 313–314
Tempelhof, 32, 52–54, 111, 115, 117–119, 137, 144, 169, 182, 188, 229, 234, 245, 254, 260, 288, 307
Teufelsberg, 71–72, 266, 285
Turcotte, Gil, 113, 115, 124–127, 218, 291; tradecraft, casing, 39, 200, 249, 308; cover, xi, 19, 21, 36, 39, 44, 69, 99, 109, 139, 158, 160, 185, 197, 199–201, 208–210, 220–223, 228–229, 238, 241, 271–274, 278, 292–293, 304, 309, 314–315; cryptography, 124, 241, 305; communications, 45–47, 75, 107, 258, 305; documentation, 109, 157, 195, 200, 221, 274, PLATE 13; intelligence, x, 10, 29, 39, 74, 85, 97, 107, 163, 239, 278; non-technical communications, 39, 107, 195, 200, 203, 241; surreptitious entry, 39, 75; surveillance, 39–41, 242; tedium of, 241, 244, 259, 272
TWA, 235

Unconventional Warfare (UW), vi–vii, x, xv, 3, 4, 6–11, 16, 21, 26–27, 31, 33–35, 37, 48–49, 61, 74–75, 82–84, 97–98, 100, 102, 127, 162, 194–196, 203, 206, 241, 250, 260, 265, 272, 274–279, 292, 306, 309
Unconventional Warfare Operational Area (UWOA), 35

Underwater Operations (UWO), *also* Combat Diver Operations, equipment, 85–93; mission, 84, 163; Team Two, 84–86, 88, 311; Team Three, 89, 91, 163; training, 85–86; 310, Baltic, 75, 86–87, 90; Eckenförde, 86, 90; Crete, 85; Key West, 84; Wannsee, 84; Tegeler See, 85, PLATE 12

Urban Unconventional Warfare Course *also* "City Training Course," 75, 83, 85, 88, 203, 249

US Army Berlin (USAB), 208, 306

US Army Europe (USAREUR), 16, 20, 29, 56, 162, 194, 206, 210, 223, 230, 264–265, 292–293, 304, 306, 314

US Army John F. Kennedy Special Warfare Center (USAJFKSWC), 95–96, 301,

US Army Special Forces *see* Special Forces

US Army Special Operations Command (USASOC), 269, 279, 315, 317

US Commander of Berlin (USCOB), 16, 26, 29, 31, 59, 61–62, 64, 210, 292

US European Command (USEUCOM), 16, 96, 137, 197, 224, 251, 276–277

US Military Advisory and Planning Group (USMAPG), *also* Greek Civil War, 5, 302

US Military Liaison Mission (USMLM), 68, 119, 277, 281, 285, 309–310, 312; Huebner/Malinin Agreement, 309; incidents, *also* "clobbers," 69, 121, 122; mission, 68; "Narks," 119; Nicholson, Arthur "Nick," 237; and *Stasi*, 119, 286–287; tours, 120, 236; vehicles, 70, 121–122

Verfassungsschutz (VS), 45

VIP Protective Security, 137, 285, 287

Vietnam, xii, 74–75, 80–81, 93, 100, 124, 135, 143, 148–149, 158, 163–164, 195, 220, 271, 278, 283, 302, 311, 313

Volckmann, Russell, 4, 8–9

Vorderbrand, Alpen Gasthof, 105–106, 157

Warsaw Pact, x–xii, xiv, 14, 16–17, 23, 25–27, 31, 48, 53, 72, 81, 89, 93, 162, 196, 206, 224, 237, 253–254, 257, 264, 268, 270–271, 276, 278, 280–281, 286, 289, 305, 316

Warsaw Pact Identification (WPID), 38, 310

Weapons, Walther MPK, 76, 89, 129–130, 132, 169, 187, 205, 207, 307, 315, PLATE 24

Walther P-38, 35, 76, 114; Walther P-5, 114; HK-21, 187, 193; HK MP-5, 111, 118, 149, 205, 207, 307, 315, PLATE 24; Mk 1 Hand Firing Device "Welrod," 76, 127, PLATE 16; High Standard HDM, 76, 169; Sten, 35, 76, 127; M-21A *also* 40XB, 76, 96; Remington 870, 111, 132, 187; Stinger, 76, 187; M2 Carbine *also* M3 submachine gun, 35; Colt M1911, 35, 114, 142; MAC-10, 76, PLATE 13; McMillan rifle, PLATE 30

West Berlin, American Sector, 20, 27–28, 64, 76; British Sector, 109, 115; French Sector, 27, 85, 247

West Germany, Bad Tölz *also* Flint Kaserne, 18, 37, 47, 54, 59, 80, 147, 220, 292; Berchtesgaden, 83, 105, 156–157; Bremerhaven, 47, 65, 67; Chiemsee, 92, PLATE 12; Eckenförde, 86, 90; Frankfurt a.M., 56, 65, 147–148, 157, 160, 162, 294; Helmstedt, 20, 147, 287, 309; Lengries, 83; Mittenwald, 83; Murnau, 75; Starnbergersee, 92; Stuttgart *also* Patch Barrack, 56, 137–138, 144, 166–167, 231, 251, 264; Vilseck, 94, 128

Wilde, Jim, 21–22, 28, 44, 79, 305, 308–310

Wise, Robert "Bob," 188, 285, 291

"Yellow Fruit," 209–210, 222, 233, 315–316